Ferguson's Guide to Apprenticeship Programs

Volume 2

C. J. Summerfield
Holli Cosgrove
editors

North Star High School Library
Boswell, PA

J. G. Ferguson Publishing Company
Chicago, Illinois

Inclusion of any program in this book should not be considered an endorsement of these apprenticeship programs by J.G. Ferguson Publishing Company. Every effort has been made to ensure the accuracy of the listings; however, J.G. Ferguson Publishing Company cannot be held liable for inaccuracies, errors, or omissions in the listings. Please notify us if you find an error in the text, and we will correct it in future editions.

Library of Congress Cataloging-in-Publication Data

Ferguson's guide to apprenticeship programs / C. J. Summerfield, Holli Cosgrove, editors.
   p. cm.
   Includes indexes.
   ISBN 0-89434-154-5
   1. Apprenticeship programs--United States--Directories.
2. Occupational training--United States--Directories.
I. Summerfield, Carol J., 1960- . II. Cosgrove, Holli, 1964- .
HD4885.U5F47   1994

331.25'922'02573--dc20   94-36764
                                                               CIP

ISBN 0-89434-154-5
Copyright © 1994 by J. G. Ferguson Publishing Company
All rights reserved

Printed in the United States of America
R-10

Contents

VOLUME 1

Foreword by Senator Paul Simon	p. ix
Acknowledgements	p. xiii
Introduction	p. xv

Part 1

Introduction to Apprenticeships	p. 1
Choosing a Program	p. 15

Part 2

Asbestos Workers and Insulators	p. 39
Boilermakers	p. 57
Bricklayers and Stone Masons	p. 67
Carpenters	p. 87
Cement Masons	p. 147
Cooks, Chefs, and Bakers	p. 167
Drywallers and Lathers	p. 173
Electricians and Line Workers	p. 185
Electronics Technicians	p. 249
Glaziers	p. 257
Ironworkers	p. 269
Laborers	p. 291
Machinists	p. 301
Mechanics	p. 321
Operating Engineers	p. 339
Painters and Paperhangers	p. 359
Pipe Trades Workers	p. 379

VOLUME 2

Plasterers	p. 429
Printing Industry Workers	p. 441
Roofers and Waterproofers	p. 465
Sheetmetal Workers	p. 483
Shipbuilding Industry Workers	p. 511
Theater Workers	p. 517
Tile Setters	p. 527
Tool, Die, Mold, and Pattern Makers	p. 539
Welders	p. 561
Additional Occupations	p. 569

Part 3

Apprenticeship Training at Colleges and Technical Schools	p. 595
Cosmetologists	p. 603
Crafts and Trades Workers at Living Historical Sites and Farms	p. 623
Dispensing Opticians	p. 631
Emergency Medical Technicians	p. 635
Firefighters	p. 675
Folk Arts Apprenticeships	p. 703
Funeral Directors and Embalmers	p. 713
Gunsmiths, Gunmakers, and Bladesmiths	p. 731
Musical Instrument Tuners and Repairers	p. 735
Ocularists	p. 739
Orthotics Technicians	p. 741
Preschool Workers	p. 745
Railroad Workers	p. 749
Vending Machine Mechanics	p. 755

Part 4

Appendix I: Glossary	p. 761
Appendix II: Regional, State, and Local BATs and SACs	p. 765
Dictionary of Occupational Titles (DOT) index	p. 783
Job Index	p. 787
State Index	p. 796

Part 2 (continued)
Traditional Apprenticeship Programs

Plasterers

Plasterers commonly work for independent contractors in the construction industry, though about one-fourth are self-employed. They are so-called because they create the outside surface of walls, ceilings, and partitions with plaster, a pasty material that hardens on drying. This material is fire resistant and helps to soundproof rooms. Plasterers also handle a variety of similar jobs, such as applying plaster veneer over drywall, applying stucco or insulation to outside walls, and casting ornamental designs in plaster.

Plaster can be applied to different types of surfaces, including cinder block, concrete, wood, metal, and lath (a framework made of wire mesh, narrow strips of wood attached to studs, or other material). With cinder block or concrete, for example, plasterers begin by applying a base of gypsum plaster (called a brown coat) onto the wall or ceiling. This plaster can either be sprayed or applied with a trowel and must be smoothed to give it an even surface. Next, a finishing, or white, coat (made of lime, plaster of Paris, and water) is applied over the surface with a hawk , a trowel, a brush, and water. The result is a smooth, durable finish, which is ready to be painted or wallpapered. Plasterers, however, can also make decorative swirls in the finishing coat.

If the supportive framework is instead made of wire mesh, an additional, preparatory step is taken. Plasterers apply a rich plaster mixture (known as the scratch coat) over the wire mesh. Before it is dry, the coat is scratched with a rakelike tool to produce ridges, which allows the following brown coat to adhere.

Apprentices work under already experienced plasterers. In addition to on-the-job training, they receive a minimum of 144 hours of classroom instruction each year and study such subjects as mathematics, drafting, and blueprint reading. Plasterers generally perform their jobs indoors, though work is done outside when applying stucco or insulation to exterior walls.

Plastering apprenticeships normally run two to three years. Most programs require that the applicant

- apply in person

- be at least 17 years old

- be a high school graduate (or GED holder)

- be physically able to perform the work of the trade

Reported beginning apprenticeship salaries range from $6.97 to $15.04 an hour.

Reported ending apprenticeship salaries range from $13.95 to $26.12 an hour.

Slow growth is expected in the number of employed plasterers. Over the years many builders have switched to drywall, which is easier and cheaper to install, though the introduction of new techniques and less costly materials have begun to make plastering more competitive. Some people, moreover, find plastered walls more durable and attractive than those made of drywall. Plaster veneer has become increasingly popular with builders. The number of job openings will also be affected by general trends in the construction industry.

For more information on plastering apprenticeships, write to the national programs listed below, as well as to any government programs located in your state. When a name is included, address your letter to that person. Because existing programs are often revised, some of the following may have changed or ceased to exist. New programs may also have been created. Additional programs might be listed with the national union or with your state's bureau of apprenticeship training. Addresses can be found in the last section of this encyclopedia.

NATIONAL SPONSOR

National Plastering Industry's JATF
1029 Vermont Avenue, NW, #1000
Washington, DC 20005
202-393-6569
ATTN: Gilbert Wolf

• • •

STATE SPONSORS

ALASKA

Alaska Trowel Trades
825 East 8th Avenue
Anchorage, AK 99501
907-272-5113
ATTN: Pat Dahl

This is a 3-year program with 432 hours of classroom instruction and 2,400 hours of on-the-job training.
Starting wage: $14.82; Ending wage: $25.55.
Annually, a varying number of people apply for a varying number of positions.
There is an initial 800-hour probationary period.
Applications are accepted by mail in February.
Call first for application.

REQUIREMENTS:

- Minimum age: 18; Maximum age: 30
- High school diploma or GED certificate
- Pass an oral interview
- Letter of recommendation
- Pass a test for illegal drugs
- Passing grade in the following high school course(s): Math

APPLICATION DOCUMENTS:

Applicants must bring the following documents when applying:
- High school transcript or GED scores
- High school diploma or GED certificate

• • •

CALIFORNIA

Kern, Inyo and Mono Counties
Plasterers and Cement Masons JAC
26 Bernard, Room 100
Bakersfield, CA 93309
805-373-6018

This is a 4-year program.
No salaries were reported by this program.
Applications are accepted in person any time of year, Monday-Friday, 8:00-10:00, 2:00-5:00.

REQUIREMENTS:

- Minimum age: 18

• • •

Butte-Shasta Area Plasterers JAC
PO Box 3729
Chico, CA 95927

This program is affiliated with Sacramento Area Plasterers JAC in West Sacramento, CA. Please see that entry for more information.

• • •

Southern California Plastering Institute
Apprenticeship Trust and JAC
9700 Flair Drive, Room 14
El Monte, CA 91731
213-283-2575
ATTN: Bill Rogers

This is a 4-year program with 576 hours of classroom instruction and 6,816 hours of on-the-job training.
Starting wage: $8.53; Ending wage: $24.83.
Annually, 21-30 people apply for 11-15 positions.
Applications are accepted in person 8:30-11:00 on the second Thursday of each month.

REQUIREMENTS:

- Minimum age: 18
- High school diploma or GED certificate
- Must be physically able to perform the work of the trade

- Pass an oral interview
- Resident of the program's jurisdiction
- Pass a test for illegal drugs

APPLICATION DOCUMENTS:

Applicants must bring the following documents when applying:
- High school diploma or GED certificate
- Social security card
- Driver's license
- Birth certificate

• • •

Fresno Area Plasterers JATC
4831 East Shields Avenue, #6
Fresno, CA 93727
209-251-8259

This is a 3-year program.
No salaries were reported by this program.
Applications are accepted in person any time of year, Tuesday-Thursday, 7:00-9:00.

REQUIREMENTS:

- Minimum age: 18
- High school diploma or GED certificate

• • •

Valley Mortar Trades Trust Fund
PO Box 245542
Sacramento, CA 95824

This program is affiliated with Sacramento Area Plasterers JAC in West Sacramento, CA. Please see that entry for more information.

• • •

Sacramento Area Plasterers JAC
1555 Overland Court
West Sacramento, CA 95691

This is a 4-year program with 576 hours of classroom instruction.
Starting wage: $7.37; Ending wage: $21.06.
Annually, 21-30 people apply for a varying number of positions.
There is an initial 90-day probationary period.
Applications are accepted in person any time of year.

REQUIREMENTS:

- Minimum age: 16
- Pass an oral interview

APPLICATION DOCUMENTS:

Applicants must bring the following documents when applying:
- Social security card
- Driver's license

ADDITIONAL PROGRAM COMMENTS:

This program is affiliated with the Butte-Shasta Area Plasterers JAC (Chico, CA) and the Valley Mortar Trades Trust Fund (Sacramento, CA).

HAWAII

Hawaii Masons and Plasterers Training Office
2nd Floor
2251 North School Street
Honolulu, HI 96819
808-845-5949

This is a 4-year program with 576 hours of classroom instruction and 8,000 hours of on-the-job training.
Starting wage: $10.56; Ending wage: $21.11.
Annually, a varying number of people apply for a varying number of positions.
Applications are accepted by mail any time of year, Monday-Wednesday, 8:00-12:00.

REQUIREMENTS:

- Minimum age: 16
- High school diploma or GED certificate
- Must be physically able to perform the work of the trade
- Pass a written test

APPLICATION DOCUMENTS:

Applicants must bring the following documents when applying:
- High school diploma or GED certificate

ADDITIONAL PROGRAM COMMENTS:

When applying for this program by mail, send a self-addressed, stamped envelope.

• • •

ILLINOIS

Plasters Union Local #5 JAC
6631 West Stanley
Berwyn, IL 60402
708-749-3660
ATTN: Kenneth Daniels

This is a 4-year program.
No salaries were reported by this program.
Applications are accepted in person a need is determined by the committee.

REQUIREMENTS:

- Minimum age: 17
- High school diploma or GED certificate
- Pass a written test
- Letter of recommendation from 2 references

APPLICATION DOCUMENTS:

Applicants must bring the following documents when applying:
- High school transcript or GED scores
- High school diploma or GED certificate
- Birth certificate

• • •

Plasterers and Cement Masons
307 East Walnut, PO Box 103
Tolono, IL 61880
217-485-3515
ATTN: Francis Ducey

Program title: Plasterers and Cement Masons Joint Apprenticeship Program
This is a 3-year program with 432 hours of classroom instruction and 6,000 hours of on-the-job training.
Starting wage: $15.04; Ending wage: $21.48.
Annually, 31-50 people apply for 0-5 positions.
There is an initial 6-month probationary period.
Applications are accepted in person Monday-Friday, 8:00-10:00 by appointment only.

REQUIREMENTS:

- Minimum age: 18
- High school diploma or GED certificate
- Must be physically able to perform the work of the trade
- Pass an oral interview
- Valid driver's license
- Resident of the program's jurisdiction for 1 year

APPLICATION DOCUMENTS:

Applicants must bring the following documents when applying:
- Social security card
- Driver's license

• • •

INDIANA

Plasterers and Cement Masons
Local Union #692
1901 North Sherman Drive, #201
Indianapolis, IN 46218
812-422-3104
ATTN: Ron Bowser

This is a 3-year program with 6,000 hours of on-the-job training.
Starting wage: $8.00; Ending wage: $18.00.
Annually, 51-100 people apply for 21-50 positions.
There is an initial 6-month probationary period.
Applications are accepted in person or by mail any time of year, Monday-Thursday, 9:00-12:00.

REQUIREMENTS:

- High school diploma or GED certificate
- Must be physically able to perform the work of the trade
- Pass an oral interview
- Valid driver's license
- Resident of the program's jurisdiction
- Letter of recommendation from former employers
- Letter of intent from a valid employer
- Pass a test for illegal drugs

APPLICATION DOCUMENTS:

Applicants must bring the following documents when applying:
- High school transcript or GED scores
- High school diploma or GED certificate
- Social security card
- Driver's license

• • •

MICHIGAN

U.P. District Council of BAC
119 South Front Street
Marquette, MI 49855
906-226-3015
ATTN: Roland Swanson

Program title: U.P. Trowel Trades Apprenticeship Program
This is a 3-year program.
No salaries were reported by this program.
Annually, over 100 people apply for 0-5 positions.
Applications are accepted by mail only when advertised.

REQUIREMENTS:

- Minimum age: 18
- High school diploma or GED certificate
- Pass a written test
- Pass an oral interview
- Resident of the program's jurisdiction for 30 days

APPLICATION DOCUMENTS:

Applicants must bring the following documents when applying:
- High school transcript or GED scores
- High school diploma or GED certificate
- Birth certificate

ADDITIONAL PROGRAM COMMENTS:

Classroom instruction lasts sixteen months. A twelve-week preapprenticeship class is offered in Detroit if needed.

• • •

MINNESOTA

Plasterers Union Local #65
312 Central Avenue SE, #386
Minneapolis, MN 55414
612-379-1515
ATTN: Richard Felber

This is a 3-year program with 432 hours of classroom instruction and 6,000 hours of on-the-job training.
Starting wage: $10.56.
Annually, 0-10 people apply for 0-5 positions.
There is an initial probationary period.
Applications are accepted in person or by mail any time of year.

REQUIREMENTS:

- Minimum age: 18
- High school diploma or GED certificate

APPLICATION DOCUMENTS:

Applicants must bring the following documents when applying:
- Social security card

ADDITIONAL PROGRAM COMMENTS:

This is an informal program which mostly refers those interested to contractors. Applicants are required to join the union.

• • •

MONTANA

International Masonry Apprenticeship Trust
PO Box 577
Anaconda, MT 59711
406-563-5397
ATTN: Robert O Geier

This is a 3-year program with 1,500 hours of classroom instruction and 6,000 hours of on-the-job training.
No salaries were reported by this program.
Annually, 51-100 people apply for 21-50 positions.
Applications are accepted in person any time of year.

REQUIREMENTS:

- Minimum age: 16
- Physician's statement of fitness
- Pass an oral interview
- Letter of recommendation from current or previous teachers

APPLICATION DOCUMENTS:

Applicants must bring the following documents when applying:
- High school transcript or GED scores
- Social security card

• • •

NEVADA

Cement Masons and Plasterers
50 East Bonanza
Las Vegas, NV 89110
ATTN: Albert Morosi

This is a 2-year program with 288 hours of classroom instruction and 4,000 hours of on-the-job training.
Starting wage: $10.37; Ending wage: $26.12.
Annually, 51-100 people apply for 11-15 positions.
Course credit is offered.
There is an initial 3-month probationary period.
Applications are accepted in person any time of year, Monday-Friday, 6:00-4:00.

REQUIREMENTS:

- Minimum age: 18
- High school diploma or GED certificate
- Must be physically able to perform the work of the trade
- Pass a written test
- Pass an oral interview
- Letter of recommendation
- Pass a test for illegal drugs

APPLICATION DOCUMENTS:

Applicants must bring the following documents when applying:
- High school diploma or GED certificate
- Birth certificate

• • •

NEW YORK

Plasterers and Cement Masons
15 East 15th Street
New York, NY 10003
212-924-8650
ATTN: Emil Riccardi

This is a 3-year program with 432 hours of classroom instruction.
Starting wage: $10.82; Ending wage: $16.83.
Annually, 31-50 people apply for 16-20 positions.
There is an initial 6-month probationary period.
Applications are accepted in person any time of year, when advertised in local papers.
The application deadline is 7 days after ads.

REQUIREMENTS:

- Minimum age: 18
- Pass a written test
- Pass an oral interview
- Letter of recommendation
- Letter of intent from a valid employer

APPLICATION DOCUMENTS:

Applicants must bring the following documents when applying:
- Social security card

• • •

OHIO

N.O.C.E.C.
4535 Hill Avenue
Toledo, OH 43615
ATTN: Ray French

Program title: Cement Mason/Plaster Joint Apprenticeship Program
This is a 4-year program.
No salaries were reported by this program.
Annually, 21-30 people apply for 6-10 positions.
Applications are accepted in person any time, Monday-Friday.

REQUIREMENTS:

- High school diploma or GED certificate
- Pass a written test
- Pass an oral interview
- Valid driver's license

APPLICATION DOCUMENTS:

Applicants must bring the following documents when applying:
- High school transcript or GED scores
- High school diploma or GED certificate
- Social security card
- Driver's license

• • •

OKLAHOMA

Eastern Oklahoma Building and Construction Trades Council
2651 East 21st Street, #405
Tulsa, OK 74114
918-742-3363
ATTN: Clayton Walker

No salaries were reported by this program.
Write or call for application information.

• • •

OREGON

Plasterers Local Union #82 JATC
2215 SE Division
Portland, OR 97202
503-232-3257
ATTN: Don McKinnon

This is a 3.5-year program with 504 hours of classroom instruction and 2,000 hours of on-the-job training.
Starting wage: $10.13.
Annually, 21-30 people apply for 0-5 positions.
Applications are accepted in person any time of year, Monday-Friday.

REQUIREMENTS:

- Minimum age: 17
- High school diploma or GED certificate
- Pass an oral interview
- Valid driver's license
- Resident of the program's jurisdiction
- Pass a test for illegal drugs

APPLICATION DOCUMENTS:

Applicants must bring the following documents when applying:
- Driver's license

• • •

PENNSYLVANIA

Plasterers Local #31 Apprenticeship Program
2227 Jane Street
Pittsburgh, PA 15203
412-481-9888
ATTN: James Lundy

This is a 4-year program with 576 hours of classroom instruction and 4,000 hours of on-the-job training.
Starting wage: $8.84; Ending wage: $17.67.
Annually, 0-10 people apply for 0-5 positions.
There is an initial 6-month probationary period.
Applications are accepted by mail at any Penna Job Service Office March 1-March 13.
The application deadline is March 13th.

REQUIREMENTS:

- Minimum age: 18
- High school diploma or GED certificate
- Physician's statement of fitness
- Must be physically able to perform the work of the trade
- Pass a written test
- Pass an oral interview
- Valid driver's license
- Resident of the program's jurisdiction for 6 months
- Pass a test for illegal drugs

APPLICATION DOCUMENTS:

Applicants must bring the following documents when applying:
- Social security card
- Driver's license

ADDITIONAL PROGRAM COMMENTS:

Applications are handled at all PENNA Job Service Offices.

• • •

RHODE ISLAND

Operative Plasterers Local Union #40
150 Ernest Street
Providence, RI 02905
401-785-2230
ATTN: Robert Damiani

This is a 4-year program.
No salaries were reported by this program.
Annually, a varying number of people apply for a varying number of positions.
Applications are accepted in person or by mail at various times. Contact for further information.

REQUIREMENTS:

- Minimum age: 18; Maximum age: 26
- High school diploma or GED certificate
- Must be physically able to perform the work of the trade
- Pass a written test
- Pass an oral interview
- Resident of the program's jurisdiction

APPLICATION DOCUMENTS:

Applicants must bring the following documents when applying:
- High school transcript or GED scores
- High school diploma or GED certificate

• • •

TENNESSEE

Cement Masons Local #521
3540 Sumner Avenue
Memphis, TN 38122
901-327-6492
ATTN: Cordis Davis

This is a 3-year program.
Starting wage: $6.97; Ending wage: $13.95.
Annually, 51-100 people apply for 11-15 positions.
Applications are accepted in person any time of year.

REQUIREMENTS:

- Minimum age: 18
- Pass an oral interview
- Resident of the program's jurisdiction
- Must attend a preapprenticeship class

APPLICATION DOCUMENTS:

Applicants must bring the following documents when applying:
- Social security card
- Driver's license
- Birth certificate

• • •

WASHINGTON

Western Washington Plasterers
Apprenticeship. and Training
Renton Technical College
3000 NE 4th Street
Renton, WA 98056
ATTN: Dale O'Brien

Plasterers

This is a 3.5-year program with 500 hours of classroom instruction and 6,500 hours of on-the-job training.
Starting wage: $9.30; Ending wage: $19.69.
Annually, over 100 people apply for 11-15 positions.
There is an initial 1,400-hour probationary period.
Applications are accepted in person any time of year, Mondays and Wednesdays by appointment only.

REQUIREMENTS:

- Minimum age: 18
- High school diploma or GED certificate
- Must be physically able to perform the work of the trade
- Valid driver's license
- Resident of the program's jurisdiction
- Letter of intent from a valid employer

APPLICATION DOCUMENTS:

Applicants must bring the following documents when applying:
- High school diploma or GED certificate
- Social security card
- Driver's license

ADDITIONAL PROGRAM COMMENTS:

Applicants must be able to lift 80 pounds and not be afraid of heights. They should have a good attitude, dependable transportation, be drug free and willing to work hard. They must also be able to speak, read, and write English.

• • •

WEST VIRGINIA

West Virginia State Building and Construction Trades Council
2301 7th Avenue
Charleston, WV 25312
304-346-1367
ATTN: E. Fisher

This is a 3-year program with 432 hours of classroom instruction and 6,000 hours of on-the-job training.

REQUIREMENTS:
- Minimum age: 17; Maximum age: 29
- Physician's statement of fitness
- Must be physically able to perform the work of the trade
- Pass a written test
- Pass an oral interview

APPLICATION DOCUMENTS:

Applicants must bring the following documents when applying:
- High school transcript or GED scores
- Birth certificate

• • •

WISCONSIN

Bricklayers
2 233 Birch Street
Eau Claire, WI 54703
ATTN: Dave Hahn

Program title: Wisconsin State Trowel Trades Apprenticeship
This is a 3-year program with 400 hours of classroom instruction and 4,280 hours of on-the-job training.
Starting wage: $8.99; Ending wage: $17.53.
Annually, 0-10 people apply for 6-10 positions.
There is an initial 6-month probationary period.
Applications are accepted in person or by mail any time of year.

REQUIREMENTS:

- High school diploma or GED certificate
- Pass an oral interview
- Letter of recommendation from previous construction employer
- Letter of intent from a valid employer

APPLICATION DOCUMENTS:

Applicants must bring the following documents when applying:
- High school transcript or GED scores
- High school diploma or GED certificate

• • •

Plasterers and Cement Masons
2025 Atwood Avenue
Madison, WI 53704
ATTN: Raymond Lauallee

This is a 2-year program with 400 hours of classroom instruction.
Starting wage: $10.53; Ending wage: $17.55.
Annually, 11-20 people apply for 0-5 positions.
Course credit is offered.
There is an initial 30-day probationary period. Applications are accepted in person any time of year, but the spring months are best. Call first for additional information.

REQUIREMENTS:

- Minimum age: 18
- High school diploma or GED certificate
- Valid driver's license
- Pass a test for illegal drugs

APPLICATION DOCUMENTS:

Applicants must bring the following documents when applying:
- High school transcript or GED scores
- Social security card
- Driver's license

• • •

Plasterers and Cement Masons
7575 North 79th Street
Milwaukee, WI 53223
414-354-4864
ATTN: John McCormick

This is a 3-year program.
No salaries were reported by this program.
Annually, 0-10 people apply for 0-5 positions.
Applications are accepted in person any time of year.

REQUIREMENTS:

- Valid driver's license
- Letter of intent from a valid employer

APPLICATION DOCUMENTS:

Applicants must bring the following documents when applying:
- Social security card
- Driver's license

• • •

Printing Industry Workers

Workers in the printing industry can be divided into three major areas—prepress, press, and bindery—reflecting the three general steps taken in the production of a book or other publication. *Prepress workers* prepare all the material needed before the pages are actually printed; for example, they typeset text, lay out pages, and produce printing plates. *Press workers,* on the other hand, are responsible for the operation of the printing presses. Finally, *bindery workers* transform printed pages into books, magazines, or other publications, often through a process of folding, sewing, and gluing pages and attaching a cover.

The prepress field has changed greatly in the late twentieth century, largely from the introduction of computers and other electronic machines. The result has been the simplifying of many jobs and a reduction in the number of workers needed. Among the prepress positions is *typesetter* (or *composer*), whose primary job is typing text into a computer or other machine; increasingly, however, authors submit manuscripts already on computer disks. The next step has been to print the text on special paper, which a *paste-up artist* would cut into columns and arrange (along with illustrations) on a layout board. The layout process can now be handled entirely on a computer; a specialized worker, sometimes called an *electronic pagination system operator,* arranges and corrects the layout on a computer screen. The layout is photographed by a *photographer* or *camera operator,* and a photographic negative is developed. (Computerized equipment run by a *scanner operator* can make negatives of existing photographs or artwork.) *Strippers* then make alterations to the film, including last-minute corrections to the text by "stripping" out and replacing type. The film images are finally transferred to thin metal printing plates by a chemical process performed by various workers, including *etchers,* who develop the plates in an acid bath, and *finishers,* who touch up irregularities on the plates.

The next stage is the actual printing of pages (several pages may be printed on one large sheet of paper), which is done on giant machines called printing presses. *Printing press operators* prepare and maintain these machines. They install the printing plates; inspect, adjust, and lubricate machine parts; load and correctly align giant rolls of paper; and inspect the print to ensure it is clear and straight. Since the introduction of computerized controls, printing press operators make many adjustments by pushing buttons on a control panel.

The final step is binding. Depending on the number of printed pages per sheet, this may require only a single fold, as for a newspaper insert, or a multistep process of folding, sewing, gluing, and covering. For mass-produced publications all steps are handled by machines, which are operated by specially trained workers. One machine, for example, may fold a group of sequentially numbered pages (called a signature), and the next machine might sew or glue the signatures together into a book. A later machine might attach the cover. Job titles sometimes reflect the type of machine operated—for example, *folding-machine operator* or *book-sewing-machine operator.* There are still a small number of *bookbinders* who perform all the stages by hand, an expensive process usually limited to special editions and the repair of old and rare books.

Apprentices work under already established printing industry workers. Classroom instruction usually comes in the form of a correspondence course. Reflecting the changing technology, the number of prepress apprenticeships have greatly declined. Those that do exist emphasize one area, such as stripping or platemaking, though apprentices are usually given some experience in all the prepress stages. In press work and binding, apprenticeships are also less common than they once were. Press apprentices might begin by cleaning the presses or by loading and unloading paper. Bindery workers might start by carrying paper from one machine to another. Apprentices also receive formal instruction either in the classroom or through correspondence courses. Because pressrooms and binderies can be noisy, some workers wear ear protectors.

Apprenticeships for printing industry workers normally run two to four years. Most programs require that the applicant

- apply in person

- be at least 18 years old

- be a high school graduate (or GED holder)

- be physically able to perform the work of the trade

Reported beginning apprenticeship salaries range from $5.56 to $12.00 an hour.

Reported ending apprenticeship salaries range from $10.10 to $20.00 an hour.

Average growth is expected in the number of employed prepress and press workers. Applicants accepted into apprenticeship programs are usually workers already employed for several years by the sponsoring company. Although improved efficiency has reduced the number of workers needed per job, there has also been a rising demand for printed material. The employment outlook for strippers in particular is good. The number of employed bindery workers, however, is expected to grow more slowly than average, in part because of improved technology. New "in-line" bindery equipment can handle several operations in a row, allowing printed paper to be fed on one end and a finished book to come out the other.

For more information on printing industry apprenticeships, write to the national programs listed below, as well as to any government programs located in your state. When a name is included, address your letter to that person. Because existing programs are often revised, some of the following may have changed or ceased to exist. New programs may also have been created. Additional programs might be listed with the national union or with your state's bureau of apprenticeship training. Addresses can be found in the last section of this encyclopedia.

NATIONAL SPONSORS

Graphic Communications International Union
Education Department
1900 L Street, NW
Washington, DC 20036
202-462-1400

This organization is affiliated with the AFL-CIO.

• • •

STATE SPONSORS

ALABAMA

Graphic Communications International Union
Local Union #211-C
Route 1 Box 768
Elmore, AL 36025
205-285-3280
ATTN: George Wyatt

Specific job title(s): Pressman
This is a 4-year program.
No salaries were reported by this program.
Annually, a varying number of people apply for 0-5 positions.
There is an initial 90-day probationary period.
Applications are accepted in person any time of year.

REQUIREMENTS:

- Minimum age: 18
- High school diploma or GED certificate
- Pass a written test
- Pass an oral interview

APPLICATION DOCUMENTS:

Applicants must bring the following documents when applying:
- Social security card

ADDITIONAL PROGRAM COMMENTS:

A hearing test will be required by OSHA. The applicant must be a union member.

• • •

CONNECTICUT

Graphic Communications International Union
Local Union #434-C
308 Bristol Street
Southington, CT 06489
203-621-4237
ATTN: William Markowski

Specific job title(s): Pressman
This is a 4-year program.
No salaries were reported by this program.
Annually, a varying number of people apply for 0-2 positions.
There is an initial 3-month probationary period.
Applications are accepted in person or by mail

any time of year. Two positions are open every four years.

REQUIREMENTS:

- High school diploma or GED certificate
- Physician's statement of fitness
- Must be physically able to perform the work of the trade
- Pass an oral interview

APPLICATION DOCUMENTS:

Applicants must bring the following documents when applying:
- Social security card

• • •

ILLINOIS

 Graphic Communications International Union
730 East Vine, Room 113
Springfield, IL 62703

Specific job title(s): Pressman
This is a 4-year program.
No salaries were reported by this program.
Annually, a varying number of people apply for 6-10 positions.
There is an initial 30-day probationary period.
Applications are accepted in person any time of year.

REQUIREMENTS:

- Minimum age: 18
- High school diploma or GED certificate
- Pass a written test
- Pass an oral interview
- Letter of recommendation

APPLICATION DOCUMENTS:

Applicants must bring the following documents when applying:
- High school diploma or GED certificate
- Social security card

• • •

 Graphic Communications International Union
Local Union #368C
3666 Johnsmanville
Waukegan, IL 60085
708-623-0037
ATTN: Larry Carrier

Specific job title(s): Pressman
This is a 4-year program.
No salaries were reported by this program.
Write or call for application information.

• • •

INDIANA

 Graphic Communications International Union
Local Union #19-M
704 West Jefferson, #101
Fort Wayne, IN 46802
219-426-0995
ATTN: Ron Dierkes

Specific job title(s): Pressman, Prepress, Bindery worker
This is a 4-year program.
No salaries were reported by this program.
Annually, a varying number of people apply for a varying number of positions.
There is an initial probationary period.
Applications are accepted in person.

REQUIREMENTS:

- Pass an oral interview

• • •

 Graphic Communications International Union
3450 South Meridan Street
Indianapolis, IN 46217
317-784-2964
ATTN: Carl Brunsman

Specific job title(s): Pressman
This is a 4-year program with 2 hours of classroom instruction.
No salaries were reported by this program.
Annually, a varying number of people apply for a varying number of positions.

There is an initial probationary period. Applications are accepted in person.

REQUIREMENTS:

- Minimum age: 18
- High school diploma or GED certificate
- Physician's statement of fitness
- Must be physically able to perform the work of the trade
- Pass a written test
- Pass an oral interview
- Pass a test for illegal drugs

APPLICATION DOCUMENTS:

Applicants must bring the following documents when applying:
- High school diploma or GED certificate
- Social security card

• • •

Graphic Communications International Union
Local Union #303
1010 North Main Street
Indianapolis, IN 46224
317-244-1572
ATTN: Woody Van Note

Specific job title(s): Pressman, Bookbinder
This is a 4-year program.
No salaries were reported by this program.
Annually, a varying number of people apply for 5-8 positions.
Applications are accepted in person any time of year.

REQUIREMENTS:

- Minimum age: 18
- Pass an oral interview

ADDITIONAL PROGRAM COMMENTS:

The bookbinder program lasts two years. A written test is required.

• • •

IOWA

Graphic Communications International Union
141 Windsor Circle
Burlington, IA 52601
319-753-5577
ATTN: Jeffrey Japsen

Specific job title(s): Pressman
This is a 4-year program.
No salaries were reported by this program.
Annually, 21-30 people apply for 0-2 positions.
Applications are accepted in person or by mail any time of year.

REQUIREMENTS:

- Minimum age: 18
- High school diploma or GED certificate
- Pass an oral interview
- Valid driver's license

APPLICATION DOCUMENTS:

Applicants must bring the following documents when applying:
- Social security card
- Driver's license

ADDITIONAL PROGRAM COMMENTS:

Press class is helpful but not required. A resume is helpful for the application process.

• • •

KANSAS

Graphic Communications International Union
Local Union #729-S
PO Box 257
Girarn, KS 66743
316-724-4006
ATTN: Robert Bone

Specific job title(s): Pressman
This is a 4-year program.
No salaries were reported by this program.
Annually, a varying number of people apply for a varying number of positions.
Course credit is offered.

There is an initial 6-month probationary period. Applications are accepted by mail any time of year.

REQUIREMENTS:

- Pass a test for illegal drugs

APPLICATION DOCUMENTS:

Applicants must bring the following documents when applying:
- Social security card

• • •

Graphic Communications International Union
Local Union #275-C
1208 West 32nd Street
Hutchinson, KS 67502
316-663-9617
ATTN: Gordon Warnken

Specific job title(s): Pressman
This is a 4-year program.
No salaries were reported by this program.
Annually, a varying number of people apply for 0-1 positions.
There is an initial 6-month probationary period. Applications are accepted in person any time of year.

APPLICATION DOCUMENTS:

Applicants must bring the following documents when applying:
- Social security card

• • •

Graphic Communications International Union
Local Union #147-C
1519 Holland Lane
Wichita, KS 67212
316-722-6886
ATTN: Robert Neice

Specific job title(s): Pressman
This is a 4-year program.
No salaries were reported by this program.
Annually, a varying number of people apply for 0-1 positions.

There is an initial 6-month probationary period. Applications are accepted in person.

REQUIREMENTS:

- High school diploma or GED certificate
- Physician's statement of fitness
- Must be physically able to perform the work of the trade
- Pass a written test
- Pass an oral interview
- Pass a test for illegal drugs

APPLICATION DOCUMENTS:

Applicants must bring the following documents when applying:
- High school transcript or GED scores
- High school diploma or GED certificate
- Social security card
- Driver's license

• • •

Graphic Communications International Union
Local Union #575-M
328 Laura
Wichita, KS 67211
316-267-3563
ATTN: Fred Quattlebaum

Specific job title(s): Bookbinder (Level 1, 2, 3), Prepress, Pressman
This is a 2-4-year program.
No salaries were reported by this program.
Annually, a varying number of people apply for 0-5 positions.
There is an initial probationary period. Applications are accepted in person or by mail.

REQUIREMENTS:

- Pass a written test
- Pass an oral interview

APPLICATION DOCUMENTS:

Applicants must bring the following documents when applying:
- Social security card

• • •

KENTUCKY

Graphic Communications International Union
Local Union #619
659 South 8th Street
Louisville, KY 40203
502-583-2709
ATTN: Robert Norton

Specific job title(s): Pressman
This is a 4-year program.
No salaries were reported by this program.
Annually, a varying number of people apply for 0-5 positions.
There is an initial probationary period.
Applications are accepted in person or by mail any time of year.

REQUIREMENTS:

- Physician's statement of fitness
- Must be physically able to perform the work of the trade

APPLICATION DOCUMENTS:

Applicants must bring the following documents when applying:
- Social security card

• • •

Graphic Communications International Union
Local Union #395-C
2241 Yewels Landing, Apt. A
Owensboro, KY 42303
502-926-4296
ATTN: Charles Berry

Specific job title(s): Pressman
This is a 4-year program.
No salaries were reported by this program.
Annually, a varying number of people apply for 0-1 positions.
Applications are accepted in person any time of year.

REQUIREMENTS:

- Minimum age: 18
- Must be physically able to perform the work of the trade
- Pass an oral interview

APPLICATION DOCUMENTS:

Applicants must bring the following documents when applying:
- Social security card

• • •

MAINE

Graphic Communications International Union
Local Union #22-C
112 Brachett Street
Portland, ME 04102
207-774-6461
ATTN: Karen Cross

Specific job title(s): Press operator/platemaker
This is a 4-year program.
No salaries were reported by this program.
Annually, a varying number of people apply for 0-5 positions.
There is an initial 3-month probationary period.
Applications are accepted by mail any time of year.

REQUIREMENTS:

- Minimum age: 18
- High school diploma or GED certificate
- Must be physically able to perform the work of the trade
- Pass a written test
- Pass an oral interview
- Letter of recommendation
- Letter of intent from a valid employer

APPLICATION DOCUMENTS:

Applicants must bring the following documents when applying:
- High school transcript or GED scores
- High school diploma or GED certificate

• • •

MASSACHUSETTS

Graphic Communications International Union
Local Union #228
25 Crossing Terrace
Pittsfield, MA 01201
413-447-8251
ATTN: Joe Scalise

Specific job title(s): Pressman, Prepress
This is a 4.5-year program.
Ending wage: $18.00.
Annually, a varying number of people apply for 0-5 positions.
There is an initial 6-month probationary period.
Applications are accepted in person or by mail any time of year. Apply to company.

REQUIREMENTS:

- Minimum age: 18

• • •

Graphic Communications International Union
516-B Dorchester Avenue
South Boston, MA 02127
ATTN: Henry Vitale

This is a 4-year program.
No salaries were reported by this program.
There is an initial 4-month probationary period.
Write or call for application information.

REQUIREMENTS:

- Minimum age: 16
- High school diploma or GED certificate
- Pass a written test
- Pass an oral interview
- Letter of intent from a valid employer

APPLICATION DOCUMENTS:

Applicants must bring the following documents when applying:
- Social security card

• • •

MICHIGAN

Graphic Communications International Union
Local Union #2
22720 Woodward Avenue, #204
Ferndale, MI 48220
313-548-0232
ATTN: David Jacobs

Specific job title(s): Pressman, Prepress, Bindery worker
This is a 4-year program.
No salaries were reported by this program.
Annually, over 100 people apply for 2-3 positions.
Course credit is offered.
There is an initial probationary period.
Applications are accepted in person any time of year.

REQUIREMENTS:

- Pass an oral interview
- Pass a test for illegal drugs

APPLICATION DOCUMENTS:

Applicants must bring the following documents when applying:
- Social security card
- Resume

• • •

Graphic Communications International Union
Local Union #12-C
1601 South Holly Way
Lansing, MI 48910
517-394-6322
ATTN: Richard Rugg

Specific job title(s): Pressman
This is a 4-year program.
No salaries were reported by this program.
Annually, a varying number of people apply for a varying number of positions.
There is an initial 1-month probationary period.
Applications are accepted in person or by mail any time of year.

REQUIREMENTS:

- Minimum age: 18
- High school diploma or GED certificate
- Physician's statement of fitness
- Must be physically able to perform the work of the trade
- Pass a test for illegal drugs

• • •

Graphic Communications International Union
Local Union #692-C
327 West Bluff
Marquette, MI 49855
906-228-6106
ATTN: Greg Ostrenga

Specific job title(s): Pressman, Compositor
This is a 4-year program.
No salaries were reported by this program.
Annually, a varying number of people apply for 3-4 positions.
There is an initial 3-month probationary period.
Applications are accepted in person or by mail any time of year.

REQUIREMENTS:

- High school diploma or GED certificate
- Pass an oral interview
- Resume

• • •

MINNESOTA

Graphic Communications International Union
Local Union #142-C
403 Park Meadows Drive, #201
Waite Park, MN 56387
612-253-9250
ATTN: David Schulzetenberg

Specific job title(s): Pressman, Prepress
This is a 4-year program.
No salaries were reported by this program.
Annually, 2-3 people apply for 0-5 positions.
There is an initial 1-month probationary period.
Applications are accepted in person any time of year.

REQUIREMENTS:

- Minimum age: 18
- Physician's statement of fitness
- Must be physically able to perform the work of the trade
- Pass an oral interview
- Pass a test for illegal drugs

• • •

Graphic Communications International Union
Local Union #237-C
1911 West 5th Street
Winona, MN 55987
507-452-2000
ATTN: Christopher Molotko

Specific job title(s): Pressman
This is a 4-year program.
Starting wage: $9.00.
Annually, 1-2 people apply for 0-2 positions.
There is an initial 1-month probationary period.
Applications are accepted in person any time of year.

• • •

MISSOURI

Graphic Communications International Union
Local Union #235
10221 East 40 Highway
Independence, MO 64055
ATTN: James Miller

Specific job title(s): Pressman
This is a 4-year program.
Starting wage: $6.50; Ending wage: $20.00.
Annually, a varying number of people apply for 10-20 positions.
There is an initial 3-month probationary period.
Applications are accepted in person any time of year.

REQUIREMENTS:

- High school diploma or GED certificate
- Physician's statement of fitness
- Must be physically able to perform the work of the trade

• • •

Graphic Communications International Union
Local Union #301-C
1707 South Engineer
Scadalia, MO 65301
816-826-1083
ATTN: Patrick Dehaven

Specific job title(s): Pressman
This is a 4-year program.
No salaries were reported by this program.
Annually, a varying number of people apply for 1-2 positions.
There is an initial probationary period.
Applications are accepted in person any time of year.

REQUIREMENTS:

- High school diploma or GED certificate
- Pass an oral interview

• • •

 Graphic Communications International Union
Local Union #203-C
3425 South Orin
Springfield, MO 65804
417-883-0874
ATTN: Dan Fuller

Specific job title(s): Pressman
This is a 4-year program.
Starting wage: $7.10; Ending wage: $10.50.
Annually, a varying number of people apply for 0-8 positions.
There is an initial 3-month probationary period.
Applications are accepted in person or by mail any time of year.

REQUIREMENTS:

- High school diploma or GED certificate
- Pass an oral interview

APPLICATION DOCUMENTS:

Applicants must bring the following documents when applying:
- Social security card
- Birth certificate

• • •

MONTANA

 Graphic Communications International Union
Local Union #227-C
1727 Oxbow Circle
Billings, MT 59105
406-259-6701
ATTN: Medric Magann

Specific job title(s): Prepress, Pressman
This is a 4-year program.
No salaries were reported by this program.
Annually, a varying number of people apply for 0-1 positions.
There is an initial 6-month probationary period.
Applications are accepted in person any time of year.

REQUIREMENTS:

- Minimum age: 18
- Pass an oral interview

APPLICATION DOCUMENTS:

Applicants must bring the following documents when applying:
- Social security card

ADDITIONAL PROGRAM COMMENTS:

Applicants' letter of intent from employer must state that they have 4,160 hours of employment currently assigned.

• • •

 Graphic Communications International Union
Missoula Typographical
PO Box 2133
Missoula, MT 59806
406-543-8311
ATTN: Nancy Lee

This is a 3-year program with 8,000 hours of on-the-job training.
No salaries were reported by this program.
Annually, 0-10 people apply for 0-5 positions.
There is an initial 90-day probationary period.
Applications are accepted in person or by mail any time of year.

REQUIREMENTS:

- High school diploma or GED certificate
- Pass an oral interview
- Resident of the program's jurisdiction

APPLICATION DOCUMENTS:

Applicants must bring the following documents when applying:
- Social security card

ADDITIONAL PROGRAM COMMENTS:

A printing background is helpful. The more you know about computers, especially graphics programs, the better.

• • •

NEW YORK

Graphic Communications International Union
Local Union #17-B
738 Ellicot Square Building
Buffalo, NY 14203
716-856-9759
ATTN: Kenneth Owen

Specific job title(s): Bindery worker
This is a 2-4-year program.
Starting wage: $12.00; Ending wage: $16.00.
Annually, a varying number of people apply for 0-3 positions.
There is an initial 3-6-month probationary period.
Applications are accepted in person any time of year when position is posted in local newspapers.

REQUIREMENTS:

- Minimum age: 18
- High school diploma or GED certificate
- Physician's statement of fitness
- Must be physically able to perform the work of the trade
- Pass a written test
- Pass an oral interview

APPLICATION DOCUMENTS:

Applicants must bring the following documents when applying:
- Social security card
- Veteran's DD-214, if applicable
- Car registration

• • •

Graphic Communications International Union
Local Union #164-C
856 Page Road
Frewsburg, NY 14738
716-569-4233
ATTN: Alton Lindstrom

Specific job title(s): Pressman
This is a 4-year program.
No salaries were reported by this program.
Annually, a varying number of people apply for 1-2 positions.
Applications are accepted in person or by mail any time of year, by applying directly to company.

REQUIREMENTS:

- Physician's statement of fitness
- Must be physically able to perform the work of the trade

APPLICATION DOCUMENTS:

Applicants must bring the following documents when applying:
- Social security card

ADDITIONAL PROGRAM COMMENTS:

Preapprenticeship classes are available if needed.

• • •

Graphic Communications International Union
Local Union #30
2495 Woodlawn Avenue
Niagara Falls, NY 14301
716-675-4661
ATTN: Bill Newell

Specific job title(s): Pressman
This is a 4-year program.
No salaries were reported by this program.
Annually, a varying number of people apply for a varying number of positions.
There is an initial 1-month probationary period. Applications are accepted in person any time of year. Write for information.

REQUIREMENTS:

- Minimum age: 18
- High school diploma or GED certificate

APPLICATION DOCUMENTS:

Applicants must bring the following documents when applying:
- High school diploma or GED certificate
- Social security card

• • •

Graphic Communications International Union
RD 1 Box 803-A Helbock Drive
Phoenix, NY 13135
315-695-3851
ATTN: James Callen

This is a 4-year program.
No salaries were reported by this program.
Annually, 0-10 people apply for 0-5 positions.
Applications are accepted in person.

ADDITIONAL PROGRAM COMMENTS:

This program is currently not accepting applications.

• • •

NORTH CAROLINA

R R Donnelley
PO Box 289
Newton, NC 28658
704-464-8110
ATTN: Ron Valentini

Specific job title(s): Bookbinder, Pressman, Cylinder corrector, Digital mechanical engraver

This is a 4-year program with 576 hours of classroom instruction and 8,000 hours of on-the-job training.
Ending wage: $15.00.
Annually, 21-30 people apply for 6-10 positions.
Course credit is offered.
There is an initial 6-month probationary period. Applications are accepted in person any time of year. In-house hires only.

REQUIREMENTS:

- Minimum age: 18
- High school diploma or GED certificate
- Physician's statement of fitness
- Must be physically able to perform the work of the trade
- Pass a written test
- Pass an oral interview
- Pass a test for illegal drugs
- Passing grade in the following high school course(s): Chemistry, Computers, Math
- Must attend a preapprenticeship class

APPLICATION DOCUMENTS:

Applicants must bring the following documents when applying:
- Social security card
- Driver's license

ADDITIONAL PROGRAM COMMENTS:

Applicants must be employed for at least six months at R R Donnelley before applying.

• • •

Graphic Communications International Union
996 Shalimar Drive
Winston Salem, NC 27107
ATTN: Reggie Moore

Specific job title(s): Pressman
This is a 4-year program.
No salaries were reported by this program.
Annually, 0-10 people apply for 0-5 positions.
Course credit is offered.
There is an initial 90-day probationary period. Applications are accepted in person or by mail any time of year.

REQUIREMENTS:

- Minimum age: 18
- High school diploma or GED certificate
- Physician's statement of fitness
- Must be physically able to perform the work of the trade
- Pass a written test
- Pass an oral interview
- Valid driver's license
- Pass a test for illegal drugs

APPLICATION DOCUMENTS:

Applicants must bring the following documents when applying:
- High school transcript or GED scores
- High school diploma or GED certificate
- Social security card
- Driver's license

• • •

NORTH DAKOTA

Graphic Communications International Union
Local Union #192-C
912 Oak Street
Grand Forks, ND 58201
701-775-9137
ATTN: Bruce Trufte

Specific job title(s): Pressman
This is a 4-year program.
No salaries were reported by this program.
Annually, a varying number of people apply for 0-3 positions.
There is an initial 3-month probationary period.
Applications are accepted in person any time of year.

REQUIREMENTS:

- High school diploma or GED certificate
- Physician's statement of fitness
- Must be physically able to perform the work of the trade
- Pass a written test
- Pass an oral interview
- Pass a test for illegal drugs

• • •

Graphic Communications International Union
503 Hamline Street
Grand Forks, ND 58203
ATTN: Steven Rude

Specific job title(s): Composer, mailroom
This is a 4-year program.
Starting wage: $5.56; Ending wage: $10.10.
Annually, 0-10 people apply for 0-5 positions.
There is an initial 3-month probationary period.
Applications are accepted in person or by mail any time of year, Monday through Friday, 9:00-5:00.

REQUIREMENTS:

- Pass a written test
- Pass an oral interview
- Valid driver's license
- Pass a test for illegal drugs

APPLICATION DOCUMENTS:

Applicants must bring the following documents when applying:
- Social security card
- Driver's license

• • •

OHIO

Graphic Communications International Union
Local Union #11-C
12159 Marwood Lane
Cincinnati, OH 45246
513-671-5073
ATTN: James Elkins

Specific job title(s): Pressman, Prepress
This is a 2-4-year program.
No salaries were reported by this program.
Annually, a varying number of people apply for a varying number of positions.
There is an initial probationary period.
Applications are accepted in person any time of year mostly through in-house workers.

REQUIREMENTS:

- Pass an oral interview

APPLICATION DOCUMENTS:

Applicants must bring the following documents when applying:
- Social security card

ADDITIONAL PROGRAM COMMENTS:

Duration of program is 2-4-years depending on experience.

• • •

Graphic Communications International Union
Local Union #508-M
2351 West McMichen Avenue
Cincinnati, OH 45245
513-621-3974
ATTN: Dexter Denney

Specific job title(s): Pressman, Prepress, Bindery worker
This is a 2-4-year program.
No salaries were reported by this program.
Annually, a varying number of people apply for 20-25 positions.
Course credit is offered.
There is an initial 6-month probationary period.
Applications are accepted in person.

REQUIREMENTS:

- Pass a written test

APPLICATION DOCUMENTS:

Applicants must bring the following documents when applying:
- Social security card

• • •

Graphic Communications International Union
Local Union #199-B
2621 East 3rd Street
Dayton, OH 45404
513-233-7734
ATTN: Ronald Gauer

Specific job title(s): Bookbinder
This is a 4-year program.
No salaries were reported by this program.
Annually, a varying number of people apply for 10-15 positions.
There is an initial probationary period.
Applications are accepted in person any time of year.

• • •

Graphic Communications International Union
Local Union #566-M
1262 North Country Road 5
Fostoria, OH 44830
419-937-2848
ATTN: Ronda Roelle

Specific job title(s): Pressman, Prepress, Bindery worker
This is a 2-4-year program.
No salaries were reported by this program.
Annually, a varying number of people apply for 11-15 positions.
There is an initial 60-day probationary period.
Applications are accepted in person from current employees

REQUIREMENTS:

- Minimum age: 18
- Physician's statement of fitness
- Must be physically able to perform the work of the trade
- Pass a written test
- Pass an oral interview
- Letter of recommendation from employers
- Pass a test for illegal drugs

ADDITIONAL PROGRAM COMMENTS:

Stripping class is available but not required, two days a week for six and a half months.

• • •

Graphic Communications International Union
Local Union #270-M
7312 Road D
Leipsic, OH 45856
419-943-2430
ATTN: Paula Siebeneck

Specific job title(s): Pressman, Prepress
This is a 3.5-year program.
No salaries were reported by this program.
Annually, a varying number of people apply for 0-2 positions.
There is an initial 2-month probationary period.
Applications are accepted in person.

REQUIREMENTS:

- Minimum age: 18
- High school diploma or GED certificate
- Physician's statement of fitness
- Must be physically able to perform the work of the trade
- Pass a written test
- Pass an oral interview
- Valid driver's license
- Pass a test for illegal drugs

APPLICATION DOCUMENTS:

Applicants must bring the following documents when applying:
- High school diploma or GED certificate
- Social security card
- Driver's license

• • •

 Graphic Communications International Union
Local Union #235-C
PO Box 116
Middletown, OH 45042
513-422-0621
ATTN: Gary Lewis

Specific job title(s): Pressman
This is a 4-year program.
No salaries were reported by this program.
Annually, a varying number of people apply for 0-2 positions.
There is an initial 3-month probationary period.
Applications are accepted in person any time of year when ad runs in local paper.

REQUIREMENTS:

- Minimum age: 18
- High school diploma or GED certificate
- Physician's statement of fitness
- Must be physically able to perform the work of the trade
- Pass a written test
- Pass an oral interview
- Letter of recommendation from previous employers
- Pass a test for illegal drugs

APPLICATION DOCUMENTS:

Applicants must bring the following documents when applying:
- High school diploma or GED certificate
- Social security card

• • •

 Graphic Communications International Union
437 North Main
Navarre, OH 44662
216-879-2619
ATTN: William Benson

Specific job title(s): Pressman
This is a 4-year program.
Starting wage: $6.55; Ending wage: $13.10.
Annually, 0-10 people apply for 0-5 positions.
There is an initial 90-day probationary period.
Applications are accepted in person or by mail any time of year, Monday-Friday, 9:00-3:00.

REQUIREMENTS:

- Minimum age: 16; Maximum age: 62
- Pass an oral interview

APPLICATION DOCUMENTS:

Applicants must bring the following documents when applying:
- Social security card
- Resume

• • •

Graphic Communications International Union
Local Union #269-M
38 East 5th Street
The Plains, OH 45780
614-797-4856
ATTN: Charles Williams

Specific job title(s): Prepress, Pressman, Bindery worker
This is a 4-year program.
No salaries were reported by this program.
Annually, a varying number of people apply for a varying number of positions.
There is an initial 1-month probationary period.
Applications are accepted in person any time of year.

REQUIREMENTS:

- Minimum age: 18
- Physician's statement of fitness

APPLICATION DOCUMENTS:

Applicants must bring the following documents when applying:
- Social security card

• • •

OREGON

Graphic Communications International Union
1120 NW C Street
Grants Pass, OR 97526
ATTN: William Dodder

Specific job title(s): Pressman
This is a 4-year program.
Ending wage: $14.32.
Annually, 0-10 people apply for 0-5 positions.
There is an initial probationary period.
Applications are accepted in person or by mail any time of year, Monday-Friday, 8:00-5:00.

REQUIREMENTS:

- Minimum age: 18
- High school diploma or GED certificate

ADDITIONAL PROGRAM COMMENTS:

Newspaper press experience is important.

• • •

PENNSYLVANIA

Graphic Communications International Union
RD 1 Box 8-A
Cambridge Springs, PA 16403
814-398-4534
ATTN: Wayne Miller

This is a 4-year program with 7,800 hours of on-the-job training.
Starting wage: $6.51; Ending wage: $11.84.
Annually, 0-10 people apply for 0-5 positions.
There is an initial 90-day probationary period.
Applications are accepted by mail any time of year.

REQUIREMENTS:

- Minimum age: 18
- High school diploma or GED certificate
- Pass an oral interview

APPLICATION DOCUMENTS:

Applicants must bring the following documents when applying:
- Social security card

• • •

Graphic Communications International Union
Local Union #141-C
RDI Box 249-A
Drums, PA 18222
717-788-1578
ATTN: William Steinman

Specific job title(s): Pressman
This is a 4-year program.
No salaries were reported by this program.
Annually, a varying number of people apply for 0-1 positions.
There is an initial 6-month probationary period.
Applications are accepted in person or by mail.

REQUIREMENTS:

- Minimum age: 18
- Pass an oral interview
- Letter of recommendation

APPLICATION DOCUMENTS:

Applicants must bring the following documents when applying:
- Social security card

• • •

 Graphic Communications International Union
Local Union #138-B
137 West Oregon Road
Lititz, PA 17543
717-560-2083
ATTN: Lynda Bennett

Specific job title(s): Bindery worker
This is a 3-year program.
No salaries were reported by this program.
Annually, a varying number of people apply for 0-5 positions.
There is an initial 3-month probationary period.
Applications are accepted in person or by mail any time of year within plant.

REQUIREMENTS:

- Minimum age: 18
- Pass an oral interview

• • •

 Graphic Communications International Union
Local Union #388-C
Road 2 117 Cree Street Box 844
Meadville, PA 16335
814-333-1972
ATTN: Richard Krasa

Specific job title(s): Pressman
This is a 4-year program.
No salaries were reported by this program.
Annually, a varying number of people apply for a varying number of positions.
There is an initial 2-month probationary period.
Applications are accepted in person or by mail any time of year.

REQUIREMENTS:

- High school diploma or GED certificate
- Pass an oral interview

• • •

 Graphic Communications International Union
Local Union #594-S
11 North 4th Street
Mount Wolf, PA 17347
717-266-4409
ATTN: Dale Sowers

Specific job title(s): Pressman
This is a 4-year program.
Starting wage: $8.50; Ending wage: $10.25.
Annually, a varying number of people apply for a varying number of positions.
There is an initial 3-month probationary period.
Applications are accepted in person any time of year.

REQUIREMENTS:

- Minimum age: 18
- High school diploma or GED certificate
- Physician's statement of fitness
- Must be physically able to perform the work of the trade
- Pass a written test
- Pass an oral interview
- Pass a test for illegal drugs

• • •

 Graphic Communications International Union
Local Union #24
1825 Boulevard of the Allies
Pittsburgh, PA 15219
412-391-1377
ATTN: Richard Nussbaumer

Specific job title(s): Prepress, Pressman
This is a 4-5-year program with 4 hours of classroom instruction.
No salaries were reported by this program.
Annually, a varying number of people apply for a

varying number of positions.
There is an initial 6-month probationary period.
Applications are accepted in person or by mail any time of year.

APPLICATION DOCUMENTS:

Applicants must bring the following documents when applying:
- Social security card

• • •

Graphic Communications International Union
Local Union #9-N
PO Box 23358
Pittsburgh, PA 15222
412-276-2649
ATTN: Joseph Stern

Specific job title(s): Pressman
This is a 4-year program.
No salaries were reported by this program.
Annually, 31-50 people apply for 0-5 positions.
There is an initial probationary period.
Applications are accepted in person or by mail any time of year.

REQUIREMENTS:

- Minimum age: 18
- High school diploma or GED certificate
- Physician's statement of fitness
- Must be physically able to perform the work of the trade
- Pass a written test
- Pass an oral interview
- Pass a test for illegal drugs

APPLICATION DOCUMENTS:

Applicants must bring the following documents when applying:
- High school diploma or GED certificate
- Social security card

• • •

Graphic Communications International Union
Local Union #160-M
1616 Muhlenberg Street
Reading, PA 19606
215-376-0517
ATTN: Scott Rathman

Specific job title(s): Prepress, Pressman, Bindery worker
This is a 4-year program.
No salaries were reported by this program.
Annually, a varying number of people apply for 10-15 positions.
There is an initial probationary period.
Applications are accepted in person or by mail any time of year. Process varies by company.

REQUIREMENTS:

- Pass a test for illegal drugs

APPLICATION DOCUMENTS:

Applicants must bring the following documents when applying:
- Social security card

• • •

Graphic Communications International Union
1904 Hillside Avenue
Windber, PA 15963
814-467-9137
ATTN: Donald Gibson

Specific job title(s): Pressman
This is a 3-year program.
Starting wage: $9.00; Ending wage: $15.00.
Annually, 0-10 people apply for 0-5 positions.
There is an initial 80-day probationary period.
Applications are accepted in person any time of year, Monday-Friday.

REQUIREMENTS:

- Minimum age: 18
- High school diploma or GED certificate
- Physician's statement of fitness
- Must be physically able to perform the

work of the trade
- Pass an oral interview
- Valid driver's license
- Letter of recommendation from personal and professional acquaintances
- Must attend a preapprenticeship class for 16 exams

APPLICATION DOCUMENTS:

Applicants must bring the following documents when applying:
- High school diploma or GED certificate
- Social security card

ADDITIONAL PROGRAM COMMENTS:

Applicants must be mechanically inclined.

• • •

Graphic Communications International Union
Local Union #329-C
305 Pinehurst Road
York, PA 17402
717-755-4260
ATTN: William Gladfelter

Specific job title(s): Pressman
This is a 4-year program.
No salaries were reported by this program.
Annually, a varying number of people apply for a varying number of positions.
Applications are accepted in person any time of year.

REQUIREMENTS:

- Minimum age: 18
- Pass an oral interview
- Pass a test for illegal drugs

APPLICATION DOCUMENTS:

Applicants must bring the following documents when applying:
- Social security card

• • •

RHODE ISLAND

Graphic Communications International Union
Local Union #12
270 West Minster Street, 2nd Floor
Providence, RI 02903
401-277-7936
ATTN: Joe O'Connor

Specific job title(s): Pressman
This is a 3-year program.
No salaries were reported by this program.
Annually, 0-10 people apply for 0-5 positions.
Applications are accepted in person any time of year.

REQUIREMENTS:

- High school diploma or GED certificate
- Must be physically able to perform the work of the trade
- Letter of intent from a valid employer
- Must attend a preapprenticeship class

• • •

TENNESSEE

Graphic Communications International Union
1418 Carroll Creek Road
Gray, TN 37615
615-283-4232
ATTN: David Sells

Program title: Apprentice Pressman Correspondence Course
Specific job title(s): Pressman
This is a 4-year program.
Starting wage: $7.00; Ending wage: $11.00.
Annually, 0-10 people apply for 0-5 positions.
There is an initial 6-month probationary period.
Applications are accepted in person any time of year.

REQUIREMENTS:

- High school diploma or GED certificate
- Physician's statement of fitness
- Must be physically able to perform the work of the trade
- Pass an oral interview

APPLICATION DOCUMENTS:

Applicants must bring the following documents when applying:
- High school diploma or GED certificate
- Social security card

ADDITIONAL PROGRAM COMMENTS:

Applicants must be mechanically inclined.

• • •

Graphic Communications International Union
Local Union #165-C
1162 West Boy Scout Road
Hixson, TN 37343
615-843-2630
ATTN: William Friar

Specific job title(s): Pressman, Press assistant, Feeder operator
This is a 1.5-2-year program.
No salaries were reported by this program.
Annually, 0-4 people apply for 0-2 positions.
There is an initial 2-3-month probationary period.
Applications are accepted in person or by mail any time of year.

REQUIREMENTS:

- Minimum age: 18
- Physician's statement of fitness
- Must be physically able to perform the work of the trade
- Pass an oral interview
- Letter of recommendation
- Pass a test for illegal drugs

APPLICATION DOCUMENTS:

Applicants must bring the following documents when applying:
- Social security card
- Proof of residency
- Proof of additional schooling

• • •

Graphic Communications International Union
Local Union #118-C
7601 Hawthorne Drive
Knoxville, TN 37919
615-691-1617
ATTN: John Hartley

Specific job title(s): Pressman
This is a 4-year program.
No salaries were reported by this program.
Annually, 0-10 people apply.
There is an initial 6-month probationary period.
Applications are accepted in person any time of year.

REQUIREMENTS:

- Minimum age: 18
- Pass a written test
- Pass an oral interview

APPLICATION DOCUMENTS:

Applicants must bring the following documents when applying:
- Social security card

• • •

VIRGINIA

Graphic Communications International Union
7654 Elkhardt Road
Richmond, VA 23235
804-276-5224
ATTN: Fred Gray

Specific job title(s): Pressman
This is a 3-year program.
Starting wage: $10.52; Ending wage: $16.65.
Annually, 51-100 people apply for 0-5 positions.
Course credit is offered.
There is an initial 6-month probationary period.
Applications are accepted in person any time of year.

REQUIREMENTS:

- High school diploma or GED certificate
- Physician's statement of fitness

- Must be physically able to perform the work of the trade
- Pass an oral interview

APPLICATION DOCUMENTS:

Applicants must bring the following documents when applying:
- High school diploma or GED certificate
- Social security card

• • •

WISCONSIN

Graphic Communications International Union
642 Putnam Street
Eau Claire, WI 54703
ATTN: Herb Ruscin

This is a 4-year program.
No salaries were reported by this program.
Annually, 0-10 people apply for 0-5 positions.
There is an initial 6-month probationary period.
Applications are accepted in person or by mail any time of year.

REQUIREMENTS:

- High school diploma or GED certificate
- Pass a written test
- Letter of recommendation from former employer

• • •

Western Publishing Company, Inc.
1220 Mound Avenue
Racine, WI 53404
414-633-2431
ATTN: Kay Kawa

Specific job title(s): Pressman, Prepress
This is a 2-4-year program.
No salaries were reported by this program.
Annually, 0-10 people apply for 1-5 positions.
Applications are accepted in person any time of year.

ADDITIONAL PROGRAM COMMENTS:

Starting and ending hourly salaries vary along with most requirements, which are based on seniority. Drug testing is pre-employment only. Prepress positions involve EPS, Stripping, B/W Camera, Platemaking, and Inkroom.

• • •

Sheboygan Paper Box Company
716 Clara Avenue
Sheboygan, WI 53081
414-458-8373
ATTN: George Schmidbuer

Specific job title(s): Pressman
This is a 5-year program.
No salaries were reported by this program.
Annually, a varying number of people apply for a varying number of positions.
There is an initial 2-5-month probationary period.
Applications are accepted by mail any time of year.

REQUIREMENTS:

- Minimum age: 18
- Letter of recommendation from teachers, past employers

APPLICATION DOCUMENTS:

Applicants must bring the following documents when applying:
- Social security card
- Driver's license

ADDITIONAL PROGRAM COMMENTS:

Classroom instruction is 300 hours or more; on-the-job instruction is 8,000 hours for Assistant Press and 10,000 hours for Head Press. Credits are obtained through Lakeshore Technical College.

• • •

Graphic Communications International Union
Local Union #556-C
1518 South 24th Street
Sheboygan, WI 53081
414-459-9605
ATTN: William Wilsing

Specific job title(s): Pressman
This is a 4-year program.
No salaries were reported by this program.
Annually, a varying number of people apply for 0-1 positions.
There is an initial 3-month probationary period.

Applications are accepted in person any time of year.

REQUIREMENTS:

- Pass an oral interview

APPLICATION DOCUMENTS:

Applicants must bring the following documents when applying:
- Social security card

• • •

Roofers and Waterproofers

Roofs can be divided into two major types—flat and pitched. Flat roofs are typically found on commercial and industrial structures and on apartment buildings. Pitched, or slanted, roofs are more commonly used on houses. *Roofers,* who install and repair roofs, often specialize in either flat or pitched roofs, though some work on both types. Most roofers are employed by roofing contractors. About one-third are self-employed. Self-employed roofers generally work on houses.

Flat roofs have traditionally been made of several layers. Roofers begin by spreading a layer of insulation on the roof deck and covering it with hot bitumen, a tarlike substance. The next layer, made of roofing felt (a fabric saturated in bitumen), is applied in overlapping pieces and covered with another coat of bitumen. Roofers alternate between roofing felt and bitumen until the desired number of layers, or plies, is reached. Finally, the top is either given a smooth finish or made rough with gravel.

Single-ply methods, using sheets of plastic or rubber material, are increasingly used on flat roofs. These sheets are rolled out over the roof's insulation and then sealed in various ways. They can, for example, be melted into place with a torch or hot anvil, or they can be covered with a layer of bitumen. Some sheets are installed with adhesives, stone ballasts, or mechanical fasteners.

For pitched roofs the first step might be tacking strips of roofing felt lengthwise across the surface. Beginning at the bottom, roofers then nail horizontal rows of asphalt shingles, which must be cut to fit around corners, chimneys, and other obstructions. Strips of metal or shingle are used to seal over the areas where two sections of the roof come together. The final step is to seal nailheads or other exposed joints with caulking or roofing cement. Such roofs can also be covered with tile or slate shingles or with metal.

Roofers sometimes waterproof other structures, such as walls, swimming pools, and tanks. Using a chisel or other tool, they might begin by smoothing out the surface and repairing imperfections. The surface is then coated with a waterproofing material or covered with a waterproofing membrane. Workers who do this type of work are sometimes called *waterproofers*.

Supervised by already established roofers and waterproofers, apprentices begin with simple tasks, such as carrying equipment or erecting scaffolding. The specialized skills of the trade are then gradually learned. Apprentices also receive each year at least 144 hours of classroom instruction in mathematics, the use of tools, and other subjects. Because roofers work high above the ground, they must have a good sense of balance and not be overly afraid of heights. Roofing, however, has one of the highest accident rates in the construction industry.

Roofing apprenticeships normally run three years. Most programs require that the applicant

- apply in person

- be at least 18 years old

- be a high school graduate (or GED holder)

- be physically able to perform the work of the trade

Reported beginning apprenticeship salaries range from $6.05 to $15.02 an hour.

Reported ending apprenticeship salaries range from $11.05 to $24.60 an hour.

The number of employed roofers and waterproofers is expected to grow at an average rate. Because roof repair accounts for some 60 percent of the work load, roofers are less affected by economic downturns than other workers in the construction industry. Most jobs are done during the spring and summer.

For more information on apprenticeships for roofers and waterproofers, write to the national programs listed below, as well as to any government programs located in your state. When a name is included, address your letter to that person. Because existing programs are often revised, some of the following may have changed or ceased to exist. New programs may also have been created. Additional programs might be listed with the national union or with your state's bureau of apprenticeship training. Addresses can be found in the last section of this encyclopedia.

NATIONAL SPONSOR

United Union of Roofers, Waterproofers, and Allied Workers
1125 17th Street NW, 5th floor
Washington, DC 20036
202-638-3228
ATTN: Robert Krul

This organization is affiliated with the AFL-CIO and has 135 locals.

ADDITIONAL PROGRAM COMMENTS:

Roofing is physically intensive work. Applicants should not be afraid of heights. Career opportunities include foreman, superintendent, estimator, and owner of one's own roofing business. Work can be seasonal in northern climates and year round in southern ones. Work is averted by rain, snow, ice, high winds, and economic downturns.

• • •

STATE SPONSORS

ALASKA

Roofers and Waterproofers
1818 West Northern Lights, #203
Anchorage, AK 99517
907-272-4311
ATTN: Richard Kraus

Program title: Alaska Roofers JATP
This is a 3-year program with 432 hours of classroom instruction and 3,600 hours of on-the-job training.
Starting wage: $13.53; Ending wage: $24.60.
Annually, 31-50 people apply for 6-10 positions.
There is an initial 350-hour probationary period.
Applications are accepted in person or by mail any time of year, Monday-Friday 8:00-12:00 and 1:00-5:00.

REQUIREMENTS:

• Minimum age: 18
• Pass an oral interview

APPLICATION DOCUMENTS:

Applicants must bring the following documents when applying:
- High school transcript or GED scores
- Birth certificate

ADDITIONAL PROGRAM COMMENTS:

Apprentices are required to attend class two nights per week for four hours each night. Courses include safety, math, drafting, fabrication and installation, blueprint reading, hoisting and rigging, testing, adjusting, and balancing, service work, indoor air quality, welding, city code, CAD and sheet metal. Extra points are given to applicants with any courses in math, algebra, geometry, trigonometry, blueprint reading, metal shop, woodworking, or construction.

• • •

REQUIREMENTS:

- Minimum age: 18
- Must be physically able to perform the work of the trade
- Pass a written test
- Pass an oral interview
- Valid driver's license
- Resident of the program's jurisdiction
- Letter of recommendation from employers or associates

APPLICATION DOCUMENTS:

Applicants must bring the following documents when applying:
- High school transcript or GED scores
- High school diploma or GED certificate
- Social security card
- Driver's license
- Birth certificate

• • •

ARIZONA

Roofers
1917 East Washington Street
Phoenix, AZ 85034
602-254-7059

No salaries were reported by this program. Write or call for application information.

• • •

ARKANSAS

Bricklayers and Allied Crafts Local #1
504 South Victory Street
Little Rock, AR 72201
501-372-3532
ATTN: Charles Martin

Specific job title(s): Waterproofer
This is a 3-year program with 432 hours of classroom instruction.
Starting wage: $15.02.
Annually, 0-10 people apply for 6-10 positions.
There is an initial 60-day probationary period.
Applications are accepted in person any time of year.

CALIFORNIA

Roofers Tri-County JAC
9901 Paramount Boulevard
Suite #211
Downey, CA 90240
310-927-2544
ATTN: Jean White

This is a 3.5-year program with 504 hours of classroom instruction.
Starting wage: $9.74; Ending wage: $20.27.
Annually, over 100 people apply.
There is an initial probationary period.
Applications are accepted in person any time of year.

REQUIREMENTS:

- Minimum age: 18
- Must be physically able to perform the work of the trade
- Pass an oral interview
- Valid driver's license
- Resident of the program's jurisdiction

Roofers and Waterproofers

APPLICATION DOCUMENTS:

Applicants must bring the following documents when applying:
- Social security card
- Driver's license

• • •

Central Valley Roofers, Waterproofers and Allied Workers JATC
4831 East Shields, Room 27
Fresno, CA 93726
209-255-0933

Specific job title(s): Roofer, Waterproofer
This is a 3-year program.
No salaries were reported by this program.
Applications are accepted in person every Wednesday and Friday, 11:00-5:00.

REQUIREMENTS:

- Minimum age: 18
- High school diploma or GED certificate

APPLICATION DOCUMENTS:

Applicants must bring the following documents when applying:
- High school transcript or GED scores
- High school diploma or GED certificate

• • •

Bay Area Roofing Industry
8301 Edgewater Drive
Oakland, CA 94621
510-635-8800
ATTN: Duane Mongerson

Specific job title(s): Roofer, Waterproofer
This is a 3.5-year program with 504 hours of classroom instruction and 4,000 hours of on-the-job training.
Starting wage: $7.93; Ending wage: $24.28.
Annually, over 100 people apply for over 100 positions.
Course credit is offered.
There is an initial 6-month probationary period.
Applications are accepted in person any time of year, 9:00-11:00.

REQUIREMENTS:

- Minimum age: 18
- Physician's statement of fitness
- Must be physically able to perform the work of the trade
- Valid driver's license
- Pass a test for illegal drugs
- Passing grade in the following high school course(s): Math
- U.S. citizenship

• • •

Roofers Local #81
8400 Enterprise Way
Oakland, CA 94621
510-632-0505

No salaries were reported by this program.
Write or call for application information.

• • •

Roofers
1074 East La Cadena Drive
Riverside, CA 92501
909-684-3645

No salaries were reported by this program.
Write or call for application information.

• • •

Roofers
2840 El Centro Road
Sacramento, CA 95833
916-646-6754

No salaries were reported by this program.
Write or call for application information.

• • •

San Diego and Imperial Counties' Slate, Tile and Composition Roofers JAC
3909 Centre Street, Suite 211
San Diego, CA 92103
619-298-3258
ATTN: Mac Colmenero

This is a 3-year program.
Starting wage: $7.44; Ending wage: $16.99.
Annually, 21-30 people apply for 16-20 positions.
Course credit is offered.
There is an initial 90-day probationary period.
Applications are accepted in person any time of year, Fridays only, 8:00-10:00.

REQUIREMENTS:

- Minimum age: 18
- Pass an oral interview
- Resident of the program's jurisdiction
- Letter of recommendation from former employers
- Pass a test for illegal drugs

APPLICATION DOCUMENTS:

Applicants must bring the following documents when applying:
- Driver's license
- Work permit or Green card

• • •

Roofers Local #40
55 Fillmore Street
San Francisco, CA 94117
415-861-9976

No salaries were reported by this program.
Write or call for application information.

• • •

Roofers Local #220
1605 North Susan, #6
Santa Ana, CA 92703
714-554-8101

No salaries were reported by this program.
Write or call for application information.

• • •

Roofers Local #56
3180 North Ad Art Road, #C-3
Stockton, CA 95215
209-931-6764
ATTN: Conrad Ensley

Program title: Roofer and Waterproofer JATC
Specific job title(s): Roofer, Waterproofer
This is a 3-year program with 325 hours of classroom instruction and 360 hours of on-the-job training.
Ending wage: $17.47.
Annually, 11-20 people apply for 6-10 positions.
Course credit is offered.
There is an initial 6-month probationary period.
Applications are accepted in person by appointment only.

REQUIREMENTS:

- Minimum age: 18
- High school diploma or GED certificate
- Must be physically able to perform the work of the trade
- Pass an oral interview
- Valid driver's license
- Resident of the program's jurisdiction
- Pass a test for illegal drugs

APPLICATION DOCUMENTS:

Applicants must bring the following documents when applying:
- High school transcript or GED scores
- High school diploma or GED certificate
- Social security card
- Driver's license

ADDITIONAL PROGRAM COMMENTS:

A good driving record and a valid driver's license are an absolute must. The applicant must be able to travel long distances to remote job sites and could also be required to drive the company truck, which requires the ability to be insured. Eighty percent of this job is having a good work ethic: show up on time, be ready to work, have all the tools necessary to do the job, and wear the correct clothing and safety equipment.

• • •

COLORADO

Roofers
404 North Spruce Street
Colorado Springs, CO 80905
719-632-5889
ATTN: Dale Solano

Program title: Southern Colorado Roofers JATP
This is a 3-year program with 400 hours of classroom instruction and 3,600 hours of on-the-job training.
Starting wage: $6.50; Ending wage: $11.05.
Annually, 0-10 people apply for 0-5 positions.
There is an initial 30-day probationary period.
Applications are accepted in person any time of year, Monday-Friday, 5:00 PM-6:00 PM.

REQUIREMENTS:

- Minimum age: 18
- Pass an oral interview
- Valid driver's license
- Letter of recommendation from a roofing contractor

APPLICATION DOCUMENTS:

Applicants must bring the following documents when applying:
- High school transcript or GED scores
- High school diploma or GED certificate
- Social security card
- Driver's license
- Birth certificate

ADDITIONAL PROGRAM COMMENTS:

Apprentices are required to attend classes two nights a month as well as study the course at home and take periodic tests. They also must complete a daily work sheet for every month of their apprenticeship.

• • •

Northern Colorado Roofers JATC
1540 Emerson Street, Suite 4
Denver, CO 80218
303-832-2269
ATTN: Gail Hamby

This is a 3-year program with 432 hours of classroom instruction and 4,500 hours of on-the-job training.
Starting wage: $6.20; Ending wage: $11.75.
Annually, over 100 people apply for 51-100 positions.
Applications are accepted in person or by mail any time of year, Monday-Friday, 7:00-11:00.

REQUIREMENTS:

- Minimum age: 18

• • •

CONNECTICUT

Roofers Local #12
679 North Avenue
Bridgeport, CT 06606
203-368-3046

No salaries were reported by this program. Write or call for application information.

• • •

Roofers Local #9
106 South Street
West Hartford, CT 06110
203-953-0665
ATTN: Brendan Finn

This is a 4-year program with 576 hours of classroom instruction.
Starting wage: $6.05; Ending wage: $16.85.
Annually, 21-30 people apply for 16-20 positions.
Course credit is offered.
There is an initial probationary period.
Applications are accepted in person during spring, summer, and fall, Monday-Friday, 8:00-2:30.

REQUIREMENTS:

- Minimum age: 18
- Pass an oral interview
- Valid driver's license
- Pass a test for illegal drugs

APPLICATION DOCUMENTS:

Applicants must bring the following documents when applying:
- Driver's license

• • •

FLORIDA

Roofers Local #181
4000 Union Hall Place
Jacksonville, FL 32205
904-384-7692

No salaries were reported by this program. Write or call for application information.

• • •

Roofers
4349 NW 36th Street
Miami, FL 33166
305-885-9759

No salaries were reported by this program. Write or call for application information.

• • •

Roofers
179 5619 North 50th Street
Tampa, FL 33610
813-620-1399

No salaries were reported by this program. Write or call for application information.

• • •

GEORGIA

Roofers and Waterproofers
374 Maynard Terrace SE
Atlanta, GA

No salaries were reported by this program. Write or call for application information.

• • •

HAWAII

Roofers and Waterproofers
Local #221 JATP
2045 Kamehameha IV Road, #201
Honolulu, HI 96819
808-847-5757
ATTN: Mariano Ponsiano

This is a 4- to 5-year program with 240 hours of classroom instruction and 7,000 hours of on-the-job training.
Starting wage: $9.79; Ending wage: $21.75.
Annually, 51-100 people apply for 31-50 positions.
There is an initial 1,000-hour probationary period.
Applications are accepted in person any time of year, Monday-Friday, 8:00-4:00.

REQUIREMENTS:

- Minimum age: 16
- High school diploma or GED certificate
- Must be physically able to perform the work of the trade
- Valid driver's license
- Pass a test for illegal drugs

APPLICATION DOCUMENTS:

Applicants must bring the following documents when applying:
- High school diploma or GED certificate

ADDITIONAL PROGRAM COMMENTS:

Apprentices should be able to lift 100 pounds. Those under 18 must have a child labor certificate and their parents' signatures on their apprenticeship agreement. Math, mechanical drawing, building construction technology, and technical science are helpful high school courses.

• • •

ILLINOIS

Roofers Local #97
212 South 1st Street
Champaign, IL 61820
217-359-3922

No salaries were reported by this program. Write or call for application information.

• • •

Decatur Roofers Local #92 JATC
PO Box 1634
Decatur, IL 62521
ATTN: Michael Shampine

This is a 4-year program with 576 hours of classroom instruction and 6,000 hours of on-the-job training.
Starting wage: $8.75; Ending wage: $17.51.
Annually, 31-50 people apply for 16-20 positions.
There is an initial 500-hour probationary period. Applications are accepted in person when advertised.

REQUIREMENTS:

- Minimum age: 18
- High school diploma or GED certificate
- Physician's statement of fitness
- Must be physically able to perform the work of the trade
- Pass a written test
- Pass an oral interview
- Resident of the program's jurisdiction for 3 years
- Pass a test for illegal drugs
- Passing grade in the following high school course(s): High school buildings and trade
- Must attend a preapprenticeship class for 4 hours

APPLICATION DOCUMENTS:

Applicants must bring the following documents when applying:
- High school transcript or GED scores
- High school diploma or GED certificate

• • •

Roofers
9838 West Roosevelt Road
Westchester, IL 60170

No salaries were reported by this program. Write or call for application information.

• • •

INDIANA

Roofers
105 Bing Boulevard
Anderson, IN 46017
317-378-0556

No salaries were reported by this program. Write or call for application information.

• • •

Indianapolis Roofers JAC Local #119
7147 Southeastern Avenue
Indianapolis, IN 46239
317-353-9281
ATTN: Broadus Asher

This is a 3-year program.
No salaries were reported by this program.
Applications are accepted in person any time of year. Call for information.

REQUIREMENTS:

- Minimum age: 18

ADDITIONAL PROGRAM COMMENTS:

This program has jurisdiction over the following counties: Marion, Hancock, Johnson, Boone, Hendricks, Hamilton, Shelby, Morgan, Union,

Jennings, Jackson, Monroe, Rush, Franklin, Bartholomew, Lawrence, Putnam, Wayne, Decatur, Brown, and Fayette.

• • •

Roofers Local #23
1345 North Side Boulevard
South Bend, IN 46615
219-288-6506

No salaries were reported by this program. Write or call for application information.

• • •

Roofers
150 31 South 13th Street
Terre Haute, IN 47807
812-232-7010

No salaries were reported by this program. Write or call for application information.

• • •

KANSAS

Roofers Local #20
10 South James Street
Kansas City, KS 66118
913-281-2527
ATTN: Richard Anderson

Program title: Roofers Apprenticeship Local #20
This is a 3-year program.
Starting wage: $7.50; Ending wage: $16.50.
Annually, over 100 people apply for 16-20 positions.
There is an initial 500-hour probationary period. Applications are accepted in person or by mail any time of year, Mondays, Wednesdays, and Fridays, 8:00-12:00.

REQUIREMENTS:

- Minimum age: 18
- Must be physically able to perform the work of the trade
- Pass a written test
- Valid driver's license
- Resident of the program's jurisdiction

ADDITIONAL PROGRAM COMMENTS:

Roofers Local #20 has different apprenticeship programs in different cities, all with different wage packages and time requirements. Statistics listed here are for Kansas City, Kansas. There are also programs in the Missouri cities of Kansas City, St. Joseph, Jefferson City, and Springfield, as well as one in Topeka, Kansas.

• • •

KENTUCKY

Roofers Local Union #147
7711 Beulah Church Road
Louisville, KY 40228
502-231-3344

No salaries were reported by this program. Write or call for application information.

• • •

LOUISIANA

Roofers Local Union #317
3260 Winbourne Avenue
Baton Rouge, LA 70805
504-355-8502

No salaries were reported by this program. Write or call for application information.

• • •

MARYLAND

Roofers Local #80 JAC
4324 York Road
Baltimore, MD 21212
301-243-5520
ATTN: Michael Brown

This is a 3-year program with 6,000 hours of on-the-job training.

No salaries were reported by this program.
Applications are accepted in person.

REQUIREMENTS:

- Minimum age: 18; Maximum age: 30
- Must be physically able to perform the work of the trade

• • •

MASSACHUSETTS

Roofers Local #33
51 Neponset Avenue
Dorchester, MA 02122
617-288-7410

No salaries were reported by this program.
Write or call for application information.

• • •

MICHIGAN

Roofers Local #149 Apprentice School
1640 Porter Street
Detroit, MI 48216
313-963-5287
ATTN: Bob Drogosch

This is a 3-year program.
No salaries were reported by this program.
Write or call for application information.

• • •

Roofers
149 G4070 North Dolan Drive
Flint, MI 48504
313-785-9222

No salaries were reported by this program.
Write or call for application information.

• • •

MINNESOTA

Roofers
312 Central Avenue NE
Minneapolis, MN 55414

No salaries were reported by this program.
Write or call for application information.

• • •

MISSOURI

Roofers
2920 Locus Street
Saint Louis, MO 63103
314-535-9683

No salaries were reported by this program.
Write or call for application information.

• • •

NEVADA

Roofers
4200 East Bonanza
Las Vegas, NV 89110
ATTN: Carl Rangen

Program title: Southern Nevada Roofers JTC
This is a 3-year program with 4,200 hours of on-the-job training.
Starting wage: $8.36; Ending wage: $15.65.
Annually, 21-30 people apply for 11-15 positions.
Course credit is offered.
There is an initial 600-hour probationary period.
Applications are accepted in person or by mail any time.

REQUIREMENTS:

- Minimum age: 18
- Physician's statement of fitness
- Pass an oral interview
- Valid driver's license
- Resident of the program's jurisdiction
- Pass a test for illegal drugs
- Must attend a preapprenticeship class for 100 hours

• • •

Roofers and Waterproofers

Roofers Local #224
1110 Greg Street
Sparks, NV 89431

No salaries were reported by this program. Write or call for application information.

• • •

NEW JERSEY

Roofers
1400 Genesee Street
Trenton, NJ 08610
609-394-2700

No salaries were reported by this program. Write or call for application information.

• • •

NEW MEXICO

Roofers
1869 Tovar Place SW
Albuquerque, NM 87121
505-836-9519

No salaries were reported by this program. Write or call for application information.

• • •

NEW YORK

Roofers Local Union #241
8903 D Street Extension
Albany, NY 12206
518-489-7646

No salaries were reported by this program. Write or call for application information.

• • •

Roofers Local #195
6780 Northern Boulevard
East Syracuse, NY 13057
315-437-1585
ATTN: Pat Redhead

This is a 4-year program with 432 hours of classroom instruction and 4,000 hours of on-the-job training.
Starting wage: $7.20; Ending wage: $18.00.
Annually, 51-100 people apply for 11-15 positions.
There is an initial 1,000-hour probationary period.
Applications are accepted in person in April and May, Mondays, Wednesdays, Fridays, 9:00-12:00, 1:00-4:00.

REQUIREMENTS:

- Minimum age: 18; Maximum age: 65
- High school diploma or GED certificate
- Must be physically able to perform the work of the trade
- Pass an oral interview

APPLICATION DOCUMENTS:

Applicants must bring the following documents when applying:
- High school diploma or GED certificate
- Social security card

• • •

Roofers Local #22
190 Dodge Street
Rochester, NY 14606
716-458-4710

No salaries were reported by this program. Write or call for application information.

• • •

OHIO

Roofers Local #88
6221 Promler Street NW
Canton, OH 44720
216-497-2848

No salaries were reported by this program. Write or call for application information.

• • •

Roofers
1579 Summit Road, #114
Cincinnati, OH 45237
513-821-3689
ATTN: Timothy Burke

Program title: JAC Composition Roofers
This is a 3-year program with 432 hours of classroom instruction and 3,000 hours of on-the-job training.
Starting wage: $10.08; Ending wage: $14.10. Annually, 31-50 people apply for 6-10 positions. Applications are accepted in person in May of each year, two weeks after the initial advertisement.

REQUIREMENTS:

- Minimum age: 18
- Pass a written test
- Pass an oral interview
- Valid driver's license
- Resident of the program's jurisdiction

APPLICATION DOCUMENTS:

Applicants must bring the following documents when applying:
- Driver's license

ADDITIONAL PROGRAM COMMENTS:

Along with classroom and on-the-job training, our apprentices also do charity work for churches and the homeless, for additional hands-on training.

• • •

Roofers and Waterproofers Local #44
1651 East 24th Street
Cleveland, OH 44114
216-781-4844

No salaries were reported by this program. Write or call for application information.

• • •

Roofers Local #86
23 West 2nd Avenue
Columbus, OH 43201
614-299-6404

No salaries were reported by this program. Write or call for application information.

• • •

Roofers Local Union #75
1407 East 3rd Street
Dayton, OH 45403
513-228-2464

No salaries were reported by this program. Write or call for application information.

• • •

Roofers Local #134
4652 Lewis Avenue
Toledo, OH 43612
419-478-3785

No salaries were reported by this program. Write or call for application information.

• • •

Roofers Local #71
2714 Martin Luther King Jr
Youngstown, OH 44216

No salaries were reported by this program. Write or call for application information.

• • •

OKLAHOMA

Roofers Local Union #143
111 NE 26th Street
Oklahoma City, OK 73105
405-524-4243

No salaries were reported by this program. Write or call for application information.

• • •

Eastern Oklahoma Building and Construction Trades Council
2651 East 21st Street
Tulsa, OK 74114
918-742-3305
ATTN: Clayton Walker

Program title: Roofers and Waterproofers JATC
Specific job title(s): Roofer, Waterproofer
No salaries were reported by this program. Write or call for application information.

• • •

OREGON

Roofers Local #49
2725 SE 21st Avenue
Portland, OR 97202
503-232-4807

No salaries were reported by this program. Write or call for application information.

• • •

Roofers
1174 Gateway Loop, Suite 106
Springfield, OR 97477
503-744-1771
ATTN: Gary Hubbard

Program title: Southwest Oregon JAC
This is a 3-year program with 1,000 hours of classroom instruction and 4,000 hours of on-the-job training.
Starting wage: $8.27; Ending wage: $16.54.
Annually, 31-50 people apply for 16-20 positions.
Course credit is offered.
There is an initial 200-hour probationary period.
Applications are accepted in person any time of year, weekdays.

REQUIREMENTS:

- Minimum age: 18; Maximum age: 51
- High school diploma or GED certificate
- Physician's statement of fitness
- Must be physically able to perform the work of the trade
- Pass an oral interview
- Valid driver's license
- Letter of recommendation from employer

APPLICATION DOCUMENTS:

Applicants must bring the following documents when applying:
- Social security card
- Driver's license

• • •

PENNSYLVANIA

Roofers Local Union #37 JAC
206 Federal Street
Pittsburgh, PA 15212
412-322-9925
ATTN: Tom Hayden

This is a 4-year program with 576 hours of classroom instruction and 5,400 hours of on-the-job training.
No salaries were reported by this program.
Annually, 51-100 people apply for 11-15 positions.
There is an initial 500-hour probationary period.
Applications are accepted in person the first of year for a two-week period. Program starts June 1st.

REQUIREMENTS:

- Minimum age: 18
- High school diploma or GED certificate
- Physician's statement of fitness

- Pass a written test
- Pass an oral interview
- Valid driver's license
- Resident of the program's jurisdiction
- Letter of recommendation from past employers
- Pass a test for illegal drugs

APPLICATION DOCUMENTS:

Applicants must bring the following documents when applying:
- High school transcript or GED scores
- High school diploma or GED certificate
- Social security card
- Driver's license

• • •

RHODE ISLAND

Roofers Local Union #169
150 Earnest Street
Providence, RI 02905
401-467-6090
ATTN: Paul Rettenmyer

Program title: Rhode Island Roofers JATP
This is a 4-year program.
No salaries were reported by this program.
Annually, a varying number of people apply for a varying number of positions.
Applications are accepted in person or by mail at various times. Contact for further information.

REQUIREMENTS:

- Minimum age: 18
- High school diploma or GED certificate
- Must be physically able to perform the work of the trade
- Pass a written test
- Pass an oral interview

APPLICATION DOCUMENTS:

Applicants must bring the following documents when applying:
- High school transcript or GED scores
- High school diploma or GED certificate

• • •

TENNESSEE

Roofers Local #115
3540 Summer Avenue
Memphis, TN 38122
901-327-6492
ATTN: Cordis Davis

This is a 3-year program with 432 hours of classroom instruction and 6,000 hours of on-the-job training.
Starting wage: $9.10; Ending wage: $12.58.
Annually, 31-50 people apply for 11-15 positions.
Applications are accepted in person any time of year.

REQUIREMENTS:

- Minimum age: 18
- Pass an oral interview
- Resident of the program's jurisdiction
- Passing grade in the following high school course(s): Math
- Must attend a preapprenticeship class

APPLICATION DOCUMENTS:

Applicants must bring the following documents when applying:
- Social security card
- Driver's license
- Birth certificate

• • •

Roofers
176 5105 Alabama Avenue
Nashville, TN 37209
615-298-5215

No salaries were reported by this program.
Write or call for application information.

• • •

WASHINGTON

Roofers Joint Apprenticeship
102 East Boone Avenue, #101
Spokane, WA 99202
509-327-2322
ATTN: Pat Bauer

Program title: Inland Empire Roofers and Employers JATC
This is a 2-year program with 288 hours of classroom instruction and 4,200 hours of on-the-job training.
Starting wage: $9.40; Ending wage: $16.00.
Annually, 31-50 people apply for 6-10 positions.
There is an initial 840-hour probationary period. Applications are accepted in person any time of year, Monday-Friday, 9:00-4:00.

REQUIREMENTS:

- Minimum age: 18; Maximum age: 45
- Must be physically able to perform the work of the trade
- Valid driver's license

APPLICATION DOCUMENTS:

Applicants must bring the following documents when applying:
- Driver's license

ADDITIONAL PROGRAM COMMENTS:

In some areas drug testing is required.

• • •

Pierce County Roofers
3049 South 36th Street, #210A
Tacoma, WA 98409
206-474-0528
ATTN: Thora Pulich

This is a 3-4-year program with 288 hours of classroom instruction and 4,900 hours of on-the-job training.
No salaries were reported by this program.
Annually, 51-100 people apply for a varying number of positions.
Course credit is offered.
There is an initial 500-hour probationary period. Applications are accepted in person.

REQUIREMENTS:

- Minimum age: 18
- High school diploma or GED certificate
- Must be physically able to perform the work of the trade
- Valid driver's license

ADDITIONAL PROGRAM COMMENTS:

This program lasts 2 to 3 years. Starting salary is approximately $8.48; ending salary ranges from $16.97 to $17.00.

• • •

WEST VIRGINIA

West Virginia State Building and Construction Trades Council
2301 7th Avenue
Charleston, WV 25312
304-346-1367
ATTN: E. Fisher

This is a 3-year program with 432 hours of classroom instruction and 6,000 hours of on-the-job training.
No salaries were reported by this program.
Write or call for application information.

REQUIREMENTS:

- Minimum age: 18
- Must be physically able to perform the work of the trade
- Pass an oral interview

APPLICATION DOCUMENTS:

Applicants must bring the following documents when applying:
- High school transcript or GED scores
- Birth certificate

• • •

Central West Virginia Roofers JATC, Local #242
1406 1/2 13th Street
Parkersburg, WV 26101
304-485-5099
ATTN: Kenneth Downie

This is a 5-year program with 750 hours of classroom instruction and 6,000 hours of on-the-job training.
Starting wage: $9.22; Ending wage: $18.44.
Annually, 0-10 people apply for 0-5 positions.
Course credit is offered.
There is an initial 1,000-hour probationary period.
Applications are accepted in person at the state Job Service Office.

REQUIREMENTS:

- Minimum age: 18
- High school diploma or GED certificate
- Pass a written test
- Pass an oral interview
- Valid driver's license
- Resident of the program's jurisdiction for 6 months
- Pass a test for illegal drugs

APPLICATION DOCUMENTS:

Applicants must bring the following documents when applying:
- High school diploma or GED certificate
- Driver's license

Sheetmetal Workers

Sheetmetal Workers

Sheetmetal workers fabricate, install, and repair products made of sheet metal. These products include ventilating, heating, and air-conditioning systems, as well as gutters, partitions, storefronts, roofing, and stainless steel kitchen and beverage equipment. Fiberglass, plastic, and other materials are sometimes used as well. About three-fourths of sheetmetal workers are employed by heating, air-conditioning, and plumbing contractors. Most of the remainder work for roofing and sheetmetal contractors. Some are also employed in the shipbuilding, aircraft, and railroad industries.

Sheetmetal workers usually produce their products in a shop. Following blueprints or other instructions, they select the proper materials and then measure and cut the metal. Saws, shears, and presses are used, as are more sophisticated machines, such as computer-controlled lasers. Once the metal is cut and shaped, the pieces are inspected to ensure they meet the specifications, and then finished with shears or hacksaws. The product is finally assembled with bolts, rivets, cement, welding, or other means. Additional assembly is usually done at the construction site. Some products—such as metal roofs—are assembled entirely at the site.

Many sheetmetal workers are involved in maintaining and repairing existing products, especially heating and air-conditioning systems. This type of work tends to be least affected by the booms and busts of the construction industry.

Apprentices are supervised by already established sheetmetal workers. They begin with such tasks as basic duct work and are gradually trained to handle the specialized jobs of the trade. In addition to on-the-job training, apprentices also receive at least 144 hours of classroom instruction each year in such subjects as mathematics, drafting, blueprint reading, computers, and welding. Most of the work is performed indoors, though the installation of roofs, gutters, and other products require workers to be outside.

Sheetmetal apprenticeships normally run four to five years. Most programs require that the applicant

- apply in person

- be at least 18 years old

- be a high school graduate (or GED holder)

- be physically able to perform the work of the trade

Reported beginning apprenticeship salaries range from $5.64 to $14.32 an hour.

Reported ending apprenticeship salaries range from $9.68 to $31.77 an hour.

Average growth is expected in the number of employed sheetmetal workers, though a growing demand for more energy-efficient heating, air-conditioning, and ventilation systems might improve the employment outlook. In general, the number of job openings will be tied to the health of the construction and manufacturing industries.

For more information on sheetmetal apprenticeships, write to the national programs listed below, as well as to any government programs located in your state. When a name is included, address your letter to that person. Because existing programs are often revised, some of the following may have changed or ceased to exist. New programs may also have been created. Additional programs might be listed with the national union or with your state's bureau of apprenticeship training. Addresses can be found in the last section of this encyclopedia.

Sheetmetal Workers

NATIONAL SPONSOR

National Training Fund for the Sheetmetal and Air Conditioning Industry
601 North Fairfax, Suite 240
Alexandria, VA 22314
703-739-7200
ATTN: Robert Martinez

• • •

STATE SPONSORS

ALABAMA

Sheetmetal Workers
PO Box 6708
Mobile, AL 36660
204-476-1900
ATTN: Bill Fisher

This is a 5-year program with 720 hours of classroom instruction.
Starting wage: $6.93; Ending wage: $13.09.
Annually, 11-20 people apply for 6-10 positions.
Applications are accepted in person or by mail any time of year.

REQUIREMENTS:

- Minimum age: 18; Maximum age: 28
- High school diploma or GED certificate
- Pass an oral interview
- Valid driver's license
- Resident of the program's jurisdiction
- Pass a test for illegal drugs
- Passing grade in the following high school course(s): Math, Drafting
- Must attend a preapprenticeship class

APPLICATION DOCUMENTS:

Applicants must bring the following documents when applying:
- Driver's license

• • •

ALASKA

SC-SE Sheetmetal Workers
1818 West Northern Lights #100
Anchorage, AK 99517
907-277-5313

This is a 4-year program with 192 hours of classroom instruction and 8,000 hours of on-the-job training.
Starting wage: $13.56; Ending wage: $27.11.
Annually, a varying number of people apply for 0-5 positions.
Applications are accepted in person February 1st-12th, Monday-Friday, 8:00-12:00, 1:00-5:00.

REQUIREMENTS:

- Minimum age: 18; Maximum age: 35
- High school diploma or GED certificate
- Pass an oral interview
- Resident of the program's jurisdiction

APPLICATION DOCUMENTS:

Applicants must bring the following documents when applying:
- High school transcript or GED scores
- High school diploma or GED certificate
- Driver's license
- Birth certificate

• • •

Fairbanks Sheetmetal Workers
3650 Braddock Street
Fairbanks, AK 99701
907-452-3864
ATTN: Donald Dokken

This is a 4-year program with 792 hours of classroom instruction and 8,000 hours of on-the-job training.
Starting wage: $14.32; Ending wage: $28.64.
Annually, 11-20 people apply for 0-5 positions.
There is an initial 6-month probationary period.
Applications are accepted in person after the first of the year.

REQUIREMENTS:

- Minimum age: 18; Maximum age: 34
- High school diploma or GED certificate
- Must be physically able to perform the work of the trade
- Pass an oral interview
- Valid driver's license
- Resident of the program's jurisdiction for 1 year

APPLICATION DOCUMENTS:

Applicants must bring the following documents when applying:
- High school transcript or GED scores
- High school diploma or GED certificate
- Driver's license
- Birth certificate
- Proof of residency
- Proof of additional schooling

• • •

ARIZONA

Phoenix Sheetmetal JATC
2534 East Adams Street
Phoenix, AZ 85034

This is a 5-year program with 1,056 hours of classroom instruction.
Starting wage: $8.25; Ending wage: $18.30.
Annually, 51-100 people apply for 16-20 positions.
Course credit is offered.
There is an initial 1-year probationary period.
Applications are accepted in person any time of year, 8:00-5:00.
The application deadline is June 30th.

REQUIREMENTS:

- Minimum age: 18
- High school diploma or GED certificate
- Pass a written test
- Pass an oral interview
- Valid driver's license
- Resident of the program's jurisdiction for 1 year
- Pass a test for illegal drugs
- Passing grade in the following high school course(s): Math

APPLICATION DOCUMENTS:

Applicants must bring the following documents when applying:
- High school diploma or GED certificate
- Social security card
- Driver's license
- Birth certificate

• • •

CALIFORNIA

Kern and Northern Los Angeles Counties Air Conditioning and Sheetmetal Workers JATC
601 Eureka Street
Bakersfield, CA 93305
805-323-4461

This is a 5-year program.
No salaries were reported by this program.
Applications are accepted in person Monday-Friday, 2:00-4:00.

REQUIREMENTS:

- Minimum age: 18
- High school diploma or GED certificate

APPLICATION DOCUMENTS:

Applicants must bring the following documents when applying:
- High school transcript or GED scores
- High school diploma or GED certificate

• • •

Fresno Sheetmetal Workers JATC
4585 East Floradora, #B
Fresno, CA 93703
209-255-3665

This is a 5-year program.
No salaries were reported by this program.
Applications are accepted in person every two years.

REQUIREMENTS:

- Minimum age: 18
- High school diploma or GED certificate

APPLICATION DOCUMENTS:

Applicants must bring the following documents when applying:
- High school transcript or GED scores
- High school diploma or GED certificate

• • •

Los Angeles Sheetmetal Workers JATC
PO Box 17096
Los Angeles, CA 90017
213-481-2088
ATTN: Lloyd Rademacher

This is a 5-year program with 1,200 hours of classroom instruction and 8,125 hours of on-the-job training.
Starting wage: $10.24; Ending wage: $25.60.
Annually, over 100 people apply for 51-100 positions.
Course credit is offered.
There is an initial 6-month probationary period.
Applications are accepted in person during the first full week of every month, Monday-Friday, 9:00-2:00.

REQUIREMENTS:

- Minimum age: 18
- High school diploma or GED certificate
- Pass a written test
- Pass an oral interview
- Valid driver's license
- Letter of recommendation
- Pass a test for illegal drugs

APPLICATION DOCUMENTS:

Applicants must bring the following documents when applying:
- High school transcript or GED scores
- High school diploma or GED certificate
- Driver's license

• • •

Modesto Area JAC for the Sheetmetal Trade
1307 7th Street, Suite B
Modesto, CA 95354
209-523-1323

This is a 4-year program.
No salaries were reported by this program.
Applications are accepted in person every two years.

REQUIREMENTS:

- Minimum age: 18
- High school diploma or GED certificate

APPLICATION DOCUMENTS:

Applicants must bring the following documents when applying:
- High school transcript or GED scores
- High school diploma or GED certificate

• • •

Air Conditioning Trade Association
900 Fulton Avenue, Suite 240
Sacramento, CA 95825
916-488-9580
ATTN: Bob Nambo

Program title: Air Conditioning Trade Association
This is a 4-year program with 408 hours of classroom instruction and 4,000 hours of on-the-job training.
Starting wage: $7.50; Ending wage: $14.00.
Annually, 11-20 people apply for 16-20 positions.
Course credit is offered.
Applications are accepted by mail any time of year.

REQUIREMENTS:

- High school diploma or GED certificate
- Must be physically able to perform the work of the trade
- Pass an oral interview
- Valid driver's license

Sheetmetal Workers

APPLICATION DOCUMENTS:

Applicants must bring the following documents when applying:
- High school diploma or GED certificate
- Social security card
- Driver's license

• • •

Sheetmetal Workers
1624 Silica Avenue
Sacramento, CA 95815
916-922-1133
ATTN: Jerry Hall

Program title: Sacramento Valley Sheet Metal/Service Tech
This is a 5-year program with 876 hours of classroom instruction and 8,000 hours of on-the-job training.
Starting wage: $8.86; Ending wage: $24.62.
Annually, 51-100 people apply for 16-20 positions.
Course credit is offered.
There is an initial 1,000-hour probationary period.
Applications are accepted in person any time of year.

REQUIREMENTS:

- Minimum age: 18
- High school diploma or GED certificate
- Pass a written test
- Valid driver's license
- Letter of recommendation
- Letter of intent from a valid employer
- Must attend a preapprenticeship class

APPLICATION DOCUMENTS:

Applicants must bring the following documents when applying:
- High school diploma or GED certificate
- Driver's license

• • •

Sheetmetal Workers Local #104
1939 Market Street
San Francisco, CA 94103
415-621-2930
ATTN: Robert Mammini

Program title: Sheetmetal Workers Local #104 JAC
This is a 5-year program with 920 hours of classroom instruction and 8,000 hours of on-the-job training.
Starting wage: $11.12; Ending wage: $31.77.
Annually, over 100 people apply for 16-20 positions.
There is an initial 1-year probationary period.
Applications are accepted in person on the 1st Tuesday of the month, 8:30-11:30.

REQUIREMENTS:

- Minimum age: 18
- High school diploma or GED certificate
- Valid driver's license

APPLICATION DOCUMENTS:

Applicants must bring the following documents when applying:
- High school diploma or GED certificate

• • •

Sheetmetal Workers
415 Chapala Street, Room 103
Santa Barbara, CA 93101
ATTN: James Lewis

Program title: Tri Counties Sheetmetal and Air conditioning Industry JAC
This is a 5-year program with 1,000 hours of classroom instruction and 8,125 hours of on-the-job training.
Starting wage: $9.66; Ending wage: $24.16.
Annually, 51-100 people apply for 6-15 positions.
There is an initial 1-year probationary period.
Applications are accepted in person or by mail any time of year, Monday-Friday, 8:00-12:00, 1:00-3:00.

REQUIREMENTS:

- Minimum age: 17
- High school diploma or GED certificate
- Must be physically able to perform the work of the trade
- Pass a written test
- Pass an oral interview
- Valid driver's license

APPLICATION DOCUMENTS:

Applicants must bring the following documents when applying:
- High school diploma or GED certificate
- Driver's license

• • •

COLORADO

Colorado Sheetmetal Workers Training Fund
688 Bryant Street
Denver, CO 80204
303-629-0717
ATTN: Gene Yale

This is a 4-year program with 850 hours of classroom instruction and 8,000 hours of on-the-job training.
Starting wage: $7.62; Ending wage: $19.13.
Annually, over 100 people apply for 21-50 positions.
Course credit is offered.
There is an initial 6-month probationary period.
Applications are accepted in person any time of year, Fridays only, 8:00-12:00.

REQUIREMENTS:

- Minimum age: 18
- High school diploma or GED certificate
- Physician's statement of fitness
- Pass a written test
- Pass an oral interview
- Valid driver's license
- Resident of the program's jurisdiction for 1 year
- Pass a test for illegal drugs
- Passing grade in the following high school course(s): Math, Algebra

APPLICATION DOCUMENTS:

Applicants must bring the following documents when applying:
- High school transcript or GED scores
- High school diploma or GED certificate
- Social security card
- Driver's license
- Birth certificate

ADDITIONAL PROGRAM COMMENTS:

Apprentices are required to attend class two nights per week for four hours each night. Courses include safety, math, drafting, fabrication and installation, blueprint reading, hoisting and rigging, testing, adjusting, and balancing, service work, indoor air quality, welding, city code, CAD and sheetmetal. Extra points are given to applicants with any courses in math, algebra, geometry, trigonometry, blueprint reading, metal shop, woodworking, or construction.

• • •

Associated General Contractors
600 South Cherry Street, #600
Denver, CO 80222
303-388-2422
ATTN: Sheri Bohti

This is a 4-year program.
No salaries were reported by this program.
Write or call for application information.

ADDITIONAL PROGRAM COMMENTS:

Starting wages range from $6.00 to $8.00 an hour; ending wages range from $12.00 to $23.05 an hour.

• • •

CONNECTICUT

General Dynamics Electric Boat Division
75 Eastern Point Road
Groton, CT 06340
203-433-3000
ATTN: Richard Taylor, Jr.

Sheetmetal Workers

Program title: Electric Boat Company Apprenticeship Program
Specific job title(s): Sheetmetal worker (Marine)
No salaries were reported by this program.
Annually, a varying number of people apply for a varying number of positions.
Applications are accepted in person or by mail.

REQUIREMENTS:

- Minimum age: 18
- High school diploma or GED certificate
- Physician's statement of fitness
- Must be physically able to perform the work of the trade
- Letter of recommendation from respective department

• • •

FLORIDA

Florida West Coast Sheet Metal JAC
5619 North 50th Street
Tampa, FL 33610
813-628-0021
ATTN: Michael Sloan

This is a 4-year program with 696 hours of classroom instruction and 8,000 hours of on-the-job training.
Starting wage: $6.68; Ending wage: $11.35.
Annually, 51-100 people apply for 6-10 positions.
Course credit is offered.
There is an initial 6- to 12-month probationary period.
Applications are accepted in person any time of year.

REQUIREMENTS:

- Minimum age: 18
- High school diploma or GED certificate
- Physician's statement of fitness
- Must be physically able to perform the work of the trade
- Pass an oral interview
- Valid driver's license
- Resident of the program's jurisdiction
- Pass a test for illegal drugs

APPLICATION DOCUMENTS:

Applicants must bring the following documents when applying:
- High school transcript or GED scores
- High school diploma or GED certificate
- Driver's license

ADDITIONAL PROGRAM COMMENTS:

Applicants are encouraged to take algebra and geometry, mechanical drafting, and any shop or trade classes.

• • •

Florida East Coast Chapter
The Associated General Contractors of America, Inc
2617 North Australian Avenue
West Palm Beach, FL 33407
407-833-3609
ATTN: A. James Pruitt

This is a 4-year program with 760 hours of classroom instruction and 8,000 hours of on-the-job training.
Starting wage: $5.91; Ending wage: $9.68.
Annually, 21-30 people apply for over 100 positions.
There is an initial 6-month probationary period.
Applications are accepted in person or by mail September through February, 9:00-5:00.

REQUIREMENTS:

- Minimum age: 18
- Pass an oral interview
- Valid driver's license
- Resident of the program's jurisdiction for 1 year
- Letter of intent from a valid employer

APPLICATION DOCUMENTS:

Applicants must bring the following documents when applying:
- Social security card
- Driver's license
- Birth certificate

• • •

GEORGIA

Sheetmetal Workers
1838 Stewart Avenue SW
Atlanta, GA 30315
ATTN: Mike Cannon

Program title: Central Georgia Sheetmetal JAC
This is a 5-year program with 918 hours of classroom instruction and 10,000 hours of on-the-job training.
Starting wage: $7.70; Ending wage: $17.35.
Annually, over 100 people apply for 51-100 positions.
There is an initial 1-year probationary period.
Applications are accepted in person at various times. Call for information.

REQUIREMENTS:

- Minimum age: 18
- High school diploma or GED certificate
- Must be physically able to perform the work of the trade
- Pass a written test
- Pass an oral interview
- Resident of the program's jurisdiction for 1 year
- Pass a test for illegal drugs

APPLICATION DOCUMENTS:

Applicants must bring the following documents when applying:
- High school diploma or GED certificate
- Birth certificate

ADDITIONAL PROGRAM COMMENTS:

Applicants should have a good understanding of math.

• • •

HAWAII

Sheetmetal Workers
1405 North King Street, 4th FL
Honolulu, HI 96817
808-841-5078
ATTN: Howard Tasaka

Program title: Hawaii Joint Apprenticeship Committee for the Sheetmetal Industry
This is a 5-year program with 900 hours of classroom instruction and 10,000 hours of on-the-job training.
Starting wage: $9.50; Ending wage: $23.75.
Annually, 31-50 people apply for 16-20 positions.
Course credit is offered.
There is an initial 3,000-hour probationary period.
Applications are accepted in person or by mail any time of year, Monday-Friday, except between 12:00 and 1:00.

REQUIREMENTS:

- Minimum age: 16
- High school diploma or GED certificate
- Physician's statement of fitness
- Must be physically able to perform the work of the trade
- Pass a written test
- Pass an oral interview
- Valid driver's license
- Pass a test for illegal drugs
- Must attend a preapprenticeship class for 2,000 hours

APPLICATION DOCUMENTS:

Applicants must bring the following documents when applying:
- High school transcript or GED scores
- High school diploma or GED certificate
- Social security card
- Driver's license

ADDITIONAL PROGRAM COMMENTS:

Applicants with a background in mechanical drawing, math, physical science, shop and language arts will find these helpful, although these courses are not required for acceptance into the program.

• • •

ILLINOIS

Sheetmetal Workers
6643 West North Avenue
Oak Park, IL 60302
708-848-9690
ATTN: Edward Donnelley

Program title: Sheetmetal Apprenticeship Program
This is a 4-year program with 600 hours of classroom instruction and 7,200 hours of on-the-job training.
Starting wage: $8.75; Ending wage: $17.50.
Annually, 11-20 people apply for 6-10 positions.
Course credit is offered.
There is an initial 6-month probationary period. Applications are accepted in person every two years.

REQUIREMENTS:

- Minimum age: 18
- High school diploma or GED certificate
- Pass a written test
- Pass an oral interview

APPLICATION DOCUMENTS:

Applicants must bring the following documents when applying:
- High school transcript or GED scores
- High school diploma or GED certificate
- Social security card

ADDITIONAL PROGRAM COMMENTS:

This program is currently inactive.

• • •

Sheetmetal Workers Local #218
2855 Via Verde
Springfield, IL 62703
217-529-0161
ATTN: Edward O'Connor

Program title: Sheetmetal Workers Local #218 JATC
This is a 4-year program with 800 hours of classroom instruction and 8,000 hours of on-the-job training.
Starting wage: $7.84; Ending wage: $19.60.
Annually, 51-100 people apply for 6-10 positions.
There is an initial 6-month probationary period. Applications are accepted in person every two years following an announcement in local newspapers.

REQUIREMENTS:

- Minimum age: 17
- High school diploma or GED certificate
- Pass a written test
- Pass an oral interview
- Valid driver's license
- Resident of the program's jurisdiction

APPLICATION DOCUMENTS:

Applicants must bring the following documents when applying:
- High school diploma or GED certificate
- Driver's license

ADDITIONAL PROGRAM COMMENTS:

Applicants are encouraged to take as many high school math courses as possible.

• • •

INDIANA

Indianapolis Sheetmetal JAC Local #20
2828 East 45th Street
Indianapolis, IN 46205
317-541-0050
ATTN: Hardie Smith

This is a 5-year program.
No salaries were reported by this program.
Applications are accepted in person usually in April for a two-week period. Call for more information.

REQUIREMENTS:

- Minimum age: 18; Maximum age: 33
- High school diploma or GED certificate

APPLICATION DOCUMENTS:

Applicants must bring the following documents when applying:
- High school transcript or GED scores
- Birth certificate

ADDITIONAL PROGRAM COMMENTS:

This program has jurisdiction over the following counties: Marion, Hancock, Johnson, Boone, Hendricks, Hamilton, Shelby, Decatur, Fayette, Franklin, Morgan, Rush, Jennings, Lawrence, Tipton, Union, Bartholomew, Brown, Jackson, Monroe, Orange, Ripley, Washington, Delaware, Henry, and Madison.

• • •

IOWA

Associated Builders and Contractors of Iowa
939 Office Park Road, #123
West Des Moines, IA 50265
515-224-9800
ATTN: Jack Dubbs

This is a 4-year program with 576 hours of classroom instruction and 8,000 hours of on-the-job training.
No salaries were reported by this program. Annually, 31-50 people apply for 21-50 positions.
Course credit is offered.
There is an initial 500-hour probationary period. Applications are accepted in person or by mail any time of year, Monday-Friday, 8:00-5:00.

REQUIREMENTS:

- Minimum age: 18
- Physician's statement of fitness

APPLICATION DOCUMENTS:

Applicants must bring the following documents when applying:
- Social security card
- Driver's license

• • •

KANSAS

Associated Builders and Contractors
5424 Antioch
Merriam, KS 46202
913-831-2221
ATTN: Roland Morreale

This is a 4-year program with 576 hours of classroom instruction and 8,000 hours of on-the-job training.
No salaries were reported by this program. Annually, 31-50 people apply for 16-20 positions.
There is an initial 500-hour probationary period. Applications are accepted in person or by mail any time of year.

REQUIREMENTS:

- Minimum age: 17
- Pass an oral interview
- Valid driver's license
- Letter of recommendation from 3 people who know applicant
- Passing grade in the following high school course(s): Math

APPLICATION DOCUMENTS:

Applicants must bring the following documents when applying:
- High school transcript or GED scores
- High school diploma or GED certificate
- Social security card
- Driver's license
- Birth certificate

• • •

LOUISIANA

Sims Mechanical, Inc.
1960 Easy Street
Lake Charles, LA 70605
318-477-8700
ATTN: David Sims

This is a 4-year program with 576 hours of classroom instruction and 8,000 hours of on-the-job training.

No salaries were reported by this program.
Annually, 0-10 people apply for 0-5 positions.
There is an initial 90-day probationary period.
Applications are accepted in person any time of year.

REQUIREMENTS:

- Minimum age: 18
- Must be physically able to perform the work of the trade
- Pass an oral interview
- Valid driver's license
- Pass a test for illegal drugs

APPLICATION DOCUMENTS:

Applicants must bring the following documents when applying:
- High school transcript or GED scores
- Social security card
- Driver's license

• • •

MAINE

Bath Iron Works
700 Washington Street
Bath, ME 04530
207-443-3311
ATTN: Jay Lemont

Program title: Bath Iron Works Apprenticeship Program
This is a 6,000-hour program with 790 hours of classroom instruction and 5,210 hours of on-the-job training.
Starting wage: $8.96; Ending wage: $13.50.
Annually, a varying number of people apply for a varying number of positions.
Course credit is offered.
There is an initial 500-hour probationary period.
Applications are accepted in person during the first quarter of the year, usually March 15th to May 1st.

REQUIREMENTS:

- Minimum age: 18
- High school diploma or GED certificate
- Pass an oral interview
- Passing grade in the following high school course(s): 2 years of college-preparatory math

APPLICATION DOCUMENTS:

Applicants must bring the following documents when applying:
- High school transcript or GED scores
- Birth certificate
- Resume

• • •

MARYLAND

Sheetmetal Workers Local #100
4705 Erdman Avenue
Baltimore, MD 21205
301-732-1849
ATTN: Neil Wilford

Program title: Sheetmetal Workers Local #100 JAC
This is a 4-year program with 672 hours of classroom instruction and 8,000 hours of on-the-job training.
No salaries were reported by this program.
Applications are accepted in person January 1st-March 31st, Monday-Friday, 8:00-4:00.

REQUIREMENTS:

- Minimum age: 18
- High school diploma or GED certificate
- Must be physically able to perform the work of the trade

• • •

Associated Sheetmetal Inc.
1244 Taylor Street NW, #1255 N
Bethesda, MD 20814
202-291-3682
ATTN: Curtis Mayfield

Program title: Associated Sheetmetal Apprenticeship Program
This is a 4-year program with 2,000 hours of classroom instruction and 1,000 hours of on-the-job training.

No salaries were reported by this program. Annually, 11-20 people apply for 0-5 positions. There is an initial probationary period. Applications are accepted in person.

REQUIREMENTS:

- Minimum age: 18
- High school diploma or GED certificate
- Pass a written test
- Pass an oral interview
- Valid driver's license
- Must attend a preapprenticeship class

APPLICATION DOCUMENTS:

Applicants must bring the following documents when applying:
- High school transcript or GED scores
- High school diploma or GED certificate
- Social security card
- Driver's license
- Birth certificate

• • •

Sheetmetal Workers Union Local #2
9703 East 53rd Street
Raytown, MD 64133
816-353-0038
ATTN: Robert Fessman

This is a 5-year program with 900 hours of classroom instruction.
Starting wage: $7.58; Ending wage: $15.75.
Annually, over 100 people apply for 21-50 positions.
There is an initial 1-year probationary period. Applications are accepted in person February through March.

REQUIREMENTS:

- Minimum age: 18; Maximum age: 36
- High school diploma or GED certificate
- Pass an oral interview
- Resident of the program's jurisdiction
- Pass a test for illegal drugs
- Passing grade in the following high school course(s): Math, Drafting

APPLICATION DOCUMENTS:

Applicants must bring the following documents when applying:
- High school transcript or GED scores
- High school diploma or GED certificate

• • •

Bethlehem Steel Corporation
Bethship
Sparrows Point, MD 21219
410-388-6759
ATTN: George Lang

This is a 3-year program with 600 hours of classroom instruction and 6,000 hours of on-the-job training.
Starting wage: $10.00.
Annually, over 100 people apply for 0-5 positions.
Course credit is offered.
There is an initial 480-hour probationary period. Applications are accepted by mail by sending a resume.

REQUIREMENTS:

- Minimum age: 18
- High school diploma or GED certificate
- Pass a written test
- Pass an oral interview
- Pass a test for illegal drugs
- Passing grade in the following high school course(s): Math

APPLICATION DOCUMENTS:

Applicants must bring the following documents when applying:
- High school transcript or GED scores
- Social security card

ADDITIONAL PROGRAM COMMENTS:

Ending hourly salary varies from $13.00 to $14.00. Additional application documents include college or military transcripts (if applicable) and a resume.

• • •

MASSACHUSETTS

Sheetmetal Workers Local Union #17
1181 Adams Street
Dorchester, MA 02124
ATTN: Edward Marks

Program title: Sheetmetal Workers Local #17 Joint Apprenticeship Training Committee
This is a 5-year program with 900 hours of classroom instruction and 10,000 hours of on-the-job training.
Starting wage: $9.00; Ending wage: $24.00.
Annually, over 100 people apply for 21-50 positions.
There is an initial 1-year probationary period.
Applications are accepted in person during the month of January.
The application deadline is January 31st.

REQUIREMENTS:

- Minimum age: 18
- High school diploma or GED certificate
- Physician's statement of fitness
- Must be physically able to perform the work of the trade
- Pass an oral interview
- Valid driver's license
- Resident of the program's jurisdiction
- Letter of recommendation from employers, teachers, friends
- Pass a test for illegal drugs
- Passing grade in the following high school course(s): Math

APPLICATION DOCUMENTS:

Applicants must bring the following documents when applying:
- High school transcript or GED scores
- High school diploma or GED certificate
- Social security card
- Driver's license
- 3 letters of reference

• • •

MISSISSIPPI

Jackson Sheetmetal Area JAC
PO Box 8851
Jackson, MS 39204
601-352-4182

This is a 5-year program with 780 hours of classroom instruction and 10,400 hours of on-the-job training.
Starting wage: $5.64; Ending wage: $10.64.
Annually, a varying number of people apply for a varying number of positions.
There is an initial 30-day probationary period.
Applications are accepted in person any time of year.

REQUIREMENTS:

- Minimum age: 18; Maximum age: 27
- High school diploma or GED certificate
- Physician's statement of fitness
- Must be physically able to perform the work of the trade
- Pass a written test
- Pass an oral interview
- Valid driver's license
- Passing grade in the following high school course(s): Math

APPLICATION DOCUMENTS:

Applicants must bring the following documents when applying:
- High school transcript or GED scores
- High school diploma or GED certificate
- Driver's license

• • •

NEVADA

Northern Nevada Associated Builders and Contractors
593 Overmeyer Road, Suite E
Sparks, NV 89431
702-358-7888
ATTN: Becki Strauss

This is a 4-year program with 576 hours of classroom instruction and 8,000 hours of on-the-job training.

No salaries were reported by this program. Annually, 11-20 people apply for 0-5 positions. There is an initial 6-month probationary period. Applications are accepted in person any time of year, Monday-Friday by appointment.

REQUIREMENTS:

- Minimum age: 17
- Pass an oral interview
- Valid driver's license
- Pass a test for illegal drugs

APPLICATION DOCUMENTS:

Applicants must bring the following documents when applying:
- High school transcript or GED scores
- High school diploma or GED certificate
- Driver's license
- Birth certificate
- Veteran's DD-214 if applicable

ADDITIONAL PROGRAM COMMENTS:

Applicants must complete their GED within six months of being in program.

• • •

NEW JERSEY

Sheetmetal Workers Local #27
322 Squankum Yellow B RD B 847
Farmingdale, NJ 07727
908-919-1999
ATTN: Thomas Stapleton

Program title: Sheetmetal Workers Local #27 JAT
This is a 4-year program with 672 hours of classroom instruction and 8,000 hours of on-the-job training.
Starting wage: $9.70; Ending wage: $18.19.
Annually, 51-100 people apply for 11-15 positions.
There is an initial 90-day probationary period. Applications are accepted in person after announcement of openings. Write for information.
The application deadline is 30 days after openings.

REQUIREMENTS:

- High school diploma or GED certificate
- Physician's statement of fitness
- Must be physically able to perform the work of the trade
- Pass a written test
- Pass an oral interview
- Valid driver's license
- Resident of the program's jurisdiction
- Must attend a preapprenticeship class for 80 hours

APPLICATION DOCUMENTS:

Applicants must bring the following documents when applying:
- High school diploma or GED certificate
- Driver's license

ADDITIONAL PROGRAM COMMENTS:

Potential applicants with some HVAC experience are preferred. Computer knowledge is helpful.

• • •

NEW MEXICO

Sheetmetal Workers
4400 Silver Avenue SE
Albuquerque, NM 87108
ATTN: Erik Emblem

Program title: New Mexico, West Texas Sheetmetal Workers JATC
This is a 5-year program with 800 hours of classroom instruction and 9,000 hours of on-the-job training.
Starting wage: $7.42; Ending wage: $14.14.
Annually, 31-50 people apply for 11-15 positions.
There is an initial 1-year probationary period. Applications are accepted in person or by mail when a need is determined.

REQUIREMENTS:

- Minimum age: 17; Maximum age: 31
- High school diploma or GED certificate
- Physician's statement of fitness
- Must be physically able to perform the

work of the trade
- Pass a written test
- Pass an oral interview
- Valid driver's license
- Resident of the program's jurisdiction for 1 year
- Pass a test for illegal drugs
- Passing grade in the following high school course(s): Math, Shop, Drafting, Home economics

APPLICATION DOCUMENTS:

Applicants must bring the following documents when applying:
- High school transcript or GED scores
- High school diploma or GED certificate
- Social security card
- Driver's license
- Birth certificate

• • •

NEW YORK

DynaBil Industries, Inc.
Flint Mine Road
Coxsackie, NY 12051
ATTN: Carol Landau

Program title: New York State Apprenticeship Program
This is a 3-year program with 432 hours of classroom instruction and 8,000 hours of on-the-job training.
Starting wage: $6.00; Ending wage: $10.00.
Annually, over 100 people apply for 0-5 positions.
There is an initial 90-day probationary period. Applications are accepted in person or by mail any time of year, Monday-Friday, 8:00-4:30.

REQUIREMENTS:

- Minimum age: 18
- High school diploma or GED certificate
- Physician's statement of fitness
- Must be physically able to perform the work of the trade
- Pass a written test
- Pass an oral interview
- Pass a test for illegal drugs

APPLICATION DOCUMENTS:

Applicants must bring the following documents when applying:
- Social security card
- Driver's license

• • •

Sheetmetal Workers Local #28
139-20 Jamaica Avenue
Jamaica, NY 11435
ATTN: Murray Liebowitz

Program title: Sheetmetal Workers Local #28 Education Fund
This is a 4-year program with 880 hours of classroom instruction and 7,000 hours of on-the-job training.
Starting wage: $8.86; Ending wage: $29.38.
Annually, over 100 people apply for 51-100 positions.
Course credit is offered.
There is an initial 6-month probationary period. Applications are accepted in person or by mail any time of year.

REQUIREMENTS:

- Minimum age: 17
- Pass a written test
- Pass a test for illegal drugs
- Must attend a preapprenticeship class for 240 hours

• • •

Sheetmetal Workers Local #46
40 Rutter Street
Rochester, NY 14606
716-254-9151
ATTN: John Mapes

Program title: Sheetmetal Workers Local #46 JATC
This is a 5-year program with 900 hours of classroom instruction and 10,000 hours of on-the-job training.
Starting wage: $6.70; Ending wage: $20.31.
Annually, 51-100 people apply for 6-10 positions.

There is an initial 5-year probationary period. Applications are accepted in person on the 1st Tuesday of every month, 9:00-11:00 and 2:00-4:00.

REQUIREMENTS:

- Minimum age: 18
- High school diploma or GED certificate
- Valid driver's license
- Resident of the program's jurisdiction for 1 year
- Pass a test for illegal drugs
- Passing grade in the following high school course(s): Algebra

APPLICATION DOCUMENTS:

Applicants must bring the following documents when applying:
- High school transcript or GED scores
- High school diploma or GED certificate
- Social security card
- Driver's license

• • •

Sheetmetal Workers Local #137
41-04-56th
Woodside, NY 11377
ATTN: Paul Collins

Program title: Apprenticeship Training Fund Local Union #137
This is a 5-year program with 120 hours of classroom instruction.
Starting wage: $6.98; Ending wage: $22.45.
Annually, 11-20 people apply for 0-5 positions.
There is an initial 6-month probationary period. Applications are accepted in person when the training program determines a need.

REQUIREMENTS:

- Minimum age: 21
- High school diploma or GED certificate
- Must be physically able to perform the work of the trade
- Pass a written test
- Pass an oral interview
- Valid driver's license

APPLICATION DOCUMENTS:

Applicants must bring the following documents when applying:
- High school diploma or GED certificate
- Social security card
- Driver's license

• • •

OKLAHOMA

Sheetmetal Workers Local #124
1404 NW 1st Street
Oklahoma City, OK 73106
405-232-1453
ATTN: Gary Nelson

Program title: Sheetmetal Workers Local #124 JAC
This is a 5-year program with 1,045 hours of classroom instruction and 8,000 hours of on-the-job training.
Starting wage: $8.66; Ending wage: $16.44.
Annually, over 100 people apply for 11-15 positions.
There is an initial 6-month probationary period. Applications are accepted in person during the last 2 weeks in February, Monday-Friday, 10:00-2:00.
The application deadline is usually in mid-March.

REQUIREMENTS:

- Minimum age: 18; Maximum age: 34
- High school diploma or GED certificate
- Pass a written test
- Pass an oral interview
- Valid driver's license
- Resident of the program's jurisdiction for 1 year

APPLICATION DOCUMENTS:

Applicants must bring the following documents when applying:
- High school transcript or GED scores
- Driver's license
- Driving record

ADDITIONAL PROGRAM COMMENTS:

Although not required, a course in algebra is highly recommended. (It increases your evaluation score.) The written exam is a math competency test. Your driving record should come from the Department of Public Safety. Classes that are also helpful are sheetmetal-related work, drafting, and industrial arts.

• • •

Eastern Oklahoma Building and Construction Trades Council
2651 East 21st Street
Suite #405
Tulsa, OK 74114
918-742-3305
ATTN: Clayton Walker

Program title: Tulsa Sheetmetal Workers JATC
This is a 4-year program with 576 hours of classroom instruction and 8,000 hours of on-the-job training.
Starting wage: $6.79; Ending wage: $15.08.
Annually, 11-20 people apply for 11-15 positions.
Course credit is offered.
Applications are accepted in person during March.
The application deadline is 45 days after opening.

REQUIREMENTS:

- Minimum age: 18
- High school diploma or GED certificate
- Physician's statement of fitness
- Pass a written test
- Pass an oral interview
- Resident of the program's jurisdiction
- Letter of recommendation from ministers, teachers, employers, etc.

• • •

OREGON

Sheetmetal Workers
825 NE 20th Avenue
Suite #130
Portland, OR 97232
503-231-4950
ATTN: Milton Hill

Program title: Sheetmetal Training Fund
This is a 5-year program with 945 hours of classroom instruction and 10,000 hours of on-the-job training.
Starting wage: $10.00; Ending wage: $20.00.
Annually, 31-50 people apply for 16-20 positions.
Course credit is offered.
There is an initial 1-year probationary period. Applications are accepted in person when a need for additional apprentices is determined by the training fund.

REQUIREMENTS:

- Minimum age: 18
- High school diploma or GED certificate
- Pass an oral interview
- Valid driver's license

APPLICATION DOCUMENTS:

Applicants must bring the following documents when applying:
- High school transcript or GED scores
- High school diploma or GED certificate
- Social security card
- Driver's license
- College transcripts

ADDITIONAL PROGRAM COMMENTS:

Applicants must have completed the following high school classes with a grade of C or better: English, general science, and geometry; they must also have completed a minimum of any 5 of the following classes with a grade of C or better: biology, chemistry, physics, calculus, trigonometry, algebra I and II, shop I and II, mechanical drawing.

Applicants must apply at the following address:

Apprenticeship Information Office
800 NE Oregon Street
Portland, OR 97232
503-731-4072

• • •

PENNSYLVANIA

Philadelphia Naval Shipyard
PO Box 36140
Philadelphia, PA 19112
ATTN: Ron Warrington

Program title: Philadelphia Naval Shipyard Apprenticeship Program
This is a 4-year program.
Starting wage: $9.00; Ending wage: $13.60.
Annually, over 100 people apply for over 100 positions.
Course credit is offered.
Applications are accepted by mail by applying to the Office of Personnel Management.

REQUIREMENTS:

- High school diploma or GED certificate
- Must be physically able to perform the work of the trade
- Pass a written test
- Pass an oral interview

• • •

Sheetmetal Workers Local #19
1301 South Delaware Avenue
Philadelphia, PA 19147
216-592-1999
ATTN: Thomas Kelly

Program title: Sheetmetal Workers JATP of Local #19
This is a 4-year program with 822 hours of classroom instruction and 7,000 hours of on-the-job training.
Starting wage: $9.39; Ending wage: $23.47.
Annually, over 100 people apply for 11-15 positions.
There is an initial 90-day probationary period.
Applications are accepted in person during the 1st two weeks of February, every two years.

REQUIREMENTS:

- Minimum age: 16
- High school diploma or GED certificate
- Physician's statement of fitness
- Must be physically able to perform the work of the trade
- Pass a written test
- Pass an oral interview
- Valid driver's license
- Resident of the program's jurisdiction for 1 year
- Pass a test for illegal drugs

APPLICATION DOCUMENTS:

Applicants must bring the following documents when applying:
- High school transcript or GED scores
- High school diploma or GED certificate
- Social security card
- Driver's license
- $10.00 application fee
- Picture ID

• • •

Sheetmetal Workers Local #12
Western Pennsylvania
1200 Gulf Lab Road
Pittsburgh, PA 15238
412-828-1386
ATTN: Paul Beehner

Program title: Sheetmetal Workers Local #12 JAP
This is a 5-year program with 900 hours of classroom instruction and 10,000 hours of on-the-job training.
Starting wage: $8.20; Ending wage: $20.49.
Annually, over 100 people apply for 16-20 positions.
Course credit is offered.
There is an initial 6-month probationary period.
Applications are accepted in person during the 1st 10 days in March, Tuesday-Saturday, 10:00-2:00.
The application deadline is March 10th.

Sheetmetal Workers

REQUIREMENTS:

- Minimum age: 17; Maximum age: 35
- High school diploma or GED certificate
- Physician's statement of fitness
- Must be physically able to perform the work of the trade
- Pass a written test
- Pass an oral interview
- Valid driver's license
- Resident of the program's jurisdiction
- Letter of recommendation from personal references
- Pass a test for illegal drugs

APPLICATION DOCUMENTS:

Applicants must bring the following documents when applying:
- High school transcript or GED scores
- High school diploma or GED certificate
- Social security card
- Driver's license

• • •

Sheetmetal Workers Local #44 JATC
116 Finn Street
Wilkes-Barre, PA 18705
717-829-0986
ATTN: Thomas Hoffman

This is a 4-year program with 144 hours of classroom instruction and 8,000 hours of on-the-job training.
Starting wage: $6.99; Ending wage: $17.49.
Annually, 51-100 people apply for 6-10 positions.
There is an initial 3-month probationary period. Applications are accepted by mail following notification in local media.

REQUIREMENTS:

- Minimum age: 17; Maximum age: 29
- High school diploma or GED certificate
- Physician's statement of fitness
- Pass a written test
- Pass an oral interview
- Valid driver's license
- Resident of the program's jurisdiction for 1 year
- Pass a test for illegal drugs
- Passing grade in the following high school course(s): Math, Drafting

APPLICATION DOCUMENTS:

Applicants must bring the following documents when applying:
- High school transcript or GED scores
- High school diploma or GED certificate

• • •

RHODE ISLAND

 Sheetmetal Workers Local #17 ATP
15 Earnest
Providence, RI
401-941-8202
ATTN: Jerry Schiano

This is a 4-year program.
No salaries were reported by this program.
Annually, a varying number of people apply for a varying number of positions.
Applications are accepted in person or by mail at various times. Contact for further information.

REQUIREMENTS:

- Minimum age: 18
- High school diploma or GED certificate
- Must be physically able to perform the work of the trade
- Pass a written test
- Pass an oral interview
- Letter of recommendation

APPLICATION DOCUMENTS:

Applicants must bring the following documents when applying:
- High school transcript or GED scores
- High school diploma or GED certificate

• • •

TENNESSEE

Sheetmetal Workers Local #177
4709 Alabama Avenue
Nashville, TN 37209
615-292-0587
ATTN: R. Paul Maloney

Program title: Local #177 Sheetmetal Apprenticeship School
This is a 3-year program with 576 hours of classroom instruction and 8,000 hours of on-the-job training.
Starting wage: $6.25; Ending wage: $15.10.
Annually, 51-100 people apply for 16-20 positions.
There is an initial probationary period.
Applications are accepted in person in the spring. Call for information.

REQUIREMENTS:

- Minimum age: 18
- High school diploma or GED certificate
- Physician's statement of fitness
- Pass a written test
- Pass an oral interview
- Valid driver's license
- Resident of the program's jurisdiction

APPLICATION DOCUMENTS:

Applicants must bring the following documents when applying:
- High school transcript or GED scores
- High school diploma or GED certificate
- Driver's license

• • •

TEXAS

Sheetmetal Workers Local #68
1020 South Industrial Blvd.
Euless, TX 76040
817-267-9213
ATTN: Richard Gatewood

This is a 5-year program with 1,100 hours of classroom instruction and 10,000 hours of on-the-job training.
Starting wage: $7.50; Ending wage: $15.25.
Annually, 31-50 people apply for 16-20 positions.
There is an initial 6-month probationary period.
Applications are accepted in person any time of year, Monday-Friday, 8:00-12:00, 1:30-4:30.

REQUIREMENTS:

- Minimum age: 17
- High school diploma or GED certificate
- Physician's statement of fitness
- Must be physically able to perform the work of the trade
- Pass a written test
- Pass an oral interview
- Valid driver's license
- Pass a test for illegal drugs

APPLICATION DOCUMENTS:

Applicants must bring the following documents when applying:
- High school transcript or GED scores
- Social security card
- Driver's license

• • •

Sheetmetal Workers Apprentice Training
900 West 34th Street
Houston, TX 77018
713-864-4594
ATTN: J. Freund

Program title: Houston Area Sheetmetal JAC
This is a 5-year program with 1,440 hours of classroom instruction and 10,000 hours of on-the-job training.
Starting wage: $7.00; Ending wage: $16.00.
Annually, 51-100 people apply for 16-20 positions.
There is an initial 6-month probationary period.
Applications are accepted in person any time of year, Monday-Friday, 8:00-4:30.

REQUIREMENTS:

- Minimum age: 18; Maximum age: 40
- High school diploma or GED certificate
- Must be physically able to perform the work of the trade

- Pass a written test
- Pass an oral interview
- Valid driver's license
- Resident of the program's jurisdiction for 6 months
- Letter of recommendation from a sheetmetal contractor in the Houston area

APPLICATION DOCUMENTS:

Applicants must bring the following documents when applying:
- High school transcript or GED scores
- Driver's license

ADDITIONAL PROGRAM COMMENTS:

Recommended high school courses are math, drafting, and shop.

• • •

Sheetmetal Workers
130 Avenue Del Rey
San Antonio, TX 78216
512-319-6584
ATTN: John Wilson

Program title: Sheetmetal Workers Local #67 Apprenticeship Training
This is a 4-year program with 162 hours of classroom instruction and 8,000 hours of on-the-job training.
Starting wage: $7.17; Ending wage: $17.92.
Annually, 51-100 people apply for 11-15 positions.
There is an initial 6-month probationary period. Applications are accepted in person in April, Monday-Friday, except between 11:30 and 1:30.

REQUIREMENTS:

- Minimum age: 18; Maximum age: 30
- High school diploma or GED certificate
- Pass an oral interview
- Valid driver's license
- Letter of recommendation from past employers

APPLICATION DOCUMENTS:

Applicants must bring the following documents when applying:
- High school transcript or GED scores
- High school diploma or GED certificate
- Birth certificate
- Veteran's DD-214 if applicable

• • •

VERMONT

Sheetmetal Specializing in HVAC, Inc.
20 D Avenue #1-A
Williston, VT 05495
ATTN: Deanna Utter

This is a 4-year program with 576 hours of classroom instruction and 8,000 hours of on-the-job training.
Starting wage: $6.50; Ending wage: $10.50.
Annually, 0-10 people apply for 0-5 positions.
There is an initial 30-day probationary period. Applications are accepted in person according to need.

REQUIREMENTS:

- Pass an oral interview
- Valid driver's license
- Resident of the program's jurisdiction

APPLICATION DOCUMENTS:

Applicants must bring the following documents when applying:
- Social security card
- Driver's license

• • •

VIRGINIA

Admissions Office
The Apprentice School Newport News Shipbuilding
4101 Washington Avenue
Newport News, VA 23607
804-380-3809

This is a 4-year program with 6,000 hours of on-the-job training.
Starting wage: $7.97; Ending wage: $13.48.
Annually, over 100 people apply for 51-100 positions.
Course credit is offered.
There is an initial 180-day probationary period.
Applications are accepted by mail any time of year, Monday-Friday, 7:30-4:30.

REQUIREMENTS:

- Minimum age: 18; Maximum age: 29
- High school diploma or GED certificate
- Must be physically able to perform the work of the trade
- Pass a written test
- Pass an oral interview
- Letter of recommendation from employers or teachers
- Pass a test for illegal drugs

APPLICATION DOCUMENTS:

Applicants must bring the following documents when applying:
- High school transcript or GED scores
- Social security card
- 2 forms ID
- College transcript

• • •

WASHINGTON

Sheetmetal Workers
1220 Tracey Street
Lacey, WA 98503
206-459-9118
ATTN: Bob Steele

Program title: Tacoma SW Washington Sheetmetal JATC
This is a 5-year program.
Starting wage: $9.39; Ending wage: $22.97.
Annually, over 100 people apply for 11-15 positions.
There is an initial 1-year probationary period.
Applications are accepted in person throughout November only, 8:00-4:30.

REQUIREMENTS:

- Minimum age: 18; Maximum age: 35
- High school diploma or GED certificate
- Must be physically able to perform the work of the trade
- Pass a written test
- Pass an oral interview
- Valid driver's license
- Letter of recommendation

APPLICATION DOCUMENTS:

Applicants must bring the following documents when applying:
- High school transcript or GED scores
- High school diploma or GED certificate
- Proof of citizenship

• • •

WEST VIRGINIA

West Virginia State Building and Construction Trades Council
2301 7th Avenue
Charleston, WV 25312
304-346-1367
ATTN: E. Fisher

This is a 5-year program with 900 hours of classroom instruction.
No salaries were reported by this program.
Write or call for application information.

REQUIREMENTS:

- Minimum age: 18
- High school diploma or GED certificate
- Must be physically able to perform the work of the trade
- Pass a written test
- Pass an oral interview

APPLICATION DOCUMENTS:

Applicants must bring the following documents when applying:
- High school transcript or GED scores
- Birth certificate

Sheetmetal Workers

ADDITIONAL PROGRAM COMMENTS:

Recommended high school courses include metal trades, geometry, mechanical drawing, welding, trigonometry, and industrial arts.

• • •

WISCONSIN

Repap Wisconsin Inc.
433 North Main Street
Kimberly, WI 54136
414-788-3511
ATTN: Dick Van Hammond

This is a 4-year program with 8,320 hours of on-the-job training.
Starting wage: $14.25; Ending wage: $16.54.
Annually, over 100 people apply for 0-5 positions.
There is an initial 6-month probationary period.
Applications are accepted in person when posted locally.

REQUIREMENTS:

- High school diploma or GED certificate
- Must be physically able to perform the work of the trade
- Pass a written test
- Pass an oral interview

APPLICATION DOCUMENTS:

Applicants must bring the following documents when applying:
- High school transcript or GED scores

ADDITIONAL PROGRAM COMMENTS:

Classroom instruction is one day every other week for three years. A drug test will be mandatory for newly hired applicants. Aptitude and reading tests are issued. Applicants are selected in-house by seniority first.

• • •

Air Comfort Inc.
5525 Bjorksten Plaza
Madison, WI 53711
608-274-5566
ATTN: Laurence Davies

This is a 5-year program with 900 hours of classroom instruction.
No salaries were reported by this program.
Annually, 0-10 people apply for 0-5 positions.
Course credit is offered.
There is an initial 6-month probationary period.
Applications are accepted by mail any time of year.

REQUIREMENTS:

- High school diploma or GED certificate
- Pass a written test
- Pass an oral interview

• • •

Briggs and Stratton
PO Box 702
Milwaukee, WI 53201
414-259-5333
ATTN: Jodi Mickalski

This is a 5-year program with 576 hours of classroom instruction and 10,400 hours of on-the-job training.
No salaries were reported by this program.
Annually, a varying number of people apply for a varying number of positions.
Applications are accepted in person in January and July.

REQUIREMENTS:

- Minimum age: 18
- High school diploma or GED certificate
- Pass a written test
- Pass an oral interview
- Letter of recommendation
- Letter of intent from a valid employer
- Pass a test for illegal drugs

APPLICATION DOCUMENTS:

Applicants must bring the following documents when applying:
- High school transcript or GED scores

ADDITIONAL PROGRAM COMMENTS:

Applicants must first be employed, then with a letter of intent they may enroll at a community college.

• • •

Milwaukee Area JATC for the Sheetmetal Industry
5425 West Vliet Street
Milwaukee, WI 53208
414-778-1100
ATTN: Kurt Nickel

Program title: same
Specific job title(s): Environmental service technician
This is a 5-year program with 1,000 hours of classroom instruction and 10,000 hours of on-the-job training.
Starting wage: $7.60; Ending wage: $20.45.
Annually, 0-10 people apply for 0-5 positions.
There is an initial 6-month probationary period. Applications are accepted in person any time of year by appointment only.

REQUIREMENTS:

- Minimum age: 18
- High school diploma or GED certificate
- Must be physically able to perform the work of the trade
- Pass a written test
- Valid driver's license

APPLICATION DOCUMENTS:

Applicants must bring the following documents when applying:
- High school transcript or GED scores
- High school diploma or GED certificate
- Social security card
- Birth certificate

• • •

Rhinelander Paper Company
515 West Davenport Street
Rhinelander, WI 54501
715-369-4100
ATTN: Bill Vancos

This is a 4-year program.
No salaries were reported by this program.
Annually, 0-10 people apply for a varying number of positions.
There is an initial 6-month probationary period. Applications are accepted in person through in-house hires.

REQUIREMENTS:

- High school diploma or GED certificate
- Physician's statement of fitness
- Must be physically able to perform the work of the trade
- Pass a written test
- Pass a test for illegal drugs

ADDITIONAL PROGRAM COMMENTS:

Salary is negotiated at approximately $10.44 to start and ending at $15.75. Classroom instruction is approximately 400 hours minimum.

• • •

Consolidated Papers Inc.
Box 8050
Wisconsin Rapids, WI 54495
715-442-3111
ATTN: Chuck Korn

This is a 4-year program with 432 hours of classroom instruction.
No salaries were reported by this program.
Annually, 51-100 people apply for 21-50 positions.
Course credit is offered.
There is an initial 60-day probationary period. Applications are accepted in person or by mail any time of year.

REQUIREMENTS:

- Pass an oral interview
- Pass a test for illegal drugs

- Passing grade in the following high school course(s): Algebra, Geometry

APPLICATION DOCUMENTS:

Applicants must bring the following documents when applying:
- High school transcript or GED scores
- High school diploma or GED certificate

• • •

Shipbuilding Industry Workers

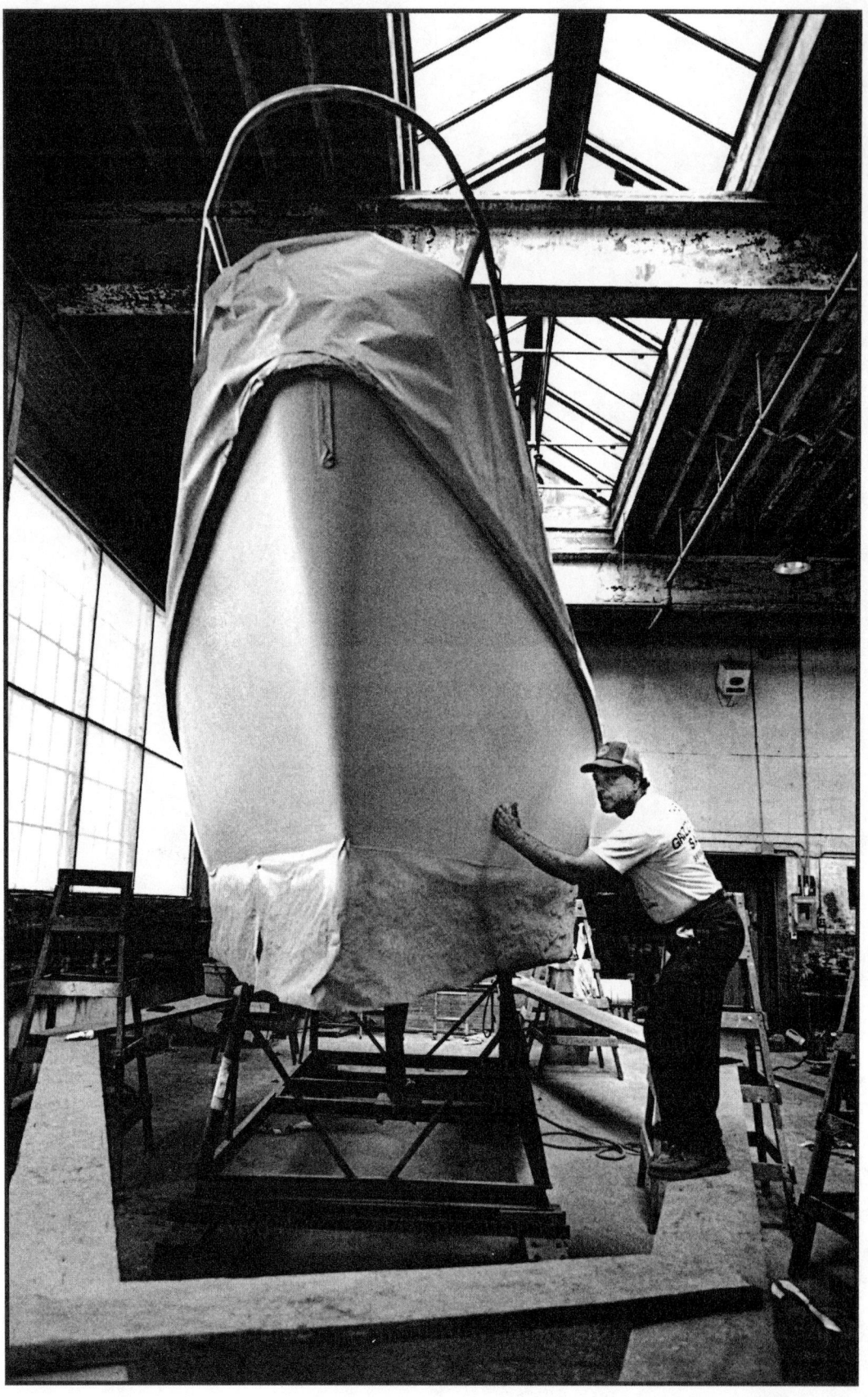

Shipbuilding Industry Workers

Building a ship is a complex process involving many specialized workers, such as welders, pipefitters, and mechanics. There are also workers specific to the shipbuilding industry. *Shipfitters,* for example, are responsible for manufacturing the metal structural parts of ships, including bulkheads and frames. They must then secure these parts in position for welding or riveting. Some shipfitters create molds for the manufacture of nonstandard parts. Shipfitters should not be confused with *shipwrights,* who are carpenters specializing in the construction and repair of ship parts.

Riggers form another important group of shipbuilding workers. Their primary responsibility is to set up and repair rigging—the various lines and chains used on a ship. Rigging, for example, is used to secure masts. On sailboats it includes the lines connected to the sails. Riggers must select the appropriate cables, ropes, pulleys, and other rigging equipment and direct their installation. Some riggers also install machinery, equipment, and structural parts on ships.

Shipbuilding apprentices receive both on-the-job and classroom instruction. Working under already experienced shipbuilders, they begin with simple tasks and move on to more difficult jobs with experience. Workers in the shipbuilding industry do most of their work inside. As with all construction trades, shipbuilding involves some risk of injury. Established safety practices must be carefully followed.

Apprenticeships for shipfitters, shipwrights, and riggers normally run three to four years. Most programs require that the applicant

- apply in person

- be at least 18 years old

- be a high school graduate (or GED holder)

- be physically able to perform the work of the trade

Reported beginning apprenticeship salaries range from $7.97 to $14.30 an hour.

Reported ending apprenticeship salaries range from $13.48 to $19.00 an hour.

Little change is expected in the number of shipbuilding workers. The overall health of the economy will have a significant impact on the shipbuilding industry, as will the number of government contracts to build and repair ships. Ships are expected to remain an important conveyor of cargo throughout the world.

For more information on shipbuilding apprenticeships, write to the national programs listed below, as well as to any government programs located in your state. When a name is included, address your letter to that person. Because existing programs are often revised, some of the following may have changed or ceased to exist. New programs may also have been created. Additional programs might be listed with the national union or with your state's bureau of apprenticeship training. Addresses can be found in the last section of this encyclopedia.

NATIONAL SPONSOR

Shipbuilders Council of America
4301 North Fairfax Drive, Suite 330
Arlington, VA 22203
703-276-1700

This is an organization of companies engaged in the construction and repair of vessels and other marine craft.

• • •

STATE SPONSORS

CONNECTICUT

General Dynamics Electric Boat Division
75 Eastern Point Road
Groton, CT 06340
203-433-3000
ATTN: Richard Taylor, Jr.

Program title: Electric Boat Company Apprenticeship Program
Specific job title(s): Shipfitter (marine), Rigger (marine)
No salaries were reported by this program.
Annually, a varying number of people apply for a varying number of positions.
Applications are accepted in person or by mail.

REQUIREMENTS:

- Minimum age: 18
- High school diploma or GED certificate
- Physician's statement of fitness
- Must be physically able to perform the work of the trade
- Letter of recommendation from respective department

• • •

MAINE

Bath Iron Works
700 Washington Street
Bath, ME 04530
207-443-3311
ATTN: Jay Lemont

Program title: Bath Iron Works Apprenticeship Program
Specific job title(s): Shipfitter, Hull outfit designer
This is a 6,000-hour program with 790 hours of classroom instruction and 5,210 hours of on-the-job training.
Starting wage: $8.96; Ending wage: $13.50.
Annually, a varying number of people apply for a varying number of positions.
Course credit is offered.
There is an initial 500-hour probationary period.
Applications are accepted in person during the first quarter of the year, usually March 15th to May 1st.

REQUIREMENTS:

- Minimum age: 18
- High school diploma or GED certificate
- Pass an oral interview
- Passing grade in the following high school course(s): 2 years of college-preparatory math

APPLICATION DOCUMENTS:

Applicants must bring the following documents when applying:
- High school transcript or GED scores
- Birth certificate
- Resume

• • •

MARYLAND

Bethlehem Steel Corporation
Bethship
Sparrows Point, MD 21219
410-388-6759
ATTN: George Lang

Specific job title(s): Shipfitter
This is a 4-year program with 600 hours of classroom instruction and 6,000 hours of on-the-job training.
Starting wage: $10.00.
Annually, over 100 people apply for 0-5 positions.
Course credit is offered.
There is an initial 480-hour probationary period. Applications are accepted by mail by sending a resume.

REQUIREMENTS:

- Minimum age: 18
- High school diploma or GED certificate
- Pass a written test
- Pass an oral interview
- Pass a test for illegal drugs
- Passing grade in the following high school course(s): Math

APPLICATION DOCUMENTS:

Applicants must bring the following documents when applying:
- High school transcript or GED scores
- Social security card

ADDITIONAL PROGRAM COMMENTS:

Ending hourly salary varies from $13.00 to $14.00. Additional application documents include college or military transcripts (if applicable) and a resume.

• • •

OHIO

Boilermakers
3625 West Tuscarawas
Canton, OH 44708
ATTN: Steven Jewell

Program title: Boilermakers Apprenticeship Program
Specific job title(s): Construction/Shop, Shipyard worker
This is a 4-year program with 1,500 hours of classroom instruction and 8,000 hours of on-the-job training.
Starting wage: $14.30; Ending wage: $19.00.
Annually, over 100 people apply for over 100 positions.
There is an initial 6-month probationary period. Applications are accepted in person any time of year. Call for information.

REQUIREMENTS:

- Minimum age: 18
- Pass a written test
- Pass an oral interview
- Passing grade in the following high school course(s): Math, Welding, Blueprint reading

APPLICATION DOCUMENTS:

Applicants must bring the following documents when applying:
- High school transcript or GED scores
- Social security card

• • •

PENNSYLVANIA

Philadelphia Naval Shipyard
PO Box 36140
Philadelphia, PA 19112
ATTN: Ron Warrington

Program title: Philadelphia Naval Shipyard Apprenticeship Program
Specific job title(s): Ship propeller finisher, Shipfitter
This is a 4-year program.
Starting wage: $9.00; Ending wage: $13.60.
Annually, over 100 people apply for over 100 positions.
Course credit is offered.
Applications are accepted by mail by applying to the Office of Personnel Management.

REQUIREMENTS:

- High school diploma or GED certificate
- Physician's statement of fitness
- Must be physically able to perform the work of the trade
- Pass a written test
- Pass an oral interview

• • •

RHODE ISLAND

Electric Boat Employment Office
General Dynamics Electric Boat
North Kingstown, RI 02852
401-268-2335
ATTN: Diane Dugan

Program title: Electric Boat Apprenticeship Program
Specific job title(s): Shipbuilder
No salaries were reported by this program.
Annually, a varying number of people apply for a varying number of positions.
Applications are accepted in person.

REQUIREMENTS:

- Minimum age: 18
- High school diploma or GED certificate
- Must be physically able to perform the work of the trade
- Pass a written test

APPLICATION DOCUMENTS:

Applicants must bring the following documents when applying:
- High school transcript or GED scores
- High school diploma or GED certificate

ADDITIONAL PROGRAM COMMENTS:

The apprenticeship term is 6,000 to 8,000-hours depending on the trade specialty. Electric Boat selects its apprentices from within its pool of current employees. In order to become eligible for training, selected persons must be employed by Electric Boat. Testing is currently being performed by Community College of Rhode Island.

• • •

VIRGINIA

Admissions Office
The Apprentice School Newport News Shipbuilding
4101 Washington Avenue
Newport News, VA 23607
804-380-3809

Specific job title(s): Shipfitter, Rigger
This is a 4-year program with 6,000 hours of on-the-job training.
Starting wage: $7.97; Ending wage: $13.48.
Annually, over 100 people apply for 51-100 positions.
Course credit is offered.
There is an initial 180-day probationary period.
Applications are accepted by mail any time of year, Monday-Friday, 7:30-4:30.

REQUIREMENTS:

- Minimum age: 18; Maximum age: 29
- High school diploma or GED certificate
- Must be physically able to perform the work of the trade
- Pass a written test
- Pass an oral interview
- Letter of recommendation from employers or teachers
- Pass a test for illegal drugs

APPLICATION DOCUMENTS:

Applicants must bring the following documents when applying:
- High school transcript or GED scores
- Social security card
- 2 forms ID
- College transcript

ADDITIONAL PROGRAM COMMENTS:

Classroom instruction is between 600 and 1,000 hours.

• • •

WASHINGTON

Shipwrights/Boat Builders Union
2415 Western Avenue
Seattle, WA 98121
206-441-8266
ATTN: Bob Scott

Specific job title(s): Shipwright
This is a 4-year program with 8,000 hours of on-the-job training.
No salaries were reported by this program.
Annually, 0-10 people apply for 0-5 positions.

Course credit is offered.
Applications are accepted in person any time of year, Monday-Friday, 7:00-4:30.

REQUIREMENTS:

- Minimum age: 18
- High school diploma or GED certificate
- Must be physically able to perform the work of the trade
- Pass a written test
- Pass an oral interview
- Pass a test for illegal drugs

APPLICATION DOCUMENTS:

Applicants must bring the following documents when applying:
- High school transcript or GED scores
- High school diploma or GED certificate
- Social security card
- Driver's license

ADDITIONAL PROGRAM COMMENTS:

Ending salary varies from $13.00 to $20.00.

Theater Workers

Theater workers who have the opportunity to learn through apprenticeships include *theater managers, stage technicians,* and *motion picture projectionists.*

Theater managers are responsible for the smooth running of the theater's business functions. They supervise box office cashiers, ticket takers, ushers, and other employees who interact with the audience at the theater. They oversee the maintenance of the physical facilities inside and outside the theater and ensure that the theater is clean. Managers are often responsible for counting and depositing money from ticket sales. They usually order food and other supplies for refreshment counters, as well as any other supplies needed for the upkeep of the theater. Managers may help to locate additional crew members or stage materials if they are needed on short notice for a performance. They are on hand before and during a performance to answer patron questions and handle any last-minute problems.

Stage technicians perform a variety of duties concerned with preparing stages for theatrical, musical, and other entertainment events in arenas, stadiums, theaters, studios, and other amusement places. They may construct, repair, paint, and set up and tear down sets; install and maintain stage lighting and electrical systems; acquire, build, and repair props and manage them during performances; rig scenery and repair and maintain rigging systems; wire and maintain audio cables and plugs, sound system setups and strikes, and operate the equipment during performances; and construct and repair sound, lighting, makeup, lasers, pyrotechnics and other physical special effects.

Motion picture machine projectionists set up and operate motion picture projection and sound-reproducing equipment to produce coordinated effects on screen. They may work in multi-plex, single-screen, and drive-in theaters. Some states require a motion picture projectionist to be licensed.

Apprentices work under already established theater workers. Classroom instruction is often geared around current productions and can vary as to content and length. Theater manager apprentices perform a variety of duties (determined by the producer or general manager) depending on the needs of their particular company. They may, for example, be responsible for the weekly payroll, paying the company's bills, or doing the nightly box office statement, or they may "run interference" for the company by handling ticket requests or problems. Stage technician apprentices learn stage carpentry, lighting, props, rigging, wardrobe, audio-visual set up, special effects, make-up, laser and pyrotechnics, and the basics of television and video production. They begin by assisting experienced workers in simple tasks and gradually work up to more complicated ones. Motion picture machine projectionists learn to operate different kinds of projection and sound equipment as they assist more skilled workers.

Apprenticeships for theater workers normally run two to three years. Most programs require that the applicant

- have some prior theater experience

- be at least 18 years old

- be a high school graduate (or GED holder)

- be physically able to perform the work of the trade

Reported beginning apprenticeship salaries range from $5.00 to $13.21 an hour.

Reported ending apprenticeship salaries range from $10.00 to $15.38 an hour.

Today, theaters tend to be concentrated in large metropolitan areas, so the number of job possibilities is greatest there, but so too is the competition for those jobs. Many people start out in local community theater or participate in their high school's or college's theater department productions. The public's demand for entertainment, especially theater and musical concerts, tends to ebb and flow with the overall economy; as people have more money to spend, they tend to go out more, but when they have less to spend, entertainment is one of the first items cut from the budget. The outlook for motion picture projections is expected to decline during the next ten years.

For more information on theater worker apprenticeships, write to the national programs listed below, as well as to any government programs located in your state. When a name is included, address your letter to that person. Because existing programs are often revised, some of the following may have changed or ceased to exist. New programs may also have been created. Additional programs might be listed with the national union or with your state's bureau of apprenticeship training. Addresses can be found in the last section of this encyclopedia.

NATIONAL SPONSOR

International Alliance of Theatrical Stage Employees and Moving Picture Machine Operators of the U.S. and Canada
1515 Broadway
Suite 601
New York, NY 10036
212-730-1770
ATTN: Keith Marshall

This organization is affiliated with the AFL-CIO and has 800 locals.

• • •

STATE SPONSORS

ALABAMA

Stage Employees Local #78
PO Box 10251
Birmingham, AL 35202
ATTN: Terry Wilkins

Specific job title(s): Stage technician
This is a 2-year program with 12 hours of classroom instruction and 12 hours of on-the-job training.
No salaries were reported by this program.
Annually, 0-10 people apply for 0-5 positions.
There is an initial 1-year probationary period. Applications are accepted by mail any time of year.

REQUIREMENTS:

- Minimum age: 18
- High school diploma or GED certificate
- Pass a written test
- Pass an oral interview
- Letter of recommendation from employer
- Letter of intent from a valid employer

APPLICATION DOCUMENTS:

Applicants must bring the following documents when applying:
- Driver's license
- Proof of citizenship

• • •

ALASKA

North County Productions
PO Box 221703
Anchorage, AK 99522
907-229-2099
ATTN: Greg McEven

Specific job title(s): Lighting and sound technician
No salaries were reported by this program.
Applications are accepted by mail any time of year.

ADDITIONAL PROGRAM COMMENTS:

This program trains apprentices in lighting and sound for large concerts. Send letter of interest to North County Productions to receive list of opening dates, specifications, and starting salaries.

• • •

CALIFORNIA

IATSE Local #33
1720 West Magnolia Boulevard
Burbank, CA 91506
818-841-9233
ATTN: Joseph Doucette, Jr.

Specific job title(s): Stage technician
No salaries were reported by this program.
Write or call for application information.

• • •

FLORIDA

IATSE Local #646
15 Southwest 7th Street
Fort Lauderdale, FL 33301
305-463-6175
ATTN: John Hubbard

Specific job title(s): Various theater workers
No salaries were reported by this program.
Write or call for application information.

• • •

IATSE Local #115
PO Box 462
Jacksonville, FL 32201
904-443-0060
ATTN: R. G. Klemmt

Specific job title(s): Stage technician
No salaries were reported by this program.
Write or call for application information.

• • •

IATSE Local #631
1206 33rd Street
Orlando, FL 32805
407-422-2747
ATTN: Harold Oakley

Specific job title(s): Stage technician
This is a 3-year program.
No salaries were reported by this program.
There is an initial probationary period.
Applications are accepted in person by telephone, Monday-Tuesday, Thursday-Friday, 1:00 PM to 12:00 AM.

REQUIREMENTS:

- Minimum age: 18
- Resident of the program's jurisdiction for

2 years
- Passing grade in the following high school course(s): TV, Electronics, Stage craft, Drama

APPLICATION DOCUMENTS:

Applicants must bring the following documents when applying:
- Social security card

ADDITIONAL PROGRAM COMMENTS:

If openings are available, individual fills out an application, then works two to three shows, which is a trial/probationary period. If hired, the applicant must apply to the union and pay an initiation fee of $350.00. Salaries vary from trade specifications. College credit is offered if enrolled at time of program.

• • •

GEORGIA

IATSE Local #320
2913 Bull Street
Savannah, GA 31405
912-233-8538
ATTN: Jean Soderlind

Specific job title(s): Various theater workers
No salaries were reported by this program.
Write or call for application information.

• • •

INDIANA

IATSE Local #30
1701 West 18th Street
Indianapolis, IN 46202
317-638-3226
ATTN: Quentin Quinn

Specific job title(s): Stage technician
No salaries were reported by this program.
Write or call for application information.

• • •

MAINE

Video Services
1065 Riverside Drive
Auburn, ME 04210
207-795-6440
ATTN: Cindy Spencer

Specific job title(s): Video production assistant
This is a 3-year program with 6,000 hours of on-the-job training.
Starting wage: $5.00; Ending wage: $10.00.
Annually, 0-10 people apply for 0-5 positions.
There is an initial 6-month probationary period.
Applications are accepted in person or by mail any time of year.

REQUIREMENTS:

- Minimum age: 21; Maximum age: 60
- High school diploma or GED certificate
- Physician's statement of fitness
- Must be physically able to perform the work of the trade
- Pass an oral interview
- Valid driver's license
- Resident of the program's jurisdiction
- Letter of recommendation
- Letter of intent from a valid employer
- Pass a test for illegal drugs
- Must attend a preapprenticeship class

APPLICATION DOCUMENTS:

Applicants must bring the following documents when applying:
- High school transcript or GED scores
- High school diploma or GED certificate
- Social security card
- Driver's license

• • •

MARYLAND

IATSE Local #22
11247-B Lockwood Drive
Silver Spring, MD 20901
301-593-4650
ATTN: Gilford Taylor

Specific job title(s): Stage technician
No salaries were reported by this program.
Write or call for application information.

• • •

MICHIGAN

Comstock Community Auditorium
Theater Technology Apprenticeship
Program
2107 North 26th Street
Comstock, MI 49041
616-388-9381
ATTN: Duwain Hunt

Specific job title(s): Stage technician
This is a 4500-hour program with 4,500 hours of classroom instruction/on-the-job training.
No salaries were reported by this program.
Applications are accepted in person.

• • •

NEVADA

Stage and Picture Operators
124 West Taylor Street
Reno, NV 89509
702-786-2286
ATTN: Brian Stedman

Program title: IATSE #368 Stagehands Apprenticeship
Specific job title(s): Stage technician
This is a 3-year program with 432 hours of classroom instruction and 4,500 hours of on-the-job training.
No salaries were reported by this program.
Annually, 11-20 people apply for 6-10 positions.
Applications are accepted in person or by mail.
The application deadline is May 30th.

REQUIREMENTS:

- Minimum age: 18
- High school diploma or GED certificate
- Must be physically able to perform the work of the trade
- Pass an oral interview
- Valid driver's license
- Pass a test for illegal drugs

ADDITIONAL PROGRAM COMMENTS:

This program does not have a rigid classroom schedule because of work scheduling, types of activities being taught, incoming work requirements, etc. Classes provide training in all technical phases of live theater, audio-visual, multi-media productions, large-scale industrial trade shows, and a brief overview of motion picture production for location work.

• • •

NEW JERSEY

IATSE Local #21
Millburn Mall, 2933 Vauxhall
Vauxhall, NJ 07041
201-379-9265
ATTN: Joy Renninghoff

Specific job title(s): Stage technician
No salaries were reported by this program.
Write or call for application information.

• • •

NEW YORK

Association of Theatrical Press Agents
and Managers
165 West 46th Street
New York, NY 10036
212-719-3666
ATTN: Berenice Weiler

Specific job title(s): Nonmember association manager, Off-Broadway manager
This is a 2-year program.
No salaries were reported by this program.
Annually, 11-20 people apply for 11-15 positions.
Applications are accepted in person or by mail any time of year.

REQUIREMENTS:

- High school diploma or GED certificate
- Pass a written test
- Letter of intent from a valid employer
- Resume

• • •

NORTH CAROLINA

IATSE Local #322
4037 East Independence, #601
Charlotte, NC 28205
704-537-8329
ATTN: Jim Duncan

Specific job title(s): Various theater workers
No salaries were reported by this program.
Write or call for application information.

• • •

OHIO

IATSE Local #364
678 North Main Street
Akron, OH 44310
216-376-2721
ATTN: Stewart Odell

Specific job title(s): Operator
No salaries were reported by this program.
Write or call for application information.

• • •

OREGON

Stagehands JATC Local #28
PO Box 1728
Portland, OR 97207
503-236-8208
ATTN: Tom Bugas

Specific job title(s): Stage technician
This is a 4-year program.
Starting wage: $13.21; Ending wage: $15.38.
There is an initial 160-hour probationary period.
Applications are accepted in person.

REQUIREMENTS:

- Minimum age: 18
- High school diploma or GED certificate
- Must be physically able to perform the work of the trade
- Pass a written test
- Pass an oral interview
- Letter of recommendation

APPLICATION DOCUMENTS:

Applicants must bring the following documents when applying:
- High school transcript or GED scores
- High school diploma or GED certificate

ADDITIONAL PROGRAM COMMENTS:

Applicant must be able to climb an eight-foot ladder and be able to see in restricted light. To be considered, applicants must know stage terminology and have at least some experience. If applicant passes written and oral interviews, he or she will be placed on an extra referral list. If shows are booked or extras are needed, applicant may be called.

• • •

PENNSYLVANIA

IATSE Local #8
1720 Delancy Place
Philadelphia, PA 19103
215-732-3316
ATTN: Drew Nolan

Specific job title(s): Stage technician
No salaries were reported by this program.
Write or call for application information.

• • •

RHODE ISLAND

IATSE Local #437
Brockton, Massachusetts
15 Barney Avenue
Lincoln, RI 02865
617-849-7798
ATTN: Marcus Weatherly

Specific job title(s): Motion picture machine operator
This is a 3-month program.
Starting wage: $8.00; Ending wage: $12.75. Annually, 0-10 people apply for 0-5 positions. Applications are accepted in person or by mail any time of year, (January-May is best) 1:00 PM-11:00 PM daily.

REQUIREMENTS:

- Minimum age: 18
- High school diploma or GED certificate
- Must be physically able to perform the work of the trade
- Pass a written test
- Pass an oral interview
- Valid driver's license

ADDITIONAL PROGRAM COMMENTS:

The state of Massachusetts and this union require a state-issued motion picture projectionist license.

• • •

TEXAS

Dallas Stage Employees Local #127 IATSE
5409 Jim Miller Road, #213
Dallas, TX 75227
ATTN: Shirley Mounsey

Starting wage: $11.10; Ending wage: $14.50. Annually, a varying number of people apply for a varying number of positions.
There is an initial 18-month probationary period. Applications are accepted in person any time of year, Monday-Friday.

REQUIREMENTS:

- Minimum age: 18
- High school diploma or GED certificate
- Physician's statement of fitness
- Pass a written test
- Pass an oral interview
- Valid driver's license
- Resident of the program's jurisdiction for 18 months
- Letter of recommendation

APPLICATION DOCUMENTS:

Applicants must bring the following documents when applying:
- Social security card
- Driver's license

ADDITIONAL PROGRAM COMMENTS:

This program primarily recruits people trained in theater technology.

• • •

UTAH

IATSE Local #99
307 West 200 Street, #2002
Salt Lake City, UT 84101
801-359-0513
ATTN: Herman Zeller

Specific job title(s): Stage technician
No salaries were reported by this program.
Write or call for application information.

• • •

WASHINGTON

IATSE Local #15
Labor Temple
2800 1st Avenue, #222
Seattle, WA 98121
206-441-1515
ATTN: Glennis Waterman

Specific job title(s): Stage technician
No salaries were reported by this program.
Write or call for application information.

• • •

Tile Setters

Tile Setters

Durable, waterproof, and easy to clean, tile has long been a popular building material for floors, walls, and ceilings. It is used, for example, in the bathrooms and kitchens of houses, as well as in office lobbies, shopping centers, schools, and hospitals. *Tile setters,* who install tiles, are typically employed by tile setting contractors. Almost two-fifths, however, are self-employed.

There are two main methods of setting tile. In the first a metal mesh is tacked to the building surface. With a trowel the tile setter coats the mesh with a cement plaster, and a small tool is used to scratch the plaster before it dries. The back of each tile is then coated with cement and carefully attached to the surface. It is essential that the tiles are aligned perfectly and that patterns are correctly matched.

The second method requires a smooth, solid surface, such as concrete, drywall, or plaster. The tile setter applies a cement adhesive or mastic (a sticky paste) either to the surface or to the back of each tile. The tiles can then be attached to the surface. With either method tile setters might need to cut tile pieces to position them around pipes, wash basins, or other obstructions. After the tiles are installed, the joints are filled with grouting cement. Workers who assist tile setters by performing such tasks as carrying materials, cleaning surfaces, and grouting are known as *tile helpers* or *tile finishers.*

Workers similar to tile setters include *marble setters* and *terrazzo workers.* Marble setters apply marble pieces to the interior and exterior surfaces of buildings. They spread a special plaster onto the marble's backing material and then attach the marble pieces to the surface. As with tile, the joints are then filled with grout. Terrazzo—developed in the sixteenth century in Venice, Italy—is a surface made of small pieces of broken stone set in mortar. It is often made of three layers—a concrete foundation on the bottom, then a sandy concrete layer, and finally a mixture of mortar and broken stone, usually marble or granite. Using colored stones, terrazzo workers can produce a variety of different designs. After the mixture is dry, they use machines to grind and polish the surface.

Apprentices are trained by already established tile setters, marble setters, or terrazzo workers. They begin with simple tasks, such as carrying material or mixing cement, and are gradually trained in the specialized skills of the trade. Apprentices also receive a considerable amount of classroom instruction in blueprint reading, basic mathematics, and other subjects. Tile setters usually work inside, while terrazzo workers and marble setters work both indoors and outdoors.

Tile, marble, and terrazzo apprenticeships normally run three years. Most programs require that the applicant

- apply in person

- be at least 18 years old

- be a high school graduate (or GED holder)

- be physically able to perform the work of the trade

Reported beginning apprenticeship salaries range from $6.80 to $12.50 an hour.

Reported ending apprenticeship salaries range from $16.59 to $26.33 an hour.

The number of jobs for tile setters, marble setters, and terrazzo workers is expected to grow at an average rate. Tile in particular will likely increase in popularity. Florida and California have been the biggest markets for terrazzo. The number of job openings will be affected by general trends in the construction industry.

For more information on apprenticeships for tile setters, marble setters, and terrazzo workers, write to the national programs listed below, as well as to any government programs located in your state. When a name is included, address your letter to that person. Because existing programs are often revised, some of the following may have changed or ceased to exist. New programs may also have been created. Additional programs might be listed with the national union or with your state's bureau of apprenticeship training. Addresses can be found in the last section of this encyclopedia.

NATIONAL SPONSOR

International Union of Bricklayers and Allied Craftsmen
815 15th Street, NW
Washington, DC 20005
202-783-3788

This organization is affiliated with the AFL-CIO and has 539 locals.

• • •

STATE SPONSORS

CALIFORNIA

Kern, Inyo and Mono Counties Bricklayers, Stone Masons, and Tile Setters JAC
26 Bernard, Room 10
Bakersfield, CA 93305
805-323-6115

This is a 3-year program.
No salaries were reported by this program.
Applications are accepted in person Mondays, 8:00-12:00.

REQUIREMENTS:

• Minimum age: 18
• High school diploma or GED certificate

APPLICATION DOCUMENTS:

Applicants must bring the following documents when applying:
• High school transcript or GED scores
• High school diploma or GED certificate

• • •

Fresno Area Bricklayers JAC
4831 East Shields, #20
Fresno, CA 93729
209-269-4577

This is a 4-year program.
No salaries were reported by this program.
Applications are accepted in person on the 1st and 3rd Tuesdays of the month, 9:00-12:00.

• • •

BAC Local #3, California
8400 Enterprise Way, #103
Oakland, CA 94621
510-632-8781
ATTN: Tim Paulson

Program title: Northern California Tile Industry JATTF
Specific job title(s): Tile setter, Tile finisher
This is a 4-year program with 4,500 hours of on-the-job training.
Ending wage: $26.33.
Annually, 30-50 people apply for 16-20 positions.

Tile Setters

Applications are accepted in person on the 1st Friday of the month, 8:00-11:00.

REQUIREMENTS:

- Minimum age: 18
- High school diploma or GED certificate

• • •

GEORGIA

Bricklayers
1323 Stewart Avenue SW
Atlanta, GA 30310
404-755-3593

Program title: BAC Apprenticeship Program
Specific job title(s): Tile setter, Stone setter, Marble setter
This is a 3-year program with 432 hours of classroom instruction.
No salaries were reported by this program.
Annually, a varying number of people apply for a varying number of positions.
Course credit is offered.
There is an initial 6-month probationary period.
Applications are accepted in person any time of year, Monday-Friday, 8:00-5:00.

REQUIREMENTS:

- Minimum age: 17; Maximum age: 24
- High school diploma or GED certificate
- Physician's statement of fitness
- Pass a written test
- Pass an oral interview

APPLICATION DOCUMENTS:

Applicants must bring the following documents when applying:
- High school transcript or GED scores
- Birth certificate

• • •

HAWAII

Hawaii Masons and Plasterers Training Office
2251 North School Street, 2nd Floor
Honolulu, HI 96819
808-845-5949

This is a 4-year program with 576 hours of classroom instruction and 8,000 hours of on-the-job training.
Starting wage: $10.29; Ending wage: $20.57.
Annually, a varying number of people apply for a varying number of positions.
Applications are accepted by mail any time of year, Monday-Wednesday, 8:00-12:00.

REQUIREMENTS:

- Minimum age: 16
- High school diploma or GED certificate
- Must be physically able to perform the work of the trade
- Pass a written test

APPLICATION DOCUMENTS:

Applicants must bring the following documents when applying:
- High school diploma or GED certificate

ADDITIONAL PROGRAM COMMENTS:

When applying by mail, send a self-addressed, stamped envelope.

• • •

ILLINOIS

Bricklayers
2317 North Western Avenue
Chicago, IL 60647
ATTN: James Murray

Program title: Terrazzo Workers Apprenticeship Local #67
Specific job title(s): Tile setter, Terrazzo worker
This is a 3-year program with 422 hours of classroom instruction and 6,000 hours of on-the-job training.

Starting wage: $11.27; Ending wage: $22.34. Annually, 11-20 people apply for 6-10 positions. Applications are accepted in person during a 2-week period when a need is determined, 9:00-2:00.

REQUIREMENTS:

- Minimum age: 17
- Pass a written test
- Pass an oral interview
- Letter of recommendation from personal acquaintence
- Must attend a preapprenticeship class for 8 weeks

APPLICATION DOCUMENTS:

Applicants must bring the following documents when applying:
- High school transcript or GED scores
- Birth certificate

ADDITIONAL PROGRAM COMMENTS:

Applicants are not paid for the 8-week preapprenticeship classes.

• • •

INDIANA

Bricklayers International Local #3
620 North East Street
Indianapolis, IN 46202
317-631-3600
ATTN: Duane Clendenson

Program title: Bricklayers International Local #3 of Indiana
Specific job title(s): Tile setter, Marble setter, Terrazzo worker
This is a 4-year program with 576 hours of classroom instruction and 6,000 hours of on-the-job training.
No salaries were reported by this program.
Annually, a varying number of people apply for a varying number of positions.
There is an initial 6-month probationary period.
Applications are accepted in person any time of year, Monday-Thursday, 8:30-4:00.

REQUIREMENTS:

- Minimum age: 18
- High school diploma or GED certificate
- Physician's statement of fitness
- Must be physically able to perform the work of the trade
- Pass a written test
- Pass an oral interview
- Valid driver's license
- Resident of the program's jurisdiction
- Letter of recommendation from 3 teachers or past employers
- Pass a test for illegal drugs
- Must attend a preapprenticeship class for 216 hours

APPLICATION DOCUMENTS:

Applicants must bring the following documents when applying:
- High school transcript or GED scores
- High school diploma or GED certificate
- Social security card

• • •

Bricklayers Local #19
4405 South Eaton Avenue
Muncie, IN 47302
317-284-2926
ATTN: Joseph Bramlett

Program title: Bricklayers Local #19 of Indiana JAC
Specific job title(s): Tile Setter, Stone setter, Marble mason
This is a 4-year program with 632 hours of classroom instruction and 6,000 hours of on-the-job training.
No salaries were reported by this program.
Annually, 4-7 people apply for 4-7 positions.
Course credit is offered.
There is an initial 2-month probationary period.
Applications are accepted in person any time of year, Monday-Friday.
The application deadline is May 31st.

REQUIREMENTS:

- Minimum age: 18
- High school diploma or GED certificate

- Pass an oral interview
- Resident of the program's jurisdiction
- Letter of recommendation from 3 employers, teachers, or counselors
- Must attend a preapprenticeship class for 18 hours

APPLICATION DOCUMENTS:

Applicants must bring the following documents when applying:
- High school transcript or GED scores
- High school diploma or GED certificate
- Social security card

• • •

MARYLAND

Bricklayers and Allied Craftsmen
Local #1 JATC
5200 Westland Boulevard
Baltimore, MD 21227
301-536-2005
ATTN: E. Edward Poarch, II

This is a 3-year program with 480 hours of classroom instruction and 4,500 hours of on-the-job training.
No salaries were reported by this program. Applications are accepted in person any time of year by appointment only.

REQUIREMENTS:

- Minimum age: 17
- Must be physically able to perform the work of the trade

• • •

Bricklayers and Allied Craftsmen
Local #1
4725 Silver Hill Road
Suitland, MD 20746
301-420-0400
ATTN: Tom McQuaid

Program title: BAC Apprenticeship Program
Specific job title(s): Tile setter, Marble setter, Terrazzo worker, Stone setter

This is a 3-year program with 432 hours of classroom instruction.
Starting wage: $6.80; Ending wage: $16.59.
Annually, 21-30 people apply for 11-15 positions.
There is an initial 3-month probationary period. Applications are accepted in person during the first two weeks in January, Monday-Friday, 7:30-3:30.

REQUIREMENTS:

- Minimum age: 18
- High school diploma or GED certificate
- Pass a written test
- Pass an oral interview

APPLICATION DOCUMENTS:

Applicants must bring the following documents when applying:
- High school diploma or GED certificate
- Social security card
- Birth certificate

• • •

MASSACHUSETTS

Bricklayers and Allied Craftsmen
Local #3
550 Medford Street
Charlestown, MA 02129
617-242-5500

Program title: Eastern Massachusetts Training Fund
Specific job title(s): Tile setter, Marble setter, Terrazzo worker, PCC restoration
This is a 3-year program with 6,000 hours of on-the-job training.
Ending wage: $24.86.
Annually, a varying number of people apply for a varying number of positions.
There is an initial 1-year probationary period. Applications are accepted in person one week per year, in February or March. Call for information.

REQUIREMENTS:

- Minimum age: 17
- High school diploma or GED certificate

- Pass a written test
- Pass an oral interview
- Valid driver's license
- Letter of recommendation

APPLICATION DOCUMENTS:

Applicants must bring the following documents when applying:
- High school transcript or GED scores
- High school diploma or GED certificate
- Social security card
- Driver's license

• • •

International Masonry Institute
84 Myron Street
West Springfield, MA 01089
413-737-5999
ATTN: Pat Murphy

Program title: Pre-Job Apprentice Program
Specific job title(s): Tile setter, Marble setter, Terrazzo worker
This is a 3-year program with 480 hours of classroom instruction and 4,500 hours of on-the-job training.
Starting wage: $12.50; Ending wage: $25.00.
Annually, over 100 people apply for 16-20 positions.
There is an initial 12-month probationary period.
Applications are accepted in person when ad is run in local paper.

REQUIREMENTS:

- Minimum age: 18
- Must be physically able to perform the work of the trade
- Pass an oral interview
- Valid driver's license
- Must attend a preapprenticeship class for 480 hours

APPLICATION DOCUMENTS:

Applicants must bring the following documents when applying:
- Social security card
- Driver's license

• • •

MONTANA

International Masonry Apprenticeship Trust
PO Box 577
Anaconda, MT 59711
ATTN: Robert Geier

Program title: International Masonry Apprenticeship Trust
Specific job title(s): Tile setter, Terrazzo worker
This is a 3-year program with 1,500 hours of classroom instruction and 6,000 hours of on-the-job training.
No salaries were reported by this program.
Annually, 51-100 people apply for 21-50 positions.
Applications are accepted in person any time of year.

REQUIREMENTS:

- Minimum age: 16
- Physician's statement of fitness
- Pass an oral interview
- Letter of recommendation from current or previous teachers

APPLICATION DOCUMENTS:

Applicants must bring the following documents when applying:
- High school transcript or GED scores
- Social security card

• • •

NEVADA

Southern Nevada Bricklayers JATC
4720 Wynn Road
Las Vegas, NV 89103
702-474-7454
ATTN: Larry Wahl

Program title: BAC Apprenticeship Program
Specific job title(s): Tile setter, Marble setter
This is a 3-year program with 864 hours of classroom instruction and 6,243 hours of on-the-job training.
Starting wage: $9.99; Ending wage: $19.92.

Annually, 51-100 people apply for 11-15 positions.
There is an initial 6-month probationary period. Applications are accepted in person when company solicits an opening.

REQUIREMENTS:

- Minimum age: 17
- High school diploma or GED certificate
- Pass an oral interview
- Pass a test for illegal drugs

APPLICATION DOCUMENTS:

Applicants must bring the following documents when applying:
- High school diploma or GED certificate
- Social security card
- Birth certificate

• • •

North Nevada Bricklayers
1150 Terminal Way
Reno, NV 89502
702-323-5451
ATTN: Les Sumner

Specific job title(s): Tile setter
This is a 3-year program with 432 hours of classroom instruction and 5,000 hours of on-the-job training.
No salaries were reported by this program.
Annually, 0-10 people apply for 0-5 positions.
Course credit is offered.
There is an initial 3-month probationary period. Applications are accepted in person any time of year, Monday-Friday, 7:00-9:30.

REQUIREMENTS:

- Minimum age: 18
- High school diploma or GED certificate
- Must be physically able to perform the work of the trade
- Pass an oral interview
- Resident of the program's jurisdiction
- Letter of recommendation from person in trade
- Letter of intent from a valid employer

APPLICATION DOCUMENTS:

Applicants must bring the following documents when applying:
- High school transcript or GED scores
- Social security card

• • •

NEW YORK

Eastern Contractors Association Local #3
6 Airline Drive
Albany, NY 12205
518-869-0961
ATTN: Jim Bradt

Program title: Bricklayers and Allied Craftsmen Apprenticeship Program
Specific job title(s): Tile setter, Terrazzo worker
This is a 4-year program with 576 hours of classroom instruction and 8,000 hours of on-the-job training.
Ending wage: $20.00.
Annually, a varying number of people apply for a varying number of positions.
There is an initial 6-month probationary period. Applications are accepted in person any time of year.

REQUIREMENTS:

- Minimum age: 17
- Must be physically able to perform the work of the trade
- Pass an oral interview
- Valid driver's license
- Resident of the program's jurisdiction for 1 year
- Pass a test for illegal drugs
- Must attend a preapprenticeship class for 480 hours

APPLICATION DOCUMENTS:

Applicants must bring the following documents when applying:
- Social security card

• • •

OKLAHOMA

Eastern Oklahoma Building and
Construction Trades Council
2651 East 21st Street, #405
Tulsa, OK 74114
918-742-3365
ATTN: Clayton Walker

Specific job title(s): Tile setter, Marble mason, Terrazzo worker
No salaries were reported by this program.
Write or call for application information.

• • •

RHODE ISLAND

Bricklayers and Allied Craftsmen
Local #1
150 Ernest Street
Providence, RI 02905
401-467-7074
ATTN: David Barricelli

This is a 3-year program with 6,000 hours of on-the-job training.
No salaries were reported by this program.
Applications are accepted in person.

REQUIREMENTS:

- Minimum age: 18
- High school diploma or GED certificate
- Must be physically able to perform the work of the trade
- Pass a written test
- Pass an oral interview
- Resident of the program's jurisdiction

• • •

TEXAS

Bricklayers Local #16, Texas
1001 Carmel Parkway, #43
Corpus Christi, TX 78411
512-854-5992

This program is affiliated with International Masonry Institute in Houston, TX. Please see that entry for more information.

• • •

BAC District Council 1, Texas
605 Safari Parkway, Suite B-4
Grand Prairie, TX 75050
214-263-8908

This program is affiliated with International Masonry Institute in Houston, TX. Please see that entry for more information.

• • •

International Masonry Institute
PO Box 34583
Houston, TX 77234
ATTN: Jack Stubbs

Program title: International Masonry Institute
Specific job title(s): Tile setter, Marble mason, Stone mason
This is a 4-year program with 912 hours of classroom instruction and 8,000 hours of on-the-job training.
Starting wage: $7.50; Ending wage: $18.00.
Annually, 51-100 people apply for 21-50 positions.
There is an initial 4-month probationary period.
Applications are accepted in person any time of year. Call for appointment.

REQUIREMENTS:

- Minimum age: 18; Maximum age: 38
- Must be physically able to perform the work of the trade
- Pass an oral interview
- Resident of the program's jurisdiction
- Letter of recommendation
- Must attend a preapprenticeship class for 480 hours

APPLICATION DOCUMENTS:

Applicants must bring the following documents when applying:
- High school diploma or GED certificate

- Social security card
- Driver's license

ADDITIONAL PROGRAM COMMENTS:

This program is affiliated with the following locals and district councils: Bricklayers Local Union #2 (San Antonio), BAC District Council 1 (Grand Prairie), Bricklayers Local Union #4 (Wichita Falls), BAC District Council Texas JAC (Houston), Bricklayers Local Union #16 (Corpus Christi).

• • •

BAC District Council Texas JAC
9105 Edgebrook
Houston, TX 77075
713-941-5668

This program is affiliated with International Masonry Institute in Houston, TX. Please see that entry for more information.

• • •

Bricklayers Local #2, Texas
611 North Flores
San Antonio, TX 78205
210-227-5422

This program is affiliated with International Masonry Institute in Houston, TX. Please see that entry for more information.

• • •

Bricklayers Local #4, Texas
3223 Milby
Wichita Falls, TX 76308
817-723-1826

This program is affiliated with International Masonry Institute in Houston, TX. Please see that entry for more information.

• • •

WASHINGTON

Seattle Area Masonry Apprenticeship School
6770 East Marginal Way South
Seattle, WA 98108
ATTN: Jerry Hays

Program title: Seattle Area Masonry Apprenticeship School
This is a 4-year program with 576 hours of classroom instruction and 6,000 hours of on-the-job training.
Starting wage: $8.98; Ending wage: $21.79.
Annually, 0-10 people apply for 0-5 positions.
Applications are accepted in person any time of year, Monday-Friday, 9:00-2:00.

REQUIREMENTS:

- Minimum age: 17
- High school diploma or GED certificate
- Must be physically able to perform the work of the trade
- Pass an oral interview
- Valid driver's license

ADDITIONAL PROGRAM COMMENTS:

This program is affiliated with the Bricklayers Local #2 of Seattle.

• • •

Bricklayers Local #2
330 Fairview Avenue North
Seattle, WA 98109
206-624-5481

This program is affiliated with Seattle Area Masonry Apprenticeship School in Seattle, WA. Please see that entry for more information.

• • •

WISCONSIN

Bricklayers
2233 Birch Street
Eau Claire, WI 54703
ATTN: Dave Hahn

Program title: Wisconsin State Trowel Trades Apprenticeship
This is a 3-year program with 400 hours of classroom instruction and 4,280 hours of on-the-job training.
Starting wage: $8.99; Ending wage: $17.53.
Annually, 0-10 people apply for 6-10 positions. There is an initial 6-month probationary period. Applications are accepted in person or by mail any time of year.

REQUIREMENTS:

- High school diploma or GED certificate
- Pass an oral interview
- Letter of recommendation from previous employer
- Letter of intent from a valid employer

APPLICATION DOCUMENTS:

Applicants must bring the following documents when applying:
- High school transcript or GED scores
- High school diploma or GED certificate
- Job service test

• • •

Tool, Die, Mold, and Pattern Makers

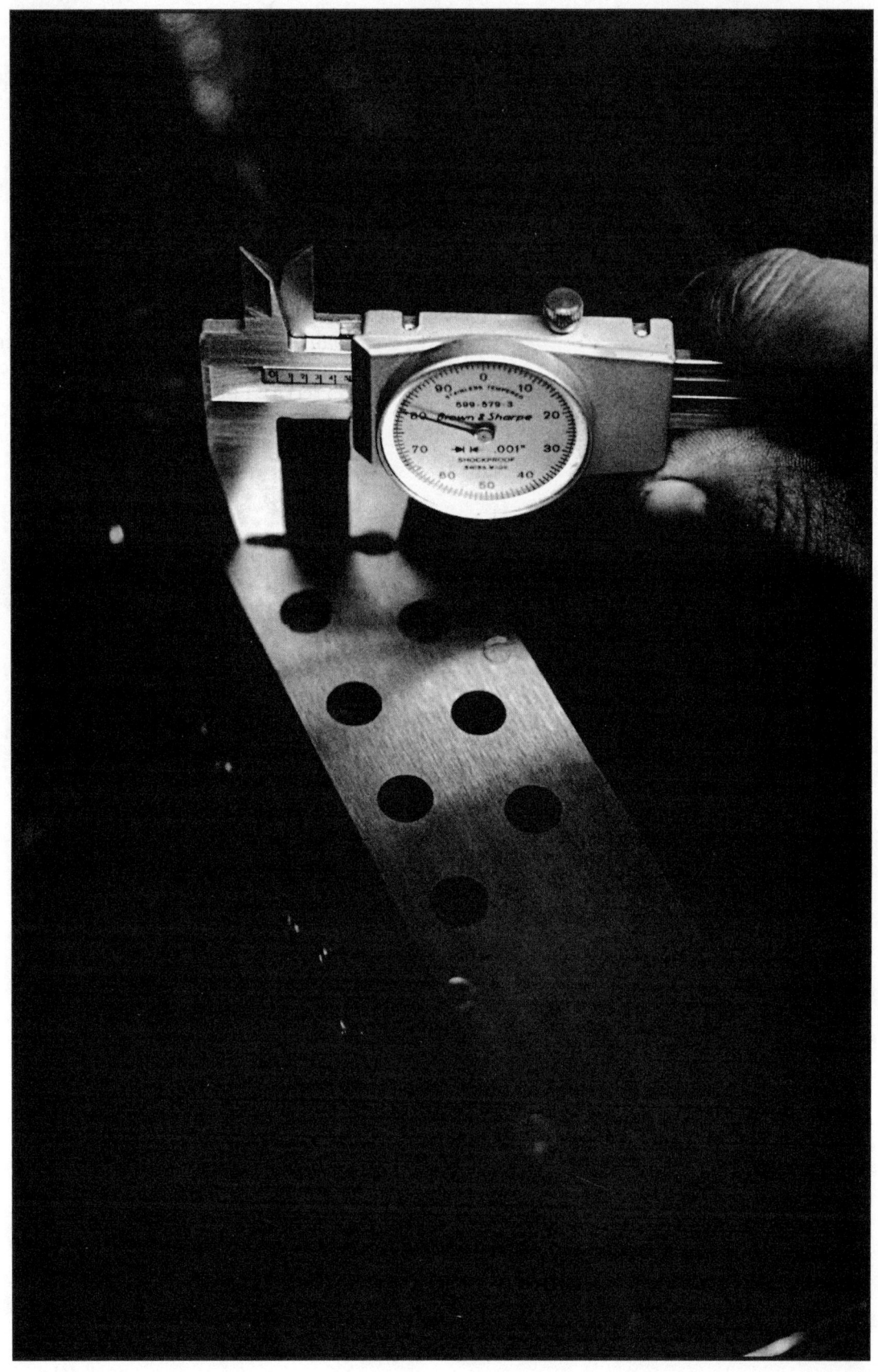

Tool, Die, Mold, and Pattern Makers

Tool and die makers are so-called because they design, produce, and repair machine tools and dies (metal molds). They also make other items, such as jigs (tool-guiding patterns), fixtures (devices that clamp workpieces in place), and gauges. Most tool and die makers are employed by manufacturing firms, especially those involved in metal-working machinery, aircraft, motor vehicles, and plastic products.

A tool, die, or other item is often produced by a single tool and die maker. The worker typically begins by reading blueprints or other instructions and planning a sequence of steps needed to produce the parts. The appropriate metal is then measured and marked according to the specifications. Next, machine tools—such as lathes or milling machines— are set up to cut, bore, or otherwise shape the parts. After the shaping operations are completed, the parts must be measured for accuracy and then assembled. Some parts might need finishing work, such as filing or grinding. Increasingly tool and die makers use automated equipment, such as numerically controlled (NC) machine tools, which can be programmed to automatically shape the parts. In such cases tool and die makers might be involved in planning and writing the computer programs.

Apprentices receive both on-the-job and classroom training. Supervised by already established tool and die makers, apprentices begin with simple tasks and are gradually trained in the specialized jobs of the trade. Because injury is possible when working with tools and machines, they must carefully follow safety rules and wear protective equipment, such as safety glasses. Apprentices are given at least 144 hours of classroom instruction each year in such subjects as mathematics, blueprint reading, tool designing, and tool programming.

Tool and die making apprenticeships normally run four to five years. Most programs require that the applicant

- apply in person

- be at least 18 years old

- be a high school graduate (or GED holder)

- be physically able to perform the work of the trade

Reported beginning apprenticeship salaries range from $5.00 to $17.48 an hour.

Reported ending apprenticeship salaries range from $9.15 to $25.59 an hour.

The number of employed tool and die makers is expected to grow at an average rate. Limiting growth will be the increasing use of automated machinery. The number of job openings will also be affected by general trends in the manufacturing industry. Because employers in some areas are having trouble attracting qualified tool and die makers, the employment outlook for well-trained workers is good.

For more information on tool and die making apprenticeships, write to the national programs listed below, as well as to any government programs located in your state. When a name is included, address your letter to that person. Because existing programs are often revised, some of the following may have changed or ceased to exist. New programs may also have been created. Additional programs might be listed with the national union or with your state's bureau of apprenticeship training. Addresses can be found in the last section of this encyclopedia.

NATIONAL SPONSORS

International Association of Machinists
and Aerospace Workers
9000 Machinists Place
Upper Marlboro, MD 20772
301-967-4500
ATTN: Charles Bradford

This organization is affiliated with the AFL-CIO and has 1,566 locals.

• • •

International Association of Tool
Craftsmen
3718 Wright Avenue
Racine, WI 53405
414-637-4371

This is an independent organization with 7 locals.

• • •

STATE SPONSORS

CALIFORNIA

Flint Glass Workers
5181 Fauna Street
Montclair, CA 91763
714-626-5780
ATTN: Robert Beatty

Specific job title(s): Mold maker
This is a 4-year program with 244 hours of classroom instruction and 8,000 hours of on-the-job training.
No salaries were reported by this program.
Write or call for application information.

REQUIREMENTS:

- Minimum age: 18
- High school diploma or GED certificate
- Must be physically able to perform the work of the trade
- Pass a written test
- Pass an oral interview
- Pass a test for illegal drugs

APPLICATION DOCUMENTS:

Applicants must bring the following documents when applying:
- High school diploma or GED certificate
- Social security card

ADDITIONAL PROGRAM COMMENTS:

Although our apprenticeship program is state- and federal-approved, it is important to know that management at the local plants has final say as to the hiring of apprentices. Applicants must also remember that the glass container industry is quite possible a dying industry.

• • •

CONNECTICUT

Prat-Whitney
400 Main Street, MS 124-36
East Hartford, CT 06108
203-565-9542
ATTN: Tom Meglin

Specific job title(s): Tool and die gauge technician
This is a 105-week program.
Starting wage: $15.00; Ending wage: $16.50.
Annually, over 100 people apply for over 100 positions.
Applications are accepted in person any time of year.

REQUIREMENTS:

- Minimum age: 18
- Pass a written test
- Must attend a preapprenticeship class

APPLICATION DOCUMENTS:

Applicants must bring the following documents when applying:
- Social security card

ADDITIONAL PROGRAM COMMENTS:

Applicant must be currently employed. The preapprenticeship class is for those who do not pass initial testing.

• • •

General Dynamics Electric Boat Division
75 Eastern Point Road
Groton, CT 06340
203-433-3000
ATTN: Richard Taylor, Jr.

Program title: Electric Boat Company Apprenticeship Program
Specific job title(s): Marine pattern maker, Tool maker, Loftsperson
No salaries were reported by this program.
Annually, a varying number of people apply for a varying number of positions.
There is an initial 90-day probationary period.
Applications are accepted in person or by mail.

REQUIREMENTS:

- High school diploma or GED certificate
- Physician's statement of fitness
- Must be physically able to perform the work of the trade
- Letter of recommendation from respective department

APPLICATION DOCUMENTS:

Applicants must bring the following documents when applying:
- High school transcript or GED scores
- High school diploma or GED certificate

• • •

GEORGIA

UAW Local #10
5407 Buford Highway, PO Box 47426
Doraville, GA 30340
ATTN: Richard Dalrymple

Program title: GM-UAW Skilled Trades Apprentice Program
Specific job title(s): Jig and fixture tool maker
This is a 4-year program with 576 hours of classroom instruction and 7,328 hours of on-the-job training.
Starting wage: $15.67; Ending wage: $18.88.
Annually, over 100 people apply for 6-10 positions.
Applications are accepted in person following public notification.
The application deadline is 30 days after posting.

REQUIREMENTS:

- Minimum age: 18; Maximum age: 44
- High school diploma or GED certificate
- Physician's statement of fitness
- Pass a written test
- Pass an oral interview
- Valid driver's license
- Letter of recommendation from former employers
- Letter of intent from a valid employer
- Pass a test for illegal drugs

APPLICATION DOCUMENTS:

Applicants must bring the following documents when applying:
- High school transcript or GED scores
- High school diploma or GED certificate
- Social security card
- Driver's license
- Proof of identity

• • •

ILLINOIS

Tooling and Manufacturing Association
1177 South Dee Road
Park Ridge, IL 60068
708-825-1120
ATTN: Jerry Biginski

Specific job title(s): Tool and die maker, Mold maker
This is a 4-5-year program with 490 hours of classroom instruction.
Starting wage: $7.50; Ending wage: $16.00.
Annually, a varying number of people apply for over 100 positions.
Course credit is offered.

Applications are accepted by mail any time of year.

REQUIREMENTS:

- Minimum age: 18; Maximum age: 23
- High school diploma or GED certificate
- Physician's statement of fitness
- Must be physically able to perform the work of the trade
- Pass a written test
- Pass an oral interview
- Pass a test for illegal drugs

APPLICATION DOCUMENTS:

Applicants must bring the following documents when applying:
- High school transcript or GED scores
- High school diploma or GED certificate
- Social security card
- Resume

ADDITIONAL PROGRAM COMMENTS:

On-the-job instruction ranges form 8,000 to 10,000 hours. Recommended high school classes include two years of math, algebra, trigonometry, industrial arts, machine shop, computers, drafting, and language skills. Member companies screen, select, and train apprentices on-the-job. TMA supplements applicants with evening classes. This program is associated with Triton, River Grove, and IIT colleges for credits.

• • •

INDIANA

Cummins Engine Company, Inc.
Mail Code 50118 Box 3005
Columbus, IN 47202
812-377-4506
ATTN: Randall Sims

Program title: Cummins Engine Company Apprenticeship Programs
Specific job title(s): Tool design drafter, Engineering model maker, Tool design drafter
This is a 4-year program with 720 hours of classroom instruction and 8,000 hours of on-the-job training.
Starting wage: $11.07; Ending wage: $16.28.
Annually, over 100 people apply for 16-20 positions.
Course credit is offered.
There is an initial 120-day probationary period.
Applications are accepted by mail following notification in local newspapers.

REQUIREMENTS:

- Minimum age: 17
- High school diploma or GED certificate
- Pass a written test
- Pass an oral interview
- Pass a test for illegal drugs
- Legal ID

• • •

Flint Glass Workers
1448 North Ford Box 332
Lapel, IN 46051
317-534-4947
ATTN: Michael Evans

Specific job title(s): Mold maker
This is a 4-year program with 576 hours of classroom instruction and 8,000 hours of on-the-job training.
Starting wage: $12.96; Ending wage: $14.35.
Annually, 0-10 people apply for 0-5 positions.
Course credit is offered.
There is an initial 90-day probationary period.
Applications are accepted in person or by mail Monday-Friday, 7:00-4:00.

REQUIREMENTS:

- Minimum age: 18; Maximum age: 27
- High school diploma or GED certificate
- Physician's statement of fitness
- Must be physically able to perform the work of the trade
- Pass a written test
- Pass an oral interview
- Pass a test for illegal drugs

APPLICATION DOCUMENTS:

Applicants must bring the following documents when applying:
- High school diploma or GED certificate
- Social security card

Tool, Die, Mold, and Pattern Makers

ADDITIONAL PROGRAM COMMENTS:

This program involves on-the-job training in the area of repairing and machining mold equipment for the glass industry, serving the food and beverage companies.

• • •

IOWA

Deco Products Company
506 Sanford Street
Decorah, IA 52101
319-382-4264

Specific job title(s): Tool and die maker
This is a 4-year program with 576 hours of classroom instruction and 8,000 hours of on-the-job training.
Starting wage: $5.75; Ending wage: $9.15.
Annually, 0-10 people apply for 0-5 positions.
There is an initial 8-month probationary period.
Applications are accepted in person or by mail weekdays, 8:00-5:00.

REQUIREMENTS:

- Minimum age: 18
- High school diploma or GED certificate
- Pass an oral interview
- Letter of recommendation
- Letter of intent from a valid employer

APPLICATION DOCUMENTS:

Applicants must bring the following documents when applying:
- High school transcript or GED scores
- High school diploma or GED certificate
- Social security card

• • •

Dubuque Stamping and Manufacturing Inc.
Box 798, 32nd and Jackson Street
Dubuque, IA 52004
319-583-5716

Specific job title(s): Tool and die maker
This is a 4-year program with 576 hours of classroom instruction and 8,000 hours of on-the-job training.
No salaries were reported by this program.
Course credit is offered.
There is an initial 500-hour probationary period.
Applications are accepted in person or by mail any time of year.

REQUIREMENTS:

- Minimum age: 18
- High school diploma or GED certificate
- Must be physically able to perform the work of the trade
- Pass an oral interview
- Valid driver's license
- Letter of recommendation
- Passing grade in the following high school course(s): 2 years of algebra and geometry

APPLICATION DOCUMENTS:

Applicants must bring the following documents when applying:
- High school transcript or GED scores
- Driver's license
- Birth certificate

• • •

Steelworkers
140 East Alta Vista
Ottomwa, IA 52501
515-684-4874
ATTN: Ronald Ruby

Specific job title(s): Tool and die maker
This is a 4-year program with 8,000 hours of on-the-job training.
No salaries were reported by this program.
Annually, 0-10 people apply for 0-5 positions.
Applications are accepted in person.

REQUIREMENTS:

- Must be physically able to perform the work of the trade

ADDITIONAL PROGRAM COMMENTS:

In order to be accepted into this program the applicant must already be an employee of Lund

International Ottumwa Industrial Airport, be accepted as a trainee to the Tool Room when a job is posted, and prove to have the ability for a tool maker.

• • •

KANSAS

A1 Pattern and Model Works
Box 68
Arma, KS 66712
316-347-8796
ATTN: Bart Maransani

Specific job title(s): Pattern maker
This is a 4-year program.
No salaries were reported by this program.
Applications are accepted in person any time of year.

REQUIREMENTS:

- High school diploma or GED certificate
- Must be physically able to perform the work of the trade
- Letter of recommendation
- Passing grade in the following high school course(s): Math

APPLICATION DOCUMENTS:

Applicants must bring the following documents when applying:
- High school transcript or GED scores
- High school diploma or GED certificate
- Social security card

• • •

Machinist Apprenticeship Program
330 Laura
Whichita, KS 67211
316-262-7030
ATTN: Anita Stone

Specific job title(s): Tool, Die, Mold, and Precision makers; CC mill, CC lather specialist, TDD
This is a 4-year program with 576 hours of classroom instruction.
No salaries were reported by this program.
Annually, over 100 people apply for 16-20 positions.
Course credit is offered.
There is an initial probationary period.
Applications are accepted in person any time of year.

REQUIREMENTS:

- Minimum age: 18
- High school diploma or GED certificate
- Pass a written test
- Letter of intent from a valid employer
- Must attend a preapprenticeship class

APPLICATION DOCUMENTS:

Applicants must bring the following documents when applying:
- High school transcript or GED scores
- High school diploma or GED certificate
- Social security card
- Photo ID

ADDITIONAL PROGRAM COMMENTS:

The Mold maker position is a 5-year program.

• • •

MAINE

Jones-Vining of Maine, Inc.
765 Webster, PO Box 1903
Lewiston, ME 04240

Specific job title(s): Last model maker
This is a 3-year program with 1,200 hours of classroom instruction and 1,200 hours of on-the-job training.
Starting wage: $6.50; Ending wage: $10.00.
Annually, 0-10 people apply for 0-5 positions.
There is an initial 6-month probationary period.
Applications are accepted in person any time of year.

REQUIREMENTS:

- Minimum age: 18
- High school diploma or GED certificate
- Physician's statement of fitness

- Pass an oral interview
- Resident of the program's jurisdiction for 6 months

APPLICATION DOCUMENTS:

Applicants must bring the following documents when applying:
- High school diploma or GED certificate

• • •

MARYLAND

Suburban Tool Manufacturing Company
PO Box 5036, 12 Emala Avenue
Baltimore, MD 21220
410-686-4894
ATTN: Paul MacEvoy

Specific job title(s): Tool and die maker
This is a 5-year program.
Starting wage: $5.00; Ending wage: $15.00.
Annually, 0-10 people apply for 0-5 positions.
Course credit is offered.
There is an initial 1-year probationary period.
Applications are accepted in person any time of year.

REQUIREMENTS:

- High school diploma or GED certificate
- Physician's statement of fitness
- Must be physically able to perform the work of the trade
- Pass an oral interview
- Valid driver's license

APPLICATION DOCUMENTS:

Applicants must bring the following documents when applying:
- Social security card

ADDITIONAL PROGRAM COMMENTS:

Classroom instruction is 8-weeks; on-the-job instruction is 32 weeks.

• • •

Poly Seal Corporation
8303 Pulaski Highway
Baltimore, MD 21237
410-682-3000
ATTN: Fred Middlestadt

Specific job title(s): Tool and die maker
This is a 5-year program with 720 hours of classroom instruction.
Starting wage: $11.40; Ending wage: $14.30.
Annually, 0-10 people apply for 0-5 positions.
Course credit is offered.
There is an initial 45-day probationary period.
Applications are accepted in person from in-house employees in August and September.

REQUIREMENTS:

- High school diploma or GED certificate
- Physician's statement of fitness
- Must be physically able to perform the work of the trade
- Pass a written test
- Pass an oral interview
- Letter of recommendation from supervisor
- Pass a test for illegal drugs

APPLICATION DOCUMENTS:

Applicants must bring the following documents when applying:
- Social security card

• • •

Marada Industries, Inc.
151 Airport Drive
Westminster, MD 21157
410-876-8000
ATTN: Suzanne Dyer-Gear

Specific job title(s): Tool and die maker
This is a 4-year program with 8,000 hours of on-the-job training.
Starting wage: $9.31.
Annually, 0-10 people apply for 0-5 positions.
Course credit is offered.
There is an initial probationary period.
Applications are accepted in person at various times.

REQUIREMENTS:

- Minimum age: 18
- High school diploma or GED certificate
- Pass a written test
- Pass an oral interview
- Letter of recommendation from supervisors, professors, etc.

• • •

MICHIGAN

Auto Workers
3731 Covington Road
Kalamazoo, MI 49002
616-381-2703
ATTN: Bruce Lee

Program title: UAW-GM Standard Apprenticeship
Specific job title(s): Tool and die maker
This is a 4-year program with 576 hours of classroom instruction and 7,328 hours of on-the-job training.
Starting wage: $17.48; Ending wage: $20.00.
Annually, 51-100 people apply for 0-5 positions.
Course credit is offered.
There is an initial 90-day probationary period.
Applications are accepted in person when a need is determined. Write for information.

REQUIREMENTS:

- Minimum age: 17
- High school diploma or GED certificate
- Physician's statement of fitness
- Must be physically able to perform the work of the trade
- Pass a written test
- Pass an oral interview
- Pass a test for illegal drugs

APPLICATION DOCUMENTS:

Applicants must bring the following documents when applying:
- High school diploma or GED certificate
- Picture ID

ADDITIONAL PROGRAM COMMENTS:

This plant is currently scheduled to close in 1998. There are no plans to hire new apprentices, although this could change as GM market conditions change.

• • •

Machinists
16215 West 12 Mile Road, #109
Southfield, MI 48076
ATTN: Robert Michela

Specific job title(s): Pattern maker
This is a 4.5-year program with 570 hours of classroom instruction and 9,000 hours of on-the-job training.
Starting wage: $8.95; Ending wage: $25.59.
Annually, 31-50 people apply for 6-10 positions.
Course credit is offered.
There is an initial 1,000-hour probationary period.
Applications are accepted in person every 2 years with notice sent out by individual shops.

REQUIREMENTS:

- High school diploma or GED certificate
- Physician's statement of fitness
- Pass a written test
- Pass an oral interview
- Valid driver's license
- Pass a test for illegal drugs

APPLICATION DOCUMENTS:

Applicants must bring the following documents when applying:
- High school transcript or GED scores
- High school diploma or GED certificate
- Driver's license

ADDITIONAL PROGRAM COMMENTS:

You also must have a reliable vehicle as well as a valid driver's license.

• • •

Tool, Die, Mold, and Pattern Makers

Chrysler UAW Apprenticeship Program
Local #372 UAW
4571 Division Street
Trenton, MI 48183
313-676-9060
ATTN: Nick Pillarelli

Specific job title(s): Tool maker
This is a 4-year program with 750 hours of classroom instruction and 7,250 hours of on-the-job training.
Starting wage: $13.44; Ending wage: $20.95.
Annually, over 100 people apply for 6-10 positions.
Course credit is offered.
There is an initial 90-day probationary period.
Applications are accepted in person or by mail following a posted notice.

REQUIREMENTS:

- Minimum age: 18
- Physician's statement of fitness
- Must be physically able to perform the work of the trade
- Pass a written test
- Pass an oral interview
- Pass a test for illegal drugs
- Passing grade in the following high school course(s): Algebra

APPLICATION DOCUMENTS:

Applicants must bring the following documents when applying:
- High school transcript or GED scores
- High school diploma or GED certificate
- Social security card
- Driver's license

ADDITIONAL PROGRAM COMMENTS:

Candidates are encouraged to take classes at community colleges to better their chances of getting an apprenticeship. Without solid educational backgrounds, working full time and attending 6-8 hours of college classes per week along with homework and family obligations can be too much. The high tech machines, computers, electrical and electronic circuits of today demand more education and continuing education. The majority of our apprentices are entering the program with degrees or at least some college behind them.

• • •

NEW YORK

Check-Mate Industries, Inc.
777 Mount Avenue
Wyandanch, NY 11798
516-491-1777
ATTN: Tom Vieweg

Specific job title(s): Tool and die maker
This is a 4-year program with 576 hours of classroom instruction and 8,400 hours of on-the-job training.
Starting wage: $6.00; Ending wage: $10.00.
Annually, 0-10 people apply for 0-5 positions.
Course credit is offered.
There is an initial 60-day probationary period.
Applications are accepted in person any time of year, 9:00-5:00.

REQUIREMENTS:

- Minimum age: 18
- High school diploma or GED certificate
- Physician's statement of fitness
- Must be physically able to perform the work of the trade
- Pass an oral interview
- Valid driver's license
- Resident of the program's jurisdiction
- Pass a test for illegal drugs
- Passing grade in the following high school course(s): Machine shop
- Must attend a preapprenticeship class

APPLICATION DOCUMENTS:

Applicants must bring the following documents when applying:
- Social security card
- Driver's license

• • •

NORTH CAROLINA

Sterling Tool and Mold, Inc.
44 Buck Shoals Road
Arden, NC 28704
704-687-0408

Program title: Mold Maker Program 20130, File 0376
Specific job title(s): Mold maker
This is a 5-year program with 576 hours of classroom instruction and 8,000 hours of on-the-job training.
Starting wage: $6.00; Ending wage: $10.50.
Annually, 0-10 people apply for 0-5 positions.
Course credit is offered.
There is an initial 3-month probationary period. Applications are accepted in person or by mail any time of year.

REQUIREMENTS:

- Minimum age: 17; Maximum age: 30
- High school diploma or GED certificate
- Must be physically able to perform the work of the trade
- Pass an oral interview
- Valid driver's license
- Pass a test for illegal drugs
- Must attend a preapprenticeship class

APPLICATION DOCUMENTS:

Applicants must bring the following documents when applying:
- High school transcript or GED scores
- Social security card
- Driver's license

ADDITIONAL PROGRAM COMMENTS:

Classes are held through AB Technical College.

• • •

Ball Incon Glass Packaging Corp. JATC
1856 Hendersonville Road
Ashville, NC 28803
704-274-2255
ATTN: E. V. Gouge

Specific job title(s): Mold craftworker, Maintenance craftworker
Starting wage: $11.80; Ending wage: $14.00.
Annually, 11-20 people apply for 6-10 positions.
Course credit is offered.
Applications are accepted in person any time of year.

REQUIREMENTS:

- Minimum age: 18; Maximum age: 42
- High school diploma or GED certificate
- Physician's statement of fitness
- Pass a written test
- Pass an oral interview
- Valid driver's license
- Pass a test for illegal drugs
- Passing grade in the following high school course(s): Math
- Must attend a preapprenticeship class

APPLICATION DOCUMENTS:

Applicants must bring the following documents when applying:
- High school diploma or GED certificate
- Driver's license

ADDITIONAL PROGRAM COMMENTS:

Mold craftworker classroom instruction and pre-apprenticeship classes are 70 quarter hours. Maintenance craftworker classroom instruction and preapprenticeship classes are 94 quarter hours. The duration of program is 2 years. The salary is the same for both.

• • •

Tool and Die maker Program
Highway US 70
Black Mountain, NC 28711
704-686-3811
ATTN: Kenneth Rinehuls

Specific job title(s): Tool and die maker
This is a 4-year program with 2,000 hours of classroom instruction and 8,000 hours of on-the-job training.
No salaries were reported by this program.
Annually, 21-30 people apply for 0-5 positions.
Course credit is offered.

Tool, Die, Mold, and Pattern Makers

There is an initial 2,000-hour probationary period.
Applications are accepted in person or by mail any time of year, during normal business hours.

REQUIREMENTS:

- Minimum age: 18
- Pass a written test
- Pass an oral interview
- Letter of recommendation
- Must attend a preapprenticeship class

• • •

Technical Design Associates, Inc.
PO Box 5100
Mills River, NC 28742
704-891-2696
ATTN: Wesley Cobb

Specific job title(s): Tool designer
This is a 4-year program with 583 hours of classroom instruction and 8,000 hours of on-the-job training.
No salaries were reported by this program.
Annually, 0-10 people apply for 0-5 positions.
Course credit is offered.
There is an initial 90-day probationary period.
Applications are accepted in person or by mail any time of year.

REQUIREMENTS:

- Minimum age: 18
- High school diploma or GED certificate
- Physician's statement of fitness
- Must be physically able to perform the work of the trade
- Pass a written test
- Pass an oral interview
- Valid driver's license
- Pass a test for illegal drugs
- Passing grade in the following high school course(s): Drafting, Math

APPLICATION DOCUMENTS:

Applicants must bring the following documents when applying:
- High school diploma or GED certificate
- Social security card
- Driver's license
- Proof of citizenship

• • •

Tool and Die Maker Program
4500-110 Preslyn Drive
Raleigh, NC 27064
919-878-7776
ATTN: Holly Borowy

Specific job title(s): Tool and die maker, Screw machine operator and setter
This is a 4-year program with 576 hours of classroom instruction and 8,000 hours of on-the-job training.
Starting wage: $7.00; Ending wage: $12.00.
Annually, 0-10 people apply for 0-5 positions.
Course credit is offered.
There is an initial 30-day probationary period.
Applications are accepted in person or by mail any time of year. See postings at colleges and job services offices.

REQUIREMENTS:

- Minimum age: 18
- High school diploma or GED certificate
- Physician's statement of fitness
- Pass an oral interview
- Letter of recommendation
- Letter of intent from a valid employer
- Passing grade in the following high school course(s): Math

APPLICATION DOCUMENTS:

Applicants must bring the following documents when applying:
- Social security card
- Driver's license

ADDITIONAL PROGRAM COMMENTS:

Courses offered at Wake Technical College.

• • •

Eagle Electric Manufacturing Company, Inc.
310 McNeil Road
Sanford, NC 27330
919-774-8015
ATTN: Richard Schauder

Specific job title(s): Tool and die maker
This is a 4-year program with 1,700 hours of classroom instruction and 8,000 hours of on-the-job training.
No salaries were reported by this program.
Annually, 0-10 people apply for 0-5 positions.
There is an initial 500-hour probationary period.
Applications are accepted in person any time of year, and openings are posted at the local college.

REQUIREMENTS:

- Minimum age: 18
- High school diploma or GED certificate
- Physician's statement of fitness
- Must be physically able to perform the work of the trade
- Pass a written test
- Pass an oral interview
- Letter of recommendation
- Pass a test for illegal drugs
- Passing grade in the following high school course(s): Drafting, Math

APPLICATION DOCUMENTS:

Applicants must bring the following documents when applying:
- High school transcript or GED scores
- Social security card
- Picture ID

ADDITIONAL PROGRAM COMMENTS:

A teacher at the local college usually recommends a student for application to the program. Employees of the company receive paid schooling, while those who are not employees must pay for schooling themselves.

• • •

 Ingersoll-Rand Company
Southern Pines, NC 28388
910-692-8700
ATTN: Dottie Fritz

Specific job title(s): Tool maker
This is a 2-year program with 4,000 hours of on-the-job training.
No salaries were reported by this program.
Annually, 0-10 people apply for 0-5 positions.
Applications are accepted in person any time of year, through the department of labor.

REQUIREMENTS:

- Minimum age: 18
- Physician's statement of fitness
- Pass an oral interview
- Resident of the program's jurisdiction
- Letter of recommendation from instructor
- Letter of intent from a valid employer
- Pass a test for illegal drugs
- Must attend a preapprenticeship class

APPLICATION DOCUMENTS:

Applicants must bring the following documents when applying:
- Social security card
- Driver's license

ADDITIONAL PROGRAM COMMENTS:

Once a student has completed a 2-year intensive technical program at Central Carolina College, the company hires the student as an apprentice.

• • •

OHIO

 Steelworkers
Route 2 Box 232
Little Hocking, OH 45742
304-422-0374
ATTN: Milton Morris

Specific job title(s): Tool and die maker, Pattern maker
This is a 4-year program with 576 hours of

classroom instruction and 8,000 hours of on-the-job training.
Starting wage: $11.00; Ending wage: $13.00.
Annually, 0-10 people apply for 0-5 positions.
There is an initial 6-month probationary period.
Applications are accepted in person when a need is determined.

REQUIREMENTS:

- Minimum age: 18; Maximum age: 40
- High school diploma or GED certificate
- Must be physically able to perform the work of the trade
- Pass a written test

APPLICATION DOCUMENTS:

Applicants must bring the following documents when applying:
- High school diploma or GED certificate
- Social security card

• • •

Jefferson Smurfit Corporation
407 Charles Street
Middletown, OH 45042
513-424-4279
ATTN: Ron McAden

Program title: Jefferson Smurfit Corporation Apprenticeship Program
Specific job title(s): Die maker
This is a 4-year program with 800 hours of classroom instruction.
No salaries were reported by this program.
Annually, 21-30 people apply for 0-5 positions.
Course credit is offered.
Applications are accepted in person from current employees when openings are available.

REQUIREMENTS:

- High school diploma or GED certificate
- Pass a written test
- Pass an oral interview
- Valid driver's license
- Passing grade in the following high school course(s): Math

APPLICATION DOCUMENTS:

Applicants must bring the following documents when applying:
- High school diploma or GED certificate
- Driver's license
- Proof of auto insurance

ADDITIONAL PROGRAM COMMENTS:

This program is offered in conjunction with the United Paperworkers Local Union #1973, 1630 Central Avenue, Middletown, Ohio 45044.

• • •

PENNSYLVANIA

Machinists
283 North Liberty Road
Grove City, PA 16127
412-458-0282
ATTN: Donald Jervis

Program title: Apprenticeship for the Pattern maker and Metal Trades
Specific job title(s): Pattern maker
This is a 5-year program with 816 hours of classroom instruction and 10,000 hours of on-the-job training.
No salaries were reported by this program.
Annually, 0-10 people apply for 0-5 positions.
Course credit is offered.
There is an initial 30-day probationary period.
Applications are accepted by mail any time of year.

REQUIREMENTS:

- Minimum age: 18; Maximum age: 25
- High school diploma or GED certificate
- Physician's statement of fitness
- Must be physically able to perform the work of the trade
- Pass a written test
- Pass an oral interview
- Valid driver's license
- Letter of recommendation from former employers
- Pass a test for illegal drugs

APPLICATION DOCUMENTS:

Applicants must bring the following documents when applying:
- High school transcript or GED scores
- High school diploma or GED certificate
- Social security card

• • •

Philadelphia Naval Shipyard
PO Box 36140
Philadelphia, PA 19112
ATTN: Ron Warrington

Program title: Philadelphia Naval Shipyard Apprenticeship Program
Specific job title(s): Tool maker, Pattern maker
This is a 4-year program.
Starting wage: $9.00; Ending wage: $13.60.
Annually, over 100 people apply for over 100 positions.
Course credit is offered.
Applications are accepted by mail by applying to the Office of Personnel Management.

REQUIREMENTS:

- High school diploma or GED certificate
- Must be physically able to perform the work of the trade
- Pass a written test
- Pass an oral interview

• • •

RHODE ISLAND

TEDCO, Inc.
20 Austin Avenue, Box 295
Greenville, RI 02828
401-949-2562
ATTN: Robert Vincent

Program title: MECHTECH Program, Tooling and Machining Industry
Specific job title(s): Tool maker, Mold maker
This is a 4-year program.
No salaries were reported by this program.
Course credit is offered.
Applications are accepted by mail.

ADDITIONAL PROGRAM COMMENTS:

MECHTECH is a registered program for the tooling and machining industry that unites general and specialized skills that are learned in metal working companies throughout Rhode Island and southeastern Massachusetts. Students are hired and paid by MECHTECH. On-the-job training is given via a rotation system throughout the tooling and machining industry. MECHTECH participants are selected from graduates of the pre-employment training program that is operated by the Rhode Island/Southeastern Massachusetts Chapter of the National Tooling and Machining Association. Applicants with industry experience, along with having been recommended by industry representatives, are also considered. Students are also required to attend the related classes presented by the Community College of Rhode Island. Further information can be obtained at:

Office of the Administrator
Ernest Cormier
40 Newton Avenue
Narragansett, RI 02882-1368
(401) 782-8978

• • •

VERMONT

Rehav Inc.
Box 319
North Springfield, VT 05150
802-886-8595
ATTN: George Trombly

Specific job title(s): Tool maker
This is a 4-year program with 576 hours of classroom instruction and 8,000 hours of on-the-job training.
Starting wage: $8.00; Ending wage: $10.00.
Annually, a varying number of people apply for a varying number of positions.
There is an initial 1,000-hour probationary period.
Applications are accepted in person or by mail on various dates. Contact for current deadlines.

REQUIREMENTS:

- Minimum age: 16
- Pass an oral interview
- Letter of intent from a valid employer
- Passing grade in the following high school course(s): Machine shop

• • •

VIRGINIA

Admissions Office
The Apprentice School Newport News Shipbuilding
4101 Washington Avenue
Newport News, VA 23607
804-380-3809

Specific job title(s): Heavy metal fabricator, Forger (heat treater), Molder
This is a 4-year program.
Starting wage: $7.97; Ending wage: $13.48.
Annually, over 100 people apply for 51-100 positions.
Course credit is offered.
There is an initial 180-day probationary period.
Applications are accepted by mail any time of year, Monday-Friday, 7:30-4:30.

REQUIREMENTS:

- Minimum age: 18; Maximum age: 29
- High school diploma or GED certificate
- Must be physically able to perform the work of the trade
- Pass a written test
- Pass an oral interview
- Letter of recommendation from employers or teachers
- Pass a test for illegal drugs

APPLICATION DOCUMENTS:

Applicants must bring the following documents when applying:
- High school transcript or GED scores
- Social security card
- 2 forms ID
- College transcript

• • •

WASHINGTON

Boeing Commercial Airplane Group
PO Box 3707, MS 7E-64
Seattle, WA 98124
206-393-8029
ATTN: Jenie Baldwin

Specific job title(s): Tooling inspector, Jig and fixture builder, Tool and die maker, Tool cutter
This is a 4-year program with 640 hours of classroom instruction and 7,360 hours of on-the-job training.
Starting wage: $14.49; Ending wage: $20.76.
Annually, 51-100 people apply for 0-5 positions.
Course credit is offered.
There is an initial 1,000-hour probationary period.
Applications are accepted by mail through in-plant mail only, during April.

REQUIREMENTS:

- Minimum age: 18
- High school diploma or GED certificate
- Pass an oral interview
- Resident of the program's jurisdiction
- Letter of recommendation from current organization management
- Pass a test for illegal drugs
- Must attend a preapprenticeship class

APPLICATION DOCUMENTS:

Applicants must bring the following documents when applying:
- High school transcript or GED scores
- High school diploma or GED certificate

• • •

WISCONSIN

Beloit Precision Die Company, Inc.
1007 Elaine Drive
Beloit, WI 53511
608-362-9085
ATTN: Rick Roth

Specific job title(s): Tool and die maker
This is a 5-year program with 575 hours of

classroom instruction and 10,000 hours of on-the-job training.
No salaries were reported by this program.
Annually, 0-10 people apply for 0-5 positions.
Course credit is offered.
There is an initial 6-month probationary period.
Applications are accepted in person in the spring.

REQUIREMENTS:

- Minimum age: 18
- High school diploma or GED certificate
- Physician's statement of fitness
- Must be physically able to perform the work of the trade
- Pass an oral interview
- Valid driver's license
- Letter of recommendation from high school shop teacher, counselor
- Pass a test for illegal drugs
- Passing grade in the following high school course(s): Trigonometry

• • •

General Pattern, Inc.
4712 North 125th Street
Butler, WI 53007
414-781-2970
ATTN: Ray James

Specific job title(s): Mold maker
This is a 5-year program with 1,000 hours of classroom instruction and 10,000 hours of on-the-job training.
Starting wage: $8.00; Ending wage: $16.00.
Annually, 0-10 people apply for 0-5 positions.
There is an initial 90-day probationary period.
Applications are accepted in person any time of year.

REQUIREMENTS:

- Minimum age: 18
- High school diploma or GED certificate
- Pass a written test
- Pass an oral interview
- Letter of recommendation from instructor
- Pass a test for illegal drugs

APPLICATION DOCUMENTS:

Applicants must bring the following documents when applying:
- High school transcript or GED scores
- Social security card
- Driver's license

• • •

Finn Pattern Company, Inc.
Box 260
Cudahy, WI 53110
414-744-5700
ATTN: Jim Larson

Specific job title(s): Pattern maker
This is a 5-year program.
No salaries were reported by this program.
Annually, 0-10 people apply for 0-5 positions.
Course credit is offered.
There is an initial 90-day probationary period.
Applications are accepted in person any time of year.

REQUIREMENTS:

- Minimum age: 18
- High school diploma or GED certificate
- Pass a written test
- Pass an oral interview
- Valid driver's license
- Letter of recommendation from shop teacher, guidance counselor
- Passing grade in the following high school course(s): Blueprint reading, Math

APPLICATION DOCUMENTS:

Applicants must bring the following documents when applying:
- High school transcript or GED scores
- Social security card
- Driver's license

ADDITIONAL PROGRAM COMMENTS:

Classroom instruction is one day per week for two years.

• • •

Tri-Tec Corporation
Precision Plastic Molding, Tooling and Assembly
455 West Maddison Street, B 70
Darien, WI 53114
414-724-3286
ATTN: Greg Holden

Specific job title(s): Tool and die maker
This is a 5-year program with 576 hours of classroom instruction.
Starting wage: $16.50.
Annually, 0-10 people apply for 0-5 positions.
Course credit is offered.
There is an initial 1,040-hour probationary period.
Applications are accepted in person any time of year, Monday-Friday, 8:00-5:00.

REQUIREMENTS:

- Must be physically able to perform the work of the trade
- Pass an oral interview
- Valid driver's license
- Letter of recommendation from high school shop teacher
- Passing grade in the following high school course(s): Shop

APPLICATION DOCUMENTS:

Applicants must bring the following documents when applying:
- Social security card
- Driver's license

ADDITIONAL PROGRAM COMMENTS:

Classroom instruction is held at

Waukesha Technical College
800 Main Street
Pewaukee, WI 53072
Bill Bulloch
(414) 691-5566

• • •

Bay Engineered Castings
1900 Enterprise Drive
De Pere, WI 54155
414-336-5781
ATTN: Jim Guyette

Specific job title(s): Foundry
This is a 4-year program with 832 hours of classroom instruction and 4,000 hours of on-the-job training.
No salaries were reported by this program.
Annually, 0-10 people apply for 0-5 positions.
Course credit is offered.
Applications are accepted in person usually through in-house workers during April.

REQUIREMENTS:

- Minimum age: 18
- High school diploma or GED certificate
- Pass a written test
- Pass an oral interview
- Letter of recommendation
- Pass a test for illegal drugs
- Passing grade in the following high school course(s): Math

APPLICATION DOCUMENTS:

Applicants must bring the following documents when applying:
- High school transcript or GED scores
- High school diploma or GED certificate
- Social security card
- Driver's license

• • •

Phillips Plastics
2930 Mondovi Road
Eau Claire, WI 54701
715-836-8452

Specific job title(s): Toolroom
This is a 5-year program with 600 hours of classroom instruction and 940 hours of on-the-job training.
Starting wage: $7.65; Ending wage: $15.32.
Annually, 0-10 people apply for 6-10 positions.
There is an initial 6-month probationary period.

Applications are accepted in person any time of year.

REQUIREMENTS:

- Minimum age: 18
- High school diploma or GED certificate
- Must be physically able to perform the work of the trade
- Pass a written test
- Pass an oral interview
- Valid driver's license
- Pass a test for illegal drugs
- Passing grade in the following high school course(s): Shop

APPLICATION DOCUMENTS:

Applicants must bring the following documents when applying:
- High school transcript or GED scores
- High school diploma or GED certificate
- Social security card

• • •

 Apex Mold and Die Inc.
Box 169
Endeavor, WI 53930
608-587-2333
ATTN: Olga Zucharias

Specific job title(s): Tool and die maker
This is a 4-year program with 576 hours of classroom instruction.
No salaries were reported by this program. Annually, 0-10 people apply for 0-5 positions.
There is an initial 90-day probationary period. Applications are accepted in person or by mail any time of year. Contact for possible openings.

REQUIREMENTS:

- Pass an oral interview
- Letter of recommendation from teacher from tech school
- Passing grade in the following high school course(s): Math, Trigonometry

APPLICATION DOCUMENTS:

Applicants must bring the following documents when applying:
- Social security card

ADDITIONAL PROGRAM COMMENTS:

This company usually hires in-house workers for this program.

• • •

Kaysun Corporation
Box 1898
Manitowoc, WI 54221
414-682-6388
ATTN: Kevin Hjort

Specific job title(s): Molding maker, Tool maker, Maintenance tool maker
This is a 5-year program.
No salaries were reported by this program. Annually, a varying number of people apply for 0-5 positions.
There is an initial 3-month probationary period. Applications are accepted in person any time of year by calling first for openings.

REQUIREMENTS:

- High school diploma or GED certificate
- Pass an oral interview
- Letter of recommendation from past employers
- Passing grade in the following high school course(s): Shop

APPLICATION DOCUMENTS:

Applicants must bring the following documents when applying:
- Social security card
- Driver's license
- Resume

• • •

Tool, Die, Mold, and Pattern Makers

Aluminum Casting and Engineering Co.
2039 South Lenox Street
Milwaukee, WI 53207
414-744-3902
ATTN: James Van Der Male

Specific job title(s): Cast metal maker (foundry)
This is a 3-year program with 576 hours of classroom instruction and 6,240 hours of on-the-job training.
No salaries were reported by this program.
Annually, 0-10 people apply for 0-5 positions.
Course credit is offered.
There is an initial 520-hour probationary period.
Applications are accepted in person any time of year.

REQUIREMENTS:

- Minimum age: 18
- High school diploma or GED certificate
- Physician's statement of fitness
- Pass an oral interview
- Valid driver's license
- Letter of recommendation
- Letter of intent from a valid employer
- Pass a test for illegal drugs

APPLICATION DOCUMENTS:

Applicants must bring the following documents when applying:
- High school transcript or GED scores
- Social security card
- Driver's license

ADDITIONAL PROGRAM COMMENTS:

Applicants must work six months at Aluminum Casting in order to qualify for an apprenticeship.

• • •

Briggs and Stratton
PO Box 702
Milwaukee, WI 53201
414-259-5333
ATTN: Jodi Mickalski

Specific job title(s): Tool and die maker (mold), Tool and die maker (stamp)
This is a 5-year program with 576 hours of classroom instruction and 10,400 hours of on-the-job training.
No salaries were reported by this program.
Annually, over 100 people apply for over 100 positions.
Course credit is offered.
There is an initial probationary period.
Applications are accepted in person during January and July.

REQUIREMENTS:

- Minimum age: 18
- High school diploma or GED certificate
- Pass a written test
- Pass an oral interview
- Letter of recommendation
- Letter of intent from a valid employer
- Pass a test for illegal drugs

APPLICATION DOCUMENTS:

Applicants must bring the following documents when applying:
- High school transcript or GED scores

• • •

J and L Fiber Service
809 Phillip Drive
Waukesha, WI 53186
414-544-1890
ATTN: Dick Prince

Specific job title(s): Pattern setter
This is a 5-year program with 1,000 hours of on-the-job training.
No salaries were reported by this program.
Annually, a varying number of people apply for a varying number of positions.
Course credit is offered.
There is an initial 90-day probationary period.
Applications are accepted in person any time of year. Most hiring is done in-house.

REQUIREMENTS:

- Minimum age: 18
- High school diploma or GED certificate
- Physician's statement of fitness
- Pass a written test

- Pass an oral interview
- Valid driver's license
- Resident of the program's jurisdiction
- Letter of recommendation from employer, teacher
- Pass a test for illegal drugs

APPLICATION DOCUMENTS:

Applicants must bring the following documents when applying:
- High school transcript or GED scores
- Social security card
- Driver's license

• • •

Welders

Welders

Welding is a process of joining metal parts, usually through the application of heat. Welding equipment can also be used to cut and shape metal pieces. *Welders* work on a variety of metal structures and manufactured products, including buildings, bridges, pipelines, automobiles, aircraft, ships, boilers, machinery, and appliances. About two-thirds work in manufacturing plants, while most of the remainder are employed by construction firms or repair shops.

Common types of welding are gas welding and arc welding. The principal equipment in gas welding is the gas torch, which produces an intensely hot flame. Also required are welding rods, which are rod-shaped pieces of a filler metal. Welders begin by adjusting the regulators on gas tanks and lighting the torch. The flame is then adjusted and applied to the edges of the metal. To supply the extra metal needed to weld two parts together, a welding rod is melted on the welding area. In arc welding, probably the most popular method, an electric current melts the metal edges and a filler wire. Other types of welding use electron beams, lasers, or friction to melt the metal.

Welders have varying levels of responsibility. Skilled welders often need to plan their work using blueprints or other specifications, and they might work on a number of different metals, such as steel, cast iron, bronze, aluminum, and nickel, and use different welding methods, depending on the needs of the job. Other welders may handle repetitive jobs that require the same tasks day after day. *Welding machine operators* run machines that do the actual welding. Welding machines are common in manufacturing plants.

Apprentices are trained under already experienced welders. They begin by handling simple tasks and by learning the tools of the trade. Each year they also receive classroom instruction in a variety of subjects, such as blueprint reading and metallurgy. Because welding equipment is potentially dangerous, and heated metal can give off toxic gases and fumes, welders follow strict safety practices and wear protective clothing, helmets, and goggles.

Welding apprenticeships normally run three to four years. Most programs require that the applicant

- apply in person

- be at least 18 years old

- be a high school graduate (or GED holder)

- be physically able to perform the work of the trade

Reported beginning apprenticeship salaries range from $7.00 to $15.67 an hour.

Reported ending apprenticeship salaries range from $13.48 to $18.88 an hour.

Little change is expected in the number of employed welders. In manufacturing, however, welding machines will be increasingly used, resulting in fewer manual welders and more welding machine operators. General trends in the manufacturing industries will also affect the number of job openings.

For more information on welding apprenticeships, write to the national programs listed below, as well as to any government programs located in your state. When a name is included, address your letter to that person. Because existing programs are often revised, some of the following may have changed or ceased to exist. New programs may also have been created. Additional programs might be listed with the national union or with your state's bureau of apprenticeship training. Addresses can be found in the last section of this encyclopedia.

NATIONAL SPONSORS

International Union of Operating
Engineers
1125 17th Street, NW
Washington, DC 20036

This organization is affiliated with the AFL-CIO and has 204 locals.

• • •

STATE SPONSORS

ALABAMA

Plumbers
PO Box 211105
Montgomery, AL 36121
205-272-9500
ATTN: Norman Elliott

Program title: Plumbers and Steamfitters Local Union #52 JAC
This is a 5-year program with 184 hours of classroom instruction.
Starting wage: $7.00; Ending wage: $14.96.
Annually, 21-30 people apply for 11-15 positions.
There is an initial 1-year probationary period.
Applications are accepted in person any time of year, Monday-Friday, 8:30-4:30.

REQUIREMENTS:

- Minimum age: 18
- High school diploma or GED certificate
- Pass an oral interview
- Valid driver's license
- Pass a test for illegal drugs

APPLICATION DOCUMENTS:

Applicants must bring the following documents when applying:
- High school diploma or GED certificate
- Social security card
- Driver's license
- Voter's registration card

• • •

CALIFORNIA

Central Valley Automotive and
Machinists JAC
544 West Olive Avenue
Fresno, CA 93728
209-264-2815

Specific job title(s): Combination welder
This is a 4-year program.
No salaries were reported by this program.
Applications are accepted in person any time of year, Monday, Wednesday, Friday, 10:00-12:00, 2:00-4:00.

REQUIREMENTS:

- Minimum age: 18
- High school diploma or GED certificate

APPLICATION DOCUMENTS:

Applicants must bring the following documents when applying:
- High school transcript or GED scores
- High school diploma or GED certificate

• • •

CONNECTICUT

General Dynamics Electric Boat Division
75 Eastern Point Road
Groton, CT 06340
203-433-3000
ATTN: Richard Taylor, Jr.

Program title: Electric Boat Company Apprenticeship Program
Specific job title(s): Welder (Marine)
No salaries were reported by this program.
Annually, a varying number of people apply for a varying number of positions.
Applications are accepted in person or by mail.

REQUIREMENTS:

- Minimum age: 18
- High school diploma or GED certificate

- Physician's statement of fitness
- Must be physically able to perform the work of the trade
- Letter of recommendation from respective department

• • •

GEORGIA

United Auto Workers Local #10
5407 Buford Highway
PO Box 47426
Doraville, GA 30340
404-457-3128
ATTN: Richard Dalrymple

Program title: GM-UAW Skilled Trades Apprentice Program
This is a 4-year program with 576 hours of classroom instruction and 7,328 hours of on-the-job training.
Starting wage: $15.67; Ending wage: $18.88.
Annually, over 100 people apply for 6-10 positions.
There is an initial 4-year probationary period.
Applications are accepted in person when notices are posted.
The application deadline is 30 days after posting.

REQUIREMENTS:

- Minimum age: 18; Maximum age: 44
- High school diploma or GED certificate
- Physician's statement of fitness
- Pass a written test
- Pass an oral interview
- Valid driver's license
- Letter of recommendation from former employers
- Letter of intent from a valid employer
- Pass a test for illegal drugs

APPLICATION DOCUMENTS:

Applicants must bring the following documents when applying:
- High school transcript or GED scores
- High school diploma or GED certificate
- Social security card

- Driver's license
- Proof of ID

• • •

Baley's Welding and Fabrication
Route #1, Box 202
Tulelake, GA 96134
916-667-4055
ATTN: Will Baley

Specific job title(s): Welder, Fabricator
This is a 1-year program.
Starting wage: $7.00.
Annually, 0-10 people apply for 0-5 positions.
There is an initial 90-day probationary period.
Applications are accepted in person or by mail any time of year (spring is peak period).

REQUIREMENTS:

- Minimum age: 18
- Must be physically able to perform the work of the trade
- Pass an oral interview
- Passing grade in the following high school course(s): Shop

APPLICATION DOCUMENTS:

Applicants must bring the following documents when applying:
- Social security card

• • •

MAINE

Bath Iron Works
700 Washington Street
Bath, ME 04530
207-443-3311
ATTN: Jay Lemont

Program title: Bath Iron Works Apprenticeship Program
This is a 3-year program with 790 hours of classroom instruction and 5,210 hours of on-the-job training.
Starting wage: $8.96; Ending wage: $13.50.
Annually, a varying number of people apply for a

varying number of positions.
Course credit is offered.
There is an initial 500-hour probationary period. Applications are accepted in person during the first quarter of the year, usually March 15th to May 1st.

REQUIREMENTS:

- Minimum age: 18
- High school diploma or GED certificate
- Pass an oral interview
- Passing grade in the following high school course(s): 2 years of college preparatory math

APPLICATION DOCUMENTS:

Applicants must bring the following documents when applying:
- High school transcript or GED scores
- Birth certificate
- Resume

• • •

MARYLAND

Bethlehem Steel Corporation
Bethship
Sparrows Point, MD 21219
410-388-6759
ATTN: George Lang

This is a 4-year program with 600 hours of classroom instruction and 6,000 hours of on-the-job training.
Starting wage: $10.00.
Annually, over 100 people apply for 0-5 positions.
Course credit is offered.
There is an initial 480-hour probationary period. Applications are accepted by mail by sending a resume during the 1st quarter of the year.

REQUIREMENTS:

- Minimum age: 18
- High school diploma or GED certificate
- Pass a written test
- Pass an oral interview
- Pass a test for illegal drugs
- Passing grade in the following high school course(s): Math

APPLICATION DOCUMENTS:

Applicants must bring the following documents when applying:
- High school transcript or GED scores
- Social security card
- College or military transcripts if applicable
- Resume

ADDITIONAL PROGRAM COMMENTS:

Ending hourly salary varies from $13.00 to $14.00.

• • •

MISSISSIPPI

Ingall's Shipbuilding
PO Box 149
Pascagoula, MS 39568
601-935-3617
ATTN: B. Robinson

This is a 2-year program with 288 hours of classroom instruction and 2,000 hours of on-the-job training.
No salaries were reported by this program.
Annually, over 100 people apply for over 100 positions.
There is an initial 2-year probationary period. Applications are accepted in person or by mail any time of year.

REQUIREMENTS:

- Minimum age: 18; Maximum age: 24
- High school diploma or GED certificate
- Must be physically able to perform the work of the trade
- Pass an oral interview
- Valid driver's license
- Letter of recommendation
- Pass a test for illegal drugs
- Passing grade in the following high school course(s): Math

APPLICATION DOCUMENTS:

Applicants must bring the following documents when applying:
- High school transcript or GED scores
- High school diploma or GED certificate
- Social security card
- Driver's license
- Birth certificate
- Voter's registration card

• • •

PENNSYLVANIA

Philadelphia Naval Shipyard
PO Box 36140
Philadelphia, PA 19112
ATTN: Ron Warrington

Program title: Philadelphia Naval Shipyard Apprenticeship Program
This is a 4-year program.
Starting wage: $9.00; Ending wage: $13.60.
Annually, over 100 people apply for over 100 positions.
Course credit is offered.
Applications are accepted by mail by applying to the Office of Personnel Management.

REQUIREMENTS:

- High school diploma or GED certificate
- Physician's statement of fitness
- Must be physically able to perform the work of the trade
- Pass a written test
- Pass an oral interview

• • •

VIRGINIA

Admissions Office
The Apprentice School Newport News Shipbuilding
4101 Washington Avenue
Newport News, VA 23607
804-380-3809

Specific job title(s): Welder, Welding equipment repair
This is a 4-year program with 6,000 hours of on-the-job training.
Starting wage: $7.97; Ending wage: $13.48.
Annually, over 100 people apply for 51-100 positions.
Course credit is offered.
There is an initial 180-day probationary period.
Applications are accepted by mail any time of year, Monday-Friday, 7:30-4:30.

REQUIREMENTS:

- Minimum age: 18; Maximum age: 29
- High school diploma or GED certificate
- Must be physically able to perform the work of the trade
- Pass a written test
- Pass an oral interview
- Letter of recommendation from employers or teachers
- Pass a test for illegal drugs

APPLICATION DOCUMENTS:

Applicants must bring the following documents when applying:
- High school transcript or GED scores
- Social security card
- 2 forms ID
- College transcript

• • •

WISCONSIN

Appleton Papers Inc.
825 East Wisconsin Avenue
Appleton, WI 54911
414-734-9841
ATTN: Kevin Larabee

This is a 4-year program.
No salaries were reported by this program.
Course credit is offered.
There is an initial 6-month probationary period.
Applications are accepted in person any time of year through in-house workers.

REQUIREMENTS:

- High school diploma or GED certificate
- Pass a written test
- Pass an oral interview

• • •

Repap Wisconsin Inc.
433 North Main Street
Kimberly, WI 54136
414-788-3511
ATTN: Dick Van Hammond

This is a 4-year program with 8,320 hours of on-the-job training.
Starting wage: $14.25; Ending wage: $16.54.
Annually, over 100 people apply for 0-5 positions.
There is an initial 6-month probationary period.
Applications are accepted in person when posted locally.

REQUIREMENTS:

- High school diploma or GED certificate
- Must be physically able to perform the work of the trade
- Pass a written test
- Pass an oral interview

APPLICATION DOCUMENTS:

Applicants must bring the following documents when applying:
- High school transcript or GED scores

ADDITIONAL PROGRAM COMMENTS:

Classroom instruction is one day every other week for three years. A drug test will be mandatory for newly hired applicants. Aptitude and reading tests are issued. Applicants are selected in-house by seniority first.

• • •

Rhinelander Paper Company
515 West Davenport Street
Rhinelander, WI 54501
715-369-4100
ATTN: Bill Vancos

This is a 4-year program.
No salaries were reported by this program.
Annually, 0-10 people apply for a varying number of positions.
There is an initial 6-month probationary period.
Applications are accepted in person through in-house hires.

REQUIREMENTS:

- High school diploma or GED certificate
- Physician's statement of fitness
- Must be physically able to perform the work of the trade
- Pass a written test
- Pass a test for illegal drugs

ADDITIONAL PROGRAM COMMENTS:

Salary is negotiated at approximately $10.44 to start and ending at $15.75. Classroom instruction is approximately 400-hours minimum.

• • •

Consolidated Papers Inc.
Box 8050
Wisconsin Rapids, WI 54495
715-442-3111
ATTN: Chuck Korn

This is a 4-year program with 432 hours of classroom instruction.
No salaries were reported by this program.
Annually, a varying number of people apply for 21-50 positions.
There is an initial 60-day probationary period.
Applications are accepted in person or by mail any time of year.

REQUIREMENTS:

- High school diploma or GED certificate
- Pass an oral interview

- Pass a test for illegal drugs

APPLICATION DOCUMENTS:

Applicants must bring the following documents when applying:
- High school transcript or GED scores
- High school diploma or GED certificate

ADDITIONAL PROGRAM COMMENTS:

This position requires a one-year vocational diploma up front.

• • •

Additional Occupations

By far the largest number of apprenticeable occupations exist in the construction industry; thousands of programs are in place across the country. There are some occupations, however, for which apprenticeships have either ceased to be a practical way to train novices, or are just beginning to be recognized as such. For the handful of occupations listed here, some may not appear in future editions, while some may move to chapters of their own.

For more information on apprenticeships, the best approach is always to check with your state's Bureau of Apprenticeship and Training for specific job titles you are interested in (whether or not they are listed in this directory). In addition, write to any of the relevant national programs listed here, as well as to any government programs located in your state. When a name is included, address your letter to that person. Because existing programs are often revised, some of the following may have changed or ceased to exist. New programs may also have been created. Additional programs might be listed with a national union or professional association or with your state's Bureau of Apprenticeship Training. Bureau addresses can be found in the last section of this encyclopedia.

INFORMATION SOURCES AND PROGRAM SPONSORS

BANK NOTE DESIGNER

U.S. Bureau of Engraving and Printing
Washington, DC
202-874-2027
ATTN: Linda Washington

This is a 7-year program.
Starting wage: $14.12; Ending wage: $32.00.
Course credit is offered.
There is an initial 1-year probationary period.
Applications are accepted by mail any time of year.

REQUIREMENTS:

- Physician's statement of fitness
- Pass an oral interview
- Letter of recommendation from teacher

- Pass a test for illegal drugs
- Passing grade in the following high school course(s): Art training
- Proof of citizenship
- Portfolio

ADDITIONAL PROGRAM COMMENTS:

Classroom instruction sometimes involves art classes (sixteen are needed). One position is open every seven years. A portfolio of artwork needs to be submitted if an opening is available.

• • •

BARTENDER

Hotel Employees and Restaurant Employees International Union
1219 28th Street, NW
Washington, DC 20007
ATTN: Information Officer

This union is affiliated with the AFL-CIO and has 198 locals.

• • •

Bartenders Local #165
PO Box 26238
Las Vegas, NV 89126
702-384-7774
ATTN: James Fisher

Program title: Bartenders Apprenticeship Program
This is a 1-year program.
Starting wage: $8.00; Ending wage: $8.00.
Annually, 51-100 people apply for 21-50 positions.
Course credit is offered.
Applications are accepted in person on the first Wednesday of every month.

REQUIREMENTS:

- Minimum age: 21
- Resident of the program's jurisdiction

APPLICATION DOCUMENTS:

Applicants must bring the following documents when applying:
- Social security card
- Clark County health card
- Birth certificate (passport or military ID okay)

ADDITIONAL PROGRAM COMMENTS:

Classroom instruction is two hours per week. On-the-job instruction consists of forty hours per week for the duration of the program. Starting salary varies from job to job. Applicants should not have any felony record.

• • •

BLACKSMITH

International Brotherhood of Boilermakers, Iron Ship Builders, Blacksmiths, Forgers and Helpers
753 State Avenue, Suite 570
Kansas City, KS 66101
ATTN: Information Officer

This union is affiliated with the AFL-CIO and has 425 locals.

• • •

International Union of Journeymen Horseshoers of the United States and Canada
C/O Jeffrey R. Cotton
3250 Nicholson Road
Fowlerville, MI 48836
ATTN: Jeffrey R. Cotton Officer

This union is affiliated with the AFL-CIO.

• • •

Horseshoers
7901 NW 3rd Street, #205 Box 2
Pembroke Pine, FL 33024
305-964-2804
ATTN: Michael Loebig

Specific job title(s): Blacksmith
Annually, a varying number of people apply for 0-5 positions.
Applications are accepted in person any time of year.

REQUIREMENTS:

- Minimum age: 18

ADDITIONAL PROGRAM COMMENTS:

This program lasts approximately two to five years and requires one hour of classroom instruction.

• • •

- Pass a test for illegal drugs
- Passing grade in the following high school course(s): Drafting

APPLICATION DOCUMENTS:

Applicants must bring the following documents when applying:
- Social security card

ADDITIONAL PROGRAM COMMENTS:

Those apprenticing with this company can continue their education at a community college through the company.

• • •

CARRIAGE SMITH

The Balloon Works
PO Box 827
Statesville, NC 28677
704-878-9501
ATTN: Sidney Conn

Program title: Aircraft Woodworker Apprenticeship
Specific job title(s): Carriage smith
This is a 3-year program with 150 hours of classroom instruction and 5,625 hours of on-the-job training.
No salaries were reported by this program.
Annually, 0-10 people apply for 0-5 positions.
Course credit is offered.
There is an initial 90-day probationary period.
Applications are accepted in person any time of year.

REQUIREMENTS:

- Minimum age: 18
- High school diploma or GED certificate
- Must be physically able to perform the work of the trade
- Pass an oral interview
- Valid driver's license
- Resident of the program's jurisdiction
- Letter of intent from a valid employer

CHEMICAL TECHNICIAN

Cummin's Engine Company, Inc.
1933 10th Street
Columbus, IN 47201
812-377-7211
ATTN: Randall Sims

Specific job title(s): Chemical technician
This is a 4-year program with 720 hours of classroom instruction and 8,000 hours of on-the-job training.
Starting wage: $11.07; Ending wage: $16.28.
Annually, over 100 people apply for 16-20 positions.
Course credit is offered.
There is an initial 120-day probationary period.
Applications are accepted by mail following announcements in local papers.

REQUIREMENTS:

- Minimum age: 17
- High school diploma or GED certificate
- Pass a written test
- Pass an oral interview
- Pass a test for illegal drugs
- Legal ID

• • •

CORRECTIONS OFFICER

International Association of Correctional Officers
PO Box 7051
Marquette, MI 49855
ATTN: Information Officer

• • •

Department of Corrections
Division of Adult Institutions
149 East Wilson, PO Box 7925
Madison, WI 53707
608-267-9082
ATTN: Jo Winston

This is a 2-year program.
No salaries were reported by this program.
Annually, over 100 people apply for over 100 positions.
Course credit is offered.
There is an initial 8-month probationary period.
Applications are accepted by mail any time of year with continuous recruitment.

REQUIREMENTS:

- Minimum age: 18
- Physician's statement of fitness
- Must be physically able to perform the work of the trade
- Pass a written test
- Pass an oral interview
- Valid driver's license
- Letter of recommendation
- Pass a test for illegal drugs
- Must attend a preapprenticeship class for 1 day

APPLICATION DOCUMENTS:

Applicants must bring the following documents when applying:
- Social security card
- Driver's license
- Birth certificate

ADDITIONAL PROGRAM COMMENTS:

Classroom instruction consists of a minimum of eight weeks. This information applies to all Officer Apprenticeships for the state of Wisconsin's prisons (e.g., Columbia, Fox Lake, Green Bay, Kettle Moraine).

The application process is as follows: 1) find listing of openings within Wisconsin's Bulletin of Opportunities; 2) fill out civil service application; 3) take civil service exam; 4) interview; 5) tentative job offer; 6) physical and drug test; 7) classroom training; 8) on-the-job training. For additional information write to:

Gary Fergot
Wisconsin State Corrections Training Center
632 Warren Road
Oshkosh, WI 54901
414-424-3153

• • •

DRAFTER

American Design Drafting Association
PO Box 799
Rockville, MD 20848-0799
ATTN: Information Officer

• • •

General Dynamics Electric Boat Division
75 Eastern Point Road
Groton, CT 06340
203-433-3000
ATTN: Richard Taylor, Jr.

Program title: Electric Boat Company Apprenticeship Program
No salaries were reported by this program.
Annually, a varying number of people apply for a varying number of positions.
There is an initial 90-day probationary period.
Applications are accepted in person or by mail.

REQUIREMENTS:

- High school diploma or GED certificate
- Physician's statement of fitness

- Must be physically able to perform the work of the trade
- Letter of recommendation from respective department

APPLICATION DOCUMENTS:

Applicants must bring the following documents when applying:
- High school transcript
- High school diploma or GED certificate

ADDITIONAL PROGRAM COMMENTS:

The Drafting Apprenticeship comprises five disciplines: Electrical, Piping, Ventilation and Arrangement, Mechanical, and Structural. Placement in a particular discipline is based upon the qualifications and background of the drafting learner and the needs of the Design Department. There is a 90-day probation period prior to starting the apprenticeship. The duration of the program is 2 to 5 years depending on the trade. There are 144 classroom hours per year. There are 4,000-10,000 hours of on-the-job instruction. Drafting recruitment is usually scheduled on an annual basis. Classes are conducted during working hours. Apprentices are evaluated every four months.

• • •

Cummin's Engine Company, Inc.
1933 10th Street
Columbus, IN 47201
812-377-7211
ATTN: Randall Sims

This is a 4-year program with 720 hours of classroom instruction and 8,000 hours of on-the-job training.
Starting wage: $11.07; Ending wage: $16.28.
Annually, over 100 people apply for 16-20 positions.
Course credit is offered.
There is an initial 120-day probationary period.
Applications are accepted by mail following announcements in local papers.

REQUIREMENTS:

- Minimum age: 17
- High school diploma or GED certificate
- Pass a written test
- Pass an oral interview
- Pass a test for illegal drugs
- Legal ID

ADDITIONAL PROGRAM COMMENTS:

This facility offers programs in Facilities engineering drafting, Mechanical engineering drafting, and Tool design drafting.

Bethlehem Steel Corporation
Bethship
Sparrows Point, MD 21219
410-388-6759
ATTN: George Lang

This is a 4-year program with 600 hours of classroom instruction and 6,000 hours of on-the-job training.
Starting wage: $10.00.
Annually, over 100 people apply for 0-5 positions.
Course credit is offered.
There is an initial 480-hour probationary period.
Applications are accepted by mail by sending a resume.

REQUIREMENTS:

- Minimum age: 18
- High school diploma or GED certificate
- Pass a written test
- Pass an oral interview
- Pass a test for illegal drugs
- Passing grade in the following high school course(s): Math

APPLICATION DOCUMENTS:

Applicants must bring the following documents when applying:
- High school transcript
- Social security card
- College or military transcripts if applicable
- Resume

Additional Occupations

ADDITIONAL PROGRAM COMMENTS:

Ending hourly salary varies from $13.00 to $14.00.

• • •

ELEVATOR CONSTRUCTOR

  International Union of Elevator Constructors
Clark Building, Suite 530
5565 Sterrett Place
Columbia, MD 21044
ATTN: Information Officer

• • •

  Eastern Oklahoma Building and Construction Trades Council
2651 East 21st Street, Suite 405
Tulsa, OK 74114
918-742-3365
ATTN: Clayton Walker

This is a 4-year program with 576 hours of classroom instruction and 8,000 hours of on-the-job training.
Starting wage: $6.60; Ending wage: $13.50.
Annually, 21-30 people apply for 16-20 positions.
Applications are accepted in person in March. The application deadline is 45 days after opening.

REQUIREMENTS:

- Minimum age: 18
- High school diploma or GED certificate
- Physician's statement of fitness
- Must be physically able to perform the work of the trade
- Pass a written test
- Pass an oral interview
- Resident of the program's jurisdiction
- Letter of recommendation from personal and professional acquaintances

• • •

  Elevator Constructors
5963 Bridle Path
Bartlett, TN 38134
901-372-6424
ATTN: Curt Wilson

Program title: National Elevator Industry Education Program
This is a 3-year program.
Annually, 11-20 people apply for 0-5 positions.
Applications are accepted by mail any time of year.

REQUIREMENTS:

- Minimum age: 18
- High school diploma or GED certificate
- Must be physically able to perform the work of the trade
- Pass a test for illegal drugs

APPLICATION DOCUMENTS:

Applicants must bring the following documents when applying:
- High school diploma or GED certificate
- Social security card
- Birth certificate

• • •

FARRIER

  International Union of Journeymen Horseshoers of the United States and Canada
C/O Jeffrey R. Cotton
3250 Nicholson Road
Fowlerville, MI 48836
ATTN: Jeffrey R. Cotton Officer

This union is affiliated with the AFL-CIO.

• • •

  American Farrier's Association
4059 Ironworks Pike
Lexington, KY 40511
606-233-7411
ATTN: Henry Heymering

This is a 4-year program.
No salaries were reported by this program.
Annually, 0-10 people apply for 0-5 positions.
There is an initial 60-day probationary period.
Applications are accepted by mail any time of year.

REQUIREMENTS:

- Minimum age: 18
- High school diploma or GED certificate
- Pass a written test
- Pass an oral interview

ADDITIONAL PROGRAM COMMENTS:

Applicants must have passed the AFA Intern Classified Test. To find out when and where tests will be in your area, contact the AFA office above. Applicants must be willing to relocate upon hire, pay a $1500 AFA fee, and support themselves from personal savings for approximately the first two years of training. If you can meet these requirements, contact the AFA Committee Chair:

Henry Heymering
PO Box 779
Cascade, MD 21719
301-241-3548

• • •

Horseshoers
120 Gladstone Street
East Boston, MA 02128
617-569-4876
ATTN: Paul Brooker

Annually, 0-10 people apply for 0-5 positions.
There is an initial 90-day probationary period.
Applications are accepted in person or by mail any time of year.

REQUIREMENTS:

- Minimum age: 16
- High school diploma or GED certificate
- Must be physically able to perform the work of the trade

APPLICATION DOCUMENTS:

Applicants must bring the following documents when applying:
- Social security card

ADDITIONAL PROGRAM COMMENTS:

On-the-job instruction consists of six days per week for the duration of the program. Applicants must take a six-hour test, which includes trimming and shoemaking and will be judged on their craft of proper fitting.

• • •

GAMING DEALER

Academy of Casino Careers
99 North Virginia Street
Reno, NV 89501
702-786-7713
ATTN: Ron Teston

Program title: Casino Gaming Dealer Apprenticeship
Specific job title(s): Gaming dealer
This is a 2-year program with 288 hours of classroom instruction and 4,000 hours of on-the-job training.
Starting wage: $6.50; Ending wage: $25.00.
Annually, 31-50 people apply for a varying number of positions.
There is an initial 90-day probationary period.
Applications are accepted in person during the fall, Monday-Friday, 9:00-5:00.

REQUIREMENTS:

- Minimum age: 21
- High school diploma or GED certificate
- Pass a written test
- Pass an oral interview
- Letter of intent from a valid employer
- Pass a test for illegal drugs

APPLICATION DOCUMENTS:

Applicants must bring the following documents when applying:
- High school diploma or GED certificate
- Social security card
- Any third form of ID

Additional Occupations

ADDITIONAL PROGRAM COMMENTS:

Applicant must be in cooperation with current casino employer. Starting salary may vary depending on company.

• • •

GENERAL WAREHOUSE WORKER

International Brotherhood of Teamsters, Chauffeurs, Warehousemen and Helpers of America
25 Louisiana Avenue, NW
Washington, DC 20001
ATTN: Information Officer

This union has 692 locals.

• • •

Graphic Communications
507 West Lackawanna Avenue
Olyphant, PA 18447
717-484-3281
ATTN: Robert Wilson

Specific job title(s): General warehouse worker
Starting wage: $5.00; Ending wage: $10.35.
Annually, 0-10 people apply for 0-5 positions.
There is an initial 60-day probationary period.
Applications are accepted in person any time of year.

REQUIREMENTS:

- Minimum age: 18
- High school diploma or GED certificate
- Physician's statement of fitness
- Must be physically able to perform the work of the trade
- Pass an oral interview
- Letter of recommendation from employers or teachers

APPLICATION DOCUMENTS:

Applicants must bring the following documents when applying:
- High school diploma or GED certificate
- Social security card

ADDITIONAL PROGRAM COMMENTS:

Classes are held one night a week for four hours from September through June.

• • •

HORSE TRAINER, BREEDER

Horse training and breeding organizations normally focus on one particular breed of horse. Check reference sources under specific breeds.

Al-Marah Arabians
4101 North Bear Canyon Road
Tucson, AZ 85749
602-749-1162
ATTN: Brenda Rice

Specific job title(s): Horse trainer, Breeder
This is a 2-year program with 288 hours of classroom instruction and 4,000 hours of on-the-job training.
No salaries were reported by this program.
Annually, 51-100 people apply for 6-10 positions.
There is an initial 90-day probationary period.
Applications are accepted in person or by mail any time of year, Monday-Friday, 8:00-5:00.

REQUIREMENTS:

- Minimum age: 18; Maximum age: 30
- High school diploma or GED certificate
- Physician's statement of fitness
- Must be physically able to perform the work of the trade
- Pass an oral interview
- Letter of recommendation from previous employers, friends, teachers
- Letter of intent from a valid employer
- Passing grade in the following high school course(s): English, Math, Science, Foreign language

APPLICATION DOCUMENTS:

Applicants must bring the following documents when applying:
- Social security card

Additional Occupations

ADDITIONAL PROGRAM COMMENTS:

Apprentices earn $747 a month for the first six months, $787 a month for the second six months, and $837 a month in their final year. The program deducts $250 a month from the above wages for living quarters, furnishings, and utilities.

• • •

LAMPWORKER

Flint Glass Workers
5 SE Boulevard, PO Box 564
Newfield, NJ 08344
609-697-4824
ATTN: Mark Homiak

This is a 4-year program.
Annually, 0-10 people apply for 0-5 positions. Applications are accepted in person any time of year.

REQUIREMENTS:

- Minimum age: 18; Maximum age: 65
- High school diploma or GED certificate
- Letter of recommendation from past employers
- Letter of intent from a valid employer

APPLICATION DOCUMENTS:

Applicants must bring the following documents when applying:
- Social security card

• • •

LEGISLATIVE LOBBYIST

American League of Lobbyists
PO Box 30005
Alexandria, VA 22310
ATTN: Information Specialist

• • •

Service Employees
18 Casino Avenue
Cranston, RI 02920
ATTN: Michael Sepe

Annually, 0-10 people apply for 0-5 positions. Applications are accepted in person during December.

REQUIREMENTS:

- Minimum age: 18
- High school diploma or GED certificate
- Valid driver's license
- Resident of the program's jurisdiction

APPLICATION DOCUMENTS:

Applicants must bring the following documents when applying:
- Social security card

• • •

MEATCUTTER

United Food and Commercial Workers International Union
Suffridge Building
1775 K Street, NW
Washington, DC 20006
ATTN: Information Officer

This union is affiliated with the AFL-CIO and has 600 locals.

• • •

Orange County and Harbor Area JAC
11515 Artesia Boulevard
Artesia, CA 90701
213-860-7744
ATTN: Greg Conger

Program title: Orange County and Harbor Area JAC
Specific job title(s): Meatcutter
This is a 2-year program with 288 hours of classroom instruction and 2,080 hours of on-the-job training.

Starting wage: $10.39; Ending wage: $14.38. Annually, 0-10 people apply for 6-10 positions. There is an initial 45-day probationary period. Applications are accepted in person any time of year.

REQUIREMENTS:

- Minimum age: 18
- High school diploma or GED certificate
- Must be physically able to perform the work of the trade
- Pass a written test
- Pass an oral interview
- Valid driver's license
- Pass a test for illegal drugs

APPLICATION DOCUMENTS:

Applicants must bring the following documents when applying:
- Social security card
- Driver's license

ADDITIONAL PROGRAM COMMENTS:

Applicant must be an employee of a participating employer before being accepted into this program.

• • •

MECHANICAL ENGINEERING TECHNICIAN

 Cummin's Engine Company, Inc.
1933 10th Street
Columbus, IN 47201
812-377-7211
ATTN: Randall Sims

Specific job title(s): Mechanical engineering technician
This is a 4-year program with 720 hours of classroom instruction and 8,000 hours of on-the-job training.
Starting wage: $11.07; Ending wage: $16.28. Annually, over 100 people apply for 16-20 positions.
Course credit is offered.
There is an initial 120-day probationary period.

Applications are accepted by mail following announcements in local papers.

REQUIREMENTS:

- Minimum age: 17
- High school diploma or GED certificate
- Pass a written test
- Pass an oral interview
- Pass a test for illegal drugs
- Legal ID

• • •

MEDICAL TRANSCRIPTIONIST

 American Association for Medical Transcription
PO Box 576187
Modesto, CA 95357
ATTN: Information Officer

• • •

 Transcription Technologies Inc.
90 West Grove Street
Reno, NV 89509
702-828-9030
ATTN: Debbie Kleinhans

No salaries were reported by this program. Annually, 0-10 people apply for 0-5 positions. Applications are accepted in person or by mail any time of year at normal business hours.

REQUIREMENTS:

- Minimum age: 18
- High school diploma or GED certificate
- Pass an oral interview
- Letter of recommendation from classroom instructor
- Must attend a preapprenticeship class

APPLICATION DOCUMENTS:

Applicants must bring the following documents when applying:
- Social security card

Additional Occupations

ADDITIONAL PROGRAM COMMENTS:

Starting salary varies on production at $7.50; ending salary ranges from $10.00 to $12.00 per hour. Applicants must take six to nine months of vocational school to receive medical transcripts at Transcription Technologies.

• • •

METAL FORGER

Philadelphia Naval Shipyard
PO Box 36140
Philadelphia, PA 19112
ATTN: Ron Warrington

Program title: Philadelphia Naval Shipyard Apprenticeship Program
Specific job title(s): Metal forger
This is a 4-year program.
Starting wage: $9.00; Ending wage: $13.60.
Annually, over 100 people apply for over 100 positions.
Course credit is offered.
Applications are accepted by mail by applying to the Office of Personnel Management.

REQUIREMENTS:

- High school diploma or GED certificate
- Must be physically able to perform the work of the trade
- Pass a written test
- Pass an oral interview

• • •

METALLURGICAL TECHNICIAN

Cummin's Engine Company, Inc.
1933 10th Street
Columbus, IN 47201
812-377-7211
ATTN: Randall Sims

Specific job title(s): Metallurgical technician
This is a 4-year program with 720 hours of classroom instruction and 8,000 hours of on-the-job training.
Starting wage: $11.07; Ending wage: $16.28.
Annually, over 100 people apply for 16-20 positions.
Course credit is offered.
There is an initial 120-day probationary period.
Applications are accepted by mail following announcements in local papers.

REQUIREMENTS:

- Minimum age: 17
- High school diploma or GED certificate
- Pass a written test
- Pass an oral interview
- Pass a test for illegal drugs
- Legal ID

• • •

NONDESTRUCTIVE TESTER

American Society for Nondestructive Testing
PO Box 28518
Columbus, OH 43228
ATTN: Information Officer

• • •

Admissions Office
The Apprentice School Newport News Shipbuilding
4101 Washington Avenue
Newport News, VA 23607
804-380-3809

Specific job title(s): Nondestructive tester
This is a 4-year program.
Starting wage: $7.97; Ending wage: $13.48.
Annually, over 100 people apply for 51-100 positions.
Course credit is offered.
There is an initial 180-day probationary period.
Applications are accepted by mail any time of year, Monday-Friday, 7:30-4:30.

REQUIREMENTS:

- Minimum age: 18; Maximum age: 29
- High school diploma or GED certificate
- Must be physically able to perform the work of the trade

- Pass a written test
- Pass an oral interview
- Letter of recommendation from employers or teachers
- Pass a test for illegal drugs

APPLICATION DOCUMENTS:

Applicants must bring the following documents when applying:
- High school transcript
- Social security card
- 2 forms ID
- College transcript

• • •

NURSING ASSISTANT

American Nursing Assistant's Association
PO Box 103
Ottawa, KS 66067
ATTN: Information Officer

• • •

Stella Maris
2300 Dulaney Valley Road
Towson, MD 21204
410-252-4500

Program title: Nursing Assistant Training Program
Specific job title(s): Nursing assistant
Starting wage: $5.00; Ending wage: $5.95.
Annually, a varying number of people apply for 16-20 positions.
There is an initial 3-month probationary period.
Applications are accepted in person when classes are posted at office.

REQUIREMENTS:

- Pass a written test
- Pass an oral interview

APPLICATION DOCUMENTS:

Applicants must bring the following documents when applying:
- Social security card
- 2 forms of ID

ADDITIONAL PROGRAM COMMENTS:

Classroom instruction is 5 days the first month. On-the-job instruction is 1 day the last three months. No minimum age, requires work permit only.

• • •

Northhampton Manor, Inc.
200 East 16th Street
Frederick, MD 21701
301-662-8700

Program title: Geriatric Nursing Assistant Training Program
Specific job title(s): Nursing assistant
Starting wage: $6.00; Ending wage: $7.75.
Annually, over 100 people apply for 51-100 positions.
Course credit is offered.
Applications are accepted in person or by mail at various times. Contact for further information.

REQUIREMENTS:

- Pass a written test
- Pass an oral interview
- Letter of recommendation
- Proof of citizenship

• • •

OIL WELL DRILLER

Oil, Chemical, and Atomic Workers International Union
PO Box 2812
Denver, CO 80201
ATTN: Information Officer

This union is affiliated with the AFL-CIO and has 400 locals.

• • •

Southern Nevada Operating Engineers
JATC
PO Box 4115
North Las Vegas, NV 89036
702-649-6888
ATTN: Wayne Grimes

This is a 3-year program with 432 hours of classroom instruction.
No salaries were reported by this program.
Annually, over 100 people apply for 0-5 positions.
There is an initial 6-month probationary period.
Applications are accepted in person at various times when company solicits.

REQUIREMENTS:

- Minimum age: 18
- High school diploma or GED certificate
- Pass a written test
- Pass an oral interview
- Pass a test for illegal drugs

APPLICATION DOCUMENTS:

Applicants must bring the following documents when applying:
- High school transcript
- High school diploma or GED certificate
- Social security card
- Birth certificate

• • •

POLICE OFFICER

International Brotherhood of Police Officers
285 Dorchester Avenue
Boston, MA 02127
ATTN: Information Officer

This union is affiliated with the AFL-CIO.

• • •

Harford County Sheriff's Department
PO Box 150
Bel Air, MD 21014
410-879-5426

Program title: Entry Level Police Officer Training Program
No salaries were reported by this program.
Annually, over 100 people apply for 11-15 positions.
Course credit is offered.
There is an initial 18-month probationary period.
Applications are accepted in person when announced at Hartford County Human Resources.

REQUIREMENTS:

- Minimum age: 21
- High school diploma or GED certificate
- Physician's statement of fitness
- Must be physically able to perform the work of the trade
- Pass a written test
- Pass an oral interview
- Valid driver's license
- Letter of recommendation
- Letter of intent from a valid employer
- Pass a test for illegal drugs

APPLICATION DOCUMENTS:

Applicants must bring the following documents when applying:
- High school diploma or GED certificate
- Driver's license

• • •

Baltimore County Police Department
7607 Parkwood Road
Baltimore, MD 21222
410-887-7276
ATTN: Michael O'Donnell

Program title: Police Academy
This is a 2-year program.
Starting wage: $24.08; Ending wage: $27.01.
Annually, over 100 people apply for 51-100 positions.

Course credit is offered.
There is an initial 2-year probationary period.
Applications are accepted by mail when advertised in local paper.

REQUIREMENTS:

- Minimum age: 21
- High school diploma or GED certificate
- Physician's statement of fitness
- Must be physically able to perform the work of the trade
- Pass a written test
- Pass an oral interview
- Valid driver's license
- Pass a test for illegal drugs

APPLICATION DOCUMENTS:

Applicants must bring the following documents when applying:
- High school diploma or GED certificate
- Driver's license

ADDITIONAL PROGRAM COMMENTS:

Applicants must also pass polygraph test.

• • •

 Eastern Shore Police Academy
317 Lemmon Hill Lane
Salisbury, MD 21801
410-543-2712

No salaries were reported by this program. Annually, a varying number of people apply for 21-50 positions.
Course credit is offered.
There is an initial 1-year probationary period. Applications are accepted in person or by mail generally in August and February. Screening is done through state agencies.

REQUIREMENTS:

- Minimum age: 21
- High school diploma or GED certificate
- Physician's statement of fitness
- Must be physically able to perform the work of the trade
- Pass a written test
- Pass an oral interview
- Valid driver's license
- Pass a test for illegal drugs

APPLICATION DOCUMENTS:

Applicants must bring the following documents when applying:
- High school diploma or GED certificate
- Social security card
- Driver's license
- Birth certificate

• • •

POWER PLANT OPERATOR

 IES Industries, Inc.
119 East Main Street
Marshalltown, IA 50158
515-754-5864
ATTN: Lloyd Jones

Program title: IES Utilities Incorporated
Starting wage: $15.54; Ending wage: $19.42.
Annually, 0-10 people apply for a varying number of positions.
There is an initial 6-month probationary period. Applications are accepted in person or by mail any time of year, Tuesdays and Thursdays, 9:00-4:00.

REQUIREMENTS:

- Minimum age: 18
- High school diploma or GED certificate
- Pass a written test
- Pass an oral interview
- Valid driver's license
- Pass a test for illegal drugs

APPLICATION DOCUMENTS:

Applicants must bring the following documents when applying:
- High school transcript
- High school diploma or GED certificate
- Driver's license

• • •

PROCESS TECHNICIAN

Glass Molders Plastics
5131 Bischoff Avenue
St. Louis, MO 63110
215-565-5051
ATTN: Richard Butler

This is a 4-year program with 566 hours of classroom instruction and 8,000 hours of on-the-job training.
Starting wage: $12.58; Ending wage: $14.05.
Annually, 11-20 people apply for 0-5 positions.
Course credit is offered.
Applications are accepted in person any time of year.

REQUIREMENTS:

- Minimum age: 18
- High school diploma or GED certificate
- Physician's statement of fitness
- Must be physically able to perform the work of the trade
- Pass an oral interview
- Must attend a preapprenticeship class

• • •

PRODUCTION CONTROLLER

National Association of Production Controllers
PO Box 4188
Warrington, FL 32507
ATTN: Violet Lane

Program title: Aircraft Production Controller
This is a 4-year program.
Starting wage: $5.25; Ending wage: $14.53.
Annually, 0-10 people apply for 0-5 positions.
Applications are accepted in person any time of year.

REQUIREMENTS:

- High school diploma or GED certificate
- Physician's statement of fitness
- Must be physically able to perform the work of the trade
- Pass a written test
- Pass an oral interview
- Letter of recommendation

• • •

PUBLIC SCHOOL WORKERS

Public School Employees of Washington JATC
4910 A Street, SE, PO Box 798
Auburn, WA 98071
206-852-3880
ATTN: Kathy Mannelly

Annually, a varying number of people apply for a varying number of positions.
There is an initial probationary period.
Applications are accepted in person by contacting the JATC for the year's schedule.

REQUIREMENTS:

- High school diploma or GED certificate
- Letter of intent from a valid employer

APPLICATION DOCUMENTS:

Applicants must bring the following documents when applying:
- High school transcript
- High school diploma or GED certificate

ADDITIONAL PROGRAM COMMENTS:

These positions are open only to current employees of the Washington Public School system. Applications are accepted through the joint labor-management committee. The local school system should be able to direct applicants through the application procedure and supply the interested candidate with a list of what positions are currently available for training. The requirements for these apprenticeships will vary slightly in each school district, because of local regulations. Although there is no minimum age requirement, anyone under the age of 18 must have a parent or guardian sign an apprenticeship agreement with the sponsoring organization. The specific requirements depend upon the position open. Contact the joint labor-management committee for details.

Apprenticeships are offered for the following job titles:

Accounts payable clerk, Central office secretary, Child care specialist, Child care technician, Data processor, Educational interpreter, Educational paraprofessional, Food service, Graphic arts technician, Grounds maintenance specialist, Instructional assistant, Payroll clerk, School bus driver, School bus mechanic, School secretary, Teachers' assistant for the vision and hearing impaired.

• • •

REAL ESTATE APPRAISER

Appraisal Institute
875 North Michigan Avenue
Suite 2400
Chicago, IL 60611
ATTN: Information Officer

• • •

Desert Appraisal Service
512 Martin Luther King Boulevard
Las Vegas, NV 89106
702-385-1414
ATTN: Ronald Rush

Starting wage: $6.00; Ending wage: $7.00.
Annually, 0-10 people apply for 0-5 positions.
Course credit is offered.
There is an initial 1,000-hour probationary period.
Applications are accepted in person any time of year.

REQUIREMENTS:

- Minimum age: 18
- High school diploma or GED certificate
- Must be physically able to perform the work of the trade
- Pass an oral interview
- Valid driver's license
- Resident of the program's jurisdiction
- Letter of recommendation from person in field
- Letter of intent from a valid employer

APPLICATION DOCUMENTS:

Applicants must bring the following documents when applying:
- High school diploma or GED certificate
- Social security card
- Driver's license

ADDITIONAL PROGRAM COMMENTS:

Course credits offered at Appraisal Institute, 225 North Michigan, Chicago, IL 60611

• • •

SECURITY OFFICER

International Union of Security Officers
2404 Merced Street
San Leandro, CA 94577
ATTN: Information Officer

• • •

Security Officer Training
University of Rochester Security, Traffic, and Safety
41 Spruce Avenue
Rochester, NY 14611
ATTN: Larry Quinn

Program title: University of Rochester Security Traffic and Safety
Starting wage: $8.29; Ending wage: $11.35.
Annually, 31-50 people apply for 0-5 positions.
Course credit is offered.
Applications are accepted in person or by mail any time of year.

REQUIREMENTS:

- High school diploma or GED certificate
- Physician's statement of fitness
- Must be physically able to perform the work of the trade
- Pass an oral interview
- Letter of recommendation from personal and professional acquaintances
- Pass a test for illegal drugs

ADDITIONAL PROGRAM COMMENTS:

All applicants must have a 2-year degree in criminal justice or equivalent experience.

• • •

SHOE REPAIRER, LEATHERWORKER

Leather Workers International Union
11 Peabody Square
PO Box 32
Peabody, MA 01960
ATTN: Information Officer

This union is affiliated with the AFL-CIO and has 15 locals.

• • •

Brotherhood of Shoe and Allied Craftsmen
PO Box 390
East Bridgewater, MA 02333
ATTN: Information Officer

This union has 16 locals.

• • •

Kingsburry Vocation Technical Center
80 West Olive Avenue
Memphis, TN 38106
901-320-6003

Starting wage: $8.00; Ending wage: $12.00.
Annually, 31-50 people apply for over 100 positions.
Course credit is offered.
Applications are accepted in person any time of year, Monday-Friday, 8:00-2:00.

REQUIREMENTS:

- Minimum age: 18
- High school diploma or GED certificate
- Physician's statement of fitness
- Must be physically able to perform the work of the trade
- Pass a written test
- Pass an oral interview

APPLICATION DOCUMENTS:

Applicants must bring the following documents when applying:
- High school transcript
- High school diploma or GED certificate
- Social security card

• • •

SOUND TECHNICIAN

Inland Sound and Communications
Apprenticeship Program
1655 East Riverview Drive
San Bernardino, CA 92408
909-796-9340
ATTN: Terry Coleman

This is a 3-year program with 640 hours of classroom instruction and 6,000 hours of on-the-job training.
Starting wage: $8.08; Ending wage: $16.25.
Annually, 31-50 people apply for 6-10 positions.
Course credit is offered.
There is an initial 12-month probationary period.
Applications are accepted in person during the last 2 weeks of March, Monday-Friday, 9:00-5:00.

REQUIREMENTS:

- Minimum age: 18
- High school diploma or GED certificate
- Pass a written test
- Pass an oral interview
- Valid driver's license
- Pass a test for illegal drugs
- Passing grade in the following high school course(s): Algebra I

APPLICATION DOCUMENTS:

Applicants must bring the following documents when applying:
- High school transcript
- High school diploma or GED certificate
- Birth certificate

ADDITIONAL PROGRAM COMMENTS:

The sound technician program covers all of Riverside, San Bernardino, Inyo, and Mono counties. Apprentices train in electronic systems such as telephone, data, CATV, alarms, electronics and sound systems. Local Unions #440 and #477 and the Southern Sierras Chapter NECA sponsor this program.

• • •

SURVEYOR

National Society of Professional Surveyors
5410 Grosvenor Lane
Bethesda, MD 20814
ATTN: Information Officer

• • •

Northern California Surveyors JAC
8105 Capwell Drive
Oakland, CA 94621
510-635-3255
ATTN: Art McArdle

This is a 5-year program with 720 hours of classroom instruction.
No salaries were reported by this program. Annually, 21-30 people apply for 11-15 positions.
There is an initial 800-hour probationary period. Applications are accepted by mail any time of year.

REQUIREMENTS:

- Minimum age: 18
- Physician's statement of fitness
- Must be physically able to perform the work of the trade
- Pass a written test
- Pass an oral interview
- Valid driver's license
- Passing grade in the following high school course(s): Mathematics to Algebra I
- Must attend a preapprenticeship class for 8 hours

APPLICATION DOCUMENTS:

Applicants must bring the following documents when applying:
- Social security card
- Driver's license
- Green card

• • •

Southern Nevada Operating Engineers JATC
PO Box 4115
North Las Vegas, NV 89036
702-649-6888
ATTN: Wayne Grimes

Program title: South Nevada Operating Engineers JATC
Specific job title(s): Surveyor
This is a 4-year program with 576 hours of classroom instruction and 8,000 hours of on-the-job training.
No salaries were reported by this program. Annually, over 100 people apply for 0-5 positions.
There is an initial 6-month probationary period. Applications are accepted in person at various times when company solicits.

REQUIREMENTS:

- Minimum age: 18
- High school diploma or GED certificate
- Pass a written test
- Pass an oral interview
- Pass a test for illegal drugs
- Passing grade in the following high school course(s): Algebra, Geometry

APPLICATION DOCUMENTS:

Applicants must bring the following documents when applying:
- High school transcript
- High school diploma or GED certificate
- Social security card
- Birth certificate

• • •

Western Washington Operating
Engineers JATC
2701 1st Avenue, Suite 120
Seattle, WA 98121
206-448-9611
ATTN: Duane Lee

Program title: Western Washington Operating Engineers JATC
Annually, a varying number of people apply for a varying number of positions.
Applications are accepted in person on the 2nd Wednesday of every month, 8:30-11:30.

REQUIREMENTS:

- Minimum age: 18
- High school diploma or GED certificate
- Must be physically able to perform the work of the trade
- Pass a written test
- Valid driver's license
- Resident of the program's jurisdiction
- Pass a test for illegal drugs
- Must attend a preapprenticeship class for 6 weeks

APPLICATION DOCUMENTS:

Applicants must bring the following documents when applying:
- High school transcript
- High school diploma or GED certificate

ADDITIONAL PROGRAM COMMENTS:

Surveyor applicants are required to take an entry-level math exam and score 80 percent or higher to be eligible. This program is affiliated with the following operating engineers locals: Local #612 (Tacoma), Local #302 (Yakima), Local #302 (East Wenatchee).

• • •

Operating Engineers Local #612
1555 Fawcett Avenue South
Tacoma, WA
206-272-6917

This program is affiliated with the Western Washington Operating Engineers JATC in Seattle, WA. Please see that entry for additional information.

• • •

Operating Engineers Local #302
2209 West Nob Hill
Yakima, WA
509-453-2567

This program is affiliated with the Western Washington Operating Engineers JATC in Seattle, WA. Please see that entry for additional information.

• • •

Operating Engineers Local #302
19 Rock Island Road
East Wenatchee, WA
509-884-2421

This program is affiliated with the Western Washington Operating Engineers JATC in Seattle, WA. Please see that entry for additional information.

• • •

TAX RETURN PREPARER

Institute for Certification of Tax Professionals
1832 Stratford Place
Pomona, CA 91768
ATTN: Information Officer

• • •

United Workers Union
2390 Central Boulevard, #L
Brownsville, TX 78520
210-541-4874
ATTN: W. Fulcher

Specific job title(s): Tax return preparer
This is a 1-year program with 45 hours of classroom instruction.

No salaries were reported by this program.
Annually, a varying number of people apply for 6-10 positions.
Course credit is offered.
Applications are accepted in person or by mail during the fall.
The application deadline is August 15th.

REQUIREMENTS:

- Minimum age: 19
- High school diploma or GED certificate

ADDITIONAL PROGRAM COMMENTS:

Applicants should already have a year or two of preparing federal income tax returns before applying.

• • •

TIN SMITH

Chrysler UAW Local #372
Apprenticeship Program
4571 Division Street
Trenton, MI 48183
313-676-9060
ATTN: Nick Pillarelli

This is a 4-year program with 750 hours of classroom instruction and 7,250 hours of on-the-job training.
Starting wage: $13.44; Ending wage: $20.95.
Annually, over 100 people apply for 6-10 positions.
Course credit is offered.
There is an initial 90-day probationary period.
Applications are accepted in person or by mail following a posted notice.

REQUIREMENTS:

- Minimum age: 18
- Physician's statement of fitness
- Must be physically able to perform the work of the trade
- Pass a written test
- Pass an oral interview
- Pass a test for illegal drugs
- Passing grade in the following high school course(s): Algebra

APPLICATION DOCUMENTS:

Applicants must bring the following documents when applying:
- High school transcript
- High school diploma or GED certificate
- Social security card
- Driver's license

ADDITIONAL PROGRAM COMMENTS:

Candidates are encouraged to take classes at community colleges to better their chances of getting an apprenticeship. The high tech machines, computers, electrical and electronic circuits of today demand more education and continuing education. The majority of our apprentices are entering the program with degrees or at least some college behind them.

• • •

Steelworkers
Route 2 Box 232
Little Hocking, OH 45742
ATTN: Milton Morris

Starting wage: $11.00; Ending wage: $13.00.
Annually, 0-10 people apply for 0-5 positions.
There is an initial 6-month probationary period.
Applications are accepted in person when a need is determined.

REQUIREMENTS:

- Minimum age: 18; Maximum age: 40
- High school diploma or GED certificate
- Must be physically able to perform the work of the trade
- Pass a written test

APPLICATION DOCUMENTS:

Applicants must bring the following documents when applying:
- High school diploma or GED certificate
- Social security card

• • •

TRUCK DRIVER

Professional Truck Driver Institute of America
8788 Elk Grove Boulevard, Suite 20
Elk Grove, CA 95624
ATTN: Information Officer

• • •

International Brotherhood of Teamsters, Chauffeurs, Warehousemen, and Helpers of America
25 Louisiana Avenue, NW
Washington, DC 20001
ATTN: Information Officer

This union has 692 locals.

• • •

Teamsters Joint Apprenticeship and Training Trust
700 Ryland Street, Suite 11
Reno, NV 89502
702-348-6060
ATTN: Lou Martino

This is a 2-year program with 288 hours of classroom instruction and 2,400 hours of on-the-job training.
No salaries were reported by this program.
Annually, 21-30 people apply for 0-5 positions.
Course credit is offered.
There is an initial 1,000-hour probationary period.
Applications are accepted in person or by mail following public notification.
The application deadline is 30 days following notice.

REQUIREMENTS:

- Minimum age: 21
- High school diploma or GED certificate
- Physician's statement of fitness
- Must be physically able to perform the work of the trade
- Pass an oral interview
- Valid driver's license
- Pass a test for illegal drugs

APPLICATION DOCUMENTS:

Applicants must bring the following documents when applying:
- High school diploma or GED certificate
- Social security card
- Driver's license
- Driving record

ADDITIONAL PROGRAM COMMENTS:

Students are encouraged to take as many math courses in high school as possible.

• • •

Eastern Oklahoma Building and Construction Trades Council
2651 East 21st Street, #405
Tulsa, OK 74114
ATTN: Clayton Walker

This is a 5-year program with 720 hours of classroom instruction and 10,000 hours of on-the-job training.
Starting wage: $6.29; Ending wage: $16.00.
Annually, 21-30 people apply for 11-15 positions.
Course credit is offered.
Applications are accepted in person during February.
The application deadline is 45 days after opening.

REQUIREMENTS:

- Minimum age: 18
- High school diploma or GED certificate
- Physician's statement of fitness
- Pass a written test
- Pass an oral interview
- Resident of the program's jurisdiction
- Letter of recommendation from minister, teachers, union members
- Passing grade in the following high school course(s): Algebra I

• • •

Additional Occupations

Teamsters Local #251
121 Brightridge Avenue
East Providence, RI 02914
401-434-0454

Applications are accepted by mail.

ADDITIONAL PROGRAM COMMENTS:

The Teamsters Union does not have a formal apprenticeship training program, but it does have a tractor trailer training program, which is limited to its members. To apply, you need to have a Class II driver's license and already be hired by a trucking company. For more information about applying to the Teamsters Union, contact the address listed.

• • •

Teamsters
PO Box 4043
Port Angeles, WA 98362
ATTN: Earl Bush

Program title: Teamster Apprenticeship Program
This is a 3-year program with 500 hours of classroom instruction and 2,400 hours of on-the-job training.
Starting wage: $14.00; Ending wage: $20.04.
Annually, 0-10 people apply for 0-5 positions.
Applications are accepted in person or by mail.

REQUIREMENTS:

- Minimum age: 21
- High school diploma or GED certificate
- Physician's statement of fitness
- Must be physically able to perform the work of the trade
- Pass an oral interview
- Valid driver's license
- Letter of recommendation from union member

APPLICATION DOCUMENTS:

Applicants must bring the following documents when applying:
- Social security card
- Driver's license

• • •

West Virginia State Building and Construction Trades Council
2301 7th Avenue
Charleston, WV 25312
304-346-1367
ATTN: E. Fisher

Specific job title(s): Truck driver
This is a 5-year program with 900 hours of classroom instruction and 10,000 hours of on-the-job training.
No salaries were reported by this program.
Write or call for application information.

REQUIREMENTS:

- Minimum age: 18
- High school diploma or GED certificate
- Must be physically able to perform the work of the trade
- Pass a written test
- Pass an oral interview
- Resident of the program's jurisdiction for 1 year
- Passing grade in the following high school course(s): Algebra I

APPLICATION DOCUMENTS:

Applicants must bring the following documents when applying:
- High school transcript
- Birth certificate

• • •

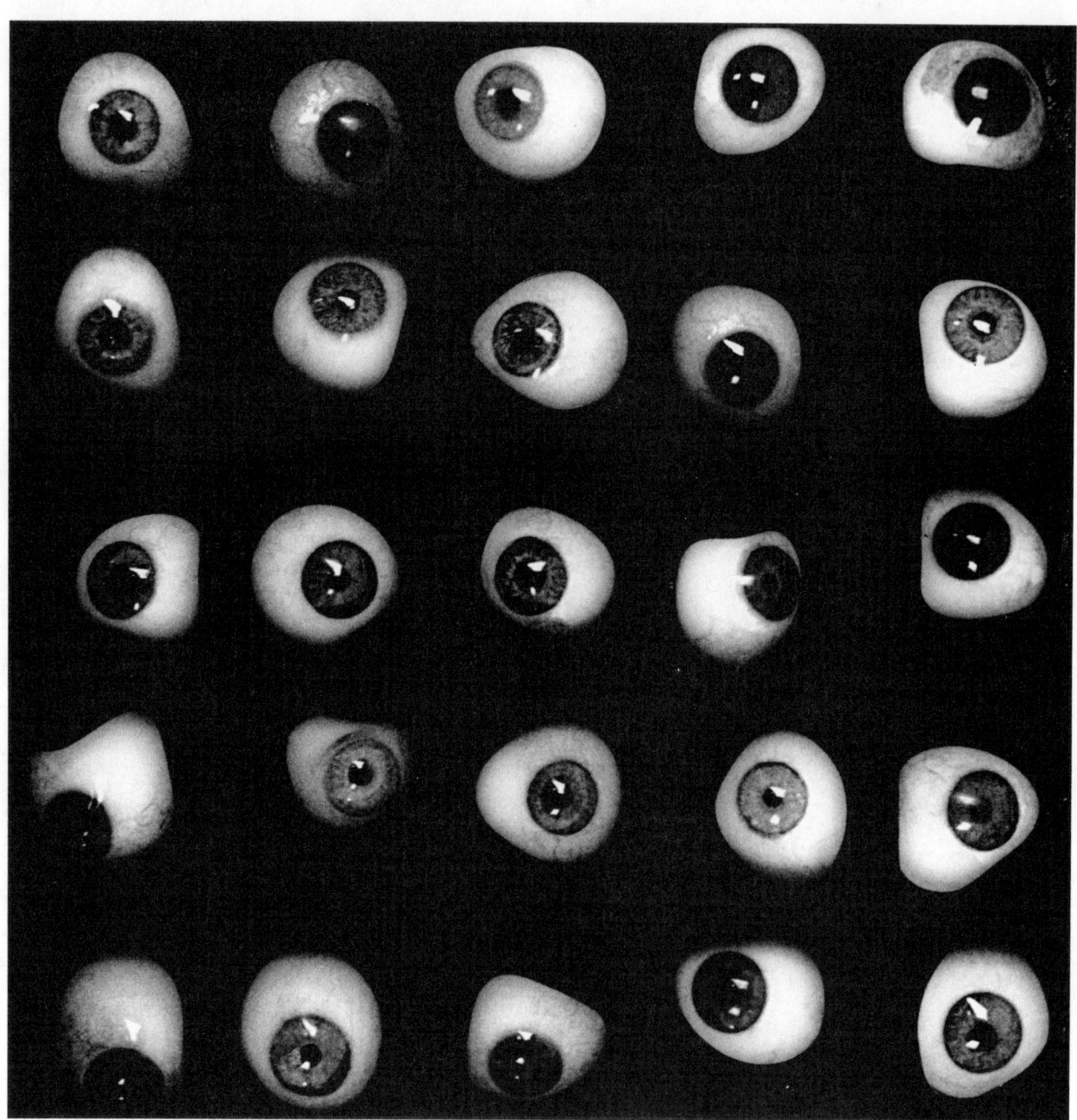

Part 3
Non-traditional Apprenticeship Programs

Apprenticeship Training at Colleges and Technical Schools

As a rule, colleges and technical schools do not sponsor apprenticeship programs. Many, however, do offer related training in cooperation with local programs, JATCs, or companies. Courses are often tailored to the specific needs of the program or company and may vary from year to year. For most programs, students must already be indentured apprentices or journeymen to participate. Some programs do not require students to be indentured and may assist them in job placement. Other programs are preapprenticeship programs; that is, they teach the basic skills that are needed to be accepted into a formal apprenticeship. The military also sponsors and trains apprentices. Check with your local recruiting office for more information.

Apprentices who take their classroom training at colleges and technical schools usually have the opportunity to earn an associate's degree in applied science by taking about a semester's worth of additional classes in general education, such as English, health, and science. Students also have the option of continuing even further to earn a bachelor's degree. Student's should know, however, that while their required apprenticeship courses are paid for by their apprenticeship program sponsor, additional courses may not be. In addition, most apprenticeship programs require apprentices who do not complete the program to reimburse the program sponsor for some or all of their classes.

For more information on apprenticeship training at colleges and technical schools, write to the organizations listed below and ask for a school catalog. Additional information might be available from your state's bureau of apprenticeship training. Addresses are found in the last section of this encyclopedia.

ARIZONA

Pima Community College
200 North Stone Avenue
Tucson, AZ 85702
ATTN: Tim Murphy
602-884-6788

THIS FACILITY OFFERS TRAINING FOR THE FOLLOWING SKILLS:

Carpenter, Ironworker, Electrician, Plumber, Pipefitter
Applicants must be indentured apprentices or journeymen to apply.

ADDITIONAL COMMENTS:

This facility works with local unions and businesses to provide currently in-demand training programs. Apprentices can earn an AAS by taking an additional 18 credit hours of general education courses.

• • •

CALIFORNIA

Associated Technical College
1670 Wilshire Boulevard
Los Angeles, CA 90017
ATTN: Richard Morano
213-353-1845

THIS FACILITY OFFERS TRAINING FOR THE FOLLOWING SKILLS:

Plumber
This is a preapprenticeship program.

• • •

ILLINOIS

Joliet Junior College
1216 Houbolt Avenue
Joliet, IL 60436
ATTN: Tim Arney
815-729-9020

THIS FACILITY OFFERS TRAINING FOR THE FOLLOWING SKILLS:

Automotives
Applicants must be indentured apprentices or journeymen to apply.

ADDITIONAL COMMENTS:

This is a 2-year program.

• • •

Triton Community College
2000 Fifth Avenue
River Grove, IL 60171
708-456-0300

THIS FACILITY OFFERS TRAINING FOR THE FOLLOWING SKILLS:

Automotives
Applicants must be indentured apprentices or journeymen to apply.

ADDITIONAL COMMENTS:

This is a 2-year program.

• • •

KANSAS

Johnson County Community College
12345 College Boulevard
Overland Park, KS 66210
ATTN: Jerry Vincent
913-469-8500

THIS FACILITY OFFERS TRAINING FOR THE FOLLOWING SKILLS:

Chef

ADDITIONAL COMMENTS:

This is a 3-year program accredited by the American Culinary Federation and the U.S. Department of Labor. Applicants must be 18 and have a high school diploma or GED. Applicants must pass a series of entry-level exams prescribed by the Apprenticeship Committee of the ACF Education Institute.

• • •

MICHIGAN

 Corporate Services
Delta College
University Center, MI 48710
ATTN: Thomas Limberg
517-686-9438

THIS FACILITY OFFERS TRAINING FOR THE FOLLOWING SKILLS:

Building trades, Industrial electrician, Jobbing molder, Machine repairer, Millwright, Pattern maker, Pipefitter (industrial maintenance), Plumber/pipefitter, Stationary boiler engineer, Tinsmith, Tool and die maker, Tool hardener
Applicants must be indentured apprentices or journeymen to apply.

• • •

MISSISSIPPI

 Mississippi Gulf Coast Community College
Box 100
Gautier, MS 39553
ATTN: Mike Killingsworth
601-497-9602

THIS FACILITY OFFERS TRAINING FOR THE FOLLOWING SKILLS:

Shipbuilding trades (shipfitter, pipefitter, sheetmetal worker, pipe welder, electrician, joiner, carpenter, painter)
Applicants must be indentured apprentices or journeymen to apply.

ADDITIONAL COMMENTS:

This facility trains apprentices exclusively for Ingall's Shipbuilding. Interested people should first apply at the Ingall's employment office. With a few additional courses, apprentices can obtain an associate's degree in applied science and occupational education.

• • •

NORTH CAROLINA

 Department of the Army
Commander, HQ XVIII Abn Corps & Ft. Bragg
Fort Bragg, NC 28307
ATTN: L. Creel
910-396-4534

THIS FACILITY OFFERS TRAINING FOR THE FOLLOWING SKILLS:

This facility offers 87 different programs for those on active duty only.

ADDITIONAL COMMENTS:

Interested applicants must take a test at a local recruiting office to determine placement in a Military Occupational Specialty (MOS). Once an applicant has a qualifying MOS, he or she can apply for a position (if there is a program available), and when spaces become available, the applicant is assigned.

Army apprenticeships range from 2,000 to 8,000 hours of work experience, parallel civilian industry standards, and are registered with the U.S. Department of Labor.

• • •

 North Carolina State University
Box 7219
Raleigh, NC 27695
ATTN: Patricia Grantham
919-515-2181

THIS FACILITY OFFERS TRAINING FOR THE FOLLOWING SKILLS:

Painter, Plumber, Locksmith, Electrician, HVAC mechanic

• • •

NEW HAMPSHIRE

New Hampshire Technical College at Laconia
Route 106
Laconia, NH 03246
ATTN: Lee Murphy
603-524-3207

THIS FACILITY OFFERS TRAINING FOR THE FOLLOWING SKILLS:

Electrician, Real estate appraiser, Insurance broker
Applicants must be indentured apprentices or journeymen to apply.

ADDITIONAL COMMENTS:

Apprentice real estate appraisers and insurance brokers are given job placement assistance.

• • •

NEW YORK

Monroe Community College
1000 East Henrietta Road
Rochester, NY 14623
ATTN: Kathie Kemp
716-325-1241

THIS FACILITY OFFERS TRAINING FOR THE FOLLOWING SKILLS:

Automotive technician
Applicants must be indentured apprentices or journeymen to apply.

• • •

Onondaga Community College
Syracuse, NY 13215
315-469-2201

THIS FACILITY OFFERS TRAINING FOR THE FOLLOWING SKILLS:

Building trades, Machine trades, Electrical trades
Applicants must be indentured apprentices or journeymen to apply.

• • •

Westchester Community College
75 Grasslands Road
Valhalla, NY 10595
ATTN: Susan Hacker
914-285-6735

THIS FACILITY OFFERS TRAINING FOR THE FOLLOWING SKILLS:

Automotive technician

• • •

OHIO

Cuyahoga Community College
700 Carnegie Avenue
Cleveland, OH 44115
ATTN: Claude Banks
216-987-4964

THIS FACILITY OFFERS TRAINING FOR THE FOLLOWING SKILLS:

Machine tools, Construction trades
Applicants must be indentured apprentices or journeymen to apply.

• • •

OREGON

Rogue Community College
3345 Redwood Highway
Grants Pass, OR 97527
ATTN: Lee Merit
503-471-3500

THIS FACILITY OFFERS TRAINING FOR THE FOLLOWING SKILLS:

Carpenter, Plumber, Sheetmetal worker, Electrician, Boiler operator, Millwright, Manufacturing plant electrician

• • •

TEXAS

 St. Philips's College
1801 Martin Luther King Drive
San Antonio, TX 78203
201-531-3319

THIS FACILITY OFFERS TRAINING FOR THE FOLLOWING SKILLS:

Chef

ADDITIONAL COMMENTS:

This is a 3-year program registered with the American Culinary Federation and the U.S. Department of Labor. There are 6,000 hours of on-the-job training, including 432 hours of classroom instruction.

• • •

UTAH

 Ogden-Weber Applied Tech Center
559 East AVC Lane
Ogden, UT 84404
ATTN: Curtis Nielsen
801-627-8300

THIS FACILITY OFFERS TRAINING FOR THE FOLLOWING SKILLS:

Electrician, Plumber, Carpenter, Bricklayer, Machinist
Applicants must be indentured apprentices or journeymen to apply.

• • •

WASHINGTON

 Shoreline Community College
16101 Greewood Avenue North
Seattle, WA 98133
ATTN: Don Schultz
206-546-4101

THIS FACILITY OFFERS TRAINING FOR THE FOLLOWING SKILLS:

Automotive technician
This facility assists students in job placement.

• • •

WISCONSIN

 Blackhawk Technical College
6004 Prairie Road, PO Box 5009
Janesville, WI 53547

THIS FACILITY OFFERS TRAINING FOR THE FOLLOWING SKILLS:

Carpenter, Electrician, Machinist, Tool and die maker, Plumber, ABC Electrician, Steamfitter, ABC Plumber, Pipefitter, Millwright

• • •

 Chippewa Valley Technical College
620 West Clairemont Avenue
Eau Claire, WI 54701
ATTN: Bill Hunt
715-833-6344

THIS FACILITY OFFERS TRAINING FOR THE FOLLOWING SKILLS:

Carpenter, Industrial electrician, Tech brick mason, Electrician, Barber/cosmetologist, Pipefitter, Steamfitter, Plumber, Sheetmetal worker, Machinist, Millwright, Painter

• • •

Fox Valley Technical College
PO Box 2277
Appleton, WI 54913
ATTN: Ronald Zenke
414-735-5777

THIS FACILITY OFFERS TRAINING FOR THE FOLLOWING SKILLS:

Carpenter, Industrial electrician, Electrician, ABC Electrician, Restaurant and cook, Tool and die maker, Welder, Operating engineer, Sheetmetal worker, Pipefitter, Steamfitter, Asbestos worker, Plumber, Machinist, Millwright

• • •

Gateway Technical College
1001 South Main Street
Racine, WI 53403
ATTN: Ralph Troeller
414-631-7404

THIS FACILITY OFFERS TRAINING FOR THE FOLLOWING SKILLS:

Carpenter, Industrial electrician, Auto mechanic, Electrician, Barber/cosmetologist, Tool and die maker, Sheetmetal worker, Pipefitter, Steamfitter, Plumber, Machinist, Machinery mechanic, Painter

• • •

Indianhead Technical College
HCR 69, PO Box 10B
Shell Lake, WI 54871
ATTN: John Graf

THIS FACILITY OFFERS TRAINING FOR THE FOLLOWING SKILLS:

Industrial electrician, Brick mason, Electrician, Utility lineman, Electrical meterman, Barber/cosmetologist, Plumber, Millwright

• • •

 Lakeshore Technical College
1290 North Avenue
Cleveland, WI 53015
ATTN: Jack Mattner
414-458-4183

THIS FACILITY OFFERS TRAINING FOR THE FOLLOWING SKILLS:

Carpenter, Industrial electrician, Printer, Brick mason, Tool and die maker, Sheetmetal worker, Plumber, Machinist, Millwright

• • •

 Madison Area Technical College
2125 Commercial Avenue
Madison, WI 53704
ATTN: Donald Lindstroth
608-757-7729

THIS FACILITY OFFERS TRAINING FOR THE FOLLOWING SKILLS:

Carpenter, Garage mechanic, Industrial electrician, HVAC ABC Mechanic, Brick mason, Electrician, ABC Electrician, Barber/cosmetologist, Ironworker, Tool and die maker, ABC Sheetmetal worker, Steamfitter, Cement and plaster finisher, Plumber, Sheemetal worker, Machinist, Millwright, Painter

• • •

 Mid-State Technical College
500 32nd Street North
Wisconsin Rapids, WI 54494
715-423-5650

THIS FACILITY OFFERS TRAINING FOR THE FOLLOWING SKILLS:

Bricklayer, Electrician, Sheetmetal worker, Carpenter, Industrial electrician, ABC Electrician, Barber/cosmetologist, Instrumentation technician, Ironworker, Welder, Pipefitter, Steamfitter, Plumber, Sheetmetal worker, Machinist, Millwright
This facility assists students in job placement.

• • •

Milwaukee Area Technical College
700 West State Street
Milwaukee, WI 53233
ATTN: Clifford Zenor
414-297-6600

THIS FACILITY OFFERS TRAINING FOR THE FOLLOWING SKILLS:

Carpenter, Cabinet maker, Truck and trailer mechanic, Industrial electrician, Brick mason, Cement mason, Electrician, ABC Electrician, Glazier, Barber/cosmetologist, Cook/chef, Tool maker, Tool and die maker, Metal fabricator, Sprinkler fitter, Pipefitter, Steamfitter, Asbestos worker, Pattern maker, Plumber, Power engineer, Sheetmetal worker, Machinist, Machine repairer, Millwright, Painter

• • •

 Moraine Park Technical College
PO Box 1940
Fond du Lac, WI 54935
ATTN: Glenn Demoske
414-929-2111

THIS FACILITY OFFERS TRAINING FOR THE FOLLOWING SKILLS:

Carpenter, ABC Carpenter, Industrial electrician, ABC Electrician, Barber/cosmetologist, Steamfitter, Plumber, ABC Plumber

• • •

 Nicolet College
PO Box 518
Rhinelander, WI 54501
ATTN: W. Dorau
715-369-4425

THIS FACILITY OFFERS TRAINING FOR THE FOLLOWING SKILLS:

Electrician, Sheetmetal worker, Pipefitter, Plumber, Millwright
This facility assists students in job placement.

• • •

 North Central Technical College
Apprenticeship Office
1000 Campus Drive
Wausau, WI 54401
715-675-3331

THIS FACILITY OFFERS TRAINING FOR THE FOLLOWING SKILLS:

Steamfitter, Bricklayer, Carpenter, Electrician, Plumber, Sheetmetal worker, Industrial electrician, Instrumentation technician, Welder, Industrial mobile equipment mechanic, Pipefitter, Machinist, Millwright
This facility assists students in job placement.

• • •

 Northeast Wisconsin Technical College
PO Box 19042
Green Bay, WI 54307
ATTN: Al Hiles
414-498-5462

THIS FACILITY OFFERS TRAINING FOR THE FOLLOWING SKILLS:

Carpenter, Floor covering installer, Industrial electrician, Brick mason, Electrician, Linesman, ABC Electrician, Electrical and instrumentation technician, Foundry worker, Cook, Instrumentation technician, Pipefitter (marine), Welder, Metal fabricator, Industrial truck mechanic, ABC Sheetmetal worker, Pipefitter, Steamfitter, Sheetmetal worker, Machinist, Millwright

• • •

 Southwest Wisconsin Technical College
Route 1, Box 500
Fennimore, WI 53809
ATTN: John Gander
608-822-3262

THIS FACILITY OFFERS TRAINING FOR THE FOLLOWING SKILLS:

Plumber

• • •

Waukesha Area Technical College
800 Main Street
Pewaukee, WI 53072
ATTN: Ron Eigenschink
414-691-5327

THIS FACILITY OFFERS TRAINING FOR THE FOLLOWING SKILLS:

Brick mason, Environmental service, Injection mold set up operator, Barber/cosmetologist, Cook/Chef, Tool and die maker, Machinist, Toolroom machinist

• • •

Western Wisconsin Technical College
PO Box 908
LaCrosse, WI 54602
ATTN: Robert Pruse
608-785-9175

THIS FACILITY OFFERS TRAINING FOR THE FOLLOWING SKILLS:

Carpenter, Industrial electrician, Brick mason, Electrician, Ironworker, Tool and die maker, Metal fabricator, Steamfitter, Plumber, Sheetmetal worker, Millwright, Machinery mechanic

• • •

Cosmetologists

Cosmetologists—often called *hairstylists, hairdressers,* or *beauticians,*—are concerned with improving the personal appearance of their customers. They cut, shampoo, straighten, curl, and color hair, for example, and give facials, manicures, and scalp treatments. Some do makeup analysis and give advice on beauty products. Cosmetologists are distinguished from *barbers,* whose range of services is generally smaller. Most cosmetologists work in beauty salons, hairstyling shops, or department stores, while others are employed in hospitals, hotels, and prisons. About three-fourths are self-employed. Although women have traditionally made up the bulk of customers, an increasing number of men prefer to have their hair cut and styled by a cosmetologist.

The three major concerns of cosmetologists are hair, skin, and nails. Cosmetologists often begin their work by talking with the customer and determining what services are wanted. They might then give the customer advice. For hair the basic services are shampooing, cutting, and styling, though cosmetologists can also straighten hair, give it a permanent wave or curl, or lighten, darken, or otherwise change hair color. Some clean and style wigs and hairpieces. For skin, cosmetologists provide facial and scalp treatments, as well as electrolysis, a method of permanently removing hair from skin. They also help women with the selection and use of makeup. Finally, cosmetologists might do the work of a *manicurist*—that is, cleaning, shaping, and polishing fingernails and toenails.

In all states cosmetologists must have a license to work. Requirements vary from state to state, though in general a person must be at least 16 years old, be a graduate from an accredited cosmetology school, and pass the state licensing examination. Some places, such as Florida, also require a high school degree (or GED), while Illinois, for example, requires only an eighth grade education. A few places, such as Oregon, have no general educational requirements at all. In some states a one- to two- year apprenticeship under an established cosmetologist can substitute for graduation from a cosmetology school. Few cosmetologists, however, learn their skills as an apprentice, and the number of apprenticeship programs across the country is decreasing.

Cosmetology programs generally last from 6 to 15 months and include both classroom instruction and practical training. Classroom subjects might include anatomy, physiology, sanitation, applied chemistry, and basic business practices. Students frequently practice on actual customers, who are drawn to such schools by their low prices on haircuts and other services.

The number of employed cosmetologists is expected to increase at an average rate. Even so, the employment outlook for licensed workers is excellent, as the number of people entering the field has not kept up with the demand for cosmetologists. Cosmetologists generally work in clean, well-lighted rooms. Evening and weekend shifts are common.

For more information on licensing and reciprocity requirements for cosmetologists, as well as information about accredited cosmetology schools, write to the organizations listed below. Additional information might be listed with your state's bureau of apprenticeship training. The bureau's address is found in the last section of this encyclopedia.

ALABAMA

Alabama Board of Cosmetology
1000-A Interstate Park Drive
Montgomery, AL 36130
205-261-5613

Cosmetologist
Education: 10th grade or equivalent
Age: 16
Training: Minimum 1,200 credit unit hours or 3,000 hours apprentice, not to exceed more than eight hours a day
Exams: twice monthly
Fees: Exam $20, Original $25, Renewal $15
License period: 9/30 odd years

Apprentice
Requirements: An apprentice must be enrolled with Board and receive permit before beginning training. Submit current health certificate including x-ray or skin test made within one year. Submit two 2"x2" photos not more than three years old (snapshots not acceptable). Submit affidavits, one signed by shop owner and manager and one signed by apprentice.
Education: Proof of 10th grade completed
Age: 16
Training: 3,000 hours, 1 year minimum duration
Fees: Original $10
Exams: twice monthly
License period: Upon completing 3,000 hours

Reciprocity
License for license with all states (exception FL licensees with less than 1,000 hours)

• • •

ALASKA

Alaska Board of Barbers and Hairdressers
Economic Development
Division of Occupational Licensing
PO Box D-Lic
Juneau, AK 99811
907-465-2547

Hairdresser
(A cosmetologist in the state of Alaska is only allowed to do facials, remove hair, and apply makeup. A hairdresser in Alaska is allowed to work with hair only. Persons wishing to do both must apply for both licenses and pay both fees.)
Training: 1,650 hours at an approved school
Fees: Student $20, Exam $25, Original $100, Renewal $100, Application fee $30
Exams: two times a year
License period: August 31

Apprentice
Training: 2,000 hours under licensed instructor
Fees: Student $20, Exam $25, Original $100, Application Fee $30
Exams: at least two times a year. Check with the board regarding further dates of examinations (generally every two months).

Reciprocity
Board of Barbers and Hairdressers. A person may be licensed in Alaska provided they have proof of 1,650 hours in school of beauty culture and a current license from another state. A person must have taken a state board practical and written examination. Board may allow 500 hours for each year of a notarized proof of experience (1,500 hours of training plus one year of current experience). Fee: $30 application fee plus initial license fee is required.

• • •

ARIZONA

Arizona Board of Cosmetology
1645 West Jefferson Street
Phoenix, AZ 85007
602-542-5301

Cosmetologist
Education: Two years high school or equivalent with 2 credits in English
Training: 1,600 hours
Fees: Original $18, Renewal $12
Exams: Continuous
License period: Birth date

Apprentice
This state does not have guidelines for apprenticeships.

Reciprocity
Granted with one year licensed work experience within the past five years immediately preceding the application and current license from the state just exited.

• • •

ARKANSAS

Arkansas State Board of Cosmetology
1515 West 7th Street, Room 400
Little Rock, AR 72201-3988
501-682-2168

Cosmetologist
Education: 10th grade or equivalent
Age: 16 years
Training: 1,500 hours
Fees: Original and Exam $30
Exams: February, April, June, August, October, December
License period: December 31

Apprentice
This state does not have guidelines for apprenticeships.

Reciprocity
License granted without examination to applicant who holds a current license in another state. Fee: $50

• • •

CALIFORNIA

California Board of Barbering and Cosmetology
PO Box 944226
Sacramento, CA 94244
916-445-7061

Cosmetologist
Education: 10th grade
Age: 17 years
Training: 1,600 hours of schooling or two years as jr. operator or four years out-of-state experience
Fees: Original and Exam $32
Exams: State examination facilities, one in LA and one in Fairfield, operate on a daily, full-time basis year-round.
License periods: two years from date of issuance

Apprentice
Requirements: The apprenticeship program lasts for twenty-four months and consists of on-the-job training in all phases of cosmetology There are weekly classes in theoretical instruction and state board preparation. At the end of program you apply to take state board exam.

Reciprocity
Out-of-state applicants must pass examination in order to obtain license in California. Credit given for every hour of training; 100 hours of credit given for each 3 months of licensed experience outside of California. Exam fee: $32

• • •

COLORADO

Colorado State Board of Barbers and Cosmetologists
1560 Broadway, Suite 1340
Denver, CO 80202
303-894-7772

Cosmetologist
Education: none
Age: 16 years
Training: 1450 hours
Fees: Exam $34, Original $19
Exams: weekly
License period: April 30

Apprentice
This state does not have guidelines for apprenticeships.

Reciprocity
Granted to licensees with hours of training equal to or higher than Colorado's requirements, who have taken a substantially equivalent examination and whose license is in good standing. Work experience can be substituted for a portion of training hours. Fee: $50.

• • •

CONNECTICUT

Connecticut Board for Barbers, Hairdressers & Cosmeticians
Department of Health Services
150 Washington Street
Hartford, CT 06106
203-566-4068

Cosmetologist
Education: 9th grade
Training: 1,500 hours
Fees: Exam $50, Original $50
Exams: Every other month

Apprentice
No apprenticeship information was available for this state.

Reciprocity
Without examination to any individual licensed in another state whose licensure requirements are commensurate to Connecticut's requirements. Fee: $25

• • •

DELAWARE

Delaware Board of Cosmetology and Barbering
Margaret O'Neil Building
PO Box 1401
Dover, DE 19903
302-739-4522

Cosmetologist
Education: 1,500 hours
Age: 8th grade
Fees: $50
Exams: No set determined days or times
License period: December 31

Apprentice
Requirements: To receive cosmetology license you must serve as an apprentice for 3,000 hours, then apply to take state board exam.

Reciprocity
All applicants otherwise qualified according to law and holding a valid license from any state, territory or District of Columbia may be granted a Delaware operator's license without being required to take the examination, but under no circumstances is the Board required to waive the requirement of examination.

• • •

FLORIDA

Florida Department of Professional Regulation
1940 North Monroe Street
Tallahassee, FL 32399-0790
904-488-5702

Cosmetologist
Education: none
Age: 16 years or high school diploma or GED
Training: 1,200 hours in no less than 7 months (1,000 hours with school permission)
Fees: $50
Exams: at least 12 times per year
License period: October 31 biennially (even numbered years)

Apprentice
No apprenticeship information was available for this state.

Reciprocity
Endorsement: Must hold current license from another state, take both the written and practical exam, and complete at least 1,000 hours of schooling. Fee: $50

• • •

GEORGIA

Georgia State Board of Cosmetology
166 Pryor Street SW
Atlanta, GA 30303
404-656-3909

Cosmetologist
Education: 9th grade
Age: 16 years
Training: none
Fees: $45

Exams: monthly
License period: biannually

Apprentice
Education: none required
Age: 16 years
Training: none
Fees: $45
Exams: monthly
License period: biannually

Reciprocity
Reciprocity without examination. Applicant must file application, submit fee, have current cosmetology license in force from another state, and letter of certification before issuance of certificate of registration entitling him or her to practice occupation of cosmetology at appropriate level. Reciprocity fee: $50.

• • •

HAWAII

Hawaii Board of Cosmetology
Professional and Vocational Licensing Division
Department. of Commerce and Consumer Affairs
PO Box 3469
Honolulu, HI 96801
808-586-2699

Cosmetologist
Education: high school diploma or GED
Age: 16 years
Training: 1,800 hours or 3,600 hours of apprenticeship
Fees: Application $10, Exam $60, Original $15.
Exams: January, May, and October
License period: December 31 every odd year

Apprentice
Education: high school diploma or GED
Age: 16 years
Training: 3,600 hours
Fees: Application $5, Original $10
License period: up to 42 months

Reciprocity
Out-of-State License: In jurisdictions with beauty training of equivalent or more hours, applicant qualifies for examination. If beauty training hours are less, then applicant shall make up difference in a school or beauty salon (requires a sanitation clearance and a licensed beauty operator) or have at least one year experience under that license.

• • •

IDAHO

Idaho State Board of Cosmetology
1109 Main Street, Suite 220
Boise, ID 83702
208-334-3233

Cosmetologist
Education: 10th grade
Age: 16 fi years
Training: 2,000 hours
Fees: Exam $35, Original $20.
Exams: 4th Monday in February, June, and October
License period: December 31

Apprentice
Education: 10th grade
Age: 16 fi years
Training: 4,000 hours
Fees: Exam $35, Original $20
Exams: 4th Monday in February, June, and October

Reciprocity
Granted to applicants having requirements equal to those of Idaho. Other states required to have three years of experience in salon within the last five years.

• • •

ILLINOIS

Illinois Department of Professional Regulation
PSS, 320 West Washington Street
3rd Floor
Springfield, IL 62786
217-785-0800

Cosmetologist
Education: 8th grade or equivalent
Age: 16 years
Training: 1,500 hours in not less than 9 months or more than 3 years
Fees: Exam $73.63, Original $25.00
Exams: Monthly alternating between Springfield and Chicago
License period: September 30, odd years

Apprentice
No apprenticeship information was available for this state.

Reciprocity
Endorsement granted to applicants on individual basis. Oral interview, if deemed necessary. Must hold current license in home state. Fee: $35

• • •

INDIANA

Indiana State Board of Cosmetology Examiners
Indiana Professional Licensing Agency
100 North Senate Avenue, Room 1021
Indianapolis, IN 46204
317-232-2980

Cosmetologist
Education: 10th grade or GED
Age: 18 years
Training: 1,500 Hours
Fees: Exam $20, Original $40
Exams: Monthly
License period: August 1 (every 4 years)

Apprentice
No apprenticeship information was available for this state.

Reciprocity
With any jurisdiction having substantially equal requirements; must have been administered written and practical examinations with an average passing score of at least 75 percent. Must have necessary paperwork completed by applicable state board. Fee: $100

• • •

IOWA

Iowa Cosmetology Board of Examiners
Arts and Sciences
Lucas State Office Building
Des Moines, IA 5019
515-281-4422

Cosmetologist
Education: High school diploma or GED
Age: No set age
Training: 2,100 hours; 8 hours continuing education required for renewal. Must be taken in biennium preceding renewal.
Fees: Exam and Original $55
Exams: February, May, August, and November
License period: Biennial

Apprentice
No apprenticeship information was available for this state.

Reciprocity
Granted to applicants from states having signed agreement with Iowa; no exam required. Applicants from other states showing proof of licensure for 12 months out of preceding 24-month period eligible for practical and theory examinations. Applicants not meeting preceding requirements must make application, and application will be reviewed to determine if additional hours are required in an Iowa school before taking the theory and practical examinations. Application fee: $50

• • •

KANSAS

Kansas State Board of Cosmetology
603 SW Topeka Boulevard, Suite 100
Topeka, KS 66603
913-296-3155

Cosmetologist
Education: High school diploma or GED if under 25 years
Age: 17 years
Training: 1,500 hours (9 months)
Fees: Exam $15

Exams: 6 times a year
License period: Birth month odd/even year

Apprentice
This state no longer has apprenticeships in cosmetology.

Reciprocity
Granted to all applicants with 1,500 hours, required to take practical exam. Temporary permit issued pending examination. Fee: $35

• • •

KENTUCKY

Kentucky State Board of Hairdressers and Cosmetologists
314 West Second Street
Frankfort, KY 40601
502-564-4262

Cosmetologist
Education: 10th grade or equivalent
Age: 16 years
Training: 1,800 hours in licensed school and pass exams
Fees: Exam $35, Original $15
Exams: September through June
License period: June 30

Apprentice
Requirements: Interested persons must write to the above address for information.
Education: 10th grade or equivalent
Age: 16 years
Training: 6 months apprenticeship after completing school and passing exams
Fees: Exam $25, Original $12
Exams: September through June
License period: June 30

Reciprocity
Applicant must be a graduate of a licensed school of cosmetology by a state which provides a prerequisite of graduation and a prescribed course of instruction of not less than 1,800 hours, and has reciprocity with Kentucky. Applicants for reciprocity from any state will not be accepted on first or apprenticeship license. Reciprocity fee: $50. Any applicant from out of state who holds a valid license and who can show proof of 2 years' current experience can come before the state board of examination (practical only) by paying a fee of $75 plus $15 for a license after passing the examination.

• • •

LOUISIANA

Louisiana State Board of Cosmetology
11622 Sunbelt Court
Baton Rouge, LA 70809
504-295-8476

Cosmetologist
Education: 10th grade
Age: 16 years
Training: 9 months, 1,500 hours
Fees: Theory $20, Practical $15, Original $15
Exams: Twice monthly
License period: March 1

Apprentice
No apprenticeship information was available for this state.

Reciprocity
Granted to anyone holding a current license with qualifications equal to those of Louisiana.
Reciprocity fees: $40

• • •

MAINE

Maine State Board of Cosmetology
122 Northern Avenue
Gardiner, ME 04345
207-582-8745

Cosmetologist
Training: 1,500 hours or 9 months' duration or apprenticeship within 3 years from date of applying to be examined
Fees: Exam $45, Original $25
Exams: Monthly
License period: 1st license June 30; renew June 30 biennially

Apprentice

Requirements: A minimum of 300 hours of instruction in theory and practice is required before an apprentice cosmetologist may practice services on patrons. You must have proof of completing at least the tenth grade, proof of being at least 17 years of age, and proof of completing 2,500 hours as an apprentice cosmetologist in not less than 18 months.
Education: 10th grade
Age: 17 years
Training: 2,500 hours of 18 months duration within 3 years from date of applying to be examined
Fees: Exam $45, Original $10
Exams: Monthly
License period: 18 months from date of issuance

Reciprocity

Full reciprocity is permitted with Arkansas, Louisiana, Massachusetts, Minnesota, Mississippi, South Carolina, Tennessee, Vermont, Texas, and Virginia. Fee $25 plus $50 application fee (biennially). Partial reciprocity: the score obtained in the written National Cosmetology Test will be honored, regardless of what participating state the exam was given in. Maine required 70 percent to pass. Candidate is subject to practical and state law exam.

• • •

MARYLAND

 Maryland State Board of Cosmetologists
501 Street Paul Place, Room 202
Baltimore, MD 21202
410-333-6320

Cosmetologist

Education: 9th grade
Age: 17 years
Training: 1,500 hours (9 months)
Fees: Exam $41, Original $50
Exams: Examinations conducted on a regular basis by vendor (call 800-359-1313)
License period: October 31, odd years

Apprentice

Requirements: Full Service Beauty Culture Apprentice/Operator: All full service beauty culture apprentices shall engage in full-time employment (minimum 30 hours per week) for a period of 24 months to be eligible to take the State Board of Examination. Each apprentice applicant shall be permitted 2 renewals of an apprentice license only.
Education: 9th grade
Age: 17 years

Reciprocity

Granted to applicants from states with requirements which are substantially equal to those of Maryland. Reciprocity fee: $50

• • •

MASSACHUSETTS

 Massachusetts Board of Registration of Cosmetologists
Leverett Saltonstall Building
Room 1520, 100 Cambridge Street
Boston, MA 02202
617-727-9940-41-42

Cosmetologist

Education: 8th grade
Age: 16 years
Training: 1,000 hours and pass exam
Fees: Exam $60, Original $60
Exams: Monthly
License period: Birth date biennially

Apprentice

Requirements: Call Board for information.
Training: 1,000 hours in licensed school and pass exam.

Reciprocity

Alabama, Arizona, Georgia, Idaho, Illinois, Louisiana, Maine, Minnesota, Mississippi, Missouri, Montana, Nevada, New Hampshire, New Mexico, North Carolina, North Dakota, Oklahoma, Pennsylvania, Puerto Rico, South Carolina, South Dakota, Utah, Virginia, New Jersey, Wisconsin, Delaware, Tennessee, Virgin Islands, Colorado, New York, and Florida (hairdressers only). Fee: $100. Massachusetts is also licensing by endorsement. Any applicant who has a license in another state will have his or her license honored by Massachusetts.

• • •

MICHIGAN

Michigan State Board of Cosmetology
611 West Ottawa, North Tower
PO Box 30018
Lansing, MI 48909
517-373-0580

Cosmetologist
Education: 9th grade
Age: 17 years
Training: 1,500 hours
Fees: Exam $42, Original $12
Exams: Contracted to private vendor
License period: August 31 biennially

Apprentice
Requirements: You must receive an apprenticeship training permit, issued by the Department, before training of the apprentice may begin. The cosmetologist program lasts 2 years. The apprentice is required to work at least an average of 20 hours per week, totaling at least 2,080 hours over the entire term of program.
Fees: Exam $42, Original $12
Exams: Contracted to private vendor

Reciprocity
Reciprocity arranged with states whose requirements are substantially equal. Reciprocity credit given for experience at ratio of 100 hours credit for each 6 months of experience.
Reciprocity fee: $35

• • •

MINNESOTA

Minnesota Department of Commerce
Cosmetology Unit
133 East 7th Street
St. Paul, MN 55101
612-297-7050

Cosmetologist
Education: 12th grade or GED
Training: 1,550 hours
Fees: Pre-registered $38, Walk-in $55
Exams: Educational Testing Service administers exams. All scheduling is performed by them.
License period: December 31 every third year

Apprentice
Exams: Educational Testing Service administers exams. All scheduling is performed by them.
License period: December 31 every third year.

Reciprocity
May be granted to currently licensed applicants from other states who successfully pass the Minnesota state exam and show proof of 1,800 hours of licensed experience within the last 3 years. Fee: $45

• • •

MISSISSIPPI

Mississippi State Board of Cosmetology
1804 North State Street
PO Box 55689
Jackson, MS 39296-5689
601-354-6623

Cosmetologist
Education: 10th grade
Age: 17 years
Training: 1,500 hours
Fees: Exam $25, Original $15
Exams: 3-4 times per month
License period: 1 year from date of issuance

Apprentice
No apprenticeship information was available for this state.

Reciprocity
Reciprocity granted to applicants from other states, provided that state grants Mississippi licensees same privilege. Must have current license. Reciprocity fee: $45 plus $15 state license fee. Total: $60

• • •

MISSOURI

Missouri State Board of Cosmetology
3605 Missouri Boulevard
PO Box 1062
Jefferson City, MO 65102
314-751-1052

Cosmetologist
Education: 10th grade
Age: 17 years of age prior to taking the exam
Training: Private: 1,500 hours, Public: 1,220
Fees: Exam $20
Exams: 6 times yearly
License period: September 30, odd years

Apprentice
Requirements: Program lasts for 18 months (approximately 3,000 hours). Applicants need an apprentice license to participate in apprenticeship training, after which they must apply to take state board cosmetology exam.
Education: 10th grade
Age: 17 years of age prior to taking exam
Training: 3,000 hours
Fees: $20
Exams: 6 times yearly

Reciprocity
Extended to applicants currently licensed in a state with requirements substantially equal or superior to Missouri, upon making application.

• • •

MONTANA

Montana Board of Cosmetologists
111 North Jackson
Helena, MT 58620
406-444-4288

Cosmetologist
Education: 10th grade
Age: 18 years
Training: 2,000 hours
Fees: Exam $20, Original $10
Exams: Every 6-8 weeks
License period: December 31

Apprentice
No apprenticeship information was available for this state.

Reciprocity
Any person who is licensed to practice cosmetology in another state upon meeting requirements may, at the discretion of the State Board, be licensed to practice in Montana without examination, provided that state in which such person is licensed grants the same privilege to persons licensed in Montana who seek a license in that state.

• • •

NEBRASKA

Nebraska State Board of Cosmetology Examiners State Department of Health
Bureau of Examining Boards
301 Centennial Mall South
PO Box 95007
Lincoln, NE 68509
402-471-2115

Cosmetologist
Education: 12th grade or equivalent
Age: 17 years
Training: 2,100 hours; 16 hours continuing education required prior to license expiration
Fees: Exam $41
Exams: At least 4 per year. All dates determined by board.
License period: Even years December 31

Apprentice
Education: none
Training: 2,100 hours
Exams: none

Reciprocity
Granted without examination to applicant holding a current license and from whom the requirements for registration were substantially equal to those of Nebraska, or upon due proof that applicant has practiced the occupation for which application for license is made within the last 5 years prior to making such application. Applicants from states with fewer than 2,100 hours are given credit for training and experience within the last 5 years (each month of full-time practice equals 100 hours of training). Fee: $41

• • •

NEVADA

Nevada State Board of Cosmetology
1785 East Sahara Avenue, Suite 255
Las Vegas, NV 89104
702-486-6541

Cosmetologist
Education: 10th grade or equivalent
Age: 18 years
Training: 1,800 hours for at least 10 months
Fees: Exam $55
Exams: Practical, monthly in alternate cities, Written, weekly in alternate cities (Reno and Las Vegas)
License period: June 30, odd years

Apprentice
This state no longer has a cosmetology apprenticeship program.

Reciprocity
Granted to applicants holding a current out-of-state license, written verification of successful passage of the National Written Exam in the form of a certification letter, and one year prior work experience within the past three years. If applicants do not meet all three requirements, they can be subject to a written exam, practical exam, or both. Fee: $100. No permits or temporary license issued.

• • •

NEW HAMPSHIRE

New Hampshire Board of Cosmetology
Health & Human Services Building
Hazen Drive
Concord, NH 03301
603-271-3608

Cosmetologist
Education: High school diploma or GED prior to taking State Board test
Age: 16 years (assume candidate is of graduating age)
Training: 1,500 hours in no less than 9 months
Fees: Exam $45, Original $25
Exams: As often as needed
License period: Renewed on birth month every 2 years

Apprentice
Education: High school diploma or GED prior to taking State Board test
Age: 16 years (assume candidate is of graduating age)
Training: 3,000 hours in not less than 24 months
Fees: Exam $45, Original $25
Exams: As often as needed
License period: June 30, odd years

Reciprocity
Granted to applicants from states with requirements which are substantially equal to those of New Hampshire. Must have current license.

• • •

NEW JERSEY

New Jersey State Board of Cosmetology and Hairstyling
PO Box 45003
Newark, NJ 07101
201-504-6400

Cosmetologist
Education: High school diploma or equivalent
Age: 17 years
Training: 1,200 hours
Fees: Exam $30, Original $15
License period: September 20

Apprentice
No apprenticeship information was available for this state.

Reciprocity
Endorsement available to out-of-state applicant who holds a license to practice barbering and a license to practice beauty culture.

• • •

NEW MEXICO

New Mexico State Board of Cosmetologists
Regulation and Licensing Department.
Plaza San Miguel
725 St. Michael's Drive
PO Box 25101
Santa Fe, NM 87504
505-827-7176

Cosmetologist
Education: 2 years high school or equivalent
Age: 16 years
Training: 1,600 hours
Fees: Exam $25, Original $20
Exams: At least 9 exams annually
License period: Birth month annually

Apprentice
No apprenticeship information was available for this state.

Reciprocity
Granted without exam if hours meet equivalency of 1,600 hours (150 hours credit for every six months of work experience within past five years). Applicants with no work experience must obtain additional hours (if hours are less than 1,500 applicant will be required to take state board examination). All applicants must be currently licensed, at least 17 years of age with two years of high school or equivalent. Fee: $100. No permits or temporary licenses.

• • •

NEW YORK

New York Department of State
Division of Licensing Services
270 Broadway
New York, NY 10007
212-587-5747

Cosmetologist
Education: Elementary
Age: 17 years
Training: 1,000 hours or 3 years' experience out-of-state
Fees: Exam $15, Original $20
Exams: 10 practical, 18 theory; dates not specified.
License period: 2 years after effective date

Apprentice
No apprenticeship information was available for this state.

Reciprocity
(Number in parentheses indicates years of experience required.) Reciprocity with states with qualifications substantially equal. Fee: $20
Reciprocity established with Alaska, Arkansas (2), Arizona (1), Colorado (5), Georgia (2), Idaho (3), Louisiana, Maine, Massachusetts (2), Minnesota (2), Mississippi, Missouri (5), Montana (4), Nevada, North Carolina, North Dakota (1), Oklahoma, Pennsylvania (2), South Carolina, South Dakota, Tennessee (2), Vermont (2), Virginia, Washington, D.C. (5), Florida, current if license by Florida examination.

• • •

NORTH CAROLINA

North Carolina Board of Cosmetology
1110 Navaho Drive
Raleigh, NC 27609
919-850-2793

Cosmetologist
Education: none
Training: 1,500 hours or 1,200 hours in approved school of beauty culture
Fees: Exam $10, Original $33
Exams: Each month
License period: September 30

Apprentice
Requirements: Must go to beauty school for 1,200 hours, take exam for apprentice license, then work under licensed cosmetologist for 6 months (have signed affidavit on work for 6 months) receive cosmetology license (not required to take exam again).
Fees: Exam $5, Original $5
Exams: Each month
License period: September 30

Reciprocity
An applicant for a North Carolina license may qualify if the following criteria are met: (1) Applicant holds a current license. (2) Applicant is currently practicing cosmetology. (3) He or she has had one year's experience within the last three years. (4) There is no disciplinary action pending. (5) The state in which the current license was issued must require a minimum of 1,200 hours in approved beauty school. Reciprocity with any other state that reciprocates with North Carolina; applicant must be currently licensed. Registration fee: $15, License fee: $33 for 3-year period, $5 for apprentices.

• • •

Cosmetologists

NORTH DAKOTA

North Dakota State Board of Cosmetology
PO Box 2177
Bismarck, ND 58502
701-224-9800

Cosmetologist
Education: 12th grade
Age: 17 years
Training: 1,800 hours
Fees: $45, Exam $20, Original $10
Exams: At least 9 times a year
License period: December 31

Apprentice
No apprenticeship information was available for this state.

Reciprocity
The applicant has complied with the requirements for registration of the District of Columbia or state, territory, foreign country, or province where the requirements are equal substantially to those in force in this state at the time the application is filed. Also granted to applicants from states with which reciprocity has been arranged. Fee shall not exceed $100. Applicants from states with less than 1,800 hours and who have not practiced for 3 years are given credit for training and experience, but they must make up the deficiency prior to taking the exam. North Dakota Law Test is always required.

• • •

OHIO

Ohio State Board of Cosmetology
8 East Long Street, Suite 1000
Columbus, OH 43214
614-466-3834

Cosmetologist
Education: 8th grade
Age: 16 years
Training: 1,500 hours
Fees: Permit $5, Exam $21, Original $20
Exams: Daily
License period: Licenses listed above are 2-year licenses with expiration of January 30 of each odd numbered year.

Apprentice
No apprenticeship information was available for this state.

Reciprocity
Reciprocity without examination granted to currently licensed applicants from states with requirements substantially equal to those of Ohio. Applicant must be 18 years of age, have the equivalent of an Ohio public school 8th grade education, and hold a current cosmetology license. Certification of cosmetology education must be supplied by state of original licensing. Ohio law does not provide for acceptance of hours earned through apprenticeship. No reciprocity for applicants with less than 1,200 hours without additional schooling. No temporary permits issued to reciprocity applicants.
Reciprocity fee: $50

• • •

OKLAHOMA

Oklahoma State Board of Cosmetology
2200 Classen Boulevard, Suite 1530
Oklahoma City, OK 73106
405-521-2441

Cosmetologist
Education: 8th grade or equivalent
Age: 16 years
Training: 1,500 hours
Fees: Exam $15, Original $15
Exams: 2nd Monday and Tuesday of January, March, May, July, September, and November
License period: Last day of birth month annually

Apprentice
Requirements: To receive information rule book for apprenticeships, send $5 cashier check to state board requesting book.
Education: 8th grade or equivalent
Age: 16 years
Training: 3,000 hours
Fees: Exam $15, Original $15
Exams: 2nd Monday and Tuesday of January, March, May, July, September, and November

License period: Last day of birth month annually

Reciprocity
License for comparable license granted to those holding a current license in any state, country, or territory with requirements substantially equal to Oklahoma license requirements or proof of 5 years of experience (recent) where there is no license law. In any circumstance an examination may be required at the Board's discretion. Fee: $63. No temporary permit. Reciprocity license must be obtained before starting work in Oklahoma. Out-of-state hours are accepted for transfer. Fee: $30

• • •

OREGON

Oregon Board of Barbers and Hairdressers
750 Front Street NE, Suite 200
Salem, OR 97310
503-378-8667

Cosmetologist
Education: none
Age: none
Training: 1,800 hours
Fees: Exam $15, Original $20
Exams: Monthly (by area)
License period: Initial practitioner's license: One year from date of issue, then every 2 years, always on the last day of the month

Apprentice
No apprenticeship information was available for this state.

Reciprocity
All applicants must take a written examination; an active license in another state qualifies applicant for examination or education, and experience must be evaluated by state Department of Education.

• • •

PENNSYLVANIA

Pennsylvania State Board of Cosmetology
PO Box 2649
Harrisburg, PA 17105
717-783-7130

Cosmetologist
Education: 10th grade
Age: 16 years
Training: 1,250 hours
Fees: Practical exam $24, Theory exam $23.50, Complete exam $47.50, Original $5
Exams: Theory examination: third Tuesday of January, April, July, and October. Practical examination: third and fourth weeks of same months
License period: January 31 biennially

Apprentice
Requirements: To qualify for apprenticeship training in a cosmetology shop, an individual shall apply to the Board for an apprentice permit. An apprentice shall work a minimum of 25 hours per week to acquire the minimum 2,000 hours of apprenticeship training.

Reciprocity
With states that recognize Pennsylvania license. Cosmetologist must show proof of two or more years of experience as licensed operator. Certification from state of licensure indicating applicant is currently licensed.

• • •

RHODE ISLAND

Rhode Island State Board of Hairdressing
3 Capitol Hill
Providence, RI 02908
401-277-2511

Cosmetologist
Education: Applicant must be a high school graduate or equivalent of all classes of licensure.
Age: 18 years
Training: 1,500 hours
Fees: $15 application fee for all classes
Exams: Written: NIC required quarterly, Practical: on or about five weeks after written

License period: June 30 of the odd or even year based on last digit of license number

Apprentice
Education: Applicant must be a high school graduate or equivalent
Fees: $15 application fee for all classes
Exams: Written: NIC required quarterly, Practical: on or about five weeks after written
License period: June 30 of the odd or even year based on last digit of license number

Reciprocity
Applications accepted for licensure by endorsement of national NIC exam and practical exam if verified by local state board of examiners. Passing grade 70 percent. Fee: $25. Credit may be given on the basis of 100 hours for each year of verified work experience up to 500 hours, for persons lacking the required 1,500 hours.

• • •

SOUTH CAROLINA

South Carolina State Board of Cosmetology
3710 Landmark Drive, Suite 205
Columbia, SC 29204
803-734-9660

Cosmetologist
Education: completion of 10th grade or equivalent
Training: 1,500 hours; 6 contact hours continuing education annually
Fees: Exam $45, original included
Exams: Monthly
License period: March 10 annually

Apprentice
No apprenticeship information was available for this state.

Reciprocity
Granted to applicants from states whose requirements are substantially equal and who grant the same privileges to South Carolina licensees, and/or the national examination.

• • •

SOUTH DAKOTA

South Dakota Cosmetology Commission
111 East Capital Avenue
PO Box 127
Pierre, SD 57501
606-224-5072

Cosmetologist
Education: High school diploma or equivalent
Age: 18 years
Training: 2,100 hours
Fees: Exam $20
Exams: At least 6 exams per year at discretion of board
License period: January 31

Apprentice
Education: High school diploma or equivalent
Age: 17 years
Training: 18 months
Fees: $25 (not renewable)
License period: Issued for 18 months (not renewable)

Reciprocity
South Dakota reciprocates with all states that have the same qualifications for licensure and if the foreign state will reciprocate. The applicant is required to present an out-of-state license. If the license is from a state not requiring at least 2,100 hours of school training, actual experience will be accepted in lieu of the difference in hours on the basis of 1 year of experience equal to 1,000 hours of school training. Reciprocity fee: $50. A test on state laws and board rules and regulations must be passed. A permit license may be issued to an out-of-state cosmetician until clearances have been completed.

• • •

TENNESSEE

Tennessee State Board of Cosmetology
First Floor, 500 James Robertson Parkway
Nashville, TN 37243-1147
615-741-2515

Cosmetologist
Education: 10th grade or equivalent
Age: 16 years
Training: 1,500 hours
Fees: Exam and Original $10
Exams: Weekly
License period: September 1 biannually

Apprentice
No apprenticeship information was available for this state.

Reciprocity
(without examination) Fee: $50. The board may, at its discretion, grant a license to any applicant who holds a license in any state, country or territory and has substantially met the qualifications for licensure in Tennessee, or furnishes satisfactory proof of continuous, lawful engagement in the occupation or practice for which a license is applied for a period of at least 5 years immediately preceding the date of application.

• • •

TEXAS

Texas Cosmetology Commission
PO Box 26700
Austin, TX 78755
512-454-4674

Cosmetologist
Education: 7th grade or equivalent
Age: 16 years
Training: 1,500 hours or 1,000 hours and 500 hours academic high school courses
Fees: Exam and Original $35
Exams: Starts 1st working day of each month until all examined
License period: Staggered by birth date

Apprentice
No apprenticeship information was available for this state.

Reciprocity
Without examination granted to states with substantially the same requirements as Texas licensees.

• • •

UTAH

Utah State Board of Cosmetology
Division of Occupational and Professional Licensing
160 East 300 South
PO Box 45802
Salt Lake City, UT 84145
801-530-6628

Cosmetologist
Training: 12 months
Fees: Exam $40, Original $40
Exams: Weekly
License period: August 31 odd year

Apprentice
Training: 15 months
Fees: Exam $40, Original $40
Exams: Weekly
License period: 15 months from issue

Reciprocity
No examination required of applicants from other states who have at least 2,000 hours and three years of experience and are currently licensed.

• • •

VERMONT

Vermont State Board of Cosmetology
Secretary of State's Office
Office of Professional Regulation
109 State Street
Montpelier, VT 05609
802-828-2373

Cosmetologist
Education: High school graduate or equivalent
Age: 17 years
Training: 1,500 hours of not less than 9 months
Fees: Exam $40, Original $20
Exams: Administered at least 6 times per year
License period: November 30 biennially

Apprentice
No apprenticeship information was available for this state.

Cosmetologists

Reciprocity
Granted to applicants from states whose requirements are substantially equal. Reciprocity may be granted to those with less than 1,500 hours of training but not less than 1,000 hours, upon proof of one year of experience gained immediately prior to application, provided all other conditions are satisfied. All applicants must pass a test pertaining to Vermont cosmetology laws.

• • •

VIRGINIA

Virginia Board for Cosmetology
3600 West Broad Street
Richmond, VA 23230
804-367-8509

Cosmetologist
Training: Competency-based program or minimum of 1,500 hours
Fees: $60 (includes original)
Exams: 12 times yearly
License period: Staggered

Apprentice
Training: 18 months or 3,000 hours
Fees: No license required with apprenticeship council

Reciprocity
License/Certification by Endorsement: Upon properly applying to the board, any person currently licensed to practice as a cosmetologist or hairdresser in any other state or jurisdiction of the United States may be issued a certificate of registration authorizing practice as a cosmetologist in this state, without an examination.

• • •

WASHINGTON

Washington State Cosmetology, Barber, Manicurist Unit
Division of Professional Licensing
PO Box 9026
Olympia, WA 98507
206-586-6359

Cosmetologist
Age: 17 years
Training: 1,600 hours
Exams: 12 annually
Fees: Exam $25
License period: Birth anniversary

Apprentice
No apprenticeship information was available for this state.

Reciprocity
Licensing may be granted with or without examination as determined by the Director, provided qualifications, training, and experience are substantially equal to the requirements regulating cosmetology in this state. Fee: $25

• • •

WASHINGTON, DC

District of Columbia Board of Cosmetology
Department of Consumer and Regulatory Affairs
Occupational and Professional Licensing Administration
614 H Street NW, Room 923
Washington, DC 20001
202-727-7454

Cosmetologist
Education: 8th grade or equivalent
Age: 16 years
Training: 1,500 hours (8 months)
Fees: $20
Exams: January, April, July, and October
License period: April 15 biennially

Apprentice
Education: 8th grade or equivalent
Age: 16 years
Training: 1,500 hours (8 months)
Exams: January, April, July, and October

Reciprocity
Granted to those whose state requirements for registration are substantially equal to those in force in the District of Columbia, or upon due proof that such applicants have continuously engaged in the practices or occupation for which a license is applied for at least 5 years imme-

diately prior to such application and upon payment of the required fee of $30.

• • •

WEST VIRGINIA

West Virginia State Board of Barbers and Cosmetologists
1716 Penn Avenue, Suite 7
Charleston, WV 25302
304-558-2924

Cosmetologist
Education: 8th grade
Age: Student 17 years, License 18 years
Training: 2,000 hours
Fees: Exam $25, Original $25
Exams: February, May, August, November
License period: December 31

Apprentice
No apprenticeship information was available for this state.

Reciprocity
Granted to applicants from all states where the training period is the same or equal to West Virginia (holds a current renewal certificate). Reciprocity applicants considered on individual basis. Applicant must have been registered by examination in state where originally registered. Requirements of less than 2,000 hours of training are usually accepted if supplemented by 1 year of practical experience for every 300 hours of schooling not to exceed 1,000 hours.
Reciprocity fee: $25, plus $25 registration fee

• • •

WISCONSIN

Wisconsin Department of Regulation and Licensing
Bureau of Business & Design Professions
Barbering & Cosmetology Examining Board
PO Box 8935
Madison, WI 53708
608-266-1630

Cosmetologist
Education: No school or specialty school may admit any applicant as a student who does not have a high school diploma or GED certificate unless that applicant passes a nationally recognized standardized, or industry-developed test, subject to criteria developed by an appropriate accredited association, measuring the applicant's aptitude to complete successfully the program for which the applicant has applied.
Age: The testing requirement is drawn from the "ability to benefit" criteria of 20 U.S.C. 1091(d).
Training: 1,800 hour student program
Fees: Exam $67 (Original included in application fee)
Exams: Approximately one each month
License period: July 1, odd-numbered years

Apprentice
Education: No school or specialty school may admit any applicant as a student who does not have a high school diploma or GED certificate unless that applicant passes a nationally recognized standardized, or industry-developed test, subject to criteria developed by an appropriate accredited association, measuring the applicant's aptitude to complete successfully the program for which the applicant has applied.
Age: The testing requirement is drawn from the "ability to benefit" criteria of 20 U.S.C. 1091(d).
Training: 4,000 hours
Fee: Apprentice permit $10 (cosmetology)
Exams: Approximately one each month
License period: July 1, odd-numbered years

Reciprocity
A current license and 4,000 hours of practice can qualify for reciprocity.

• • •

WYOMING

Wyoming State Board of Cosmetology
PO Box 4480
Casper, WY 82604
307-265-2917

Cosmetologist
Education: 10th grade
Age: 16 years
Training: 2,000 hours

Cosmetologists

Fees: Exam $20, Original $15
Exams: 6 times a year
License period: December 31

Apprentice
No apprenticeship information was available for this state.

Reciprocity
Licensure without exam granted to applicants from other states if applicants have current licenses, provided applicant took state board exam, practical and written. Reciprocity not provided to instructors.

• • •

Crafts and Trades Workers at Living Historical Sites and Farms

There are scores of living historical sites and farms across the United States. Their common mission is to present the physical appearance and activities of another time period. At a historical farm, for example, workers dressed in period costumes might raise crops using horse-drawn farm equipment, prepare food using the methods of the time, and demonstrate to the public such skills as blacksmithing, weaving, coopering, pottery making, and silversmithing. A historical site might include restored buildings and reenactments of notable events. In addition to educating visitors, these sites and farms might support historical and scientific research and maintain a museum where pertinent artifacts are collected, exhibited, and interpreted.

Living historical sites, farms, and agricultural museums present a different kind of apprenticeship opportunity from the more formal, structured programs presented elsewhere in this directory. Most programs, for example, are highly flexible, depending on the interests of the apprentice and the needs of the site, which may vary from year to year. Training may last for a few days to several months, or even several years. Some sites accept only one or two apprentices at a time, with new apprentices accepted only after current "apprentices" (who may actually have completed their training months or years before) decide to leave.

People seeking apprenticeship training at historic sites are quite often just as (or maybe more) interested in the historic aspect and the overall experience of working at such a site than in the particular craft they are learning. Some, on the other hand, may be experts in the modern methods of, say, carpentry, but have an interest in the historic tools and skills of the trade. Still others may have an interest in museum work in general and may find a curatorial, educational interpretive apprenticeship at a historic site valuable experience.

Requirements at historic sites are often minimal, with no age or educational specifications; however, some programs give preference to applicants with demonstrated interest or skills in particular areas. Nearly all sites expect apprentices to be able to interact with the public by lecturing on and answering questions about their skill or craft. Applications can normally be made any time of year by writing to the organization to express interest and request more information. Apprentices may be housed on the premises and given a small stipend, or they may have to find their own housing and support themselves.

Only a small segment of historical sites offer apprenticeships; many are considering beginning such programs. Most nonprofessional staff positions, however, are nonpaying internships (usually available only to college students as part of their course of study for college credit) or volunteerships. Some facilities rely heavily on volunteers to demonstrate and interpret historic skills or staff museum gift shops, reception areas, and information centers. Keep in mind that volunteering at such sites is an excellent way to get on-the-job training in a variety of areas and may even lead to a paying position.

For more information on apprenticeships for crafts and trades workers at living historical sites and farms, write to the organizations listed below. Additional information might be available from your state's bureau of apprenticeship training. The bureau's address is found in the last section of this encyclopedia.

NATIONAL SPONSOR

Association for Living Historical Farms
and Agricultural Museums
El Rancho de las Golondrinas
Route 14, Box 214
Santa Fe, NM 87505
505-471-2261
ATTN: George Paloheimo

PROGRAM COMMENTS

This organization publishes a directory of living historical sites and agricultural museums.

• • •

STATE SPONSORS

COLORADO

Cross Orchards Living History Farm
3073 F Road
Grand Junction, CO 81504
303-434-9814
ATTN: George Woolsey

SITE DESCRIPTION

This facility depicts a farm in the period 1896-1923. It seeks to acquire, preserve, interpret, and exhibit information and materials primarily deriving from relevant social and natural history of western Colorado.

PROGRAM DESCRIPTION

Specific job title(s): Museum curating and administering
Applications are accepted by mail any time of year.

PROGRAM COMMENTS

This is a nonpaid program that exposes the trainee to all aspects of museum curating and administration, including educational and special events programming, marketing, and promotion.

• • •

INDIANA

Conner Prairie Farm
13400 Allisonville Road
Noblesville, IN 46060
317-776-6000

SITE DESCRIPTION

This facility is an outdoor living history museum depicting the lives and times of the first generation of Indiana settlers using first- and third-person interpretation and hands-on experience for visitors.

PROGRAM DESCRIPTION

Specific job title(s): Blacksmith, Potter

• • •

KENTUCKY

The Homeplace
Tennessee Valley Authority
Land Between the Lakes
100 Van Morgan Drive
Golden Pond, KY 42211
502-924-1310
ATTN: George Bartnik

SITE DESCRIPTION

This facility is an agricultural recreation facility depicting life in this area around 1850.

PROGRAM DESCRIPTION

Specific job title(s): Environmental communications, Forester, Graphic designer, Leadership development, Photographer, Recreation administrator, Research administrator, Wildlife manager
This is a 1-year program.
Applications are accepted in person or by mail any time of year.

PROGRAM COMMENTS

Applicants must have a bachelor's degree and not be currently enrolled in school in order to apply.

Apprentices receive a weekly stipend of $150 and receive free housing on site.

MAINE

Norlands Living History Center
Intern Program
Route 2, Box 1740
Livermore Falls, ME 04254
207-897-4366
ATTN: Kurt Bonnie

SITE DESCRIPTION

This facility is a historic house and farm depicting rural life in nineteenth-century Maine. It preserves the family home of the Washburns, national political and business figures in the late nineteenth century.

PROGRAM DESCRIPTION

Specific job title(s): Blacksmith, Carpenter, Farm worker
This is a 3-6 month program.
Annually, 3-5 positions are available.
Applications are accepted in person or by mail.

REQUIREMENTS

- Pass an oral interview
- Letter of recommendation from 2 personal contacts

PROGRAM COMMENTS

This program requires a commitment from the apprentice for the length of the training. There are no educational requirements, although many apprentices train here following college and before studying for a master's degree. Apprentices receive a $50 a week stipend. Programs vary from year to year depending on the museum's plans and needs. Past programs have included construction of a post and beam barn, restoration of buildings, and rebuilding of antique machines. Skills learned include working with draft animals (oxen) and horses, blacksmithing, and wood joinery.

MARYLAND

Furnace Town
PO Box 207
Snow Hill, MD 21863
410-632-2032
ATTN: Kathy Fisher

SITE DESCRIPTION

This facility preserves and interprets the site of the Nassawanjo Iron Furnace, which operated between 1828 and 1850.

PROGRAM DESCRIPTION

Specific job title(s): Printer, Gardener, Blacksmith, Broom maker, Weaver
This is a 6-8 week program.
Starting wage: $5.00.
Annually, 11-20 people apply for 6-10 positions.
Applications are accepted by mail January-March.

REQUIREMENTS

- Minimum age: 16

APPLICATION DOCUMENTS

Applicants must bring the following documents when applying:
- Social security card
- Work permit (if 16)

MASSACHUSETTS

Plimoth Plantation
Box 1620
Plymouth, MA 02362
508-746-1622
ATTN: Nancy Gedraitis

SITE DESCRIPTION

This facility is a living history museum of seventeenth-century New England depicting the lives of early settlers and the Native Wampanoag Indians.

PROGRAM COMMENTS

This facility offers internships, but these are not limited to college students, although applicants with some college are preferred. The only program with a small stipend is the internship in agriculture and rare breeds. All other such programs are not compensated, although the museum makes an effort to place its interns in part-time paid positions elsewhere in the museum.

• • •

Gore Place
52 Gore Street
Waltham, MA 02154
617-894-2798

SITE DESCRIPTION

This facility preserves the country seat of Christopher Gore, early Massachusetts governor, and depicts a farm of the period 1750-1825.

PROGRAM COMMENTS

This facility sets no age or education requirements (other than the person must be able to read and cannot be a child). It offers non-paying internships and volunteer programs in interpretation, curatorial work, and office work, any of which can lead to paid positions.

• • •

Hancock Shaker Village
PO Box 898
Pittsfield, MA 01202
413-443-0188
ATTN: Todd Burdick

SITE DESCRIPTION

This facility depicts Shaker life, farming, and crafts of the nineteenth century.

PROGRAM DESCRIPTION

Specific job title(s): Crafts such as basket making, oval box making, cabinet making, spinning, weaving, and blacksmithing
Applications are accepted by mail any time of year.

REQUIREMENTS

• Minimum age: 18

PROGRAM COMMENTS

Applicants to this facility must commit to serving at least one day a week during the season (May to October).

• • •

Old Sturbridge Village
1 Old Sturbridge Village Road
Sturbridge, MA 01566
508-347-3362
ATTN: Personnel Department

SITE DESCRIPTION

This facility is a living history museum depicting everyday life in a small New England town during the period 1790 to 1840.

PROGRAM DESCRIPTION

Specific job title(s): Interpreters in various historic trades
Applications are accepted by mail.

PROGRAM COMMENTS

This facility offers paid interpreterships for which it provides on-the-job training. It prefers applicants with at least one year of college or related experience, as well as those with experience working with the public and a degree in history or museum study. The work is seasonal (April to October) and the staff turnover is slow. Applicants who lack sufficient qualifications may be directed to one of the facility's many one- or two-day workshops, which teach such skills as tinsmithing, blacksmithing, coopering, hearth cooking, shoemaking, textiles, pottery, dairying, and historical gardening. Applicants should keep in mind that, if hired, they will be placed where they are most needed, not necessarily in the craft or skill of their choice.

• • •

NEW JERSEY

Allaire Village, Inc.
Route 524, Allaire Road
Allaire, NJ 07727
908-938-2253
ATTN: Victoria Dzenis

SITE DESCRIPTION

This facility is located within a state park and depicts the period between 1822 and 1850.

PROGRAM COMMENTS

This facility relies on volunteer "guilds," groups of volunteers organized around a particular craft or skill, to demonstrate and interpret for the public. Examples of guilds include blacksmithing, carpentry, fiber arts, food ways, gardening, and a militia. Volunteers are asked to participate at least three times a year, and thus the level of experience and expertise gained is left up to the individual.

• • •

NEW YORK

The Farmers' Museum
Box 800
Cooperstown, NY 13326
607-547-2593
ATTN: Katie Boardman

SITE DESCRIPTION

This facility is an agricultural museum depicting rural life in upstate New York during the period 1820 to 1860.

PROGRAM DESCRIPTION

Specific job title(s): Blacksmith
This is a 10-month program.
Applications are accepted in person or by mail from April to December.

PROGRAM COMMENTS

Apprentices are taught historic nineteenth-century blacksmithing techniques as well as interpretation. Only one apprenticeship is available at a time for this 10-month seasonal position. As a condition of the apprenticeship, students are asked to stay at least one additional season, preferably two, following completion of the program. Openings vary depending on the previous apprentice's length of stay. This is not a beginner's position. Applicants are expected to know something about horses and blacksmithing.

• • •

OHIO

Lake Metropark Farm
8800 Euclid-Chardon Road
Kirtland, OH 44094
216-256-2122

SITE DESCRIPTION

This facility is an educational recreational agricultural facility depicting farming and rural life of the past, present, and future.

PROGRAM DESCRIPTION

Specific job title(s): Volunteers in various historic and modern skills
Applications are accepted by mail.

REQUIREMENTS

• Minimum age: 12

PROGRAM COMMENTS

This facility offers an extensive volunteer training program in a variety of areas, including draft horse training, tractor training, animal care, horticulture (hydroponics, beekeeping, gardening, etc.), library work, retail training, and data entry. Training periods depend on the area selected and can last from 3 days to 240 days. The facility asks that volunteers serve at least 10 hours a month.

• • •

VIRGINIA

 The Colonial Williamsburg Foundation
Human Resources Education and
Support Team
PO Box 1776
Williamsburg, VA 23187
804-220-7713
ATTN: Nancy Uram

SITE DESCRIPTION

This facility is a restored colonial village depicting colonial life in the late eighteenth century.

PROGRAM DESCRIPTION

Specific job title(s): Cabinet maker, Musical instrument maker, Cooper, Blacksmith, Gunsmith, Silversmith, Engraver, Foundry worker, Printer, Bootmaker, Harness maker, and Building trades worker
This is a 4-6 year program.
Starting wage: $8.47.
Annually, 50-100 people apply for 0-5 positions.
Applications are accepted in person or by mail Monday through Friday, 8:30 to 4:30 following posted notice.
The application deadline is 72 hours after posting.

REQUIREMENTS

- Pass an oral interview
- Pass a test for illegal drugs
- Passing grade in the following high school course(s): History

APPLICATION DOCUMENTS

Applicants must bring the following documents when applying:
- Social security card
- Photo ID

PROGRAM COMMENTS

Applicants with a documented interest in eighteenth century history and prior experience in demonstrating and interpreting a specific craft will have a higher chance of selection. Current employees of Colonial Williamsburg are given hiring preference.

• • •

Dispensing Opticians

Dispensing opticians fit prescription eyeglasses and contact lenses. They help customers select appropriate frames and take measurements of the face to ensure a proper fit. About half of the country's dispensing opticians are employed by ophthalmologists or optometrists. Others work in optical shops or in other retail outlets, such as department stores or drug stores.

An important part of the dispensing optician's job is customer service. Opticians must be patient when customers are considering frames and be able to provide helpful guidance. In giving advice opticians might consider the customer's occupation, facial features, hairstyle, and weight and thickness of the required corrective lenses.

Once the frame is selected, the dispensing optician examines the written prescription to determine the lens specifications. If the customer does not have a prescription, the optician can sometimes use a "lensmeter" to determine the prescription of the customer's present eyeglasses. They also take measurements of the customer's face. For example, the distance between the pupils is measured because the center of each lens must be positioned in front of a pupil. Also measured is the distance between the eye surface and the lens. Opticians then prepare a work order for an ophthalmic laboratory, which does the actual fabrication of the lenses. The work order includes information about the prescription, lens size, type of material, color, and style. Extra thin lenses can be ordered. Some opticians grind and polish their own lenses; these workers are sometimes called *optical mechanics*.

After the glasses have returned from the laboratory, the optician checks the prescription, optical center, and surface quality of the lenses. He or she then places the glasses on the customer's face and adjusts them for fit and comfort. Opticians use a number of hand tools for fitting, including screwdrivers, optical pliers, and files. Opticians also fix broken glasses.

A smaller number of dispensing opticians fit contact lenses, artificial eyes, and cosmetic shells (which cover blemished eyes). Fitting contact lenses takes considerably more skill and care than than fitting eyeglasses. The general steps for fitting contact lenses include measuring the shape and size of the eyes, selecting the lens material, and filling out the work order. When the contacts arrive, opticians help the customer insert, remove, and care for the lenses. They must ensure that the contacts fit properly and use specialized instruments to observe the customer's eyes. Customers are frequently asked to return for follow-up examinations. When customers experience a major problem with the contacts, they are referred to a ophthalmologist or optometrist.

Some dispensing opticians are trained on the job, while others attend a two-year program in opticianry at a community college or trade school. A few colleges and universities also have such programs. Course work might focus on mechanical optics, geometric optics, ophthalmic dispensing procedures, contact lenses, and business practices, as well as laboratory work in grinding and polishing.

In more than 20 states opticians are required to have a license. Licensing criteria might include an educational requirement, a written test, and a practical examination. In these states a person who is trained on the job must register as an apprentice; the required length of an apprenticeship varies from two to four years. Most other states also have apprenticeship programs for dispensing opticians. Programs tend to be more structured in large companies than in small shops.

National apprenticeship and training standards have been established by a group of opticianry associations—the National Academy of Opticianry, the National Committee of State Opticianry Licensing Boards, the National Federation of Opticianry Schools, and the Opticians Association of America. The core of the program is 4,000 hours (24 months) of on-the-job training, along with related formal instruction. Apprentices are trained in 33 specified tasks, such as how to establish a rapport with customers, how to determine a customer's needs and wants, how to make recommendations to a customer, how to operate and maintain equipment, how to compute and analyze ophthalmic data, and how to document and place orders. The related instruction must cover a minimum of 24 specified topics, including the anatomy and physiology of the eye, basic optical principles, communication techniques, ophthalmic terminology, and lens design. Applicants to apprenticeship programs must be at least 18 years old, have a high school degree (or GED), and be physically able to perform the job. Some applicants are given an aptitude test, which is intended to judge whether an applicant is capable of learning the necessary skills for the job.

The number of employed dispensing opticians is expected to grow at a rate much faster than average, in part because of an increasing number of elderly people, who are the most likely to need corrective lenses. Other factors include a growing public awareness about eye care, as well as the introduction of new products. More than half of all Americans now wear corrective lenses. Some people own more than one pair of glasses for fashion reasons.

For more information on training programs and apprenticeships for dispensing opticians, write to the organization listed below. Additional information might be available from your state's bureau of apprenticeship training. The bureau's address is found in the last section of this encyclopedia.

 The National Academy of Opticianry
10111 Martin Luther King, Jr. Highway
Suite 112
Bowie, MD 20720-4299
301-577-4828

The NAO is an independent, nonprofit educational organization dedicated to providing its members with programs and services to meet the educational requirements for state licensure or certification by the American Board of Opticianry.

Emergency Medical Technicians

Emergency medical technicians, or *EMTs*, are often the first specialists to arrive at a medical emergency. They are sent to the scene of automobile accidents, for example, as well as heart attacks, burns, poisonings, gunshot wounds, and even unscheduled childbirths. They must identify the nature of the emergency, provide immediate medical care, and transport patients to a hospital. Many lives are saved by their ability to make quick, well-informed decisions. About two-fifths of EMTs are employed by private ambulance services; a third by fire, police, or rescue squad departments; and much of the remainder by hospitals. Most paid EMTs work in cities. Rural areas are generally serviced by volunteers.

EMTs, who drive specially equipped emergency vehicles, are usually assigned to a two-person team. Their work begins when they receive a call from a dispatcher, who provides any available information about the medical emergency. Although EMTs must then travel as quickly as possible to the scene, they follow the traffic laws that apply to emergency vehicles in order to avoid causing an accident themselves. After arriving at the scene, they quickly evaluate the nature and extent of the emergency and attempt to bring the area under control. This might include asking bystanders for help with directing traffic or with clearing debris. They might also ask bystanders for information.

EMTs must be prepared for any type of emergency. A patient might be bleeding profusely, a heart attack victim could be lying unconscious, or a person might be trapped under a heavy object, such as a car. Sometimes EMTs are confronted with emotionally disturbed patients. A delay in treatment could cost the patient's life. Emergency treatments include opening up breathing passages, controlling bleeding, and performing cardiac resuscitation. If a victim is trapped under an object, medical care is sometimes given first and then, using specialized equipment and techniques, the person is removed. In many cases EMTs receive assistance from police officers or firefighters.

Victims who must be transported are placed on a stretcher and lifted into the emergency vehicle. The dispatcher might then tell them where to take the patient, but sometimes EMTs must make this decision themselves. In any case, the details of the medical problems are given to the dispatcher so that the hospital can be prepared for the patient. While being transported, patients often need to be monitored and to receive additional medical care. At the hospital the EMTs bring the patient to the emergency department and sometimes assist with the first steps of in-hospital care.

After leaving the hospital, EMTs must be prepared for another emergency. They replace the linens and blankets, for example, get new supplies of oxygen and drugs, and sterilize equipment. They must also periodically check the gas, oil, brakes, battery, and other systems to ensure the proper running of the vehicle.

All states require EMTs to be certified. Some states have their own certification requirements, but many follow those established by the National Registry of Emergency Medical Technicians (NREMT). The NREMT has set up three levels of competency. The first, called EMT-Basic, enables an EMT to perform such emergency techniques as opening airways, controlling bleeding, administering oxygen, immobilizing fractures, bandaging wounds, and assisting in childbirth. These skills are taught in an 80- to 120-hour training program developed by the U.S. Department of Transportation. The program is offered in numerous community colleges; police, fire, and health departments; and hospitals. Candidates must spend an additional 10 hours as an intern in a hospital or emergency room. Those who pass the training course, as well as a written and practical examination administered by the state (or the NREMT), earn the title *Registered EMT-Basic.*

The next level, EMT-Intermediate, is obtained through an additional 35 to 55 hours of training. Students learn new means of patient assessment, as well as various medical treatments, including the use of intravenous fluids and antishock garments. A specified amount of clinical and field experience is also required, in addition to an examination.

Finally, the highest level is EMT-Paramedic, which requires extensive training lasting from 750 to 2,000 hours. The program includes classroom instruction, clinical experience, and an internship in the field. To gain certification the candidate must also have six months of experience as an EMT-Paramedic and pass a written and practical examination. EMT-Paramedics are certified to administer drugs orally and intravenously, interpret EKGs, and handle other complex equipment. Compared with other EMTs, they make more physician-like judgments.

All EMTs must periodically reregister, usually every two years, to keep their certification. Requirements for reregistering include working as an EMT and taking additional courses.

The number of employed EMTs is expected to grow at an average rate. The increasing population of older people, who need emergency medical services more often than do other age groups, will help boost the job prospects for EMTs, but this trend might be offset by constraints and cutbacks in government spending. The most job opportunities are anticipated in hospitals and private ambulance services. In fire, police, and rescue squad departments—where pay and benefits are the most generous—competition for positions will likely remain fierce.

EMTs work both indoors and outdoors and in all types of weather. They must be in good physical shape, be efficient, and have an even temperament. The field of emergency medical care brings with it a number of risks. EMTs might be exposed to various diseases, such as hepatitis B and AIDS, from bleeding patients. They risk physical harm from emotionally disturbed persons or those under the influence of drugs. Many EMTs, however, find the challenges exciting and derive great satisfaction in knowing their work provides a vital public service.

For more information on training programs and apprenticeships for EMTs, write to the organizations listed below. Additional information might be available from your state's bureau of apprenticeship training. The bureau's address is found in the last section of this encyclopedia.

ALABAMA

 Division of Emergency Medical Services
Department of Public Health
434 Monroe Street
Montgomery, AL 36130-1701
Rick Harris, Director
(205) 613-5383

BASIC EMT

Hours of training: 110 minimum (didactic and clinical)
Certification requirements: 8 contact hours annually to maintain licensure
License duration: 36-month intervals
Recertification requirements: Annual recertification based on completion of CEU requirements

INTERMEDIATE EMT

Hours of training: 268 hours minimum
Certification requirements: 10 contact hours annually to maintain licensure.
License duration: 36-month intervals
Recertification requirements: Annual recertification based on completion of CEU requirements.

PARAMEDIC

Hours of training: 350-400 minimum
Certification requirements: Completion of state-approved Paramedic training course. Pass National Registry EMT-Paramedic written and practical exams. License duration: 36-month intervals.
Recertification requirements: Annual recertification based on completion of CEU requirements of 15 contact hours annually.
Responsible certification agency: State Board of Health.
Reciprocity: Pass National Registry at Basic and Paramedic levels. Intermediate level pass National Registry plus additional skills for Alabama - intubation, defibrillation, EKG recognition.

SALARY RANGES

Basic EMT: Minimum wage to $12.500/year.
Intermediate EMT: $12,500/year to $15,000/year.
Paramedic: $15,000/year to $22,000/year.

• • •

ALASKA

Department of Health and Social Services
Division of Public Health
Emergency Medical Services Section
PO Box 110616
Juneau, AK 99811-0616
Matt Anderson, EMS Training Coordinator
(907) 465-3027

BASIC EMT

Hours of training: 110 hours minimum
Certification requirements: DOT Basic EMT curriculum including instruction in application of pneumatic antishock device (MAST suit). Also must show need for certification and pass state EMT-I written and practical examinations. Must have (Option 1) 48 hours of continuing education, current CPR card and pass written and practical recertification examinations; or (Option 2) 24-hour refresher course with skills check-off and written examination, 24 hours of continuing education, and current CPR CARD.

EMT II

Hours of training: 50 hours minimum above basic.
Certification requirements: Basic EMT certification, approval from sponsoring physician and must take and pass the state written and practical EMT-II examination.
Recertification requirements: Every 2 years. Must recertify as an EMT-I, have letter from sponsoring physician, and must take and pass EMT II recertification examination.

EMT-III

Hours of training: 50 hours minimum over EMT-II
Certification requirements: EMT-III must have letter from sponsoring physician and must take and pass the EMT-III examination.
Recertification requirements: As an EMT-II, every 2 years have a letter from a physician and must take and pass the EMT-III examination.

PARAMEDIC

Hours of training: There are no number of hours specified in EMT-P regulations.
Certification requirements: Course taken must have met DOT standards and prepare the student to demonstrate skills outlined by the NAS/NRTF on EMT

PERFORMANCE

Recertification requirements: Every 2 years. MICPs must provide evidence of 60 hours of CME/year, ACLS certification, BCLS certification, recommendation from physician medical director and fees.
Responsible certification agency: EMT-I, EMT-II, OR EMT-III: EMS Section, Department of Health and Social Services. Mobile Intensive Care Paramedics: Alaska State Medical Board, Department of Commerce and Economic Development.
Reciprocity: EMT-I, EMT-II, OR EMT-III: Must have National Registry certification, or current certification from a state that meets or exceeds Alaska's standards, and a letter of recommendation from a supervisor and sponsoring physician. All out-of-state applicants for EMT-II and EMT-III certification, as well as EMT-I applicants not certified by the National Registry of Emergency Medical Technicians, must pass the written and practical examinations at the appropriate level. EMT-P must be 19 years of age or older; be a high school graduate; be of acceptable moral character; be a currently certified EMT by the National Registry or the Alaska Department of Health and Social Services and pass the written and practical examination for the EMT-P administered by the NREMT; be under the supervision of a sponsoring physician approved by the Alaska State Medical Board; have successfully completed an approved training program; have satisfactorily completed an approved internship.

SALARY RANGES

Basic EMT: $15,000/year to $25,000
Intermediate EMT: $15,000/year to $30,000/year
Paramedic: $18,000/year to $40,000/year

• • •

ARIZONA

Office of EMS
Arizona Department of Health Services
Office of Emergency Medical Services
1651 East Morten, Suite 120
Phoenix, AZ 85020
(602) 255-1170
Victor Dominguez, State Training Manager

BASIC EMT

Hours of training: Certification - 110 hours minimum; recertification-24 hours minimum
Certification requirements: Successful completion of Department-certified course; current certification in BLS by American Heart Association or other agency approved by the Department; pass physical examination; pass written examination.
Recertification requirements: Must recertify every two years. Successful completion of Department-certified refresher course or continuing education program approved by the Department; current certification in BLS by the American Heart Association or other agency approved by the Department; pass written examination every four years.

INTERMEDIATE EMT

Hours of training: Certification 317 hours minimum: recertification 40 hours minimum.
Certification requirements: Successful completion of Department-certified course, certification in BLS by American Heart Association or other agency approved by the Department; pass National Registry examinations; pass state written examinations; pass IV medications and endotracheal intubation practical examinations.
Recertification requirements: Must recertify every 2 years. Successful completion of Department certified refresher course or continuing education program approved by the Department; current certification in BLS by American Heart Association or other agency approved by the Department; provide letter of recommendation from base hospital Medical Director.

PARAMEDIC

Hours of training: Certification 625 hours minimum; recertification 60 hours minimum
Certification requirements: Successful completion of Department certified course; current certification in ACLS by the American Heart Association or other agency approved by the Department; pass physical and written examinations; pass National Registry examinations.
Recertification requirements: Must recertify every 2 years. Successful completion of continuing-education program approved by the Department; current certification in ACLS by American Heart Association or other agency approved the Department; verification of 60 hours of vehicular time for each 6-month period during previous certification; letter of recommendation from base hospital Medical Doctor.
Responsible certification agency: Arizona Department of Health Services.
Reciprocity: Basic EMTs certified and in good standing in another state, and who have National Registry certification will receive BEMT certification in Arizona. I-EMTs and Paramedics who are National Registry-certified are required to take a written pharmacology examination. I-EMTs must also pass endotracheal intubation and IV medications practical examinations.

SALARY RANGES

Basic EMT: $8,000/year to $20,000/year
Intermediate EMT: $12,000/year to $24,000/year
Paramedic: $20,000/year to $35,000/year

• • •

ARKANSAS

Division of Emergency Medical Services
Arkansas Department of Health
4815 West Markham Street, Slot 38
Little Rock, AR 72205-3867
(501) 661-2262
Virginia K. Williams, State Training Director

BASIC EMT

Hours of training: 120 hours minimum
Certification requirements: Must complete approved NSC course and be recommended by instructor. EMT-Ambulance applicant must pass 200-question state written exam and state practical exam.
Recertification requirements: Basic EMT (non-active), current CPR certification plus 2 of following: NSC Refresher Course, 48 hours approved CEUs, pass state recertification exam. Basic EMT (active), EMT-Ambulance: Current CPR, 1 of following: NSE Refresher Course, 48 hours approved continuing education, current National Registry, pass state Recertification.

INTERMEDIATE EMT

Hours of training: N/A
Certification requirements: Must meet objectives of National Standard Curriculum, complete approved NSC course, pass National Registry written and practical exam; successful completion of course includes being recommended by primary instructor and medical director of approved training program.
Recertification requirements: Application card, $10 fee, current AHA, Arkansas Affiliate CPR certification (course C) letter verifying employment with an Arkansas-licensed ALS ambulance service, recommendation of medical director of that service, and one of the following: Basic EMT refresher course and 12 hours of continuing education at the intermediate level; 48 hours of continuing education; Basic EMT recertification exam and 12 hours of continuing education at intermediate level; or maintain National Registry at EMT-I level.

PARAMEDIC

Hours of training: Minimum 710; must included didactic-300, clinical-260, and field internship-150
Certification requirements: Successfully complete approved training programs (NSC guideline) and be recommended by the instructor/coordinator and medical director, successfully pass the EMT-P National Registry written and practical exams.
Recertification requirements: Non-active: 2 of the following: NSC refresher course, recertification exam, current National Registry, 48 hours continuing education; document 6 IVs and 3 ETs within previous 90 days, have current ACLS. Active: 1 of the 4 listed above, plus current ACLS certification letter from employer, and recommendation of medical director of the service.
Responsible certification agency: Division of EMS, Arkansas Department of Health.
Reciprocity: Basic: Verification of current certification from another state, document need for Arkansas certification (Arkansas resident, working in arkansas or full-time student in Arkansas), current AHA, Arkansas Affiliate CPR certification, must be within original certification period or have recertified in the state from which you're transferring. State with reciprocity: GA, IL, KS, LA, ME, MI, MO, NY, ND, OR, SD, VA, DC. Must verify written exam or take Arkansas written: AK, CT, ID, MA, MN, MT, NH, NJ, NM, UT, VT, WV, WI, WY. Must take Arkansas practical: AL, AZ, CO, FL, IN, MD, NC, OH, OK, SC, TN, TX. Must verify written exam and take Arkansas practical or written and practical: KY, MS NE, NV, PA, RI, WA. Must take both Arkansas written and practical exams: CA, IA. States that do not meet training, certification, or recertification requirements or were not included in survey: DE, HI. Intermediate: Must verify certification in another state and be Nationally Registered. If not Nationally Registered, have to take NR exam. Paramedic: Must verify state and National Registry. If not Nationally Registered, must take National Registry exam.

SALARY RANGES

Basic and Intermediate EMT: Minimum wage to $17,000/year.
Paramedic: $12,000/year-$22,000 year.

• • •

CALIFORNIA

Emergency Medical Services Authority
State of California
1930 9th Street, Suite 100
Sacramento, CA 95814
(916) 322-4336
Joseph E. Morales, MD, MPA, Director

BASIC EMT

Hours of training: 110
Certification requirements: Pass a competency-based written and skills examination.
Recertification requirements: Every two years - must complete a 24-hour refresher course and pass a competency-based written and skills examination. The optional skill of defibrillation has been added, but may only be used at local EMS agency option.

INTERMEDIATE EMT

Hours of training: 306, which included 210 hours of didactic and skill laboratory and 96 hours of clinical field internship; also a minimum 20 ALS patient contacts in the combined hospital clinical field internship. Of the 20 ALS patient contacts, 5 ALS patient contacts must be in the field.
Certification requirements: Every 2 years, must complete 48 hours continuing education, including CPR and field care audits, satisfy any minimal work requirements, pass a competency-based written and skills examination for both basic and intermediate skills.

PARAMEDIC

Hours of training: Minimum of 1,032 hours, which included 320 hours didactic and skills laboratory and 160 clinical training and 480 hours field internship. Also a minimum of 40 ALS patient contacts in the field.
Certification requirements: Pass a competency-based written and skills state certifying examination.
Recertification requirements: Same as EMT-II with the exception of no skills test. Written testing is done every 4 years.
Responsible certification agency: Certification of EMTI and II levels is the responsibility of the medical director of the local EMS agency; however, testing EMT-P certification is now administered by the (state) EMS Authority.
Reciprocity: An EMT-I (Basic) from another state would have to challenge and pass a written/skills examination An EMT-II (Intermediate) would have to take our EMT-II course. An EMT-P (Paramedic) from another state would have to provide evidence of completion of a paramedic course that meets DOT standards, complete any additional training required by the county where certification is being requested, and pass a written skills certification examination.

• • •

COLORADO

 Colorado Department of Health
Emergency Medical Services Division
4300 Cherry Creek Drive, South
Denver, CO 80222
(303) 692-2980
Larry L. McNatt, Director

BASIC EMT

Hours of training: Minimum 110 hours, but most courses are 126-180 hours.
Certification requirements: Successful completion of a course that includes practical skills evaluations done following departmental standards, and successful completion of practical and written examinations.
Recertification requirements: Completion of 36 hours of continuing education or a refresher course. Successful completion of a practical examination, successful completion of a written examination, done every 3 years.

INTERMEDIATE EMT

Hours of training: 200
Certification requirements: Successful completion of a course including a practical evaluation and successful completion of a state written and practical examination.
Recertification requirements: Every 3 years, documentation of 36 hours of continuing education or refresher training, a practical examination, and successful completion of a state written examination, and approved physician advisor sign-off.

PARAMEDIC

Hours of training: 900+
Certification requirements: Successful completion of an approved course including a practical skills evaluation, successful completion of a state written examination, Physician advisor sign-off.

Recertification requirements: Every 3 years, documentation of 45 hours of continuing education or refresher training including practical skills evaluations and successful completion of a state-prepared written examination.
Responsible certification agency: EMS Division
Reciprocity: State evaluated on individual basis. Must have current certification in approved state or National Registry.

SALARY RANGES

Basic EMT: $9,000/year to $22,000/year
Intermediate EMT: $10,000/Year to $25,000/year
Paramedic: $15,000/year to $40,000/year

• • •

CONNECTICUT

Office of Emergency Medical Services
State of Connecticut
Department of Health Services
150 Washington Street
Hartford, CT 06106
(203) 566-7336
Paul Winfield Smith, Chief, Education and Training

BASIC EMT

Hours of training: 120 hours
Certification requirements: For the purpose of maintaining certification, a person must complete 25 hours of commissioner-approved training, which includes both practical and written evaluations.
Recertification requirements: This requirement must be complied with every two years for persons who have been continuously certified for less than six years. For persons certified for six years or more, their certification training requirement must be met every 3 years.

INTERMEDIATE EMT

Hours of training: 60-80
Certification requirements: Initial certification is offered only to MIC personnel who are affiliated with an approved Mobile Intensive Care Service provider. Satisfactory completion of a state-approved course of study, skills evaluation, and recommendation by medical programs and regional director.
Recertification requirements: Before the end of 24-month period.

PARAMEDIC

Hours of training: 750-950
Certification requirements: EMT-Paramedic written examination by Professional Examination Services administered by the Office of Emergency Medical Services. The skills evaluation and oral board may be provided and administered on a region-by-region basis with physician's input.
Recertification requirements: Attend continuing education program of a minimum of 48 hours every 24 months. The standardized written examination is administered by the Office of Emergency Medical Services before the end of a 24-month period.
Responsible certification agency: Certification is the responsibility of the State of Connecticut, Department of Health Services through the Office of Emergency Medical Services.
Reciprocity: As of April 1, 1988, personnel certified from 41 states may gain legal recognition in our state at the Basic level.

SALARY RANGES

Hospital: EMT, $10.40-$13.26/hour
EMT-Intermediate $11.27-$14.34/hour
EMT-Paramedic, $12.37/$17.43/hour
Flight Nurse,$22.00-$28.37+differential

Municipal: EMT, $10.23-$12.40/hour
EMT-Intermediate, $12.20-$16.35/hour
EMT-Paramedic, $13.36-$16.35/hour

Commercial: EMT, $8.40-$12.00/hour
EMT-Intermediate, $8.35-$12.07/hour
EMT-Paramedic, $9.70-$18.30/hour.

• • •

DELAWARE

Division of Public Health
Department of Health and Social Services
Office of Paramedic Administration
PO Box 637
Dover, DE 19903
(302) 739-6637, (302) 739-6638
Ruth Oates-Graham, Administrator

AMBULANCE ATTENDANT

Hours of training: 60

EMT

Hours of Training: 110+ hours
Certification requirements: Students are required to complete all blocks of the DOT curriculum. Must possess current certification in CPR. Must be a member of an ambulance squad, fire department, or rescue squad to be eligible for certification.
Recertification requirements: CPR recertification, patient assessment, and application to the Delaware State Fire School.

PARAMEDIC

Hours of training: 1200+
Certification requirements: Be employed by one of three counties. Paramedics are certified by the Office of Paramedic Emergency Medical Services following guidelines adopted by the Board of Medical Practice. Must successfully pass National Registry Paramedic exam within 1 year after completion of paramedic school.
Responsible certification agency: Ambulance Attendants-Delaware State Fire School
Paramedics - Office of Paramedic Administration, Division of Public Health.
Reciprocity: Paramedic (ALS): Must be nationally registered paramedic and complete state clinical/field evaluation period. Ambulance Attendant(BLS): Must challenge the ambulance attendant test

SALARY RANGES

N/A

• • •

FLORIDA

Emergency Medical Services
Department of Health and Rehabilitative Services
1317 Winewood Boulevard
Tallahassee, FL 32399-0700
(904) 487-1911
Michael S. Williams, Director

BASIC EMT

Hours of training: 110
Certification requirements: Complete the most current U.S. Department of Transportation standard EMT training program of 110 hours. Currently certified in CPR, pay certification fee of $35 and exam fee of $40, pass state certification examination within 1 year of course completion.
Recertification requirements: Compete 30-hour refresher course, be currently certified in CPR, pay $20 recertification fee.

PARAMEDIC

Hours of training: 800-1000
Certification requirements: Complete most current U.S. DOT standard paramedic training curriculum consisting of six DOT Divisions, be certified in CPR or ACLS, pay $45 certification fee and $40 examination fee, pass certification examination within one year of course completion.
Responsible certification agency: Office of EMS, Department of Health and Rehabilitative Services
Reciprocity: No full reciprocity. EMTs and Paramedics certified out of state are allowed to challenge appropriate certification exam and become certified upon passing that exam.

SALARY RANGES

Basic EMT: $12,000/year to $20,000/year
Paramedic: $17,000//year to $27,000/year

• • •

GEORGIA

Emergency Medical Services Section
Division of Public Health
Department of Human Resources
2 Peachtree Street, South West
7th Floor Annex
Atlanta, GA 30303
(404) 657-6700
Keith Wages, Director

BASIC EMT

Hours of training: 220 clock hours.
Certification requirements: Successfully complete an approved 220-hour course. Successfully pass state practical and written exam
Recertification requirements: All levels of EMT must meet work requirements of 80 hours per month for 9 months of he immediately preceding12 month or for 80 hours per month during 18 months of the immediately preceding 24 months by rendering or being on call to render any service which such person's certificate authorizes that person to render. Also,continuing education requirements must be met annually by all levels of EMTs: Basic EMT, 10 hours; Cardiac Technician, 15 hours; and Paramedic, 20 hours

CARDIAC TECHNICIAN

Hours of training: 260 didactic, 200 clinical (460 total). ACLS
Certification requirements: Complete department approved course plus ACLS and successfully challenge state Cardiac Technician test. Prerequisite; Georgia-certified Basic.
Recertification requirements: Successfully complete 15 hours of recertification training by December 31 each year and to have worked or been on call as an EMT for 80 hours for 9 of the past 12 months or 18 of the past 24 months.

PARAMEDIC

Hours of training: 400 hours didactic, 350 clinical (750 total).
Certification requirements: Approved course and successfully challenge the state Paramedic test.
Recertification requirements: Successfully complete 20 hours of recertification training by December 31 each year and have worked or been on call as an EMT-P for 80 hours for 9 of the past 12 months or 18 of the past 24 months.
Responsible certification agency: Basic EMTs are certified by the Emergency Medical Services Section, Department of Human Resources. Cardiac Technicians and Paramedics are certified by the Composite Board of medical Examiners.
Reciprocity: National Registry Paramedic only. Basic current in state or National Registry with equal training must take state practical and written. If training is not equivalent, a 40-hour course must be completed before taking state practical and written.
Cardiac Technician: Must be certified as Georgia Basic, have quality training and ACLS, then take written exam. Paramedic must have equal training, ACLS, and take written exam.

SALARY RANGES

Basic EMT: $15,225-$28,875/Year
Cardiac Technician: $16,275-$30,350/year
Paramedic: $17,640-$33,500/year

• • •

HAWAII

State of Hawaii
Department of Health
Emergency Medical Services System Branch
3627 Kilauea Avenue, Room 102
Honolulu, HI 96816
(808) 735-5267
Edward Kalinowski, RN, State Training Director

BASIC EMT

Hours of training: 315 hours.
Certification requirements: Those applicants who have fulfilled the requirements of the National Registry to be registered as emergency medical technicians (EMT) and also present evidence of completion of a state-approved training program or its equivalent to be determined by the Board of Medical Examiners shall be certified by the board as EMT.

Recertification requirements: EMTs not certified by the National Registry shall submit documentary evidence that they have complied with requirements equal to the requirements of the National Registry for EMTs.

MICT

Hours of training: 1,215 hours
Certification requirements: Those applicants who have fulfilled the requirements of the National Registry to be registered as emergency medical technician-Paramedic (MICT) and also present evidence of completion of a state-approved training program or its equivalent to be determined by the Board of Medical Examiners which will entail a practical skills examination, a period of observation, or both, shall be certified by the board as MICT.
Recertification requirements: MICTs not certified by the National Registry shall submit documentary evidence that they have complied with requirements equal to those requirements of the National Registry for MICTs.
Responsible certification agency: Board of Medical Examiners
Reciprocity: If the Board of Medical Examiners determines that the applicant has the equivalency in training and holds a current National Registry Certificate, the candidate will be allowed to take the equivalency examination

SALARY RANGES

EMT: + $24,600
MICT: + $32,400

• • •

IDAHO

Idaho EMS System
450 West State Street
Boise, ID 83720
(208) 334-5994
Perry B. Lamb, Certification & Licensure Coordinator

BASIC EMT
Hours of training: 90 hours didactic, 11 hours extrication, 10 hours clinical observation time in hospital emergency department
Certification requirements: Successful completion of state EMT course, written and practical exams. Certification is for 2 years
Recertification requirements: 30 hours of continuing education, written and practical recertification exams every 2 years. CEUs are obtained through several methods: (1) Teleconferences: This program can have up to 30 separate locations on line at any given item; (2) Mobile Interactive Training Unit (MITU): This unique program provides training in rural communities of Idaho using interactive laser video disc computer programs; (3) Annual Emergency Medical Conferences; (4) Regional Conferences and Workshops; (5) Individual Unit Training.

EMT-INTERMEDIATE

Hours of training: 50 didactic, 24 clinical.
Certification requirements: Successful completion of state EMT-intermediate course, written and practical exams. Candidates must be actively engaged in the delivery of emergency medicine with an approved intermediate-level program. Certification by the Idaho State Board of Medicine is for 2 years. Physician program director recommendation is required.
Recertification requirements: Skill requirements must be reported quarterly. Biennial continuing education requirements include 30 hours BLS and 16 hours ILS; written and practical recertification exams are required every 2 years.

EMT-PARAMEDIC

Hours of training: 500-hour minimum required by state law. Actual training program consist of an average of 800 hours.
Certification requirements: Successful completion of state EMT-Paramedic course, written and practical exams. Active affiliation with an approved program and physician program director recommendation are required. Certification by the Idaho State Board of Medicine is for 2 years.
Recertification requirements: 80 hours of continuing education biennially as well as quarterly skills maintenance. Written and practical recertification exams are required after the first 2 years of certification. Written and practical recertification exams are required every 4 years thereafter, allowing recertification based on continuing education and physician program

director recommendation every other 2-year period.
Responsible certification agency: All EMTs are certified by the Idaho Emergency Medical Services Bureau.
EMT-Intermediates and EMT-Paramedics are certified by the Idaho State Board of Medicine.
Reciprocity: The state of Idaho is currently utilizing "legal recognition" as a standard for recognizing competency at the Basic EMT level as defined by the National Council of State EMS Training Coordinators. EMT-Intermediate and EMT-Paramedic certifications are considered on a case-by-case basis and must be approved by the Board of Medicine SWPCALS to challenge the Idaho state certification exams.

SALARY RANGES

Basic EMT: $9,000/year-$25,000/year
EMT-Intermediate:$12,000/year-$25,000/year
E MT-Paramedic: $17,000/year-$31,000/year

• • •

ILLINOIS

Division of Emergency Medical Services & Highway Safety
Illinois Department of Public Health
525 West Jefferson Street, Third Floor
Springfield, IL 62761
(217) 785-2080

BASIC EMT

Hours of training: 116 hours, federal DOT Curriculum
Licensing requirements: Successfully complete a Department-approved training program; be 18 years of age or older, hold a high school diploma or high school equivalency certificate; successfully complete the required testing procedures.
Renewal requirements: Completion of a minimum of 20 hours at a Department-approved refresher training program or BTLS or PHTLS at the basic level; current CPR certificate; completion of a minimum of 40 hours of continuing education, seminars, and workshops. Licensure period is two years.

INTERMEDIATE EMT

Hours of training: minimum 56 hours, federal DOT Curriculum
Licensing requirements: Currently licensed as an EMT-A; be 18 years of age or older, successfully complete a Department-approved training program; successfully complete the required testing procedures; receive a recommendation from the Project Medical Director. Licensure period is two years.
Renewal requirements: Completion of a minimum of 20 hours at a Department-approved refresher training program or BTLS or PHTLS at the basic level; current CPR certificate; completion of 48 hours of continuing education,seminars, and workshops (12 hours of which are directed at intermediate skills); recommendation for renewal from Project Medical Director.

PARAMEDIC

Hours of training: Minimum of 390 hours, federal DOT Curriculum.
Licensing requirements: Satisfactory completion of a Department-approved training program; successfully complete the required testing procedures consisting of practical, supervised clinical, supervised field experience, and state licensure exam; be currently state licensed as an EMT-A or EMT-I; receive a recommendation from the Project medical Director. Licensure period is two years.
Renewal requirements: A minimum of 40 hours of continuing education each year; current CPR certificate; receive a letter of recommendation from the Project Medical Director.
Responsible licensing agency: Department of Public Health
Reciprocity: On the EMT-A level, Illinois is participating in the Legal Recognition Plan established by the National Association of State Emergency Medical Services Directors. On the EMT-I AND EMT-P levels, recommendation for licensure by reciprocity is at the discretion of the Project medical director. Upon recommendation, the EMT-I or EMT-P must successfully complete the state licensing

exam (if National Registry, the exam is waived).

SALARY RANGES

Basic EMT: Mostly volunteer minimum wage or paid on call
Intermediate EMT: Mostly volunteer minimum wage or paid on call
Paramedic: Medium range averages between $15,000 and $24,000/year.

• • •

INDIANA

Indiana Government Center
Room 208E
Indianapolis, IN 46204
(317) 232-3980
Tony Pagano, Director EMS Training and Certification

BASIC EMT

Hours of training: 135 hour minimum, includes 10 hours ED observation.
Certification requirements: Successful completion of Commission-approved Basic EMT Training Course, plus state practical skills and written examinations for initial certification.
Recertification requirements: Annual participation in and reporting of 24 hours of continuing education (17 hours lecture/didactic and 7 hours in BLS skill areas; CPR, mechanical aids to breathing, bandaging, splinting, patient assessment, patient handling, MAST)

INTERMEDIATE EMT

Hours of training: 60-80, depending upon clinical performance.
Certification requirements: EMT certification plus successful completion of state-approved training curriculum and state practical skills and written examinations.
Recertification requirements: Annual accumulation of 10 hours of continuing education in ALS including 6 hours medical director audit and review, 4 hours medical director skill and 4 hours of lectures provided by the organization's supervising hospital-and maintain EMT certification.

PARAMEDIC

Hours of training: 860 to 1,500.
Certification requirements: Current EMT certification plus successful completion of Commission-approved Paramedic Training Program and National Registry Paramedic examination for initial certification.
Recertification requirements: Recertify every 13 months; 60 hours continuing education credits, including skills and audit and review.
Responsible certification agency: Indiana EMS Commission, State Emergency Management Agency.
Reciprocity: Verification of successful completion of comparable training program plus successful completion of Indiana practical skills and written certification examinations. Testing is waived for National Registry-certified EMTs and Paramedics.

SALARY RANGES

Basic EMT: $10,000/year-$22,000/year
Intermediate EMT: $10,000/year-$24,000/year
Paramedic: $12,000/year-$30,000/year

• • •

IOWA

Iowa Department of Public Health
Emergency Medical Services
Lucas State Office Building
Des Moines, IA 50319-0075
(515) 281-3741
Gary L. Ireland, EMS Program Manager

BASIC EMT

Hours of training: 120 hours (102 hours classroom, 18 hours clinical)
Certification requirements: Must be able to speak, read, and write English, be physically able to perform skills, be at least 17 years old prior to enrollment, pass state written and practical examinations. Practical is administered by

training program using state-provided forms; written is administered by state EMS staff.
Recertification requirements: Must complete at least 24 hours during each two-year certification period and have a current CPR certification.

INTERMEDIATE EMT

Hours of training: EMT-D (manual), 16; EMT-D (auto), 4; EMT-I, approximately 160.
Certification requirements: Must be currently certified as an EMT-A for enrollment, high school diploma or equivalent, EMT-D: Complete training program (written and practical). EMT-I: Complete training, complete state-approved practical; written administered by state EMS staff.
Recertification requirements: EMT-D: 24 hours plus current CPR certification. EMT-I: 48 hours during 2-year certification.

PARAMEDIC

Hours of training: The EMT-P received a minimum of 600 hours of training: 150 hours of clinical experience, 150 hours of in-field training, and 300 classroom.
Certification requirements: The paramedic must be certified as an EMT-A for enrollment, have a high school diploma or equivalent, be at least 18, and be able to read, speak, and write English.
Recertification requirements: 60 hours of continuing education during two-year certification period.
Responsible certification agency: Certification group includes a physician. Only advanced service programs require a medical director. Basic and Advanced programs are administered through the EMS section, Iowa Department of Health
Reciprocity: State written and practical examinations to obtain reciprocity for all levels.

SALARY RANGES

N/A

• • •

KANSAS

Board of Emergency Medical Services
109 South West 6th Street
Topeka, KS 66603-3805
(913) 296-7296
Bob McDaneld, Administrator

FIRST RESPONDER

Hours of training: Successful completion of at least 45-hour training program approved by Board of Emergency Medical Services and successful completion of state-administered written and practical examinations.
Recertification requirements: Completion of 8 hours annually prescribed by board.

BASIC EMT

Hours of training: 120 hours
Certification requirements: Successful completion of approved program and successful completion of state-administered written and practical examination.
Recertification requirements: Completion of continuing education prescribed and approved annually by the Board of Emergency Medical Services. Averages about 14 hours annually. Basic EMTs are eligible to take training and gain approval to use AED/SAED. First responders are also now allowed to be trained in and use AED/SAED.

INTERMEDIATE EMT

Hours of training: Minimum of 40 hours for program approval by the Board of EMS.
Certification requirements: Successful completion of approved program and successful completion of state-administered written and practical examinations.
Recertification requirements: Completion of all Basic level continuing education, plus 4 hours of IV therapy prescribed and approved annually by the Board of EMS

EMT-DEFIBRILLATOR

Hours of training: Minimum of 26 hours.
Certification requirements: successful completion of approved program and of state-admin-

istered written and practical examinations
Recertification requirements: completion of Basic level continuing education plus 4 hours defibrillation training, prescribed and approved annually by the Board of EMS.

PARAMEDIC

Hours of training: Minimum of 1,200 hours for program approval by the Board of EMS.
certification requirements: Successful completion of approved program and completion of state-administered written and practical examinations.
Recertification requirements: 30 hours of continuing education prescribed and approved annually by the Board of EMS.
Reciprocity: Must be certified in another state or with National Registry to be eligible to challenge the state written and practical exams for Kansas certification.

SALARY RANGES

Basic EMT: From $12,000/year-$20,000/year
Intermediate EMT: From $12,000/year-$22,000/year
Paramedic: From $18,000/year to$30,000/year.

• • •

KENTUCKY

 Emergency Medical Services Branch
Division of Health Systems Development
Department for Health Services
Cabinet for Human Resources
275 East Main Street
Frankfort, KY 40621
(502) 564-8963
Marcia A. Burklow, State Training Director

EMT-FIRST RESPONDER

Hours of training: 40 hours
Certification requirements: One written, one practical skills exam for initial certification.
Recertification requirements: Every 3 years. Requirements include at least 12 hours of continuing education, plus current CPR certification.

BASIC EMT

Hours of training: 120 hours.
Certification requirements: 4 written exams, 1 final skill exam for initial certification.
Recertification requirements: Every 2 years. Requirements include at least 24 hours of continuing education (a minimum of 12 of the 24 hours shall be in practical skills) plus current CPR certification. Plans are underway to amend present statutes and regulations to allow a written test and skills examination as an option to continuing education hours for recertification requirements. April 1991, automatic or semiautomatic external defibrillation training introduced as optional training for the EMT. November 1991, regulations adopted to allow optional training for the EMT in the maintenance and discontinuation of a pre-established peripheral IV infusion of a stable patient during an interfacility or facility to home transport.

PARAMEDIC

Hours of training: 1,500 (total clinical and didactic).
Certification requirements: Within a 30-month period the trainee must complete the training curriculum, field clinical evaluation of at least 5 months' duration, must receive a written recommendation of the medical advisor, and must pass a written, oral, and practical examination.
Recertification requirements: Must obtain 40 hours of inservice training annually and must pass renewal examination within 30 months of issuance of last certificate.
Responsible certification agency: Kentucky State Board of Medical Licensure
Reciprocity: No full reciprocity. An EMT currently certified in another state may challenge Kentucky written and practical exams; must submit a letter of request, along with proof of current certification in another state. Plans are underway to revise the regulations to also accept current National Registry certification to be eligible to take the challenge exam. Regulations for a re-entry challenge exam for previously Kentucky-certified EMTs whose certification has been expired no more than 5 years were adopted in March 1989. A Paramedic currently certified in another state may challenge oral, written, and practical exams upon submission of a letter from a potential employer and ALS medical director.

SALARY RANGES

Basic EMT: $9,000/year-$22,000/year
Paramedic: $9,500/year-$29,000/year

• • •

LOUISIANA

Bureau of Emergency Medical Services
Department of Health and Hospitals
Office of Public Health
PO Box 94215
1201 Capitol Access Road, 5th Floor
Baton Rouge, LA 70804
(504) 342-4881
Nancy Bourgeois, Director

BASIC EMT

Hours of training: 110
Certification requirements: Successful completion of state-approved National Standard DOT training program. Successful completion of the National Registry Basic EMT written exam and a State Basic EMT practical exam in accordance with National Registry guidelines. Must have evidence of residence and/or employment in Louisiana.
Recertification requirements: Maintain National Registry certification according to Registry guidelines.

INTERMEDIATE EMT

Hours of training: 80-100 didactic, 80 clinical, 80 field internship.
Certification requirements: Successful completion of state-approved training program adhering to DOT National Standard Curriculum for EMT-I, successful completion of National Registry EMT-I exam (practical and written), documentary evidence of residence and/or employment in Louisiana, submission of an application for a certificate from Louisiana State Board of Medical Examiners.
Recertification requirements: Maintain current National Registry certification according to Registry guidelines.

PARAMEDIC

Hours of training: 350 didactic, 240 clinical, 240 field internship.
Certification requirements: Successful completion of state-approved training program adhering to DOT National Standard Curriculum for EMT-P, successful completion of the National Registry EMT-P exam (practical and written), documentary evidence of residence and/or employment in Louisiana, submission of an application for a certificate from the Louisiana State Board of Medical Examiners.
Recertification requirements: Maintain National Registry certification according to Registry guidelines.
Responsible certification agency: Basic Emt - certified by Office of Public Health, Emergency Medical Services
Intermediate Paramedic EMTs: Louisiana State Board of Medical Examiners.
Reciprocity: Full reciprocity with National Registry only.

SALARY RANGES

Basic EMT: $10,000/year-$17,000/year
Intermediate EMT:$14,000/year-$20,000/year
Paramedic: $17,000/year-$25,000/year

• • •

MAINE

Maine Emergency Medical Service
16 Edison Drive
Augusta, ME 04330
(207) 287-3953
Kevin McGinnis, MPS, EMT-P, Director

BASIC EMT

Hours of training: 111
Certification requirements: Completion of MEMS-approved course for Basic EMTs, CPR certification, and MEMS practical/written exams.
Recertification requirements: Completion of MEMS-approved refresher course or MEMS continuing education hours equivalent; current CPR certification; passing of MEMS written and practical test.

EMS INTERMEDIATE

Hours of training: 124
Certification requirements: Completion of MEMS-approved course; Basic EMT licensure (or equivalent BLS training provided in a combined BLS/ALS original course)
Recertification requirements: Completion of BLS/ALS combined refresher or continuing education hours at this level; current CPR certification; pass practical/written exams or skills lab.

EMT CRITICAL CARE

Hours of training: 300
Certification requirements: training and practical and written testing.
Recertification requirements: training/continuing education and practical and written testing or skills lab.

PARAMEDIC

Hours of training: 400
Certification requirements: Completion MEMS-approved combined BLS/ALS refresher or continuing education hours at this level; current CPR certification; pass MEMS practical/written exams or skills lab.
Responsible licensure agency: Maine Board of Emergency Medical Services
Reciprocity: No automatic reciprocity is granted. Out-of-state Paramedic credentials will be promptly reviewed. If out-of-state tests and training are equivalent, a license will be granted.

SALARY RANGES

N/A

• • •

MARYLAND

Maryland Institute e for Emergency Medical Services Systems
636 West Lombard Street Baltimore, MD 21201-1528
(410) 706-5074
Ronald B. Schaefer, State Training Director

BASIC EMT

Hours of training: 110 minimum.
Certification requirements: written and practical exams.
Recertification requirements: Every 3 years through an approved EMT-A refresher program. Reciprocity for EMT-A with most states and National Registry.

CARDIAC RESCUE TECHNICIAN

Hours of training: Basic EMT hours plus minimum of 160 hours
Recertification requirements: 10 hours of CE a year, affiliation with an ALS unit, and demonstration of skills proficiency.

PARAMEDIC

Hours of training: Basic EMT hours plus a minimum of 300 hours.
Recertification requirements: Successful recertification of National Registry EMP-P; affiliation with an ALS unit.
Responsible certification agency: The Maryland Institute for Emergency Medical Services Systems certifies EMT-As. The Maryland Board of Physician Quality Assurance certifies CRTs and EMT-Ps.
Reciprocity: Equal training and testing based on national DOT objectives.

SALARY RANGES

Basic EMT: $14,000/year-$22,000/year
Intermediate EMT: $14,000/year-$28,000/year
Paramedic: $24,000/year-$35,000/year

• • •

MASSACHUSETTS

Department of Public Health
Office of Emergency Medical Services
150 Tremont Street, 2nd Floor
Boston, MA 02111
(617) 727-8338
Louise Goyette, Director

BASIC EMT

Hours of training: Effective 11/85, 110-hour DOT curriculum as minimum
Certification requirements: Initial certification-pass course and state-administered written and practical examinations.
Twenty-hour refresher course and twenty-eight additional hours of continuing education every two years.

INTERMEDIATE EMT

Hours of training: 220
Certification requirements: Basic EMT certification, complete an approved course that includes: DOT curriculum at a minimum; hospital clinical practicum; field internship, 80 hours minimum. There are minimum skills performance numbers for hospital and field.
Recertification requirements: Annual CPR recertification, active EMT-S must have "credentials" (that is, authorization-to-practice) from system physician medical director, thirty-hour refresher course, and twenty-eight hours of additional continuing education every two years.

PARAMEDIC

Hours of training: 800-1500
Certification requirements: Basic EMT certification, ACLS certification, complete an approved P course and includes: DOT curriculum at a minimum; hospital clinical practicums in ED, IV, OB/Gyn, or (for ETT), pedi/neonate, psych; field internship, 80 hours minimum. There are minimum skill performance numbers for hospital and field.
Recertification requirements: Annual CPR recertification, active EMT-Ps must have "credentials" (authorization-to-practice) from system physician medical director, ACLS, 48-hour refresher course, and 25 hours of additional continuing education every two years.
Responsible certification agency: Commonwealth of Massachusetts, Office of Emergency Medical Service.
Reciprocity: Out-of-state Basic EMTs must complete written and practical examinations. All Advanced EMTs must complete written and/or practical examinations.

SALARY RANGES

Basic EMT: $15,000/year-$23,000/year
Intermediate EMT: $16,000/year-$25,000/year
Paramedic: $20,000/year-$32,000/year

• • •

MICHIGAN

Michigan Department of Public Health
Division of Emergency Medical Services
PO Box 30195
Lansing, MI 48909
(517) 335-8570
John Hubinger, State Chief,
Training/Education/Trauma

BASIC EMT

Hours of training: 145
Licensure requirements: Pass state written and practical examinations
Relicensure requirements: 30 credits ongoing education or DOT refresher course

INTERMEDIATE EMT

Hours of training: 85
Licensure requirements: Pass state written and practical examinations
Relicensure requirements: 30 credits ongoing education or DOT refresher course.

PARAMEDIC

Hours of training: 85
Licensure requirements: Pass state written and practical examinations
Relicensure requirements: 45 ongoing education hours or DOT refresher course.
Responsible certification agency: Department of Public Health
Reciprocity: All states, provided person is currently licensed (in good standing) elsewhere., Must participate in and pass Michigan examination.

SALARY RANGES

N/A

• • •

MINNESOTA

Minnesota Department of Health
717 South East Delaware Street
PO Box 9441
Minneapolis, MN 55440
(612) 623-5482
Jennifer Deschaine, Chief, EMS Section

BASIC EMT

Hours of training: 110 hours of instruction with a minimum of 100 hours classroom and 10 hours field training.
Certification requirements: State-approved course based on DOT standards. NREMT exam following initial EMT course, practical and written test approved by health commissioner.
Recertification: Every 2 years. State recertification required; NREMT recertification optional.

INTERMEDIATE EMT

Hours of training: at least 52 hours including both classroom instruction and practical skills, plus supervised clinical and field experience.
Certification requirements: State-approved courses based on DOT standards. Must be currently certified as EMT-Basic. NREMT-I exam. Rule making which may change these requirements is underway.
Recertification requirements: Every 2 years. State recertification required; NREMT-I recertification optional.

PARAMEDIC

Hours of training: State-approved courses based on DOT standards.
Certification: NREMT-P exam required.
Recertification requirements: Every two years. State recertification with continuing education and physician verification of skills are required; NREMT- P recertification optional.
Responsible certification agency. State coordinates all exams. Certification group includes physicians. State law requires each EMS System to have a medical director or advisor.
Reciprocity: Minnesota recognizes national board certification (NREMT) at basic, intermediate, and paramedic levels. State certificate is issued upon request to individuals holding NREMT certification.

SALARY RANGES

Basic EMT: volunteer to $20,000/year.
Intermediate EMT: volunteer to $20,000/year.
Paramedic: volunteer from $16,000/year-$35,000/year. All ranges are estimated.

• • •

MISSISSIPPI

Office of EMS
Mississippi State Department of Health
PO Box 1700
2423 North State Street
Jackson, MS 39215-1700
(601) 987-3880
Wade Spruill, Jr., Director

BASIC EMT

Hours of training: 110
Certification requirements: We are a National Registry state (same requirements as National Registr)y.
Recertification requirements: Same requirements as National Registry.

INTERMEDIATE EMT

Hours of training: didactic 150, clinical 40, field 40.
Certification requirements: We are a National Registry state (same requirements as National Registry).
Recertification requirements: Same requirements as National Registry, plus defibrillation.

PARAMEDIC

Hours of training: didactic 500, clinical 250, field 150.
Certification requirements: We are a National Registry state (same requirements as National Registry).
Recertification requirements: Same requirements as National Registry.
Responsible certification agency: State Division

of EMS. This certification group includes a physician. A physician adviser is required for basic services.
Reciprocity: Applicants must be Nationally Registered.

SALARY RANGES

N/A

• • •

MISSOURI

Bureau of Emergency Medical Services
1738 East Elm
PO Box 570
Jefferson City, MO 65102
(314) 751-6356
Robert W. Renick, State Training and Licensing Coordinator

BASIC EMT

Hours of training: 124 class hours, 24 clinical hours.
Certification requirements: Approved EMT-Basic course, then pass state practical and written exams.
Recertification requirements: Every 3 years through either continuing education or refresher training and state testing.

PARAMEDIC

Hours of training: 850-1500 hours.
Certification: All training entities meet or surpass DOT guidelines. Must pass state written and practical examination.
Recertification requirements: Every 3 years with either continuing education or refresher training and state testing.
Responsible certification agency. State Bureau of Emergency Medical Services, Missouri Department of Health.
Reciprocity. DOT EMT-Basic or DOT EMT-P minimum curriculum training; National Registry and/or state certification; all must pass Missouri state written examination.

SALARY RANGES

Basic EMT: rural average, $13,748, urban average, $22,981.
Paramedic: rural average, $18,583, urban average, $26,486.

• • •

MONTANA

Emergency Medical Services Bureau
Montana Department of Health and Environmental Sciences
PO Box 200901
Cogswell Building
Helena, MT 59620-0901
(406) 444-3895

BASIC EMT

Hours of training: minimum 110.
Certification requirements: National Registry, written/practical examination.
Recertification requirements: National Registry, current CPR, 48 hours CE, 24 hours refresher, current affiliation with prehospital care service.

INTERMEDIATE

Hours of training: minimum of 116
Certification requirements: National Registry, written and practical, and Montana written and practical for intubation and defibrillation.
Recertification requirements: National Registry, current CPR, 36 hours CE, 36 hours refresher, current affiliation with prehospital-care service, skills sign-off by MD.

PARAMEDIC

Hours of training: minimum of 780
Certification requirements: National Registry, written and practical.
Recertification requirements: National Registry, current CPR, 24 hours CE, 48 hours refresher, current affiliation with prehospital-care service, skills sign-off by MD, ACLS current
Responsible certification agency: Montana Board of Medical Examiners.
Reciprocity: EMT-Basic, National Registry;

Emergency Medical Technicians

EMT-I, National registry plus intubation and defibrillation exam; EMT-P National Registry.

SALARY RANGES

N/A

• • •

NEBRASKA

Nebraska State Department of Health
Division of EMS
PO Box 95007
Lincoln, NE 68509
(402) 471-2158
Bob Leopold, Director

BASIC EMT

Hours of training: 110 hours.
Certification requirements: Successful completion of DOT standards.
Recertification requirements: Every 3 years (30 hours continuing education to renew certificate of competency to act as ambulance attendant)
EMT-A/D. training: 7 hours plus EMT-A.
Recertification: Every 3 years
EMT-A/M. training: 7 hours + EMT-A.
Recertification: Every 3 years
EMT-I/V training: 22 hours. Recertification every 3 years

ADVANCE EMT-I

Hours of training: 172 plus field training.
Recertification requirements: Every 2 years.

PARAMEDIC

Hours of training: 415 hours plus field training.
Certification requirements: Successful completion of DOT standards.
Recertification requirements: Every 2 years. All advanced EMT-I-II, and Paramedics are required to take 96 hours continuing education every 2 years.

EMT-D

Hours of training: successful completion of 14-hour course devised by state AEMC Board, plus 2-hour certifying examination.
Recertification requirements: Must complete 6 hours of approved classroom instruction and 24 hours of clinical experience providing advanced emergency care every 2 years.
Responsible certification agency: Department of Health. A physician is included in the certification group.
Reciprocity: Full reciprocity (no exams) for EMT-A. Law effective after 8/26/83 allows reciprocity for Paramedics. Must meet full DOT and have passed National Registry. Need not be certified.

SALARY RANGES

Basic EMT: volunteer to $16,000/year
Intermediate EMT: $12,000/year-$18,000/year
Paramedic: $15,000/year-$28,000/year

• • •

NEVADA

EMS and Trauma Systems
Nevada State Health Division
Room 204, Kinkead Building
505 East King Street
Carson City, NV 89710
(702) 687-3065

BASIC EMT

Hours of training: 110
Certification requirements: Successful course completion and passing a written and practical exam.
Recertification requirements: DOT refresher course or provide documentation of attendance in programs of continuing medical education and training approved by the emergency medical services section of the health division. The requirement for attendance at such programs of education and training is not less than 30 hours.

INTERMEDIATE EMT

Hours of training: N/A
Certification requirements: Successful passage of course, clinical experience, and testing. Renew EMT, provide proof of skill retention and testing. Employed by an operator of a service or

firefighting agency endorsed to operate at the intermediate or advanced level of care for renewal.

PARAMEDIC

Hours of training: N/A
Certification requirements: Successful completion or course, field internship and testing.
Recertification requirements: 40 hours CME every 2 years and certification ACLS or paramedic refresher curriculum. Also must demonstrate ALS skills annually to the Service Medical Director. May not renew if not a licensed ambulance attendant.
Responsible certification agency: State Health Division for all of state except Clark County (Las Vegas area) and Washoe County (Reno area).
Reciprocity: Valid current certification from state of origin or National Registry.

SALARY RANGES

Basic EMT, $15,000/year.
Intermediate EMT, $18,000/year.
Paramedic, $22,000-$38,000/year.

• • •

NEW HAMPSHIRE

Division of Public Health Services
Bureau of EMS
H&W Building, 6 Hazen Drive
Concord, NH 03301
(603) 271-4568
Liza Burrill, State Training Coordinator

BASIC EMT

Hours of training: 110
Certification requirements: Must met National Registry requirements.
Recertification requirements: Refresher course, including practical and written exams.

INTERMEDIATE EMT

Hours of training: 85
Certification requirements: Must become nationally registered and state registered.
Recertification requirements: National Registry requirements and state re-registration

PARAMEDIC

Hours of training: Two-year associate's degree program and 800+ hours in a nondegree program.
Certification requirements: Meet National Registry requirements and become state registered.
Recertification requirements: Maintain National Registration and apply for state re-registration.
Responsible certification agency: National Registry.

SALARY RANGES

Basic EMT: from $18,000/year.
Intermediate EMT: from $20,000/year.
Paramedic: from $22,000/year.

• • •

NEW JERSEY

New Jersey Office of Emergency Medical Services
300 Whitehead Road, CN367
Trenton, NJ 08625-0367
(609) 588-3720
Robert S Dinetz, State Education Coordinator

BASIC EMT

Hours of training: More than 120
Certification requirements: Written and practical examinations.
Recertification requirements: 48 continuing education credits every 3 years.

EMT-DEFIBRILLATOR

Hours of training: 8 hours of didactic/clinical training in semiautomatic defibrillation.
Certification requirements: NJ certified EMT-A, state EMT-D written and practical examinations.
Recertification requirements: Annual recertification through continuing education and clinical competency.

PARAMEDIC

Hours of training: 350 didactic and 600 clinical with field internship.
Certification requirements: Continuing education plus skills competency requirements. Certification examinations are the National Registry written and practical examinations.
Recertification requirements: Every 2 years. Recertification is based on continuing education, ACLS certification, and clinical competency.
Responsible certification agency: The New Jersey Department of Health, Office of Emergency Medical Services. ALS systems have medical directors.
Reciprocity: Valid DOT-approved EMT training from other states is recognized. Those holding EMT certification from New York and Pennsylvania are automatically recognized and do no need to seek "legal recognition" or become dually certified. Paramedics should be full 15-Module DOT course and need to do an internship with a sponsoring New Jersey MICU hospital, as well as pass National Registry written and practical examinations within one year.

SALARY RANGES

Basic EMT: $12,000-$23,000/year.
Paramedic: $20,000-$30,000/year

• • •

NEW MEXICO

 Department of Health
PO Box 26110
1190 St. Francis Drive
Santa Fe, NM 87502-6110
(505) 827-2509
Kevin Henson, State Training Coordinator

BASIC EMT

Hours of training: 120 hours minimum.
Certification requirements: Upon successful course completion, candidate must pass state licensure examination (written and practical).
Recertification requirements: Every 2 years, including 24-hour refresher course, current CPR certification and 24 contact hours of state-approved continuing education, of which at least 12 hours must be medically oriented from the EMT-B curriculum. By early 1994, it is anticipated that semi-automatic defibrillation, pulse oximetry, automated glucometry, and use of the multi-lumen airway, i.e., PTL, will be added to the curriculum and scope of practice.

EMT-INTERMEDIATE

Hours of training: 72.
Certification requirements: Successful course completion and written and practical state licensing examination.
Recertification requirements: Basic refresher (24 hours). Intermediate refresher (16 hours). Bureau-approved CEs, 30 hours, of which 15 must be medically oriented and 6 specific to Intermediate skills. By early1994 it is anticipated that epinephrine, (l:l,000) S.C., and multi-lumen airways, i.e., PTL, will be added. There is also discussion about adding albuterol.

PARAMEDIC

Hours of training: 932 total (560 didactic, 192 clinical, 180 internship).
Certification requirements: Successful course completion and National Registry licensing examination.
Recertification requirements: EMT-P refresher, 48 hours approved CE of which 24 must be medically oriented and at least 12 must be specific to paramedic skills and current ACLS.
Responsible licensing agency: The Primary Care and EMS Bureau of the New Mexico Department of Health.
Reciprocity: At this time, NM fully recognizes 38 states as equivalent at the Basic level, provided the individual is in the first two years of licensure. This means no state exam is required. All others must take the appropriate state licensing examinations.

SALARY RANGES

N/A

• • •

NEW YORK

Emergency Medical Services Program
New York State Department of Health - EMS
74 State Street
Albany, NY 12237-0616
(518) 474-0911
Edward Wronski, Associate Director

CERTIFIED FIRST RESPONDER

Hours of training: 36 hours didactic/labs.
Certification requirements: At least 16 years of age, successfully complete the course, pass the state practical skills examination, pass New York State CFR certifying examination.
Recertification requirements: Every 3 years refresher and exams.

BASIC EMT

Hours of training: 109 minimum.
Certification requirements: At least 18 years of age, successfully complete the course, pass the state practical skills examination, pass New York State EMT certifying examination.
Recertification requirements: Must recertify every three years, pass practical skills examination, pass New York State EMT certifying examination.

EMT-DEFIB

Hours of training: 6 minimum
Certification requirements: At least 18 years of age and hold a current EMT card. Must complete the course, pass a local written and state-approved practical skills exam.
Recertification requirements: Every 3 years concurrent with EMT, must take a combined EMT/EMT-D refresher.

INTERMEDIATE EMT

Hours of training: 75 hours didactic/labs, 48 hours clinical and complete an internship.

EMT-CRITICAL CARE

Hours of training: Minimum 128 hours didactic, 62 hours clinical
Minimum requirements: Satisfactorily complete an A-EMT course, complete an internship, and pass a state practical skills exam and a state certifying written exam.
Recertification requirements: Every 3 years. Must pass a practical skills exam and state certifying written exam.

PARAMEDIC

Hours of training: minimum 300 hours didactic, 232 hours clinical. Complete an internship.
Certification requirements: Satisfactorily complete an EMT-P refresher course and pass a state practical skills and the state certifying written exam.
Recertification requirements: N/A
Responsible certification agency: New York State Department of Health
Reciprocity: EMT-most; Advanced EMT test required of all candidates who are not National Registered and hold a current state certification

SALARY RANGES

N/A

• • •

NORTH CAROLINA

North Carolina Office of Emergency Medical Service
PO Box 29530
Raleigh, NC 27626-0530
(919) 733-2285
Ed Browning, State Training Director

BASIC EMT

Hours of training: 110
Certification requirements: 18 years old, complete an approved training program following EMT National Standard Curriculum, pass state written and practical examination.
Recertification requirements: Complete 27-hour refresher course or an approved 72-hour continuing education program. Pass practical skills examination. Revised educational requirements established January 1, 1994

EMT-DEFIB

Hours of training: 13
Certification requirements: Current NC EMT, affiliation with EMT-D service or approved first responder organization, ALS skills performance exam by local medical director, pass state administered/approved BLS practical exam, pass state EMT-D written exam.
Recertification requirements: 36 hours of approved continuing education annually, ALS skills exam by local medical director, pass state-administered/approved BLS practical exam, pass state-approved/administered EMT-D written exam or pass state-approved local examination. Revised educational requirements will be established January 1, 1994.

INTERMEDIATE EMT

Hours of training: 98
Certification requirements: Current NC EMT, affiliation with EMT-I service, physical capability and suitable character, complete approved training program, ALS skills performance exam by local medical director, oral interview panel in local program, pass state BLS practical exam, pass state EMT-I written exam.
Recertification requirements: 48 hours continuing education annually, ALS skills exam by local medical director, pass state BLS practical exam, pass state EMT-I written exam or pass state-approved local examination. Revised educational requirements will be established January 1, 1994.

EMT ADVANCED INTERMEDIATE

Hours of training: 216
Certification requirements: Current North Carolina EMT, affiliation with EMT-AI service, physical capability and suitable character, ALS skills exam administered by local medical director, oral interview panel in local program, pass state BLS practical exam, pass state EMT-AI written exam.
Recertification requirements: 48 hours continuing education annually, ALS skills exam by local medical director, pass state BLS practical exam, pass state EMT-AI written exam or pass state-approved local examination. Revised educational requirements will be established January 1, 1994.

PARAMEDIC

Hours of training: 558
Certification requirements: Current NC EMT, affiliation with EMT-P service, physical capability and suitable character, ALS skills exam by local medical director, oral interview panel in local program, pass state BLS practical exam, pass state EMT-P written exam.
Recertification requirements: 48 hours continuing education annually, ALS skills exam by local medical director, pass state BLS practical exam, pass state EMT-P written exam or pass state-approved local examination. Revised educational requirements will be established January 1, 1994.
Responsible certification agency: NC Medical Care Commission is responsible for certifying EMTs; NC Board of Medical Examiners is responsible for certifying EMT-D, EMT-I, EMT-AI, and EMT-P.
Reciprocity: Full reciprocity for out-of-state personnel who hold current certification from state that meets or exceeds NC training requirements at appropriate level.

SALARY RANGES

Basic EMT: $9,500/year-$13,000/year.
Intermediate EMT: $10,500/year-$14,000/year.
Paramedic: $14,500/year-$22,000/year.

• • •

NORTH DAKOTA

 Division of Emergency Health Services
North Dakota State Department of
Health and Consolidated Laboratories
600 East Boulevard Avenue
Bismarck, ND 58505-0200
(701) 224-2388
Larry Weber, State Training Coordinator

BASIC EMT

Hours of training: 110
Certification requirements: National Registry certification.
Recertification requirements: Biannual CPR, 48 hours continuing education, 24-hour refresher course and written and practical testing.

INTERMEDIATE EMT

Hours of training: 100
Certification requirements: National Registry requirements and state licensure, which consists of submission of a physician preceptor form and $10 annual license fee.
Recertification requirements: National Registry requirements.

PARAMEDIC

Hours of training: 444 plus a state-mandated 300-hour field internship with a North Dakota-licensed ALS ambulance service.
Certification requirements: National Registry requirements and state licensure, which consists of submission of a physician preceptor form and $10 annual license fee.
Recertification requirements: National Registry requirements.
Responsible certification agency: Division of Emergency Health Services and National Registry.
Reciprocity: National Registry certification of Basic EMTs, EMT-Intermediates, and EMT-Paramedics.

SALARY RANGES

Basic EMT: Volunteer to $20,000/year.
Intermediate EMT: Volunteer to $20,000/year
Paramedic: Volunteer to $28,000/year.

• • •

OHIO

Ohio Department of Public Safety
240 Parsons Avenue
PO Box 7167
Columbus, OH 43266-0563
(614) 466-9447
Linda Ishler, EMS Liaison

BASIC EMT

Hours of training: 110
Certification requirements: Successful completion of U.S./DOT National Standard curriculum for Emergency Medical Technician-Ambulance through programs accredited by the Department of Education. Individual accredited by the Department of Education. Individual accredited programs may exceed the minimum hours as needed to meet the objectives. National Registry examination as of January 1990.
Recertification requirements: Every 3 years, successful completion of U.S./DOT National Standard curriculum for Basic refresher course and functioning as an EMT-A.

ADVANCED EMT

Hours of training: Minimum of 60 hours of didactic in addition to in-hospital training.
Certification requirements: Successful completion of U.S./DOT National Standard curriculum for the intermediate EMT through programs accredited by the Department of Education. Individual accredited programs may exceed the minimum hours as needed to meet U.S./DOT objectives. National Registry examination.
Recertification requirements: Minimum of 6 hours of clinical and classroom instruction during each year of the 3-year certification period, functioning as an Advanced EMT during the certification period; successful completion of Basic EMT refresher course.

ADVANCED-=EPINEPHRINE

Hours of training: Minimum of 6 hours
Certification requirements: same as Advanced EMT plus Ohio Department of Education approved training program in the administration of epinephrine.
Recertification requirements: In addition to requirements for Advanced EMT, 3 hours of continuing education each year in the administration, pharmacology of epinephrine, and the assessment of and treatment for persons suffering allergic reactions. Must be approved by medical director.

ADVANCED-DEFIB

Hours of training: In addition to advanced skills, minimum of 20 hours of training.
Certification requirements: Same as Advanced EMT plus Ohio Department of Education approved training program in defibrillation.
Recertification requirements: In addition to requirements for Advanced EMT, 4 hours of

continuing education annually in monitoring-defibrillations skills. Must be approved by Medical Director.

EMT-PARAMEDIC

Hours of training: 500 hours
Certification requirements: Successful completion of U.S/DOT National Standard curriculum for Emergency Medical Technician-Paramedic through programs accredited by the Department of Education. Individual accredited programs may exceed the minimum hours as needed to meet these objectives. National Registry examination.
Recertification requirements: Successful completion of U.S./DOT course or successful completion of a 48-hour paramedic refresher course; current Advanced Cardiac Life Support (provider and/or instructor) by American Heart Association or an equivalent by a program accredited by Department of Education; 72 hours of continuing education during the 3-year certification period (no less than 20 in any one year). All hours must be approved by a medical director or a medical advisory board. Must be currently functioning in the field of emergency medicine.
Responsible certification agency: Ohio Department of Public Safety Division of Emergency Medical Services.
Reciprocity: National Registry examination is used at all levels.

SALARY RANGES

N/A

• • •

OKLAHOMA

 Oklahoma State Department of Health, EMS Division
1000 North East 10th Street Oklahoma City, OK 73117-1299
(405) 271-4062

BASIC EMT

Hours of training: Minimum of 124 hours (100 didactic, 24 clinical)

Licensure requirements: successful completion of a state-approved Basic EMT training program and successful completion of state-administered National Registry written and practical skills examinations results in co-issuance of Oklahoma state license and National Registration at the EMT-A (Basic) level.
Recertification requirements: Every 2 years, candidate must complete a minimum 24-hour EMT Basic refresher, 48 hours of approved continuing education; and annual CPR refresher (AHA or ARC). Fee requirements: $50 for initial licensure, retests, and National Registration (NR fee of $15 is paid by state), and a $10 state renewal fee every two years (does not include NR re-registration).

INTERMEDIATE EMT

Hours of training: Minimum of 63 didactic hours and 128 clinical hours.
Certification requirement: Must be currently licensed as an EMT-Basic, successfully complete a state-approved Intermediate training program and successfully complete the NR Intermediate written and practical. In addition, successful completion of the Oklahoma state practical for extra skills leads to co-issuance of NR Intermediate and Oklahoma license at EMT Intermediate leave. Fee requirements: $475 for initial licensure, re-tests, and NR registration (NR fee is paid by state), and a $15 state renewal fee every two years (does not include NR re-registration).

PARAMEDIC

Hours of training: Minimum of 310 didactic hours and 358clinical hours above the hours required for EMT Intermediate.
Certification requirements: Must be currently licensed as an EMT Basic, successfully complete a state-approved Paramedic training program, and successfully complete the National Registry Paramedic written and practical examinations. Completion of the above leads to the co-issuance of National Registration and an Oklahoma state Paramedic license.
Recertification requirements: Same as for National re-registration. Fee requirements: $85 for initial licensure and National Registration (NR fee is paid by state) and a $20 state renewal fee every two years (does not include NR re-registration).

Responsible certification agency: The OSDHEMS Division

Reciprocity: Technicians who are currently certified with the National Registry are allowed to apply for Oklahoma EMT licensure, without further testing. Exception is the EMT-Intermediate, who must show proof of Oklahoma EMT-Intermediate requirements and pass the Oklahoma examination before licensure. All others must successfully complete National Registry examination before licensure is granted in Oklahoma. A nine-month temporary permit is available until national registration is obtained for $150 plus some additional restrictions. This is for EMTs who only have a state license or certification (not nationally registered).

SALARY RANGES

Basic EMT: $9,600/year-$15,360/year.
Intermediate EMT: $10,000/year-$18,000/year.
Paramedic: $15,000/year-$25,000/year

• • •

OREGON

Emergency Medical Services and Systems
Oregon Health Division
800 North East Oregon Street #607
Portland, OR 97232
(503) 731-4011

EMT-BASIC

Hours of training: 118.
Certification requirements: Initial certification, completion of approved course, make application, submit $55 fee, pass both written and practical examinations.
Recertification requirements: 25 hours continuing education in specified subject areas every 2 years, plus quarterly AED/SAD.

EMT-INTERMEDIATE

Hours of training: 76 lecture, 44 laboratory.
Certification requirements: Initial certification, completion of approved course, make application, submit $75 fee, pass both written and practical examinations.
Recertification requirements: 45 hours continuing education in specified subject areas every 2 years, including quarterly AED/SAD requalification.

EMT-PARAMEDIC

Hours of training: 255 didactic, 240 clinical, 200 field internship (including 40 ALS ambulance calls).
Certification requirements: Initial certification, completion of approved course, make application, submit $165 fee, pass both written and practical examinations.
Recertification requirements: 75 hours continuing education in specified subject areas every 2 years.
Reciprocity: In accordance with complex regulations. Generally, EMT-Basic reciprocity is not complicated once additional training is obtained for items unique to Oregon scope of practice. No reciprocity at EMT-Intermediate level due to no known equivalent certification. At EMT-Paramedic level, provisional certification is granted to NREMT-Ps pending on completion of state written and practical exams (policy is currently under review.) Final reciprocity for EMT-Ps usually involves additional training in pediatrics/neonatology.

• • •

PENNSYLVANIA

Division of Emergency Medical Services Systems
Pennsylvania Department of Health
PO Box 90
Harrisburg, PA 17108
(717) 787-8740

BASIC EMT

Hours of training: 126
Certification requirements: Complete training program and successfully pass a 3-station practical skills exam involving 9 skills, and written knowledge exams.
Recertification requirements: At a minimum pass the skills (3-station practical involving 9 skills) and written knowledge exams with a passing grade of 70 percent.

PARAMEDIC

Hours of training: Minimum of 212 didactic and 232 clinical hours set by course medical director, programs average 1,000 hours.
Certification requirements: Attain 75 percent on state written certification exam.
Recertification requirements: Completion of continuing education requirements set by system medical director and skill maintenance requirements. Completion of EMT skill exam and passing state written recertification exam with a score of 75 percent.
Responsible certification agency: Division of Emergency Health Services, PA Department of Health
Reciprocity: Full EMT reciprocity with MD, WA, WV, NJ, NY. These EMTs need to present a current EMT certification, a need for certification, and verification of having completed skills and knowledge exams for certification. All other EMTs must take our skills and knowledge exams. Paramedic: No direct reciprocity. Certification from another state paramedic training program must meet or exceed Pennsylvania's program. Must be Pennsylvania EMT-certified before granting paramedic reciprocity. Completion of skill evaluation and state certification exam.

SALARY RANGES

N/A

• • •

RHODE ISLAND

 Division of Emergency Medical Services
Rhode Island Department of Health
3 Capitol Hill, Room 404
Providence, RI 02908-5097
(401) 277-2401
Peter Leary, Chief

BASIC EMT

Hours of training: 120
Certification requirements: Written and practical exam.
Recertification requirements: Successful completion of DOT standard refresher training program every three years.

INTERMEDIATE

Hours of training: 27. The EMT-I or Intermediate program was consolidated into the EMT-A course as described above in January 1989. While existing EMT-I licenses are renewed, no new EMT-I licenses are issued.
Recertification requirements: Successful completion of DOT standard refresher training program every three years.

EMT-CARDIAC

Hours of training: 170
Certification requirements: Pass a written and practical exam.
Recertification requirements: Successful completion of DOT standard refresher training program every three years.

EMT-PARAMEDIC

Hours of training: 1,414
Certification requirements: National Registry Paramedic written and practical examinations.
Recertification requirements: Maintenance of current NREMT-P certification.
Responsible certification agency: Rhode Island Department of Health
Reciprocity: Those certified from other states may challenge the Rhode Island EMTs at examination providing that such training from other state was conducted in compliance with DOT National Standard curricula.

SALARY RANGES

Basic EMT: $18,000/year-$25,000/year.
Intermediate EMT: $18,000/year-$25,000/year.
EMT-Cs: $20,000/year-$28,000/year

• • •

SOUTH CAROLINA

South Carolina Department of Health
and Environmental Control
2600 Bull Street
Columbia, SC 29201
(803) 737-7204
Albert M. Futrell, Jr., Director

BASIC-EMT

Hours of training: 117 hours theory and 10 hours in hospital emergency department or ambulance service training. EMT-Defibrillation has been approved at the provider level. Providers interested must apply to the division and meet the requirements for approval.
Certification requirements: Completion of course and pass state-administered written and practical examination.
Recertification requirements: Basic EMTs have the following options: (1) Complete 36 hours of a state-approved refresher course. Student must pass state-administered written and practical examination. (2) If the service has a state-approved In-Service Training (IST) program, students may complete 54 hours of state-approved IST. (3) Earn 36 hours of continuing education units. The medical control physician can examine the student in lieu of the state. Certification is good for 3 years.

INTERMEDIATE EMT

Hours of training: 54 hours theory and 16 hours clinical.
Certification requirements: Completion of course pass state-administered written and practical examinations.
Recertification requirements: I-EMTs have the following options: (1) Complete 36-hour state-approved continuing education. (2) Complete 36 hours state-approved refresher course (student must pass state-administered written and practical examination). (3) If the service has a state-approved IST program, students may complete 60 hours of IST. The medical control physician can examine the student in lieu of the state. Certification is good for 3 years.

PARAMEDIC

Hours of training: 212 hours of theory, 130 clinical, 72 field internship, and 10 hours testing.
Certification requirements: Completion of course and pass state-administered written and practical examination.
Recertification requirements: Paramedics have the following options: (1) Complete 48 hours state-approved continuing education. (2) Complete 48 hours at approved refresher course (students must pass state written and practical examinations). (3) If the service has a state-approved IST program students may complete 90 hours of IST. The medical control physician can examine the student in lieu of the state. Certification is good for 3 years.
Responsible certification agency: Division of MS.
Reciprocity: All EMTs who are certified by National Registry have full reciprocity. All advanced EMTs must provide course outline and take state written and practical examinations. All advanced EMTs must be sponsored by an emergency physician who must be the unit's medical control physician. The advanced EMTs must also be associated with an EMS provider. Out-of-state EMTs must furnish a copy of their certificate from their original state and must take the state-administered written and practical examinations.

SALARY RANGES

Basic EMT: $16,174/year-$19,968/year.
Intermediate EMT: $16,745/year-$20,677/year.
Paramedic: $18,806/year-$24,516/year.

• • •

SOUTH DAKOTA

South Dakota Department of Health
Emergency Medical Services
445 East Capitol Street
Pierre, SD 57501
(605) 773-4928
Robert J. Fines, State Training Director

BASIC EMT

Hours of training: 110
Certification requirements: To become certified a person must complete the class and pass the state-administered practical and written examinations.

Recertification requirements: 30 hours of refresher training every 2 years.

EMT-INTERMEDIATE

Hours of training: 40 hours didactic, 24 hours ride time with ALS service.
Certification requirements: Compete class, pass National Registry practical and written examinations for EMT-I.
Recertification requirements: 20 hours of refresher training annually.

EMT-SPECIAL SKILLS

Hours of training: 152 didactic, 96 hours ride time with ALS service, 65 hours in hospital.
Certification requirements: Complete class and pass state-administered practical and written examinations. Thirty hours of refresher training is needed annually for recertification.

PARAMEDIC

Hours of training: 360 hours didactic, 200 hours hospital clinical, 240 hours ride time with ALS service.
Certification requirements: Complete class and pass EMT-P National Registry written and practical examinations. National Registry requirements for recertification.
Responsible certification agency. EMT-3As are certified by the State Department of Health for a period of 2 years and all ALS personnel are licensed by the State Board of Medical and Osteopathic Examiners for a 1-year period. Medical directors are required for all ALS personnel, but not for EMT-As.
Reciprocity. EMT-A reciprocity is granted upon proof of current certification by another state or by the National Registry. They also must be living in South Dakota. All ALS personnel must be working for a South Dakota ambulance service and be currently certified by the National Registry.

SALARY RANGES

Basic EMT: $12,000/year-$20,000/year.
Intermediate EMT:$12,000/year-$20,000/year.
Paramedic $18,000/year-$30,000/year.

• • •

TENNESSEE

 Division of Emergency Medical Services
Tennessee Department of Health
287 Plus Park Boulevard
Nashville, TN 37247-0701
(615) 367-6278
Judy K. Gaffron
State Training Director

BASIC EMT

Hours of training: 150 minimum (150 didactic and at least 10 hours of clinical).
Licensure requirements: 18 years of age, high school graduate or GED, physician examination, completion of DOT curriculum and additional hours specific to Tennessee: 20 CEUs, score of 80 percent on written exam with successful examination in skills proficiency. Licensure and testing fees total $20 for initial testing.
Recertification requirements: Document continuing education of 20 CEUs or greater of score 80 percent or greater on the certification renewal examination. Must recertify every 2 years.

INTERMEDIATE EMT

Hours of training: Automatic or semiautomatic defibrillation, 6hours; IV therapy, 40 hours. Renewal every 2 years, 2.0 continuing education or renewal exam.

PARAMEDIC

Hours of training: 500 minimum clinical, didactic and field, and practicum.
Licensure requirements: Maintain Basic certification; complete state-approved EMT-P course; successful completion of state written and practical examinations; licensure and testing fees total $50 for initial test.
Recertification requirements: Renew every 2 years; renewal exam or 3.0 CEUs
Responsible licensure agency: Department of Health EMS Board.
Reciprocity: Reciprocity for EMTs and Paramedics is conditional upon meeting all applicable certification requirements.

SALARY RANGES

Basic EMT: $12,000/year-$25,000/year.
Paid Intermediate EMT: $12,000/year-$28,000/year.
Paramedic: $15,000/year- $35,000/year.

• • •

TEXAS

EMS Division
Texas Department of Health
1100 West 49th Street
Austin, TX 78756-3199
(512) 834-6740
Debra Bradford, State Training Coordinator

EMERGENCY CARE ATTENDANT

Hours of training: 40 minimal.
Certification requirements: Didactic test (50-question exam), and basic skills examination.
Recertification requirements: Every 4 years.

BASIC EMT

Hours of training: 120
Certification requirements: Didactic test (100-question test for EMT), and Basic skills examination.
Recertification requirements: Every 4 years.

INTERMEDIATE EMT.

Hours of training: 160
Certification requirements: 100-question didactic test and Basic and Advanced skills examination.
Recertification requirements: Every 4 years.
Responsible certification agency: Texas Department of Health
Reciprocity: We have full reciprocity. If candidates are currently registered from another state of with the National Registry, they will be certified for 1 year. At the end of that time, the certificate must have completed 25 percent of the required C.E. and pass written and skills examinations.

SALARY RANGES

Basic EMT: $12,000/year-$24,000/year
Intermediate EMT: $15,000/year-$27,000/year
Paramedic: $20,000/year-$30,000/year

• • •

UTAH

Bureau of Emergency Medical Services
Utah Department of Health
PO Box 16990
Salt Lake City, UT 84116-0990
(801) 538-6435
Jan M. Buttrey, Director

BASIC EMT

Hours of training: 120
Certification requirements: Complete course exams, written and practical.
Recertification requirements: Every 3 years by completing 60 hours of continuing medical education and successfully completing a written and practical test.
Special Modules: Defibrillation training (4 hours automatic, 12 hours manual).
Certification requirements: Completion of course, pass written and practical examinations.
Recertification requirements: Quarterly practical examination, pass written examination, IV training (25 hours).
Certification requirements: Completion of course, pass written and practical examination.
Recertification requirements: Pass written examination and physician evaluation.

INTERMEDIATE EMT

Hours of training: 50
Certification requirements: Completion of course and pass written test
Recertification requirements: 60 hours of continuing medical education during 3-year time period, pass written and practical test, and physician evaluation.
Defibrillator training: 16 hours manual, 6 hours automatic.
Certification requirements: Completion of course and pass written and practical test.
Recertification requirements: Pass written and practical test.

PARAMEDIC

Hours of training: 880
Certification requirements: Completion of course and pass written test
Recertification requirements: 25 hours of continuing medical education each year, plus ACLS certification, physician review, peer review, and pass written test. Recertification is required two years after initial certification and thereafter every four years.
Responsible certification agency: Utah Department of Health, EMS Bureau
Reciprocity: Reciprocity for applicant certified outside of the state of Utah will be based on the following considerations: must be 18 years of age or older, provide the department with a current copy of EMT certification, provide proof that the certifying course meets the standards established by the department, successfully complete the department's written and practical exam unless the state in which the applicant is currently certified has a reciprocal agreement with the department or is on the approved legal recognition list as promulgated by the State EMS Directors Association.

SALARY RANGES

Paramedic: $20,000/year-$30,000/year

• • •

VERMONT

Vermont Department t of Health
Emergency Medical Services Division
PO Box 70, 108 Cherry Street
Burlington, VT 05402
(802) 863-7310
Michael O'Keefe, State Training Coordinator

BASIC EMT

Hours of training: 110 minimum
Certification requirements: 18 years of age minimum, demonstrate need for certification, complete approved training program, pass written and practical examinations; training program follows National Standard curriculum.
Recertification requirements: Must recertify every year with 15 hours of continuing education; test, both written and practical, every 3 years.

INTERMEDIATE EMT

Hours of training: 60+
Certification requirements: Current Vermont EMT, be sponsored by a service licensed at the intermediate level or above, complete approved training program, and pass the state written and practical exams. Certification is good for 1 year.
Recertification requirements: Must recertify every year with 5 hours of continuing education, plus IV starts as required by their district. Retesting of both written and practical exams is not required unless requested by the local medical director.

DEFIBRILLATION

Hours of training: 15-20 hours above the EMT-I level. Certification and recertification requirements: Parallel other Advanced EMT certification levels. A pilot program using semiautomatic defibrillators is currently in place.

PARAMEDIC

Hours of training: 544
Certification requirements: Current Vermont EMT Basic certification, demonstrate need for Paramedic certification, complete approved training program, and pass National Registry written and practical examinations. For Vermont Paramedic certification, the individual must be affiliated with a Vermont EMS service that provides ALS at the Paramedic level as part of an approved prehospital ALS program.
Recertification requirements: Recertification every 2 years per National Registry standards.
Responsible certification agency: EMS Division, Vermont Department of Health.
Reciprocity: Any person with current certification from a state that meets Vermont's standards can be automatically certified as a Vermont EMT for one year. To continue certification the person must show 15 hours of continuing education and pass state written and practical examinations. We recognize only National Registered Paramedics. States and territories accepted: AK, CT, IL, IN, IA, KS, KY, LA, MA, ME, MD, MI, MO, MS, MT, NV, NH, NJ, NM, NY, NC, OK, OR, PA, SD, TN,

UT, VI, VA, WV, DC. Must show evidence of MAST training: AR, CO, ID, MA, NE, ND, RI, SC, TX, WY. Remaining considered on a case by case basis.

SALARY RANGES

Basic EMT: $10,000/Year-$16,000/year
Intermediate EMT: $12,000/year-$18,000/year
Paramedic: $14,000/year-$20,000/year

• • •

VIRGINIA

Office of Emergency Medical Services
Virginia Department of Health
1538 East Parham Road
Richmond, VA 23228
(804) 371-3500
Bill L. Meadows, State Training Manager

BASIC EMT

Hours of training: 110
Certification requirements: Must be at least 16 years of age. DOT course used. Pass state written and practical examination.
Recertification requirements: Every 4 years and pass state written and practical exam.

INTERMEDIATE EMT

Hours of training: Shock Trauma Technician, 87 hours; Cardiac EMT, 142 hours.
Certification requirements: Must be at least 18 years of age. Shock Trauma: DOT ALS curriculum and must pass state written and practical exam; cardiac EMT: Must be at least 18 years of age, DOT ALS curriculum and must pass state written and practical exam.
Recertification requirements: Must recertify every 2 years.

PARAMEDIC

Hours of training: 400
Certification requirements: Must be at least 18 years of age. DOT Paramedic Curriculum. Must pass National Registry written and practical exam.
Recertification requirements: Must recertify every 2 years.

Responsible certification agency: The Office of EMS, State Health Department
Reciprocity: We have reciprocity with MD, PA, DC, NC, and WV. Applicants from other states eligible for certification by legal recognition.

SALARY RANGES

Basic EMT: $7,280/year-$39,372/year.
Intermediate EMT: not available
Paramedic: $10,400/year-$49,600/year

• • •

WASHINGTON

Department of Health
Emergency Medical Services, Licensing and Certification
PO Box 47853
Olympia, WA 98504-7853
(206) 705-6710
Jack Cvitanovic, Section Manager

FIRST RESPONDER

Hours of training: DOT 44-hour course.
Certification period: 3 years.
Certification requirements: Pass the course, written and practical examination. CME requirements, 5-hour annual.

BASIC EMT

Hours of training: EMT-I 10 hours minimum.
Certification requirements: Attend the course, pass written exam (70) and pass practical exam.
Recertification requirements: 30 hours of continuing education, pass written and skill exams/evaluation.

INTERMEDIATE EMT

Hours of training: 50 hours didactic, clinical and field training (local option)
Certification requirements: Written and skill test required.
Recertification requirements: Proof of performance based on IVs and 1 airway per month and 15 hours a year continuing education for each level of training.

PARAMEDIC

Hours of training: 600 minimum
Certification requirements: Must be certified EMT, one year experience working in the system. Must complete the training program, NREMT exams, be endorsed by physician director.
Recertification requirements: Perform IVs to the satisfaction of the medical director and 1 intubation per month, and receive 50 hours a year of continuing education.
Responsible certification agency: DOH, EMS Section. State law requires a medical director for each county EMS system.
Reciprocity: EMT: Proof of completion of DOT 110-hour course, current certification, and proof of EMS affiliation within the state of Washington. Advanced skills: Paramedics must be, or have been, nationally registered as a paramedic. Current certification and transcript of training. Individual must be recommended to the state by the County Medical Program Director. Testing at county EMS level.

SALARY RANGES

Basic EMT: $12,000/year-$16,000/year
Intermediate EMT: $12,000/year-$18,000/year
Paramedic: $18,000/year-$36,000/year

• • •

WASHINGTON, DC

Office of Emergency Health and Medical Services
Commission of Public Health
Department of Human Services
1660 L Street, North West, Room 1223
Washington, DC 20036
(202) 673-6744
Alma Gonzalez, Training Director

BASIC EMT

Hours of training: 120 minimum
Certification requirements: Successfully pass an approved DOT EMT course. Maintenance of a valid certificate depends on successful completion of 8 hours CPR training each year.
Recertification requirements: Successful completion of 12 hours minimum of continuing medical education per year, and 24 hours of refresher EMT training in the second year. EMT certification is for a 2-year period.

INTERMEDIATE PARAMEDIC

Hours of training: 200 minimum in addition to being an EMT.
Certification requirements: Certification is issued upon recommendation of the Paramedic Review Board.
Recertification requirements: Successful completion of 8 hours of CPR training each year; successful completion of 18 hours minimum of continuing medical education per year, and 24 hours of refresher training in the second year with 16 hours of ACLS training over a 2-year period.

PARAMEDIC

Hours of training: 400-600 hours
Certification requirements: Certification is for a 2-year period. Certification is issued upon recommendation by the Paramedic Review Board.
Recertification requirements: Maintenance of a valid certificate depends on successful completion of 8 hours CPR training each year, successful completion of 36 hours minimum of continuing medical education per year, and 16 hours of ACLS training over a 2-year period, in-field evaluation needed for recertification.
Responsible certification agency: Office of Emergency Health and Medical Services
Reciprocity: There is reciprocity agreement in the District of Columbia for EMS personnel from other states, providing that the state EMS offices verify EMT status for certification to the OEHMS, Paramedics and Intermediate Paramedics must be recommended by the Paramedic Review Board for certification through reciprocity.

SALARY RANGES

Basic EMT: $22,67/year-$28,215/year
Intermediate Paramedic: $24,385/year-$30,568/year
Paramedic: $29,594/year-$37,154/year

• • •

WEST VIRGINIA

Office of Emergency Medical Services
Department of Health and Human Resources
1411 Virginia Street, East
Charleston, WV 25301
(304) 558-3956
Carl L. Baker, Jr., State Training Director

BASIC EMT

Hours of training: 110 hours
Certification requirements: National Registry examination. Initial certification for 2-3 years, ending December 31.
Recertification requirements: Recertification periods three years based on 33-hour refresher course or alternative approved in squad continuing education program of 40 hours. State written and practical examinations required.

EMT-CRITICAL CARE

Hours of training: 200
Certification requirements: Written and practical examinations lead to 2-3 year certification.
Recertification requirements: Every 3 years based on continuing education and written and practical examinations.

PARAMEDIC

Hours of training: 500
Certification requirements: National Registry examination, initial certification 2-3 years, ending December 31.
Recertification requirements: Every 3 years via 100 CE hours plus written and practical examinations. Those nationally registered will recertify for a two-year period, with fewer required hours (72) and with a program to simplify National Registry reregistration.
Responsible certification agency: State Department of Health and Human Resources. This certification group does include a physician. State law requires a medical director for each EMS system
Reciprocity: Demonstrated need (residency or employment) and verified equal training and current certification. Examinations required. Full reciprocity with National Registry.

SALARY RANGES

Basic EMT: $11,000/year-$17,800/year
Paramedic: $14,000/year-$26,600/year

• • •

WISCONSIN

Department of Health and Social Services
Division of Health
EMS Section
PO Box 309
Madison, WI 53701
(608) 266-1568

BASIC EMT

Hours of training: 120
Certification requirements: Training must be equivalent to National Standard DOT Basic EMT course. Licensure examination is the National Registry exam. Licensure is renewed biennially. Continuing education is 30-hour DOT refresher course every 2 years; current CPR.

EMT-DEFIBRILLATION

Hours of training: 5 (automatic), 20 (manual)
Certification requirements: Training course objectives set by EMS Section, standard written and practical skills examination distributed by EMS Section. Certification is renewed biennially.
Recertification requirements: Competency in performing defibrillation must be demonstrated every 3 months for manual defibrillator, every 6 months for automatic defibrillator. CPR certification must be maintained.

INTERMEDIATE EMT

Hours of training: Minimum of 100
Certification requirements: 40 hours didactic, 60 hours clinical and supervised field experience. Certification requires successful completion plus

National Registry exam. Local medical director must provide and certify continuing education for recertification.
Recertification requirements: Biennially. Continuing education 30-hour DOT refresher course (Basic); 12-hour intermediate refresher course; current CPR.

PARAMEDIC

Hours of training: Minimum of 750
Certification requirements: Clinical and didactic and supervised field experience. Successful completion of training. Must take state written exam or National Registry EMT-Paramedic exam and documentation by system medical director that applicant is proficient in clinical skills. Local medical director must provide and certify continuing education for recertification.

Recertification requirements: Biennially. Continuing education 48 hours based on DOT curriculum, current ACLS an CPR. Responsible certification agency. Licensure of all ambulance personnel is the responsibility of the EMS Section, Division of Health, Department of Health and Social Services. Medical director is required for each Advanced Life support system.

Reciprocity. EMT-Basic requires current registration with National Registry. Such persons are granted licensure by reciprocity. Other person who can document training and certification to the National Standard are allowed to take the Registry exam in Wisconsin to qualify for licensure. No formal reciprocity exists for licensure. No formal reciprocity exists for EMT-D, EMT-I or EMT-P. Evaluation is done on case-by-case basis.

SALARY RANGES

Basic and Intermediate EMT: $15,000/year-$25,000/year.
Paramedic: $18,500/year-$30,000/year

• • •

WYOMING

 Office of Emergency Medical Services
State Division of Health
Hathaway Building, #527
Cheyenne, WY 82002
(307) 777-7955
Jim Mayberry, State Training Coordinator

BASIC EMT

Hours of training: 120 hours.
Certification requirements: DOT course, plus added hours in practical areas. Must pass state written with 80 percent and also pass practical.
Recertification requirements: Every two years. 40 hours plus CPR, plus written and practical testing.

INTERMEDIATE EMT

Hours of training: Minimum 40 hours, depending on Modules taken.
Certification requirements: Course based on appropriate DOT Paramedic Modules. Must pass written and practical.
Recertification requirements: Every 2 years. Quarterly and semiannual inservices plus testing.

PARAMEDIC

Certification requirement: DOT Paramedic Module course.
Recertification requirements: Every 2 year. Practical demonstrations, quarterly inservices, written and practical testing.
Responsible certification agency: Basic, Intermediate, and Paramedic are state EMS office. This certification group does include physicians. State law requires a medical director for each EMS system and EMTs.
Reciprocity: State EMS evaluates/tests all out-of-state applicants.

SALARY RANGES

Basic EMT: $14,000/year-$19,000/year.
Intermediate EMT: $15,000/year-$21,000/year.
Paramedic: $16,000/year-$28,000/year

• • •

Firefighters

The primary responsibility of *firefighters* is to protect lives and property from fire. They try to prevent fires by inspecting buildings and organizing public education programs. When fires occur, firefighters immediately travel to the site, attempt to extinguish the flames, and rescue trapped or injured people. They might also need to determine the cause of the fire. Additional responsibilities include helping with emergency medical care and with recovery efforts after natural disasters. Most career firefighters are employed by municipal fire departments. A small number work at state and federal facilities, such as airports. Rural areas frequently use volunteer firefighters.

Although communities have always needed to protect themselves from fires, their methods were quite primitive until the twentieth century. In the colonial period, for example, townspeople would form bucket brigades, in which people stood in a line and passed buckets of water from one person to another. Hand-pulled fire vehicles, equipped with water hoses, were subsequently used, but these had a number of limitations: the vehicle's water tank still had to be filled and refilled by a fire brigade; the water force, generated by a hand pump, was weak; and, because the hoses were short and stiff, the vehicles had to be brought close to the fire. Firefighting became much more effective with the development of huge motorized fire trucks, powerful mechanized water pumps, and other types of new equipment, such as fire extinguishers. Firefighters themselves have also become better trained to handle fire emergencies.

Firefighters today spend much of their time preparing for emergencies. Firefighting equipment, for example, must be kept in perfect condition. Firefighters lubricate mechanical equipment, and water hoses are kept dry and stretched into shape. Firefighters also hold practice drills to maintain readiness.

While waiting in the fire station, firefighters must be ready to head out immediately. Any delay could result in additional loss of property and lives. Because of the potential for mass confusion at the site of a fire, firefighters are given well-defined responsibilities. Some, for example, are responsible for connecting hoses to fire hydrants, while others operate water pumps; raise ladders; break through doors, windows, or walls with fire axes; or rescue people caught in the fire. To prevent burns, firefighters wear protective suits, gloves, helmets, and boots. A self-contained breathing apparatus might also be used to prevent suffocation. After the flames are extinguished, firefighters must remain at the site to ensure the fire is completely out. *Fire investigators* might then examine the cause of the fire, especially if there were injuries or deaths.

Some firefighters work actively to prevent fires by inspecting buildings for violations of municipal fire codes. They look for flammable materials, such as chemicals or trash, as well as worn-out or exposed wiring. They also check for fire alarms and escape routes, as a blocked hallway or exit could cost many lives. Property owners are then notified if improvements need to be made, and in some cases owners are fined. Firefighters sometimes give speeches on fire prevention to school assemblies, civic groups, or other organizations.

Firefighters are typically required to handle other emergencies unrelated to fires. For example, they assist emergency medical technicians with medical emergencies (such as heart attacks), help control and clean up the site of oil spills and hazardous chemical accidents, and assist recovery efforts after such natural disasters as hurricanes and tornadoes. They are frequently called to help at the site of automobile accidents.

Requirements for firefighters vary from place to place, though in general applicants must be at least 18 years old, have a high school degree (or GED), and be physically able to perform the work of the job (some departments require 20/20 eyesight and the ability to lift 70-100 pounds). Candidates usually take both written and physical tests and, in some areas, a civil service examination. An increasing number of firefighters have postsecondary education. Some colleges and universities offer two- or four-year degrees in fire engineering or fire science. Fire departments sometimes pay already employed firefighters to pursue such degrees.

In a large fire department, new firefighters spend the first few weeks at a training center, where they receive practical and classroom instruction. They are then assigned to a fire company. A growing number of fire departments have three- or four-year apprenticeship programs, which also combine classroom and on-the-job training. Working under experienced firefighters, they begin with simple tasks, such as holding a hose, and are gradually trained to handle more difficult jobs. Among the subjects they study are fire prevention, relevant city ordinances, the use and care of equipment, and emergency medical procedures.

Competition is often fierce for job openings, in part because only a high school degree is required, the pay is relatively high, and the work is seen as exciting. Moreover, firefighters provide a valuable and high-profile public service. The work, however, can be quite dangerous. Firefighters must enter burning buildings and are exposed to intense heat, smoke, chemicals, and gases. Floors, walls, and even entire buildings can cave in on a firefighter.

The number of employed firefighters is expected to grow at an average rate. Employment will probably increase little in the fire departments of large cities, but smaller communities with growing populations will likely need to hire additional firefighters.

For more information on training programs and apprenticeships for firefighters, write to the organizations listed below. Additional information might be available from your state's bureau of apprenticeship training. The bureau addresses are found in the last section of this encyclopedia.

ALABAMA

 Alabama Fire Collage
2015 McFarland Boulevard East
Tuscaloosa, AL 35404
205-759-1508

SPECIFICATIONS:

Certification is mandatory.
Certification is not required before hiring.
Paid firefighters must be certified as firefighter I.
There are 100 paid fire departments in the state.

• • •

ALASKA

 Alaska State Fire Marshal's Office
Fire Services Training
5700 East Tudor Road
Anchorage, AK 99507-1225
907-269-5789

SPECIFICATIONS:

Certification is voluntary.
There are 4 paid fire departments in the state.

• • •

ARIZONA

 Arizona State Fire Marshal's Office
1540 West Vanburen Street
Phoenix, AZ 85007
602-255-4964

SPECIFICATIONS:

Certification is voluntary.
There are 40 paid fire departments in the state.
Send written request with $10 for directory.

• • •

ARKANSAS

 Arkansas Fire Academy
PO Box 3499
East Camden, AR 71701
501-574-1521

SPECIFICATIONS:

Certification is voluntary.
There are 27 paid fire departments in the state.
Information on certification is restricted to firefighters currently on a fire department.

• • •

CALIFORNIA

 California State Fire Fighters Association
3246 Ramos Circle
Sacramento, CA 95827
916-368-2578

SPECIFICATIONS:

Certification is voluntary.
For information on certification training contact:

Office of State Fire Marshal
Training Division
7171 Bowling Drive, Suite 600
Sacramento, CA 95823
916-262-1958

To receive a brochure and to have your name put on application mailing list (for fire departments who request JAC's assistance in locating recruits) contact:

California Fire Fighter JAC
1780 Creekside Oaks, Suite 201
Sacramento, CA 95833
916-648-1717

• • •

National Fire Fighters Association
4600 Northgate Boulevard, #240
Sacramento, CA 95834
916-648-3000

Program title: Wildland Firefighter's Apprenticeship Program
Specific job title(s): Wildland firefighter
This is an 18-month program with 320 hours of classroom instruction and 3,000 hours of on-the-job training.
Starting wage: $7.60; Ending wage: $7.60.
Annually, over 100 people apply for 51-100 positions.
Course credit is offered.
There is an initial 18-month probationary period.
Applications are accepted by mail typically at the end of August.

REQUIREMENTS:

- Minimum age: 18; Maximum age: 35
- High school diploma or GED certificate
- Physician's statement of fitness
- Must be physically able to perform the work of the trade
- Valid driver's license
- Letter of recommendation
- Letter of intent from a valid employer

• • •

COLORADO

Colorado Division of Fire Safety
Department of Public Safety
700 Kipling Street, Suite 1200
Denver, CO 80215-5865
303-239-4463

SPECIFICATIONS:

There are 50 paid fire departments in the state.

• • •

Avon Fire Department
Box 935
Avon, CO 86120
303-949-6425

Program title: Avon Fire Department Resident Program
Specific job title(s): Resident firefighter
This is a 2-year program.
No salaries were reported by this program.
Annually, 51-100 people apply for 6-10 positions.
There is an initial 3-month probationary period.
Applications are accepted in person or by mail at the beginning of year, send letter of interest for application.

REQUIREMENTS:

- Minimum age: 18
- High school diploma or GED certificate
- Must be physically able to perform the work of the trade
- Pass a written test
- Pass an oral interview
- Valid driver's license
- Pass a test for illegal drugs

APPLICATION DOCUMENTS:

Applicants must bring the following documents when applying:
- High school diploma or GED certificate
- Social security card
- Driver's license
- Car Insurance

ADDITIONAL PROGRAM COMMENTS:

Resident firefighter works one 24-hour shift per week and attends one class at local community college or attends an approved seminar (one per semester minimum). Resident firefighter also completes the necessary course work and hands-on exercises required to attain the certification of Firefighter Level I by the end of probationary period.

Program administered at Avon Fire Department. There is no salary per hour. Fire department provides lodging at fire station and college tuition for an associate's degree in fire science. Individual is responsible for meals and books.

• • •

Firefighters

 Vail Fire Department
42 West Meadows Drive
Vail, CO 81657
303-479-2250

Program title: Student/Resident Firefighter Program
This is a 2-3-year program.
Starting wage: $5.00; Ending wage: $5.00.
Annually, 51-100 people apply for 0-5 positions.
There is an initial 1-year probationary period.
Applications are accepted by mail any time of year via typewritten resume; include driver's license number.

REQUIREMENTS:

- Minimum age: 21
- High school diploma or GED certificate
- Physician's statement of fitness
- Must be physically able to perform the work of the trade
- Pass an oral interview
- Valid driver's license
- Pass a test for illegal drugs

APPLICATION DOCUMENTS:

Applicants must bring the following documents when applying:
- High school diploma or GED certificate
- Social security card
- Driver's license

ADDITIONAL PROGRAM COMMENTS:

During program individual lives and works at fire department while attending local community college. At this time, individual fulfills course work and practicals at a minimum of 63 hours to attain Firefighter Level I certification. Individual receives room and board in lieu of paycheck unless out on call wherein they are paid per hour. Individual is responsible for tuition and meals. At end of program individual is certified as firefighter and degreed. This does not mean he or she is a permanent member of Vail Fire Department. Openings may exist after program, yet individual may need to find employment elsewhere.

• • •

CONNECTICUT

 Commission on Fire Prevention and Control and Connecticut Fire Academy
PO Box 3383
Windsor Locks, CT 06096
203-627-6363, ext. 230

SPECIFICATIONS:

Certification is voluntary.
There are 44 paid fire departments in the state.
Enrollment is restricted.
Applicants must be a member of a fire department or fire service.

• • •

DELAWARE

 Wilmington Fire Personnel Department
300 North Walnut
Wilmington, DE 19802
302-571-4280

SPECIFICATIONS:

Certification is voluntary.
Restricted enrollment.
There is one paid fire department in the state. Although the state of Delaware does not mandate certification, the only paid fire department in the state requires its new hires to be certified to the level of Firefighter II within the one-year probationary period. For information on certification/training contact:

Delaware State Fire School
R.D. #2, Box 166-A
Dover, DE 19901
302-739-4773

• • •

FLORIDA

 Florida State Fire Marshal
Fire College
11655 NW Gainesville Road
Ocala, FL 34482
904-732-1330

SPECIFICATIONS:

Certification is mandated by the state.
Most fire departments require applicants be certified before hiring consideration.
There are 500-600 paid fire departments in the state.

• • •

GEORGIA

Fire Fighter Standards and Training Council
1000 Indian Springs Drive
Forsythe, GA 31029
912-993-4521

SPECIFICATIONS:

Certification is mandatory.
Certification before hiring varies.
There are 138 paid fire departments in the state.
Applicants must be sponsored by a fire department.

• • •

HAWAII

State Fire Council's Office Training Center
890 Valkenburgh
Honolulu, HI 96818
808-422-0827

SPECIFICATIONS:

Certification is voluntary.
There are 4 paid fire departments in the state.
For information on applying to paid fire staffs contact:

Kuai County Department of Personnel
808-241-6595

City/County of Honolulu Department of Personnel
808-523-4301

Maui County
808-243-7850

Hawaii County Department of Personnel
808-961-8361

• • •

IDAHO

Fire Service Training
Division of Vocation Education
PO Box 83720
Boise, ID 83720
208-334-3216

SPECIFICATIONS:

Certification is voluntary.
There are 8 paid fire departments in the state.
For information on location of fire staffs write and send $5.00 fee with written request to:

Idaho State Fire Marshal
Department of Insurance
Division of Fire Marshal
500 South 10th Street
Boise, ID 83720

• • •

ILLINOIS

Office of State Fire Marshal
Division of Personnel Standards
1035 Stevenson Drive
Springfield, IL 62703-4259

SPECIFICATIONS:

Training/certification restricted to member of fire departments at Fire Academy, University of Illinois Fire Service Institute.
Certification is voluntary.
There are 68 paid fire departments in the state.

• • •

Fire Fighters
PO Box 8796
Waukegan, IL 60079
ATTN: John Schmidt

This is a 3-year program with 500 hours of classroom instruction and 1,000 hours of on-the-job training.
No salaries were reported by this program. Annually, over 100 people apply for 6-10 positions.
There is an initial probationary period. Applications are accepted in person about every 2 years as determined by Civil Service Commission.

REQUIREMENTS:

- Minimum age: 21; Maximum age: 35
- High school diploma or GED certificate
- Physician's statement of fitness
- Must be physically able to perform the work of the trade
- Pass a written test
- Pass an oral interview
- Valid driver's license
- Resident of the program's jurisdiction
- Pass a test for illegal drugs

APPLICATION DOCUMENTS:

Applicants must bring the following documents when applying:
- High school diploma or GED certificate
- Social security card
- Driver's license

ADDITIONAL PROGRAM COMMENTS:

This apprenticeship is geared toward the State of Illinois Advanced Firefighter III. Six weeks at the Firefighter Academy is necessary to bring the recruit to Firefighter II level. Various departmental programs are given to enhance training, such as Hazardous Materials ID. Additional requirements include certification as an EMT-Paramedic within 3 years of being hired.
Previous fire department experience is helpful, as is any emergency medical services experience and education in fire science. Physical fitness and a good driving record are necessary. There will be a background check for employment and any criminal history.

• • •

INDIANA

Public Safety Training Institute
402 West Washington Street, Room 208
Indianapolis, IN 46204
317-232-2169 or 1-800-666-7784

SPECIFICATIONS:

Certification is mandatory.
There are 18 full paid fire departments in the state.
Enrollment restricted.

• • •

City of Kokomo Fire Department
215 West Superior
Kokomo, IN 46901
317-457-2636

This is a 3-year program with 432 hours of classroom instruction and 6,000 hours of on-the-job training.
Starting wage: $9.16; Ending wage: $9.60.
Annually, 51-100 people apply for 0-5 positions.
There is an initial 1-year probationary period. Applications are accepted in person any time of year at personnel office.

REQUIREMENTS:

- Minimum age: 21; Maximum age: 35
- High school diploma or GED certificate
- Physician's statement of fitness
- Must be physically able to perform the work of the trade
- Pass a written test
- Pass an oral interview
- Valid driver's license
- Pass a test for illegal drugs

ADDITIONAL PROGRAM COMMENTS:

New applicants must fill out application at personnel office and also complete the agility test. When an opening is available and applicant is chosen, a medical exam needs to be taken. Residency is not required until applicant is hired.

• • •

Fort Wayne Fire Department
1 Main Street, Room 280
Fort Wayne, IN 46801
219-427-1170

This is a 3-year program with 432 hours of classroom instruction and 6,000 hours of on-the-job training.
Starting wage: $8.51; Ending wage: $9.42.
Annually, over 100 people apply for 6-10 positions.
There is an initial 1-year probationary period.
Applications are accepted in person when announcement is posted.
The application deadline is 3 weeks after announced.

REQUIREMENTS:

- Minimum age: 21; Maximum age: 35
- High school diploma or GED certificate
- Must be physically able to perform the work of the trade
- Pass a written test
- Pass an oral interview
- Valid driver's license
- Resident of the program's jurisdiction
- Pass a test for illegal drugs
- Must attend a preapprenticeship class for 400 hours

APPLICATION DOCUMENTS:

Applicants must bring the following documents when applying:
- High school transcript or GED scores
- High school diploma or GED certificate
- Social security card
- Driver's license
- Birth certificate

ADDITIONAL PROGRAM COMMENTS:

Apply to:

Personnel Department
County Building, 3rd Floor
Fort Wayne, IN 46801

• • •

Fire Chief/Administration Office
Firefighter Apprenticeship Program
443 North Fourth
Lafayette, IN 47901
317-742-6309

This is a 2-year program with 500 hours of classroom instruction and 3,000 hours of on-the-job training.
Starting wage: $9.40; Ending wage: $10.33.
Annually, 31-50 people apply for 0-5 positions.
There is an initial 6-month probationary period.
Applications are accepted in person usually in April and October, Monday-Friday, 8:00-4:00.
The application deadline is 1 week before testing.

REQUIREMENTS:

- Minimum age: 18
- High school diploma or GED certificate
- Must be physically able to perform the work of the trade
- Pass a written test
- Valid driver's license
- Resident of the program's jurisdiction

APPLICATION DOCUMENTS:

Applicants must bring the following documents when applying:
- High scho ! transcript or GED scores
- High school diploma or GED certificate

• • •

IOWA

Fire Service Institute
Iowa State University
Haber Road
Ames, Iowa 50011
515-294-6817

SPECIFICATIONS:

Certification voluntary.
There are 30 full paid fire departments in the state.

• • •

KANSAS

Kansas State Fire Marshal Department
700 SW Jackson, Suite 600
Topeka, Kansas 66603
913-296-3401

SPECIFICATIONS:

Certification is voluntary.
There are 35 full paid fire departments in the state.

• • •

Mission Township Fire Department
3101 Urish Road
Topeka, KS 66614
913-478-4053

Program title: Mission Township Fire Department Apprenticeship Program
Specific job title(s): Fire medic
This is a 3.5-year program with 504 hours of classroom instruction and 6,496 hours of on-the-job training.
Starting wage: $4.92; Ending wage: $6.00.
Annually, 0-10 people apply for 0-5 positions.
There is an initial 6-month probationary period.
Applications are accepted in person or by mail any time of year, Monday-Friday, 8:00-5:00.

REQUIREMENTS:

- Minimum age: 21
- High school diploma or GED certificate
- Pass a written test
- Valid driver's license
- Letter of recommendation from Fire Chief

APPLICATION DOCUMENTS:

Applicants must bring the following documents when applying:
- Social security card
- Driver's license
- EMT Certificate

ADDITIONAL PROGRAM COMMENTS:

Applicant must have 2-years' experience (volunteer firefighter experience accepted). Must be certified as an EMT.

• • •

KENTUCKY

Fire Commission
1049 U.S. Highway 127 South, Suite 5
Frankfort, KY 40601
502-564-3473

SPECIFICATIONS:

Certification is mandatory.
Certification is required within one year of hire.

• • •

LOUISIANA

Louisiana State University
Louisiana Firefighter Certification System
Room 327, Pleasant Hall
Baton Rouge, LA 70803
504-388-5051

SPECIFICATIONS:

Certification is voluntary.
There are 20 full paid fire departments in the state.
For information on location of fire departments in this state contact:

Fire and Police Civil Service
PO Box 44366
Baton Rouge, LA 70804-4366
504-342-2875

• • •

MAINE

State Fire Administrator
Southern Maine Technical College
Fort Road North
South Portland, ME 04106
207-767-9556

SPECIFICATIONS:

Certification is voluntary.
There are 4 full paid fire departments in the state.

• • •

MARYLAND

Maryland Fire and Rescue Institute
University of Maryland
College Park, Maryland 20742
301-220-7240

SPECIFICATIONS:

Certification is voluntary.
There are 20 full paid fire departments in the state.
For information on the location of fire departments in this state contact:

Fire Chief's Office
9201 Basil Court, Suite 452
Landover, Maryland 20785
301-925-5200

Restricted enrollment

• • •

MASSACHUSETTS

Massachusetts State Fire Academy
PO Box 1025
State Road
Stow, MA 01775
617-727-9635

SPECIFICATIONS:

Certification is voluntary.
There are 170 full paid fire departments in the state.
Restricted enrollment

• • •

Prince George's County Fire Training Academy
PO Box 370
Cheltenham, MA 20623
301-856-3410

This is a 3-year program with 756 hours of classroom instruction and 6,244 hours of on-the-job training.
Starting wage: $8.65; Ending wage: $16.32.
Annually, over 100 people apply for 21-50 positions.
There is an initial 1-year probationary period. Applications are accepted in person or by mail through openings once a year.

REQUIREMENTS:

- Minimum age: 18
- High school diploma or GED certificate
- Must be physically able to perform the work of the trade
- Pass a written test
- Pass an oral interview
- Valid driver's license
- Pass a test for illegal drugs

APPLICATION DOCUMENTS:

Applicants must bring the following documents when applying:
- High school diploma or GED certificate
- Social security card
- Driver's license
- Birth certificate
- Fire Service Certifications

ADDITIONAL PROGRAM COMMENTS:

In order to enter the apprenticeship program, individuals must be hired as a recruit Fire

Fighter. For an application, apply to:

Prince George's County Fire Department
Bureau of Administrative Services
Large Government Center
9201 Basil Court, Suite 356
Landover, MA 20785

• • •

MICHIGAN

Michigan Fire Fighters Training Council
7150 Harris Drive
Lansing, MI 48913
517-322-1922

SPECIFICATIONS:

Certification is mandatory.
Some departments require certification within one year of hire and some before hire in this state.
There are 150 full paid fire departments in the state.

• • •

MINNESOTA

Minnesota State Fire Service Certification Board
10983 South Jackson Drive
Solon Springs, WI 54873
800-743-0911

SPECIFICATIONS:

Certification is voluntary.
There are 8 full paid fire departments in the state.
For information on the location of fire departments in this state contact:

Fire Center
550 Cedar Street
St. Paul, Minnesota 55101
612-296-6516

• • •

MISSISSIPPI

N.F.P.A. Certification Division
Mississippi State Fire Academy
1 Fire Academy U.S.A.
Jackson, Mississippi 39208
601-932-2444

SPECIFICATIONS:

Certification is mandatory.
Some departments require certification within one year of employment and some before hire.
There are 23 full paid fire departments in the state.
For information on the location of fire departments in this state contact:

Division of Fire Services Development
PO Box 22542
Jackson, MS 39225-2542
Enrollment restricted

• • •

MISSOURI

State Fire Marshal's Office
Division of Fire Safety
PO Box 844
Jefferson City, MO 65102
800-877-5688

SPECIFICATIONS:

Certification is voluntary.
There are 70 full paid fire departments in the state.

• • •

MONTANA

State Fire Service
Fire Training school
2100 16th Avenue, South
Great Falls, MT 59405
406-761-7885

SPECIFICATIONS:

Certification is voluntary.
There are 18 full paid fire departments in the state.
For information on the location of fire departments in this state contact:

Montana State Fire Marshal
Department of Justice
Fire Prevention & Investigations Bureau
303 North Roberts, Room 375
Helena, MT 59620-1417
406-444-2050

• • •

NEBRASKA

Nebraska State Fire Marshal's Office
246 South 14th Street
PO Box 94677
Lincoln, NE 68508
402-471-2027

SPECIFICATIONS:

Certification is voluntary.
There are 3 full paid fire departments in the state.
For information on the location of fire departments in this state send a written request with $5.00 to the above address.

• • •

NEVADA

Nevada State Fire Marshal's Office
Training Division
107 Jacobsen Way
Carson City, NV 89710
702-687-4290

SPECIFICATIONS:

Certification is mandatory and required before hire.
There are 63 full paid fire departments in the state.

• • •

NEW HAMPSHIRE

Fire Standards & Training
222 Sheep Davies Road
Concord, NH 03301
603-271-2092

SPECIFICATIONS:

Certification is voluntary
There are 60 full paid fire departments in the state.
For a list of all fire departments send a written request with a check for $5.00.

• • •

NEW JERSEY

Division of Fire Safety
101 South Broad Street, CN809
Trenton, NJ 08625-0809
609-633-6070

SPECIFICATIONS:

Certification is voluntary.
There are 39 full paid fire departments in the state.

• • •

NEW MEXICO

New Mexico Firefighters Training Academy
PO Box 239
Socorro, NM 87801
505-835-7500

SPECIFICATIONS:

Certification is voluntary.
There are 21 full paid fire departments in the state.
For information on the location of fire departments in this state contact:

Office of State Fire Marshal
PO Drawer 1269
Santa Fe, NM 87504-1269
505-827-3550

• • •

NEW YORK

 State Fire Administrator
Office of Prevention & Control
162 Washington Avenue
Albany, NY 12231
written requests only)

SPECIFICATIONS:

Certification is mandated for fire departments with six or more paid firefighters.
New hires are given 18-36 months to achieve certification, depending on the amount of time worked.
There are 38 full paid fire departments in the state.
For questions by phone contact:

Fire Service Bureau/Standards
518-474-6746
24-hour answering system

• • •

NORTH CAROLINA

 Fire and Rescue Commission
PO Box 26387
Raleigh, NC 27611
919-733-5435

SPECIFICATIONS:

Certification is voluntary.
There are 45-50 full paid fire departments in the state.

• • •

 Asheville Fire Department
PO Box 7148
Asheville, NC 28801
704-259-5527

This is a 3-year program with 432 hours of classroom instruction and 5,568 hours of on-the-job training.
Starting wage: $6.43; Ending wage: $10.20.
Annually, over 100 people apply for 0-5 positions.
There is an initial 6-month probationary period. Applications are accepted in person or by mail any time for mailing list. Dates/deadlines vary.

REQUIREMENTS:

- Minimum age: 18
- High school diploma or GED certificate
- Must be physically able to perform the work of the trade
- Pass a written test
- Pass an oral interview
- Valid driver's license
- Resident of the program's jurisdiction
- Pass a test for illegal drugs

APPLICATION DOCUMENTS:

Applicants must bring the following documents when applying:
- High school diploma or GED certificate
- Social security card
- Driver's license

ADDITIONAL PROGRAM COMMENTS:

Apply to:

City Hall
Civil Service
100 Court Plaza
Asheville, NC 28801
704-259-5523

• • •

 Thomasville Fire Department
712 East Main Street
Thomasville, NC 27306
910-475-4293

This is a 2-year program with 480 hours of classroom instruction and 3,520 hours of on-the-job training.
Starting wage: $7.97; Ending wage: $8.77.
Annually, 31-50 people apply for 0-5 positions.
There is an initial 12-month probationary period.
Applications are accepted in person any time of year.

REQUIREMENTS:

- Minimum age: 21
- High school diploma or GED certificate
- Must be physically able to perform the work of the trade
- Pass a written test
- Pass an oral interview
- Valid driver's license
- Pass a test for illegal drugs

APPLICATION DOCUMENTS:

Applicants must bring the following documents when applying:
- High school transcript or GED scores
- High school diploma or GED certificate
- Social security card
- Driver's license

• • •

Wilmington Fire Department
20 South 4th Street
Wilmington, NC 28401
910-341-7846

Program title: Standards of Apprenticeship for Wilmington Fire Department
This is a 3-year program with 6,000 hours of on-the-job training.
No salaries were reported by this program.
Annually, 0-10 people apply for 0-5 positions.
Course credit is offered.
There is an initial 18-month probationary period.
Applications are accepted in person when advertised locally.

REQUIREMENTS:

- Minimum age: 21
- High school diploma or GED certificate
- Physician's statement of fitness
- Must be physically able to perform the work of the trade
- Pass a written test
- Pass an oral interview
- Valid driver's license
- Letter of recommendation from past employer, etc.
- Pass a test for illegal drugs

APPLICATION DOCUMENTS:

Applicants must bring the following documents when applying:
- High school diploma or GED certificate
- Driver's license

ADDITIONAL PROGRAM COMMENTS:

The starting annual salary is $ 18,350. Applicants must live within 18 miles from department. Other documents of training in fire-related matters are recommended for the application process.

• • •

NORTH DAKOTA

Firemen's Association
176 1st Street NE
Beach, NJ 58621
701-872-4392

SPECIFICATIONS:

Certification is voluntary.
There are 4 full paid fire departments in the state.

• • •

OHIO

Department of Public Safety
Division of EMS
240 Parsons Avenue
PO Box 7167
Columbus, OH 43205
800-233-0785

SPECIFICATIONS:

Certification is mandatory.
Certification may be required before hire in some departments or within one year of appointment to fire department by others.
There are 300 full paid fire departments in this state.
For information contact:

Division of State Fire Marshal
8895 East Main Street
PO Box 525
Reynoldsburg, OH 43068
614-752-7167

Send $3.00 for a list of all fire departments in the state.

• • •

OKLAHOMA

Fire Service Training
Oklahoma State University
Fire Building
Stillwater, OK 74078-0114
405-744-5727

SPECIFICATIONS:

Certification is voluntary
There are 40 full paid fire departments in the state.

• • •

OREGON

State Fire Marshal's Office
Public Safety Standards and Training
4760 Portland Road, NE
Salem, OR 97305-1760
503-378-3473

SPECIFICATIONS:

Certification is voluntary.
There are 8-10 full paid fire departments in the state.
For information on the location of fire departments in this state send $10 for a directory.
Oregon is in the process of establishing an apprenticeship system. For apprenticeship update contact:

Oregon State Fire Fighters Council
191 Chapel Drive, Suite 200
Eugene, OR 97404-1678
503-689-5388

• • •

PENNSYLVANIA

State Fire Academy
1150 Riverside Drive
Lewistown, PA 17044
717-248-1115

SPECIFICATIONS:

Certification is voluntary.
There are 47 full paid departments in the state.
For information on locations contact:

State Fire Commission
PO Box 3321
Harrisburg, PA 17105
717-783-5061

• • •

Chester Fire Department
320 East 14th Street
Chester, PA 19013
610-447-7765

This is a 3-year program.
Starting wage: $12.06; Ending wage: $14.63.
Annually, 51-100 people apply for 0-5 positions.
Course credit is offered.
There is an initial 6-month probationary period.
Applications are accepted in person when advertised locally.

REQUIREMENTS:

- Minimum age: 18
- High school diploma or GED certificate
- Must be physically able to perform the work of the trade
- Pass a written test
- Pass an oral interview
- Valid driver's license
- Resident of the program's jurisdiction for 1 year
- Pass a test for illegal drugs

APPLICATION DOCUMENTS:

Applicants must bring the following documents when applying:
- High school diploma or GED certificate
- Driver's license
- Birth certificate

ADDITIONAL PROGRAM COMMENTS:

Classroom instruction ranges from 900 to 1,500 hours. On-the-job instruction ranges from 4,500 to 5,100 hours. Starting and ending salaries may vary.

• • •

City Hall
Personnel Office
10 North Market
Harrisburg, PA 17101
717-255-6475

Program title: Harrisburg Firefighter Apprenticeship Program
This is a 3-year program with 1,900 hours of classroom instruction and 4,100 hours of on-the-job training.
Starting wage: $13.42; Ending wage: $14.58.
Annually, over 100 people apply for 0-5 positions.
Course credit is offered.
There is an initial 6-month probationary period.
Applications are accepted in person or by mail when recruiting testing date is posted. Contact for further info.

REQUIREMENTS:

- Minimum age: 18
- High school diploma or GED certificate
- Must be physically able to perform the work of the trade
- Pass a written test
- Pass an oral interview
- Valid driver's license

APPLICATION DOCUMENTS:

Applicants must bring the following documents when applying:
- High school transcript or GED scores
- High school diploma or GED certificate
- Social security card
- Driver's license

• • •

City Hall
Human Resources
120 North Duke Street
Lancaster, PA 17602
717-291-4720

Program title: Lancaster Bureau Apprenticeship Program
This is a 3-year program with 832 hours of classroom instruction and 800 hours of on-the-job training.
Starting wage: $10.07; Ending wage: $14.65.
Annually, 11-20 people apply for 0-5 positions.
There is an initial 6-month probationary period.
Applications are accepted in person.

REQUIREMENTS:

- Minimum age: 21
- High school diploma or GED certificate

- Must be physically able to perform the work of the trade
- Pass a written test
- Pass an oral interview
- Valid driver's license
- Resident of the program's jurisdiction for 1 year
- Pass a test for illegal drugs

APPLICATION DOCUMENTS:

Applicants must bring the following documents when applying:
- High school transcript or GED scores
- Social security card
- Driver's license

ADDITIONAL PROGRAM COMMENTS:

There are two applications: A municipal application, which can be filled out any time during year, and a civil service application, which is only taken at certain times of the year. Applicants who have filled out the municipal application will be notified about dates and deadlines for the civil service application. Applicants must live within a 13-mile radius of downtown Lancaster.

• • •

RHODE ISLAND

Rhode Island State Fire Marshal
Division of Fire Safety
272 West Exchange Street
Providence, RI 02903
401-277-2335

SPECIFICATIONS:

Certification is voluntary.
There are 11-19 full paid fire departments in the state.

• • •

SOUTH CAROLINA

South Carolina State Budget and Control Board
Division of Fire & Safety
141 Monticello Trail
Columbia, SC 29203
803-896-9800

SPECIFICATIONS:

Certification is voluntary.
There are 150 full paid fire departments in the state.
Fire school is restricted to members of SC fire departments.
For information on the location of fire departments in this state send $10 for directory to:

State Firemen Association
PO Box 67
Simpsonville, SC 29681
803-967-8311

• • •

SOUTH DAKOTA

South Dakota State Fire Marshal
118 West Capitol
Pierre, SD 57501
605-773-3562

SPECIFICATIONS:

Certification is voluntary
There are 5 full paid fire departments in the state.

• • •

TENNESSEE

Firefighting Commission
500 James Robertson Parkway
Nashville, TN 37243
615-741-6780

SPECIFICATIONS:

Certification is voluntary in this state
There are 60 full paid fire departments in the state.
For information on the location of fire departments contact:

State Fire Marshal's Office
500 James Robertson Parkway
Nashville, TN 37243
615-741-2981

• • •

TEXAS

Texas Commission on Fire Protection
Standards and Licensing Division
3006 B Longhorn Boulevard
PO Box 2286
Austin, TX 78768-2286

SPECIFICATIONS:

Certification is mandatory.
There are 400 full paid fire departments in the state.
For written information on the location of fire departments and certification in this state send $5.00 to the above address.

• • •

UTAH

Utah Valley State College
Utah Fire and Rescue Academy
800 West 1200 South
Orem, UT 84058
801-222-8000, ext. 508

SPECIFICATIONS:

Certification is voluntary.
There are 60-80 full paid fire departments in the state.

• • •

City Hall
Human Resources Department
405 South 200 East
Salt Lake City, UT 84111
801-535-7900

Program title: Salt Lake City Firefighter Apprenticeship Program
This is a 2-year program with 660 hours of classroom instruction and 3,340 hours of on-the-job training.
Starting wage: $8.41; Ending wage: $8.84.
Annually, over 100 people apply for 6-10 positions.
There is an initial 1-year probationary period.
Applications are accepted in person or by mail twice a year during testing. Write for testing dates/deadlines.

REQUIREMENTS:

- Minimum age: 18
- High school diploma or GED certificate
- Must be physically able to perform the work of the trade
- Pass a written test
- Pass an oral interview
- Valid driver's license
- Pass a test for illegal drugs
- Must attend a preapprenticeship class for 480 hours

ADDITIONAL PROGRAM COMMENTS:

Associated with:

Salt Lake City Fire Department Training
315 East 200 South, 7th Floor
Salt Lake City, UT 84111
Chuck Querry, Training Division
801-596-5249

• • •

VERMONT

Fire Service Training
PO Box 53
Pittsford, VT 05763
802-483-9407

SPECIFICATIONS:

Certification is mandatory.
There are 10 full paid fire departments in the state.

• • •

VIRGINIA

Department of Fire Programs
Parham164 Building, Suite 200
2806 Parham Road
Richmond, VA 23294
804-527-4236

SPECIFICATIONS:

Certification is voluntary.
There are 25-30 full paid fire departments in this state.

• • •

WASHINGTON

Fire Protection Services
PO Box 48350
Olympia, WA 98504-8350
206-493-2736

SPECIFICATIONS:

Washington does not have a certification process currently in place. For more information on locations of fire departments in the state, send $20.00 for a directory to:

Washington Fire Commissioner's Association
PO Box 134
Olympia, WA 98507

• • •

King County Fire District #16
18030 - 73rd Avenue Northeast
Bothell, WA 98011
206-486-2784

Program title: King County Fire District #16 Apprenticeship Program
This is a 3-year program with 432 hours of classroom instruction and 5,568 hours of on-the-job training.
Starting wage: $12.56.
Annually, over 100 people apply for 0-5 positions.
There is an initial 1-year probationary period.
Applications are accepted in person or by mail when advertised locally.

REQUIREMENTS:

- Minimum age: 18
- High school diploma or GED certificate
- Must be physically able to perform the work of the trade
- Pass a written test
- Pass an oral interview
- Valid driver's license
- Pass a test for illegal drugs
- Must attend a preapprenticeship class for 400 hours

APPLICATION DOCUMENTS:

Applicants must bring the following documents when applying:
- Social security card
- Driver's license

• • •

Centralia Fire Department
512 North Pearl Street
Centralia, WA 98531
206-736-3338

Program title: Centralia Fire Department Fire-Medic Apprenticeship Program
This is a 3.5-year program.
No salaries were reported by this program.
Annually, a varying number of people apply for a varying number of positions.
Applications are accepted in person from department employees only.

REQUIREMENTS:

- Minimum age: 21; Maximum age: 55
- High school diploma or GED certificate

- Must be physically able to perform the work of the trade
- Pass a written test
- Pass an oral interview
- Valid driver's license
- Resident of the program's jurisdiction
- Pass a test for illegal drugs

• • •

Hoquiam Fire Department
625 8th Street
Hoquiam, WA 98550
206-532-3312

Program title: Hoquiam Fire Department Apprenticeship Program
This is a 3-year program with 432 hours of classroom instruction and 5,568 hours of on-the-job training.
Starting wage: $10.58; Ending wage: $12.77.
Annually, 31-50 people apply for 0-5 positions. There is an initial 6-month probationary period. Applications are accepted in person or by mail when advertised locally. Pick up application at fire department.

REQUIREMENTS:

- Minimum age: 18
- High school diploma or GED certificate
- Must be physically able to perform the work of the trade
- Pass a written test
- Pass an oral interview
- Valid driver's license
- Pass a test for illegal drugs

APPLICATION DOCUMENTS:

Applicants must bring the following documents when applying:
- High school transcript or GED scores
- High school diploma or GED certificate
- Social security card
- Driver's license

• • •

Cowlitz County 2 Fire and Rescue
701 Vine Street
Kelso, WA 98626
206-577-3056

This is a 3-year program with 432 hours of classroom instruction and 5,568 hours of on-the-job training.
Starting wage: $12.65; Ending wage: $13.83.
Annually, 51-100 people apply for 0-5 positions. There is an initial 1-year probationary period. Applications are accepted in person or by mail once a year.

REQUIREMENTS:

- Minimum age: 18
- High school diploma or GED certificate
- Must be physically able to perform the work of the trade
- Pass a written test
- Pass an oral interview
- Valid driver's license
- Letter of recommendation from previous employers, personal references
- Pass a test for illegal drugs

APPLICATION DOCUMENTS:

Applicants must bring the following documents when applying:
- High school diploma or GED certificate
- Social security card
- Driver's license
- Paramedic certification

ADDITIONAL PROGRAM COMMENTS:

Send a self-addressed, stamped envelope and a $15.00 check or money order (administrative fee) to the above address to receive an application packet.

• • •

City Hall
PO Box 6108
Kennewick, WA 99336
509-586-4181

Program title: Kennewick Firefighter Apprenticeship Program
This is a 3-year program with 432 hours of classroom instruction and 5,568 hours of on-the-job training.
Starting wage: $11.81; Ending wage: $15.49.
Annually, over 100 people apply for 6-10 positions.
Course credit is offered.
There is an initial 1-year probationary period. Applications are accepted in person or by mail through an entrance exam, once a year.

REQUIREMENTS:

- Minimum age: 18
- High school diploma or GED certificate
- Must be physically able to perform the work of the trade
- Pass a written test
- Pass an oral interview
- Valid driver's license
- Pass a test for illegal drugs

APPLICATION DOCUMENTS:

Applicants must bring the following documents when applying:
- Driver's license

ADDITIONAL PROGRAM COMMENTS:

Applicants may contact to be placed on notification list of exam date and deadline.
Application packets are mailed out only once a year one month prior to entrance exam.
Applicants must become EMT certified during first year of hire on their own time. Not part of apprenticeship program.

• • •

Kent Fire Department
24611 116th Avenue SE
Kent, WA 98031
206-859-3322

Program title: Kent Fire Department Apprenticeship Program
This is a 3-year program with 432 hours of classroom instruction and 5,568 hours of on-the-job training.
Starting wage: $11.75; Ending wage: $15.67.
Annually, over 100 people apply for 0-5 positions.
There is an initial 1-year probationary period. Applications are accepted in person or by mail through exam given once a year. Call to be placed on notification.

REQUIREMENTS:

- Minimum age: 18
- High school diploma or GED certificate
- Must be physically able to perform the work of the trade
- Pass a written test
- Pass an oral interview
- Valid driver's license

APPLICATION DOCUMENTS:

Applicants must bring the following documents when applying:
- High school diploma or GED certificate
- Social security card
- Driver's license

• • •

Westinghouse Hanford Fire Department
PO Box 1970, #H2-22
2425 Stevens Center
Richland, WA 99352
509-373-2830

This is a 3-year program with 300 hours of classroom instruction and 5,700 hours of on-the-job training.
Starting wage: $12.67; Ending wage: $18.11.
Annually, 31-50 people apply for 0-5 positions.
Course credit is offered.
There is an initial 6-month probationary period. Applications are accepted in person or by mail Monday-Friday, 7:30-4:00.

REQUIREMENTS:

- Minimum age: 18
- High school diploma or GED certificate
- Must be physically able to perform the work of the trade
- Pass an oral interview
- Valid driver's license

- Letter of recommendation from previous employers, teachers
- Pass a test for illegal drugs

APPLICATION DOCUMENTS:

Applicants must bring the following documents when applying:
- High school transcript or GED scores
- High school diploma or GED certificate
- Social security card
- Driver's license

ADDITIONAL PROGRAM COMMENTS:

The Westinghouse employment number is 800-438-1305

• • •

Spokane City Fire Department #9
14 West Graves Road
Spokane, WA 99218
509-466-4602

This is a 3-year program with 700 hours of classroom instruction and 5,300 hours of on-the-job training.
Starting wage: $8.97; Ending wage: $12.82.
Annually, over 100 people apply for 0-5 positions.
There is an initial 6-month probationary period.
Applications are accepted in person or by mail once every two years through entrance exam.

REQUIREMENTS:

- Minimum age: 18
- High school diploma or GED certificate
- Must be physically able to perform the work of the trade
- Pass a written test
- Valid driver's license
- Pass a test for illegal drugs

APPLICATION DOCUMENTS:

Applicants must bring the following documents when applying:
- Driver's license

ADDITIONAL PROGRAM COMMENTS:

Applicants may enter themselves upon the interest list where they will be notified on test dates and deadlines.

• • •

Pierce County Fire District #2
5000 Steilacoom Boulevard SW
Tacoma, WA 98499
206-582-4600

Program title: Pierce County Fire District #2 Apprenticeship Program
This is a 3-year program with 432 hours of classroom instruction and 5,568 hours of on-the-job training.
Starting wage: $12.22; Ending wage: $17.16.
Annually, over 100 people apply for 0-5 positions.
There is an initial 1-year probationary period.
Applications are accepted in person or by mail only during entrance exam, once every two years.

REQUIREMENTS:

- Minimum age: 18
- High school diploma or GED certificate
- Must be physically able to perform the work of the trade
- Pass a written test
- Pass an oral interview
- Valid driver's license

APPLICATION DOCUMENTS:

Applicants must bring the following documents when applying:
- High school diploma or GED certificate
- Social security card
- Driver's license

ADDITIONAL PROGRAM COMMENTS:

There is a pre-employment medical exam. Applicant must be certified as an EMT within one year of employment.

• • •

Wenatchee Fire Department
136 South Chelon Avenue
Wenatchee, WA 98801
509-664-3950

Program title: Wenatchee Firefighter Apprenticeship Committee
This is a 3-year program with 432 hours of classroom instruction and 6,000 hours of on-the-job training.
Starting wage: $12.48; Ending wage: $15.60.
Annually, over 100 people apply for 0-5 positions.
There is an initial 1-year probationary period.
Applications are accepted in person or by mail.

REQUIREMENTS:

- Minimum age: 21
- High school diploma or GED certificate
- Physician's statement of fitness
- Must be physically able to perform the work of the trade
- Pass a written test
- Pass an oral interview
- Valid driver's license
- Pass a test for illegal drugs

APPLICATION DOCUMENTS:

Applicants must bring the following documents when applying:
- High school diploma or GED certificate
- Social security card
- Driver's license

ADDITIONAL PROGRAM COMMENTS:

Credit of up to 2.5 years can be given if applicant has proof of previous training or experience can be shown. Applications are given out at the beginning of June. The application must be returned by deadline (which varies from year to year) with a $25.00 administrative fee. Applicants are then mailed a book for study in preparation for testing which is conducted in September.

• • •

WASHINGTON, DC

District of Columbia Personnel
404 4th Street, NW
Washington, DC 20001
202-939-8734

SPECIFICATIONS:

Certification is mandatory but not required before hire.
There is 1 full paid fire department in the district.
Applicants must already be hired as a firefighter to attend the training academy.

• • •

WEST VIRGINIA

State Fire Commission
PO Box 50140
2100 Washington Street, East
Charleston, WV 25305-0140

SPECIFICATIONS:

Certification is mandatory.
Certification is required within one year of hire.
There are 9 full paid fire departments in the state.

• • •

Beckley Fire Department
City of Beckley
PO Drawer A J
Beckley, WV 25802
304-256-1768

Program title: WV Professional Firefighters' Certification and Apprenticeship
This is a 3-year program with 720 hours of classroom instruction and 5,280 hours of on-the-job training.
No salaries were reported by this program.
Annually, over 100 people apply for 0-5 positions.
Course credit is offered.
There is an initial 6-month probationary period.

Applications are accepted in person or by mail when advertised. Entrance exam given every three years.

REQUIREMENTS:

- Minimum age: 18
- High school diploma or GED certificate
- Must be physically able to perform the work of the trade
- Pass a written test
- Valid driver's license
- Resident of the program's jurisdiction for 1 year

APPLICATION DOCUMENTS:

Applicants must bring the following documents when applying:
- High school transcript or GED scores
- High school diploma or GED certificate
- Social security card
- Driver's license

ADDITIONAL PROGRAM COMMENTS:

Starting salary approximately $6.97; ending salary approximately $7.05.

• • •

Charleston Fire Department
Box 2749
Charleston, WV 25330
304-348-0732

This is a 3-year program with 750 hours of classroom instruction and 5,250 hours of on-the-job training.
No salaries were reported by this program.
Annually, over 100 people apply for 0-5 positions.
Course credit is offered.
There is an initial 6-month probationary period. Applications are accepted in person or by mail 8:00-4:00 at entrance. Contact for further information.

REQUIREMENTS:

- Minimum age: 18; Maximum age: 35
- High school diploma or GED certificate
- Must be physically able to perform the work of the trade
- Pass a written test
- Valid driver's license
- Pass a test for illegal drugs

APPLICATION DOCUMENTS:

Applicants must bring the following documents when applying:
- High school transcript or GED scores
- High school diploma or GED certificate
- Social security card
- Driver's license

ADDITIONAL PROGRAM COMMENTS:

Starting salary is approximately $9.13; ending salary approximately $10.09. For application contact:

Charleston City Hall
City Clerk's Office
(corner of Court and Virginia)
Charleston, WV 25301
304-348-8179

• • •

Clarksburg Fire Department
465 West Main Street
Clarksburg, WV 26301
304-624-1669

This is a 3-year program with 750 hours of classroom instruction and 5,250 hours of on-the-job training.
Starting wage: $4.47; Ending wage: $6.75.
Annually, 51-100 people apply for 0-5 positions.
Course credit is offered.
There is an initial 6-month probationary period. Applications are accepted in person between 8:00-4:30, Monday-Friday, when announced locally.

REQUIREMENTS:

- Minimum age: 18; Maximum age: 35
- High school diploma or GED certificate
- Must be physically able to perform the work of the trade
- Pass a written test

- Pass an oral interview
- Valid driver's license
- Resident of the program's jurisdiction for 1 year
- Pass a test for illegal drugs

APPLICATION DOCUMENTS:

Applicants must bring the following documents when applying:
- High school diploma or GED certificate
- Driver's license
- Birth certificate
- College diploma

ADDITIONAL PROGRAM COMMENTS:

Contact:

Chief Spencer
City Hall
227 West Pike Street
Clarksburg, WV 26301
304-624-1673

• • •

Dunbar Fire Department
907 Dunbar Avenue
Dunbar, WV 25064
304-766-0215

Program title: Dunbar Fire Department Apprenticeship & Training Program
This is a 3-year program with 6,000 hours of classroom instruction.
Starting wage: $6.33; Ending wage: $6.33.
Annually, 21-30 people apply for 0-5 positions.
There is an initial 6-month probationary period.
Applications are accepted in person or by mail when testing is called for Civil Service.

REQUIREMENTS:

- Minimum age: 18; Maximum age: 35
- High school diploma or GED certificate
- Physician's statement of fitness
- Must be physically able to perform the work of the trade
- Pass a written test

- Valid driver's license
- Letter of recommendation from employers and friends
- Pass a test for illegal drugs

APPLICATION DOCUMENTS:

Applicants must bring the following documents when applying:
- High school diploma or GED certificate
- Driver's license

ADDITIONAL PROGRAM COMMENTS:

References and background will be checked.

• • •

Huntington Fire Department
839 Seventh Avenue
PO Box 1659
Huntington, WV 25701
304-696-5950

This is a 3-year program with 756 hours of classroom instruction and 2,592 hours of on-the-job training.
Starting wage: $5.57; Ending wage: $6.78.
Annually, over 100 people apply for 6-10 positions.
Course credit is offered.
There is an initial 6-month probationary period.
Applications are accepted in person or by mail when recruitment is announced in local paper.

REQUIREMENTS:

- Minimum age: 18; Maximum age: 36
- High school diploma or GED certificate
- Must be physically able to perform the work of the trade
- Pass a written test
- Pass an oral interview
- Valid driver's license
- Pass a test for illegal drugs

APPLICATION DOCUMENTS:

Applicants must bring the following documents when applying:
- High school transcript or GED scores
- High school diploma or GED certificate
- Driver's license

ADDITIONAL PROGRAM COMMENTS:

Apply to:

City Clerk
Room 16
800 Fifth Avenue
Huntington, WV 25701
304-696-5530

• • •

 Moundsville Fire Department
804 Sixth Street
Moundsville, WV 26041
304-845-2050

This is a 3-year program with 432 hours of classroom instruction and 6,000 hours of on-the-job training.
Starting wage: $8.33; Ending wage: $9.05.
Annually, 31-50 people apply for 0-5 positions.
There is an initial 6-month probationary period. Applications are accepted in person only when published in local newspaper.

REQUIREMENTS:

- Minimum age: 18; Maximum age: 35
- High school diploma or GED certificate
- Physician's statement of fitness
- Must be physically able to perform the work of the trade
- Pass a written test
- Valid driver's license
- Resident of the program's jurisdiction for 1 year

APPLICATION DOCUMENTS:

Applicants must bring the following documents when applying:
- High school diploma or GED certificate
- Social security card
- Driver's license

ADDITIONAL PROGRAM COMMENTS:

Residency is not required after hire.

• • •

WISCONSIN

 Fire Education & Training
310 Price Road
PO Box 7874
Madison, WI 53707
608-266-7289

SPECIFICATIONS:

Certification is voluntary.
There are 64 full paid fire departments in this state.

• • •

 City of Green Bay
Personnel Department
100 North Jefferson
Green Bay, WI 54301
414-448-3147

This is a 3.5-year program with 630 hours of classroom instruction and 6,370 hours of on-the-job training.
Starting wage: $12.36; Ending wage: $16.95.
Annually, over 100 people apply for 6-10 positions.
There is an initial 1-year probationary period. Applications are accepted in person or by mail any time of year. Personnel will notify those on interest list.

REQUIREMENTS:

- Minimum age: 18
- High school diploma or GED certificate
- Physician's statement of fitness
- Must be physically able to perform the work of the trade
- Pass a written test
- Pass an oral interview
- Valid driver's license
- Resident of the program's jurisdiction for 1 year
- Pass a test for illegal drugs
- Must attend a preapprenticeship class for 60 hours

APPLICATION DOCUMENTS:

Applicants must bring the following documents when applying:
- High school transcript or GED scores
- High school diploma or GED certificate
- Social security card
- Driver's license
- Birth certificate

ADDITIONAL PROGRAM COMMENTS:

Candidates are subject to a background investigation. Job requirements include an associate's or bachelor's degree in fire science or one year's full-time experience as a paid fire fighter or paramedic. Unpaid experience considered if candidate has documentation of 2,500 hours of training and experience or is certified as a Fire Fighter III by the State of Wisconsin.

• • •

City of Waukesha
Personnel Department
201 Delafield Street
Waukesha, WI
414-524-3745

Program title: City of Waukesha Fire Department Apprenticeship Program
This is a 3-year program with 432 hours of classroom instruction and 5,568 hours of on-the-job training.
Starting wage: $8.80; Ending wage: $11.46.
Annually, 0-10 people apply for 0-5 positions.
There is an initial 12-month probationary period.
Applications are accepted in person when given out in person during recruitment.

REQUIREMENTS:

- Minimum age: 21
- High school diploma or GED certificate
- Physician's statement of fitness
- Must be physically able to perform the work of the trade
- Pass a written test
- Pass an oral interview
- Valid driver's license

APPLICATION DOCUMENTS:

Applicants must bring the following documents when applying:
- Social security card
- Driver's license

• • •

WYOMING

Department of Fire Prevention and Electrical Safety
Herschler Building
1st Floor, West Wing
Cheyenne, WY 82002
307-777-7909

SPECIFICATIONS:

Certification is voluntary.
There are 12 full paid fire departments in the state.

• • •

Folk Arts Apprenticeships

Apprenticeships in the folk arts are nothing like the formal, legally binding job training apprenticeships presented elsewhere in this directory. Created in 1977 by the National Endowment for the Arts, the Folk Arts Program seeks to support traditional arts that are identified with a specific cultural community, whether ethnic, occupational, religious, regional, or a community defined by age or gender. Programs are state based and may be funded entirely by a particular state or share funding with the NEA.

"Traditional art" suggests an art form that has a history or has evolved over time within a community. Frequently traditional arts are passed from one generation to the next, whether it is parents teaching children, village elders teaching youths, or masters teaching apprentices.

Folk arts apprenticeships stress the one-to-one communication between master and apprentice. They are about more than just learning a skill or a craft, for through his teaching, the master passes on a part of himself and a part of the culture he comes from. For this reason folk arts apprenticeships usually require the master and the apprentice to be of the same cultural background and that the craft being taught be a traditional craft of that culture.

Examples of traditional crafts and skills taught in folk arts apprenticeships include musical instrument making, Ukranian egg painting, Native American quillwork, canoe building, basket making, lace making, storytelling, Acadian singing, fiddling, step dancing, rug braiding, gospel singing, snowshoe making, saddle making, Laotian weaving, and African drumming. Most states require that the master be recognized by his or her community as one of the finest practitioners of the craft and that the apprentice, too, already have some skill in the craft, as well as a commitment and determination to continue to practice it. Some states fund only crafts and skills that are considered "endangered," i.e., on the verge of being lost forever because of the limited number of practitioners.

Before applying for an apprenticeship grant, the master and the apprentice should formulate a plan for the apprenticeship. What is the goal? How often will they meet? What skills will be learned? How long will it take? How much will it cost? The state organizations (usually the state arts council) can assist in this process, and may even insist on it as a condition of the application. Once a plan has been formalized, the master and the apprentice together fill out the application for the grant. Most states require that, in addition to the application, both master and apprentice submit several slides or photographs of their work, or several minutes of audio or videotape if it is of a performance nature, as proof of their skill. (Nearly all states stress that they do not want physical samples of the work.) Some also ask for letters of recommendation from other community members attesting to the master's skill or the apprentice's commitment.

Grants can range from $1,500 to $5,000 and are usually intended to compensate the master for his or her time, although some consideration is often given for material and travel expenses. Most states require that the apprentice be a legal resident of the state; in most cases, the master need not be a state resident.

Apprenticeships normally range from three months to a year, during which time a representative from the state arts council may visit the training site to observe the work and interview the master and apprentice. In some states, following the apprenticeship training, the master and the apprentice are asked to participate in a public demonstration of their skills, or to write a report of their experience. After the completion of the apprenticeship, in most cases, masters are permitted to apply for additional grants with new apprentices, but apprentices are not allowed to reapply. New applicants who are not successful the first time, however, may reapply.

Applications are normally evaluated by a committee, which bases its decision on such criteria as the traditionality of the art, the quality of work of both the master and the apprentice, whether they are both members of the same cultural community, how dedicated the apprentice is to the art form, and how likely the apprenticeship timetable and work plan are to succeed.

Most states do not fund art forms that are not traditional in nature or that are re-creations of historic traditions that have already passed. They also do not fund the work of professional teachers, contemporary studio craftspeople, or those who make reproductions of antiques. Most apprenticeships must be one-on-one training, although some exceptions are made for skills that are primarily group activities.

Following are the addresses for the national and state organizations that sponsor folk arts apprenticeships. Remember to contact them first for assistance in planning an apprenticeship program, and any time thereafter for additional counseling.

NATIONAL PROGRAM

 Public Information Office
Room 803
National Endowment for the Arts
Nancy Hanks Center
1100 Pennsylvania Avenue, NW
Washington, DC 20506
202-682-5400

• • •

STATE SPONSORS

ALABAMA

 Alabama State Council on the Arts
323 Adams Avenue
Montgomery, AL 36130
205-242-4076
ATTN: Joey Brackner

• • •

Folk Arts Apprenticeships

ALASKA

Alaska State Council on the Arts
411 West 4th Avenue, Suite 1E
Anchorage, AK 99501
907-279-1558
ATTN: Vernon Chimegalrea

• • •

ARIZONA

The Southwest Folklore Center
1053 East 8th Street, Suite B
Tucson, AZ 85719
602-621-3392
ATTN: James Griffith

• • •

ARKANSAS

Arkansas Arts Council
The Heritage Center
225 East Markham Street, #200
Little Rock, AR 72201
501-371-2539

• • •

COLORADO

Arvada Center for the Arts and Humanities
10 Ridge Road
Colorado Springs, CO 80904
719-633-5793
ATTN: Bea Roeder

• • •

CONNECTICUT

Institute for Community Research
2 Hartford Square West, #100
Hartford, CT 06106
203-278-2141
ATTN: Lynne Williamson

• • •

DELAWARE

Division of Parks and Recreation
PO Box 1401
Dover, DE 19903
302-739-4413
ATTN: Gregory Jenkins

• • •

FLORIDA

Florida Folklife Program
Florida Department of State
PO Box 265
White Springs, FL 32096
904-397-2192
ATTN: Ormond Loomis

• • •

GEORGIA

Georgia Folklife Program
Georgia Council for the Arts
530 Means Street, NW, #115
Atlanta, GA 30318
404-651-7920
ATTN: Maggie Holtzberg

• • •

HAWAII

 The State Foundation on
Culture and the Arts
335 Merchant Street, Room 202
Honolulu, HI 96813
808-586-0302
ATTN: Lynn Martin

• • •

IDAHO

 Idaho Commission on the Arts
c/o Statehouse Mail
Boise, ID 83720
208-334-2119
ATTN: Deborah Fant

• • •

ILLINOIS

 Folk and Ethnic Arts Program
Illinois Arts Council
State of Illinois Center
100 West Randolph, #10-500
Chicago, IL 60601
312-814-6750
ATTN: Loretta Rhoads

• • •

INDIANA

 Indiana Arts Commission
Arts: Rural and Multicultural
402 West Washington, Room 072
Indianapolis, IN 46204
317-232-1268

• • •

IOWA

 Community Arts and Cultural
Heritage Program
Iowa Arts Council
1223 East Court Avenue
Des Moines, IA 50319
515-281-4008

• • •

KANSAS

 Kansas State Historical Society
120 West 10th Street
Topeka, KS 66612
913-272-8681
ATTN: Jennie Chinn

• • •

KENTUCKY

 Kentucky Folklife Program
PO Box H
Frankfort, KY 40602
502-564-3016
ATTN: Robert Gates

• • •

LOUISIANA

 State of Louisiana
Department of Culture,
Recreation, and Tourism
PO Box 44247, 1051 N. Third
Baton Rouge, LA 70804
504-342-8180
ATTN: Maida Owens

• • •

MAINE

Maine Arts Commission
55 Capitol Street
State House Station 25
Augusta, ME 04333
207-287-2724
ATTN: Kathleen Mundell

• • •

MARYLAND

Maryland State Arts Council
601 North Howard Street, 1st floor
Baltimore, MD 21201
410-333-8232
ATTN: Charles Camp

• • •

MASSACHUSETTS

Massachusetts Cultural Council
80 Boylston Street, Room 1000
Boston, MA 02116
617-727-3668

• • •

MICHIGAN

Michigan Traditional Arts
Apprenticeship Program
Michigan State University Museum
East Lansing, MI 48824
517-353-9678
ATTN: Yvonne Lockwood

• • •

MINNESOTA

Minnesota State Arts Board
432 Summit Avenue
St. Paul, MN 55102
612-297-2603
ATTN: Philip Nusbaum

• • •

MISSISSIPPI

Mississippi Arts Commission
239 North Lamar Street
Jackson, MS 39201
601-359-6030
ATTN: Deborah Boykin

• • •

MISSOURI

Missouri Folk Arts Program
Museum of Art and Archaeology
Packard Hall
University of Missouri, Columbia
Columbia, MO 65211
314-882-3591
ATTN: Dana Everts-Boehm

• • •

MONTANA

Montana Arts Council
48 North Last Chance Gulch
Helena, MT 59620
406-444-6430
ATTN: Nicholas Vrooman

• • •

NEBRASKA

Nebraska Arts Council
3838 Davenport
Omaha, NE 68131
402-595-2122
ATTN: Gwendolyn Meister

• • •

NEVADA

Nevada State Council on the Arts
Capitol Complex
100 South Stewart Street
Carson City, NV 89710
702-687-6680
ATTN: Andrea Graham

• • •

NEW HAMPSHIRE

New Hampshire State
Council on the Arts
40 North Main Street
Concord, NH 03301
603-271-2789

• • •

NEW JERSEY

Folklife Program
New Jersey Historical Commission
113 West State Street
Trenton, NJ 08625
609-292-6062
ATTN: David Cohen

• • •

NEW MEXICO

New Mexico Arts Division
224 East Palace Avenue
Santa Fe, NM 87501
505-827-6490
ATTN: Claude Stephenson

• • •

NEW YORK

Folk Arts Program
New York State Council on the Arts
915 Broadway
New York, NY 10010
212-387-7031
ATTN: Robert Baron

• • •

NORTH CAROLINA

Office of Folklife Programs
North Carolina Department of
Cultural Resources
109 East Jones Street, #316
Raleigh, NC 27611
919-733-7897
ATTN: George Holt

• • •

NORTH DAKOTA

North Dakota Council on the Arts
Black Building, #606
Fargo, ND 58102
701-237-8959
ATTN: Troyd Geist

• • •

OHIO

Ohio Arts Council
Traditional Arts Apprenticeship Program
727 East Main Street
Columbus, OH 43205
614-466-2613
ATTN: Noreen Mulcahy

• • •

OKLAHOMA

State Arts Council of Oklahoma
Jim Thorpe Building, Room 640
2101 North Lincoln Boulevard
Oklahoma City, OK 73105
405-521-2931
ATTN: Dayna Lee

• • •

OREGON

Oregon Folk Arts Program
Oregon Historical Society
1230 SW Park Avenue
Portland, OR 97205
503-221-1741
ATTN: Nancy Nusz

• • •

PENNSYLVANIA

Governor's Heritage Affairs Commission
309 Forum Building
Harrisburg, PA 17120
717-783-8625
ATTN: Amy Skillman

• • •

RHODE ISLAND

Rhode Island Folklife Project
The Old State House
150 Benefit Street
Providence, RI 02903
401-781-5531
ATTN: Michael Bell

• • •

SOUTH CAROLINA

South Carolina Arts Commission
1800 Gervais Street
Columbia, SC 29201
803-734-8696
ATTN: Lesley Williams

• • •

SOUTH DAKOTA

State Folk Arts and Folklife
Cultural Heritage Center
900 Governors Drive
Pierre, SD 57501
605-773-3458
ATTN: Michael Miller

• • •

TENNESSEE

Tennessee Arts Commission
320 6th Avenue, North, #100
Nashville, TN 37219
615-741-1701
ATTN: Robert Cogswell

• • •

TEXAS

Texas Folklife Resources
PO Box 49824
Austin, TX 78765
512-320-0022

• • •

UTAH

Utah Arts Council Folk Arts Program
617 East South Temple
Salt Lake City, UT 84102
801-533-5760

• • •

VERMONT

Vermont Folklife Center
Gamaliel Painter House, Box 442
Middlebury, VT 05753
802-388-4964
ATTN: Greg Sharrow

• • •

VIRGINIA

Virginia Foundation for the Humanities
The Virginia Folklife Program
145 Ednam Drive
Charlottesville, VA 22901
804-924-3776
ATTN: Gary Barrow

• • •

WASHINGTON

Washington State Arts Commission
234 East 8th Avenue, PO Box 42675
Olympia, WA 98504
206-753-3860
ATTN: Willie Smyth

• • •

WASHINGTON, DC

D.C. Commission of the
Arts and Humanities
410 Eighth Street, NW, 5th Fl.
Washington, DC 20004
202-724-5613
ATTN: Michael Licht

• • •

WEST VIRGINIA

Division of Culture and History
Capitol Complex
Charleston, WV 25305
304-348-0220
ATTN: Danny Williams

• • •

WISCONSIN

Wisconsin Arts Board
101 East Wilson Street
Madison, WI 53703
608-266-0190
ATTN: Richard March

• • •

WYOMING

American Studies Program
University of Wyoming
Box 4036, Cooper House
Laramie, WY 82071
307-766-6197
ATTN: Timothy Evans

• • •

Funeral Directors and Embalmers

Embalmers are responsible for disinfecting, preserving, and improving the appearance of dead bodies. Most are employed by funeral homes. There they assist *funeral directors,* whose primary job is to make funeral and burial arrangements. Other embalmers work in hospitals and medical schools, where they prepare bodies for autopsies and dissection classes, assist pathologists, and maintain records.

Embalming has long been practiced in the United States. It first became popular during the Civil War, when bodies needed to be preserved before shipping them home. President Lincoln himself was embalmed. Embalming allows the body to maintain a lifelike appearance and to be presentable for viewing for an extended period after death. In some states all bodies must be embalmed if more than 48 hours pass between the death and burial.

The work of an embalmer begins when a body is brought to the funeral home. If the body was not given an autopsy, the first step is to clean the skin and hair. An incision is then made either at the base of the neck or in the groin, where tubes can be inserted into a major artery and vein. A mechanical pump injects a preservative and disinfecting solution into the tube connected to the artery, causing the solution to fill the circulatory system. In the process the body's blood is forced out through the vein connected to the other tube. Fluid and gases from the trunk are then removed with a long hollow needle and replaced with a disinfecting chemical. The embalmer might use cosmetics to improve the facial appearance, and the body is then dressed and placed in a casket.

More complex is the preparation of a body after an autopsy. Autopsies frequently leave parts of the body disfigured, and the embalmer tries to restore the body's original appearance using various materials, including wax, cotton, plaster of paris, and cosmetics.

Requirements for embalmers and funeral directors vary from state to state, but in general they must have some postsecondary education in mortuary science, undergo an apprenticeship lasting one to three years (though most commonly just one year), and then pass a state examination, which might include written, oral, and practical testing. In school students typically study such subjects as anatomy, embalming practices, and public health laws. Apprenticeships allow those entering the field to gradually learn practical skills under an established embalmer or funeral director. Work study programs are sometimes arranged between schools of mortuary science and funeral homes. In some states embalmers must continue to take classes in order renew their license.

The number of employed embalmers is expected to grow at an average rate. Because there tends to be a shortage of people entering the field, the employment outlook for qualified workers is excellent. The field, moreover, is rarely affected by downturns in the economy, and funeral homes tend to be stable institutions. The average funeral home has been in business more than forty years. Mergers, acquisitions, and consolidation of funeral homes, however, could limit job growth in the future.

Embalmers and funeral directors generally work indoors in exceptionally clean settings. Although most work regular hours, evening or weekend shifts might be necessary. Although embalmers sometimes work on the remains of someone who died of a contagious disease, the risk of infection is quite small, as strict sanitation practices are maintained.

For more information on training programs and apprenticeships for embalmers and funeral directors, write to the organizations listed below. Additional information might be available from you state's bureau of apprenticeship training. The bureau's address is found in the last section of this encyclopedia.

ALABAMA

Alabama Board of Funeral Services
100 Commerce Street, Suite 104
Montgomery, AL 36130
205-242-4049

Embalmer

REQUIREMENTS:

- Minimum age: 16
- High school graduate or GED holder
- Two years of mortuary school
- Two-year apprenticeship with Alabama licensed embalmer
- Pass state embalmers exam

APPLICATION DOCUMENTS:

Applicants must present proof of the following when applying:
- High school diploma or GED

• • •

ALASKA

State of Alaska
Department of Commerce
Economic Development
Division of Occupational Licensing
333 Willoghby Avenue, 9th Floor
PO Box 110806
Juneau, AK 85007
907-465-2580

Funeral Director

REQUIREMENTS:

- High school graduate or GED holder
- Letter of intent from employer
- 30 semester hours of college
- One-year apprenticeship with licensed director
- Pass state board exam
- Pass jurisprudence exam

Embalmer

REQUIREMENTS:

- High school graduate or GED holder
- Letter of intent from employer
- Graduate from mortuary college
- One-year apprenticeship with licensed embalmer
- Pass national board exam

• • •

ARIZONA

Arizona State Board of Funeral Directors and Embalmers
1645 West Jefferson, Room 410
Phoenix, AZ 85007
602-542-3095

Embalmer

REQUIREMENTS

- Must graduate with diploma from an American board-approved mortuary school
- One-year apprenticeship (including at least 25 embalmings) with a licensed Arizona funeral director
- Pass national board exam or state exam
- Get embalming license

APPLICATION DOCUMENTS:

Applicants must present proof of the following when applying:
- Mortuary school
- Apprenticeship

Funeral Director

REQUIREMENTS:

- All requirements for embalmer in addition to holding an embalming license for one year

• • •

ARKANSAS

Arkansas State Board of Embalmers and Funeral Directors
400 Harrison, Suite 203
Batesville, AR 72501
501-698-2072

Embalmer

REQUIREMENTS:

- Minimum age: 18
- High school graduate or GED holder
- Letter of intent from employer
- One year of embalming school
- One-year apprenticeship (Need to have served a position before applying to board for apprenticeship.)
- Letter of recommendation
- Character references

APPLICATION DOCUMENTS:

Applicants must present proof of the following when applying:
- High school diploma or proof of GED
- Employment

Funeral Director
- May do two-year apprenticeship instead of school
- Minimum Age: 18
- High school graduate or GED holder
- Pass an oral interview with funeral home
- Letter of intent from employer
- Letter of recommendation
- Character references

APPLICATION DOCUMENTS:

Applicants must present proof of the following when applying:
- High school diploma or GED
- Employment

• • •

CALIFORNIA

California Board of Funeral Directors and Embalmers
400 R Street, Suite 2060
Sacramento, CA 95814-6213
916-445-2413

Embalmer

REQUIREMENTS:

- Minimum age: 18
- High school graduate or GED holder
- Residency in area
- Letter of intent from employer
- One year of embalming school
- Two-year apprenticeship under California-licensed embalmer (including 100 embalmings)
- Pass tests on embalming
- Pass jurisprudence test

APPLICATION DOCUMENTS:

Applicants must present proof of the following when applying:
- High school diploma
- Police report

• • •

CONNECTICUT

Board of Examiners of Embalmers and Funeral Directors
150 Washington Street
Hartford, CT 06106
203-566-1039

Embalmer

REQUIREMENTS:

- High school graduate or GED holder
- Letter of intent from employer
- Associate's degree in mortuary science
- One-year apprenticeship with Connecticut-licensed embalmer (3 months pregraduate and 9 months postgraduate)

• • •

DELAWARE

Delaware State Board of Funeral Service
Practitioners
PO Box 1401
Margaret O'Neil Building
Dover, DE 19903
302-739-4522

Funeral Director

REQUIREMENTS:

- Minimum age: 18
- High school graduate or GED holder
- Letter of recommendation from other than funeral directors
- 60 credit hours of general schooling plus 30 credit hours of mortuary service
- One-year apprenticeship with licensed funeral director

APPLICATION DOCUMENTS:

Applicants must present proof of the following when applying:
- Schooling
- Police report

• • •

FLORIDA

Florida Department of Professional
Regulation
Board of Funeral
Directors and Embalmers
1940 North Monroe Street
Suite #60
Tallahassee, FL 32399
904-488-8690

Embalmer

REQUIREMENTS:

- One year of school in mortuary science
- One-year internship or apprenticeship with a licensed Florida funeral home
- Minimum age: 18
- High school graduate or GED holder
- Oral interview with a funeral home
- Letter of intent from employer

APPLICATION DOCUMENTS:

Applicants must present proof of the following when applying:
- High school diploma or GED
- Mortuary science school

Funeral Director

REQUIREMENTS:

- Minimum age: 18
- High school graduate or GED holder
- Oral interview with a funeral home
- Letter of intent from employer
- Associate's degree plus one year of mortuary science, or, an associate's degree in funeral service

APPLICATION DOCUMENTS:

Applicants must present proof of the following when applying:
- High school diploma or GED
- Schooling past high school

• • •

GEORGIA

Georgia State Examining Boards
166 Pryor Street SW
Atlanta, GA 30303
404-656-3933

Funeral Service

REQUIREMENTS:

- Minimum age: 18
- High school graduate or GED holder
- Oral interview
- Letter of intent from employer
- One year at a mortuary college
- Pass national boards
- Two-year apprenticeship with a Georgia-licensed and registered funeral director

Funeral Directors and Embalmers

APPLICATION DOCUMENTS:

Applicants must present proof of the following when applying:
- High school diploma or GED
- Mortuary schooling

• • •

IDAHO

Idaho Bureau of Occupational Licenses
Idaho State Board of Morticians
Statehouse
Boise, ID 83720
208-334-3233

Mortician

REQUIREMENTS:

- Minimum age: 18 to go to school, 21 to get a mortician's trainee license
- High school graduate or GED holder
- Letter of intent from employer
- Letter of recommendation from a mortician or a funeral director
- 60 credit hours in liberal arts, business or science
- One year in a mortuary school with a "C" average or better
- Pass conference exam at mortuary school
- Mortician's Trainee License
- One-year apprenticeship with a licensed mortician or funeral director in Idaho

APPLICATION DOCUMENTS:

Applicants must present proof of the following when applying:
- High school diploma or GED scores
- Conference exam at mortuary school

• • •

ILLINOIS

Illinois Department of Professional Regulation
Funeral Directors and Embalmers
License and Discipline Boards
320 Washington Street, 3rd Floor
Springfield, IL 62786
217-782-8556

Funeral Director, Embalmer

REQUIREMENTS:

- Minimum age: 18
- Physician's statement of fitness
- Residency in the area
- Letter of intent from employer
- Birth certificate
- 30 hours in college plus one year of mortuary science or an associate's degree in mortuary science plus a one-year apprenticeship involving embalming and funeral arrangements for 24 bodies
- Pass national board exam

APPLICATION DOCUMENTS:

Applicants must present proof of the following when applying:
- Additional schooling

• • •

INDIANA

Indiana State Board of Funeral and Cemetery Service
100 Senate Avenue, Room 1021
Indianapolis, IN 46204
317-232-7209

Funeral Director

REQUIREMENTS:

- Minimum age: 18
- High school graduate or GED holder
- Letter of intent from employer
- Police record
- 30 semester hours in general college courses

and 4 academic quarters in mortuary science or 21 months of mortuary science
- Pass exam required by board
- One-year apprenticeship

• • •

IOWA

Iowa Professional Licensure
State Department of Health
Lucas State Office Building, 4th Floor
Des Moines, IA 50319-0075
515-281-4416

Funeral Director

REQUIREMENTS:

- High school graduate or GED holder
- Letter of intent from employer
- 60 hours in a regionally accredited college with a 2.0 grade average plus a course in mortuary science
- Pass national board exam with a 75 percent grade or better
- Pass Rules and Laws of the state of Iowa
- Three references from people who are not funeral directors
- Transcripts from all schooling
- One-year internship
- Pass practical exam

• • •

KANSAS

Kansas State Board of Mortuary Arts
700 SW Jackson, Suite 904
Topeka, KS 66603
913-296-3980

Embalmer

REQUIREMENTS:

- Minimum Age: 17
- High school graduate or GED holder
- Oral interview after apprenticeship with a licensed funeral director in Kansas
- An "A" in mortuary science
- One-year apprenticeship with a licensed embalmer (any state)
- Pass national board exam

APPLICATION DOCUMENTS:

Applicants must present proof of the following when applying:
- High school diploma
- College transcript
- National board letter

Funeral Director

REQUIREMENTS:

- 60 credit hours
- One-year apprenticeship with a funeral director licensed in Kansas (must work with 25 families)
- Pass state exam on state laws

• • •

KENTUCKY

Kentucky State Board of Embalmers and Funeral Directors
210 East 4th Street, Cagel Building
PO Box 335
Beaver Dam, KY 42320
502-274-4515

Funeral Director

REQUIREMENTS:

- Three-year apprenticeship to Kentucky licensed funeral director
- Pass state boards
- Residency in the area
- Letter of intent from employer

APPLICATION DOCUMENTS:

Applicants must present proof of the following when applying:
- High school diploma

Embalmer

REQUIREMENTS:

- One year of mortuary school
- Two-year apprenticeship to Kentucky licensed embalmer
- Pass state board
- Residency in the area
- Letter of intent from employer

APPLICATION DOCUMENTS:

Applicants must present proof of the following when applying:
- High school diploma

• • •

LOUISIANA

Louisiana State Board of Embalmers and Funeral Directors
3500 Causeway Boulevard North
Executive Towers, Suite 1232
Metaire, LA 70011
504-838-5109

Funeral Director

REQUIREMENTS:

- Minimum Age: 18
- High school graduate or GED holder
- Oral interview
- Letter of intent from employer
- 30 semester hours in a SACS associated school
- One-year internship with a licensed funeral director
- Pass national board exam with score of 75 percent or better
- 15 months at an American Board-accredited mortuary science school
- One-year apprenticeship with a licensed embalmer/funeral director (may serve six months of apprenticeship prior to mortuary school and six months past mortuary school)
- Pass national board exam with 75 percent or better

APPLICATION DOCUMENTS:

Applicants must present proof of the following when applying:
- High school diploma or GED
- Birth certificate
- Additional schooling

Embalmer

- Minimum age: 18
- High school graduate or GED holder
- Oral interview
- Letter of intent from employer
- 15 months at an American Board-accredited mortuary science school
- One-year apprenticeship with a licensed embalmer/funeral director (may serve six months of apprenticeship prior to mortuary school and six months past mortuary school)
- Pass national board exam with 75 percent or better

APPLICATION DOCUMENTS:

Applicants must present proof of the following when applying:
- High school diploma or GED
- Birth certificate
- Additional schooling

• • •

MAINE

Maine Board of Funeral Service
State House Station 35
Augusta, ME 04333
207-582-8723, ext. 2325

Embalmer

REQUIREMENTS:

- Minimum age: 18
- High school graduate or GED holder
- Pass conference boards
- Letter of intent from employer
- Letter of recommendation
- Two years of school
- Pass conference boards
- 2,000-hour apprenticeship

- Practical exams (perform autopsy)
- Laws of Maine exams

APPLICATION DOCUMENTS:

Applicants must present proof of the following when applying:
- High school diploma
- Birth certificate
- Conference board exam

• • •

MARYLAND

Maryland State Board of Morticians
4201 Patterson Avenue
Baltimore, MD 21215
410-764-4792

Mortician

REQUIREMENTS:

- 2,000-hour apprenticeship under licensed mortician (must participate in 25 funerals and 25 embalmings)
- Associate's degree in mortuary science or 60 credit hours in any college plus a certificate in mortuary science
- Pass national conference test
- Pass state law test
- Pass practical exam
- High school graduate or GED holder
- Oral interview with sponsor present

APPLICATION DOCUMENTS:

Applicants must present proof of the following when applying:
- High school transcript

• • •

MICHIGAN

Michigan Bureau of Occupational and Professional Regulation
Testing Services Division
PO Box 30018
Lansing, MI 48909
527-373-1699

Practitioner of mortuary science

REQUIREMENTS:

- Minimum age: 18
- High school graduate or GED holder
- Three-year course in mortuary science at accredited school
- One-year resident training under the supervision of the holder of a license for the practice of mortuary science (must include embalming of 25 bodies and assistance at 20 funerals)
- Pass national or state board exam
- Pass state laws exam

APPLICATION DOCUMENTS:

Applicants must present proof of the following when applying:
- High school diploma

• • •

MINNESOTA

Minnesota Mortuary Science Unit
717 SE Delaware Street
PO Box 9441
Minneapolis, MN 55440
612-623-5492

Mortician

REQUIREMENTS:

- Minimum age: 18
- High school graduate or GED holder
- Letter of intent from employer
- Two years of college
- Graduation from college of mortuary science
- Pass national board exam
- One-year apprenticeship

Funeral Director

REQUIREMENTS:

- Minimum age: 18
- High school graduate or GED holder
- Letter of intent from employer
- Two years of college

- Graduation from college of mortuary science
- One-year apprenticeship
- Pass tests given by commissioner

• • •

MISSISSIPPI

Mississippi State Board of Funeral Service
802 North State Street
Executive Building, Suite 401
Jackson, MS 39202
601-354-6903

Funeral Director

REQUIREMENTS:

- Minimum age: 18
- High school graduate or GED holder
- Oral interview
- Letter of recommendation
- Two-year apprenticeship with a licensed funeral director
- Pass state board exam with score of 75 percent or better

APPLICATION DOCUMENTS:

Applicants must present proof of the following when applying:
- High school diploma or GED scores
- Schooling
- Birth certificate

• • •

MISSOURI

Missouri State Board of Funeral Directors and Embalmers
3605 Missouri Boulevard
PO Box 423
Jefferson City, MO 65102
314-751-0813

Embalmer

REQUIREMENTS:

- High school graduate or GED holder
- Graduate from mortuary school
- Pass national conference exam
- One-year apprenticeship with licensed embalmer
- Get application from state board
- Oral state board test

APPLICATION DOCUMENTS:

Applicants must present proof of the following when applying:
- High school transcript
- National scores

• • •

MONTANA

Montana Board of Morticians
Arcade Building
111 North Jackson
Helena, Mt 59620
406-444-5433

Mortician

REQUIREMENTS:

- Minimum age: 18
- 90 quarter credits at an accredited university
- Diploma from college of mortuary science
- Pass national board exam
- Pass state law exam
- One-year internship
- Assist in complete funeral service for at least 25 bodies

• • •

NEBRASKA

Nebraska Bureau of Examining Boards
Department of Health
PO Box 95007
Lincoln, NE 68509-5007
402-471-2115

Funeral Director

REQUIREMENTS:

- Minimum age: 18
- High school graduate or GED holder
- Letter of intent from employer
- Letter of recommendation
- 39 hours of general college
- One year of mortuary science
- One-year apprenticeship with Nebraska-licensed funeral director (may be split up with six months before mortuary school and six months after)
- Pass national board exam
- Pass state jurisprudence test

Embalmer

REQUIREMENTS:

- Minimum age: 18
- High school graduate or GED holder
- Letter of intent from employer
- Letter of recommendation
- 39 hours of general college
- One year of mortuary science
- One-year apprenticeship with Nebraska-licensed funeral director (may be split up with six months before mortuary school and six months after)
- Pass national board exam
- Pass state jurisprudence test

• • •

NEW HAMPSHIRE

Board of Registration of Funeral Directors and Embalmers
Health and Human Services
New Hampshire
603-271-4648

Embalmer

REQUIREMENTS:

- High school graduate or GED holder
- Pass oral interview with sponsor
- Letter of intent from employer
- Letter of recommendation from a licensed New Hampshire funeral director
- Must attend preapprenticeship class
- One-year apprenticeship with licensed New Hampshire funeral director
- 30 credit hours of general studies plus one year of mortuary science

APPLICATION DOCUMENTS:

Applicants must present proof of the following when applying:
- High school diploma or GED

• • •

NEW JERSEY

State Board of Mortuary Science of New Jersey
124 Halsey St, 6th Floor
PO Box 45009
Newark, NJ 07101

Funeral Service

REQUIREMENTS

- High school graduate or GED holder
- Two years of college
- One year of mortuary science school
- Two-year internship at a funeral home in New Jersey
- Pass the national board examination
- Pass a mortuary jurisprudence examination
- Pass a practical embalming examination

• • •

NEW MEXICO

New Mexico Board of Thanatopractice
725 Saint Michael's Drive
PO Box 25101
Santa Fe, New Mexico 87504
505-827-7177

Funeral Service Practitioner

REQUIREMENTS:

- Minimum age: 18
- High school graduate or GED holder
- Letter of intent from employer
- Letter of recommendation from a licensed practitioner
- Associate's degree plus one year of mortuary school
- Pass conference board exam
- Pass New Mexico jurisprudence exam
- One-year apprenticeship with licensed funeral service practitioner

APPLICATION DOCUMENTS:

Applicants must present proof of the following when applying:
- High school diploma or GED
- Additional schooling

• • •

NEW YORK

New York Bureau of Funeral Directing
New York City Department of Health,
Corning TWR, ESP
Albany, NY 12237-0681
518-453-1989

Registered Residency for Funeral Director

REQUIREMENTS:

- High school graduate or GED holder
- Letter of intent from employer
- Must go to school first and must register with Bureau of Funeral Directing as a student
- 60 credit hours in mortuary science or 30 credit hours in general studies plus one year of mortuary science
- Pass national board exam
- One-year residency apprenticeship
- Pass Rules and Regulations of New York exam

APPLICATION DOCUMENTS:

Applicants must present proof of the following when applying:
- Birth certificate
- Armed forces service card
- U.S. citizen or alien card
- Marriage certificate
- Record of convictions for misdemeanors or felonies

• • •

NORTH CAROLINA

North Carolina State Board of Mortuary Science
412 North Wilmington Street
Raleigh, NC 27601
919-733-9380

Funeral Director

REQUIREMENTS:

- Minimum age: 18
- High school graduate or GED holder
- Letter of intent from employer
- 32 hours of mortuary science or graduate
- One-year apprenticeship
- Pass oral or written funeral director exam
- Pass state law exam

APPLICATION DOCUMENTS:

Applicants must present proof of the following when applying:
- High school diploma
- Additional schooling or training

Embalmer

REQUIREMENTS:

- Minimum age: 18
- High school graduate or GED holder
- Letter of intent from employer
- Graduate of a mortuary science program
- One-year apprenticeship
- Pass oral or written embalmer exam
- Pass state law exam

APPLICATION DOCUMENTS:

Applicants must present proof of the following when applying:
- High school diploma
- Additional schooling or training

Funeral Service

REQUIREMENTS:

- Minimum age: 18
- High school graduate or GED holder
- Letter of intent from employer
- Graduate of a mortuary science program
- One-year apprenticeship
- Pass oral or written funeral service exam
- Pass state law exam

APPLICATION DOCUMENTS:

Applicants must present proof of the following when applying:
- High school diploma
- Additional schooling or training

• • •

OHIO

Board of Embalmers and
Funeral Directors of Ohio
77 South High Street, 16th Floor
Columbus, Ohio 43266-0313
614-466-4252

Embalmer

REQUIREMENTS:

- Minimum age: 18
- High school graduate or GED holder
- Letter of intent from employer
- Two years of general college
- Register with board prior to entering mortuary science school for 12 months
- Take state board exam for embalmers
- One-year apprenticeship (embalming at least 25 bodies)

APPLICATION DOCUMENTS:

Applicants must present proof of the following when applying:
- High school diploma or GED
- Birth certificate
- Police report
- College transcript

Funeral Director

REQUIREMENTS:

- Minimum age: 18
- High school graduate or GED holder
- Letter of intent from employer
- Bachelor's degree
- Register with board and have completed all the requirements for an embalmer's license and after mortuary science school serve one-year apprenticeship with licensed Ohio state funeral director or have completed one-year apprenticeship in lieu of mortuary science
- Pass funeral director's exam

APPLICATION DOCUMENTS:

Applicants must present proof of the following when applying:
- High school diploma or GED
- Birth certificate
- Police report
- College transcript

• • •

OREGON

State Mortuary and Cemetery Board
800 NE Oregon Street, #21, Suite 430
Portland, OR 97232
530-731-4040

Funeral Service Practitioner

REQUIREMENTS:

- Minimum Age: 18
- High school graduate or GED holder
- Letter of intent from employer
- Two-year apprenticeship with a licensed Oregon funeral director
- Pass test on state laws

APPLICATION DOCUMENTS:

Applicants must present proof of the following when applying:
- High school diploma

Embalmer

REQUIREMENTS

- Minimum age: 18
- High school graduate or GED holder
- Letter of intent from employer
- One-year apprenticeship
- Complete course and graduate from an accredited mortuary science school

APPLICATION DOCUMENTS:

Applicants must present proof of the following when applying:
- High school diploma

• • •

PENNSYLVANIA

Pennsylvania Board of Funeral Directors
Transportation and Safety Building
PO Box 2649
Harrisburg, PA 17105-2649
717-983-1253

Funeral Director

REQUIREMENTS:

- Minimum age: 18
- High school graduate or GED holder
- Letter of intent from employer
- 60 credits of liberal arts studies
- One year minimum at mortuary school
- One-year internship under licensed Pennsylvania funeral director
- Pass national boards
- Pass state test

APPLICATION DOCUMENTS:

Applicants must present proof of the following when applying:
- High school diploma
- Mortuary school
- College

• • •

RHODE ISLAND

Board of Examiners in Embalming and Funeral Directors
Department of Health, Room 104
3 Capitol Hill
Providence, RI 02980
401-277-2827

Embalmer

REQUIREMENTS:

- Minimum age: 18
- High school graduate or GED holder
- Letter of intent from employer
- Two-year apprenticeship under supervision of licensed funeral director (including embalming of 50 bodies)
- Graduation from an accredited embalming school
- Pass national board exam
- Pass state laws test

• • •

SOUTH CAROLINA

South Carolina Department of Labor, Licensing and Regulation
Board of Funeral Service
424 Calhoun Street
PO Box 305
Johnston, SC 29832

Embalmer

REQUIREMENTS:

- Minimum age: 18
- High school graduate or GED holder
- Residency in the area
- Letter of recommendation plus two affidavits of good character
- One year in accredited mortuary college
- Two-year apprenticeship (including embalming 50 bodies)

Funeral Director

REQUIREMENTS:

- Minimum age: 18
- High school graduate or GED holder
- Residency in the area
- Letter of recommendation plus two affidavits of good character
- One year in accredited mortuary college
- Two-year apprenticeship (including conducting 50 funerals)

• • •

SOUTH DAKOTA

South Dakota Board of Funeral Service
115 East Sioux
PO Box 1115
Pierre, SD 57501
605-224-6281

Funeral Service Licensee

REQUIREMENTS:

- Minimum age: 18
- High school graduate or GED holder
- Residency in the area
- 60 semester hours of college
- One year at a mortuary science school
- Pass national board exam
- Pass state board exam and state law exam
- One-year apprenticeship (including 25 embalmings)

• • •

TENNESSEE

Tennessee Board of Funeral Directors and Embalmers
Volunteer Plaza, 2nd Floor
500 James Robertson Parkway
Nashville, TN 37219
615-741-2378

Funeral Director

REQUIREMENTS:

- Minimum age: 18
- High school graduate or GED holder
- Physician's statement of fitness
- Two-year apprenticeship with a licensed funeral director and assist in 25 funerals or a complete course of study at a school for funeral directors and one-year apprenticeship with a licensed funeral director
- Pass a state of national board exam
- Pass a state laws exam

APPLICATION DOCUMENTS:

Applicants must present proof of the following when applying:
- High school transcript
- High school diploma or GED

Embalmer

REQUIREMENTS:

- Minimum age: 18
- Must be a citizen of the U.S.
- Must be of good moral character
- High school graduate or GED holder
- One year of schooling at a board-accredited school in the science and art of embalming, disinfection, and sanitation
- One-year apprenticeship under a licensed embalmer and funeral director having an established place of business (including at least 25 embalmings)
- Pass a board exam
- An application accompanied with a fee as set by the board

APPLICATION DOCUMENTS:

Applicants must present proof of the following when applying:
- High school transcript
- High school diploma or GED

• • •

TEXAS

Texas Funeral Service Commission
8100 Cameron Road
Building B, Suite 550
Austin, TX 78753
512-834-9992

Funeral Director

REQUIREMENTS:

- Minimum age: 18
- High school graduate or GED holder
- Letter of intent from employer
- Graduation from an accredited mortuary school
- Pass national board exam
- Pass state laws exam
- One- to two-year apprenticeship
- Pass oral interview with board

APPLICATION DOCUMENTS:

Applicants must present proof of the following when applying:
- High school diploma
- Additional schooling
- Exam scores

Embalmer

REQUIREMENTS:

- Minimum age: 18
- High school graduate or GED holder
- Letter of intent from employer
- Graduation from an accredited mortuary school
- Pass national board exam
- Pass state laws exam
- One- to two-year apprenticeship
- Pass oral interview with board

APPLICATION DOCUMENTS:

Applicants must present proof of the following when applying:
- High school diploma
- Additional schooling
- Exam scores

• • •

UTAH

Utah Department of Commerce
PO Box 45805
Salt Lake City, UT 84145-0805
801-530-6628

Funeral Service

REQUIREMENTS:

- Minimum age: 18
- High school graduate or GED holder
- Letter of intent from employer
- Two years of mortuary science (2,000 hours)
- Pass test on laws
- One-year apprenticeship (including 50 embalmings) under licensed funeral service director
- Pass funeral service exam with score of 70 percent or better

• • •

VERMONT

Vermont Division of Licensing and Registration
Board of Funeral Service
109 State Street, Pavilion Office Building
Montpelier, VT 05609-1106
802-828-2390

Embalmer

REQUIREMENTS:

- Minimum age: 18
- High school graduate or GED holder
- One year of mortuary science
- One-year apprenticeship served with Vermont licensed embalmer
- Pass national conference exams

APPLICATION DOCUMENTS:

Applicants must present proof of the following when applying:
- Verification of training

• • •

VIRGINIA

Commonwealth of Virginia
Virginia Board of Funeral Directors and Embalmers
6606 West Broad Street, 4th Floor
Southern States Building
Richmond, VA 23230-1717
804-662-9907

Funeral service licensee

REQUIREMENTS:

- Minimum age: 18
- High school graduate or GED holder
- Letter of intent from employer
- 18-month apprenticeship with licensed funeral service practitioner
- Graduate of a board-approved school of mortuary science
- Pass state and national exams

APPLICATION DOCUMENTS:

Applicants must present proof of the following when applying:
- High school transcript
- High school diploma or GED
- Birth certificate

• • •

WASHINGTON

Washington Funeral and Cemetery Boards
PO Box 9012
Olympia, WA 98507-9012
206-586-4905

Funeral Director

REQUIREMENTS

- One-year apprenticeship with accredited funeral home
- Two years of college
- Pass national exams and/or state boards

APPLICATION DOCUMENTS:

Applicants must present proof of the following when applying:
- High school diploma

Embalmer

REQUIREMENTS

- Two-year apprenticeship with accredited funeral home
- Two years of college
- One year of mortuary school
- Pass national exams and/or state boards

APPLICATION DOCUMENTS:

Applicants must present proof of the following when applying:
- High school diploma

• • •

WEST VIRGINIA

West Virginia Board of Funeral Directors and Embalmers
179 Summers Street, Suite 305
Charleston, WV 25301
304-558-0302

Embalmer

REQUIREMENTS:

- Minimum age: 18
- Associate's degree
- Oral interview with board
- One-year apprenticeship under West Virginia-licensed embalmer
- One-year program at mortuary science college
- Pass conference national board exam

APPLICATION DOCUMENTS:

Applicants must present proof of the following when applying:
- High school diploma

Funeral Directors and Embalmers

- Birth certificate
- Schooling

• • •

WISCONSIN

 Wisconsin Funeral Directors Examining Board
Wisconsin Department of Regulation and Licensing
1400 East Washington Avenue
PO Box 8935
Madison, WI 53708
608-266-1630

Funeral Director

REQUIREMENTS:

- High school graduate or GED holder
- Letter of intent from employer
- 60 college credits
- One year of mortuary school
- One-year apprenticeship
- Pass conference board exam
- Pass state exam

APPLICATION DOCUMENTS:

Applicants must present proof of the following when applying:
- High school diploma
- College sophomore standing

• • •

Gunsmiths, Gunmakers, and Bladesmiths

Strictly speaking, *gunmakers* build firearms, while *gunsmiths* repair them. In general usage, however, gunsmiths handle all stages of building, repairing, and modifying guns. Fewer than 2,500 gunsmiths are employed full-time in the United States, and most work for gun shops, hunting supply stores, sporting goods stores, or manufacturers and distributors of guns and hunting products. *Bladesmiths,* who forge blades or knives, have almost no job opportunities. People train to become bladesmiths because of a love for the craft.

There are three main parts of a gun—the stock (the basic framework, the grip, for example, on a handgun), the barrel (the tube through which the bullet is discharged), and the action (the firing mechanism). Gunsmiths often begin their work by reading blueprint orders or instructions from customers. They select a stock, attach the barrel and action, and then align the gun. They might also attach an optical sight for aiming, a pistol grip, and decorative pieces. Gunsmiths treat the metal parts with a process called blueing, which involves stripping the old finish and immersing the metal in a blueing salt bath. The result is a bluish, rust-resistant surface.

Because assembly lines are not well suited to the manufacture of quality firearms, much of the gunsmith's work is still done by hand. Gun stocks, for example, are made either by machine or by hand, but even those from the factory are often only partially completed, and the gunsmith must then carve it into the correct shape. For a custom-made gun, the gunsmith might handcraft all the parts, including carving a design in the gun's handle. It is with custom work that gunsmithing becomes a true craft or art.

Gunsmiths might also be asked to modify, repair, or restore guns. For example, they might convert a military rifle into a hunting rifle or repair a gun that has historic or sentimental value. When repairing and restoring old guns, the gunsmith might need to custom build the replacement parts.

In the past apprenticeships were a common means for becoming a gunsmith. Working under an already established gunsmith, apprentices were gradually trained in the various tasks of the trade, a process that might last as long as four years. Gunsmithing apprenticeships are now rare. In the United States, however, there are more than a dozen schools or colleges that offer two-year gunsmithing programs. These provide classes in firearms design and function, bench metal work, stockmaking, gun blueing and metal finishing, and other subjects. Some schools also offer short-term courses that last from one day to two weeks.

The number of employed gunsmiths has declined over the years, and the employment outlook is not expected to improve. In the early 1990s, in fact, there were many more trained gunsmiths than jobs available. Employed gunsmiths generally work indoors and often around noisy machinery. They are usually busiest just before and during the hunting season.

The forging of blades is also a serious craft requiring years of study and hard work. The American Bladesmith Society (ABS) sponsors classes on bladesmithing and sets the guidelines for becoming a journeyman and master smith. An introductory class, for example, might involve both lectures and hands-on training. Metal selection and various blade designs might be discussed. Students might also perform basic hammer forging in order to shape, anneal, heat treat, grind, and temper a blade. In 1988 the ABS opened its first bladesmithing college in Texarkana, Texas. Another was later established in Washington, Arkansas.

There are three requirements for becoming a journeyman smith. First, the applicant must be a regular member (apprentice smith) of the ABS for two years. Second, the applicant must forge a blade at least ten inches long that can pass a series of cutting, chopping, and bending tests. For example, the blade must be able to cut a free-hanging, one-inch hemp rope in a single stroke. Finally, the applicant must submit five more blades of various styles, which are judged on their design, workmanship, and finish. An even more difficult battery of tests is required for the master smith rating, which can be achieved only after being a journeyman smith for at least two years.

For more information on training programs and apprenticeships for gunsmiths and bladesmiths, write to the organizations listed below. Additional information might be available from your state's bureau of apprenticeship training. The bureau's address is found in the last section of this encyclopedia.

National Rifle Association
1600 Rhode Island Avenue, NW
Washington, DC 20036
202-828- 6000

The NRA can send you a list of schools that offer both short-term and full-time gunsmithing courses.

• • •

American Bladesmith Society
4204 Ballenger Creek Pike
Frederick, MD 21701
301-663-6923

The ABS offers its own training program.

• • •

Musical Instrument Tuners and Repairers

Musical instrument tuners and repairers usually specialize in one family of musical instruments. Some, for example, work on bowed instruments, such as violins and cellos, while others work on guitars, pianos, organs, brass instruments, woodwinds, or percussion instruments. Essential for this work are a good sense of hearing, mechanical aptitude, and manual dexterity. Music stores, repair shops, and musical instrument manufacturers all employ tuners and repairers. Most, however, are self-employed.

By far the largest group of tuners and repairers work on pianos. Sometimes called *piano technicians,* they tune pianos and locate, identify, and correct problems in the operating mechanisms. Pianos frequently go out of tune, usually from use, age, temperature change, or moving.

Piano tuners travel to houses, schools, churches, and other places where people have pianos. They typically begin their work by striking a tuning fork and comparing its sound with that made by one of the piano's "A" strings. The tuner then adjusts the string by tightening or loosening it with a tuning hammer, also called a tuning wrench. The other strings can be properly adjusted by comparing their sounds in relation to the A string. It might take an hour and a half to tune all 230 strings on a standard piano.

Pianos sometimes develop more serious problems than simply being out of tune. These problems can occur in any of the thousands of moving parts, the sounding board, or the frame. Piano technicians might begin a repair job by talking with the customer and trying to obtain clues. The piano might then be partially dismantled and inspected. After the problem is identified, the technician makes the necessary adjustments or repairs, often with the use of hammers, screwdrivers, and pliers, as well as various specialized tools, such as those for restringing. Pianos rarely need a major overhaul during their first 20 years.

Those who repair stringed instruments are called *luthiers.* Luthiers, who make instruments as well, can be further divided into those who work on guitars, for example, and those who specialize in bowed instruments—violins, violas, cellos, and stand-up basses. To locate and identify defects, they not only inspect the instruments but also play them. To repair a crack in a violin, the repairer might begin by removing the cracked section. The crack is then washed with warm water and bonded with special glue. To prevent further splitting, the section is reinforced with cleats, studs, or other supportive material. The section is then reattached to the violin, the outside of the crack is covered with "fill varnish," and the crack is finally treated with "retouch varnish" to make it invisible. The whole process may take as long as three weeks. For an especially expensive violin (some are worth millions of dollars), the job must be done with the utmost care, and repairing just a few cracks could take 2,000 or more hours.

Other instruments also have special repair problems. Repairers of woodwinds—for example, clarinets and oboes—might need to solder together broken keys. Brass instruments, such as trumpets or French horns, sometimes become dented, and the repairer must unsolder the dented piece and work the dent out with a hammer and then with more delicate tools. Even drums, bells, cymbals, and other percussion instruments require repair work. A new skin, for example, might need to be stretched over a drum.

The traditional way to become an instrument tuner or repairer was to enter an apprenticeship. Working under an already established craftsman, the apprentice was gradually taught the trade in exchange for providing free or cheap labor. As the apprentice became more experienced, his or her pay was increased. This type of arrangement is now rare. Few journeymen can afford to take on an apprentice, as apprentices often need to be trained for a considerable amount of time before their work can justify even a minimum wage salary. Moreover, many journeymen do not want to train their own competition. Apprentices today generally pay journeymen for their training.

Tuners and repairers are more likely to find training at a technical school or college. Some offer one- or two-year programs. Correspondence, or home-study, programs are also available, but these do not provide practical experience. (Some correspondence programs do help students find practical training.) In general, programs require at least a high school degree or GED. Depending on the type of program, students might study such subjects as acoustics, buffing, dent removal, machine tool operation, or soldering, as well as small business practices. They generally have to purchase their own tools. While in school some students are able to arrange additional training or an apprenticeship with an experienced repairer. Contacts for such arrangements can sometimes be made at a trade organization meeting, and many professional societies can offer assistance in matching an apprentice with a journeyman.

The number of musical instrument tuners and repairers is expected to grow little if at all. Even so, there will probably still be excellent job opportunities. The average age of piano technicians, for example, is over 50, and many new technicians will be needed to replace these workers as they retire. In fact, unless more people start entering the field, there could be a shortage of piano tuners and repairers. Because it is a luxury for many owners to have their instruments tuned or repaired, craftsmen tend to lose business during recessions.

For more information on training programs and apprenticeships for musical instrument tuners and repairers, write to the organizations listed below. Additional information might be available from your state's bureau of apprenticeship training. The bureau's address is found in the last section of this encyclopedia.

The Piano Technicians Guild
3930 Washington
Kansas City, MO 64111
816-753-7747
ATTN: Mary Kinman

The PTG can provide a list of all places in the United States where individuals can be trained as a piano technician and can also assist in matching apprentices with sponsors.

• • •

American Institute of Organbuilders
PO Box 130982
Houston, TX 77219
ATTN: Howard Maple

Although this organization has no formal apprenticeship program, it does have an informal guide, and may eventually have a formal program.

• • •

Guild of American Luthiers
8222 South Park Avenue
Tacoma, WA 98408
206-472-7853

The GAL can provide a list of schools or individual luthiers who offer training. Its quarterly journal also is a source for individuals seeking sponsors, as is its National Convention.

• • •

Ocularists

Ocularists make and fit artificial eyes for humans. They are highly skilled craftsmen who must have artistic talent, an attention for detail, and an understanding of the necessary materials. They are sometimes called *artificial eye makers*. Ocularists are not spread evenly around the country. Some states, in fact, do not have any ocularists.

Artificial eyes are made of either plastic or glass. Some are manufactured in standard sizes and colors, while many others are specially made for a patient. To create a custom-made plastic eye, the first step might be to measure the patient's empty eye socket with calipers. Also measured is the natural eye, including the size and location of the pupil and iris. A stock plastic eye is then placed in the empty socket, and the patient is asked questions about how the new eye feels. Using information from the patient, the ocularist builds up and correctly shapes the stock eye with additional plastic.

The next step is to create a mold by placing the stock eye in plaster of paris. When the plaster is dry, the ocularist pours plastic into the mold—thus forming the patient's artificial eye—and the plastic is set by boiling it in water. The ocularist then paints the iris and the white of the eye to match the colors of the patient's natural eye. Veins are drawn onto the plastic eye with a colored pencil or scratched into the eye and filled with a pigment. The ocularist immerses the artificial eye in a clear plastic solution to create a glassy look. Irregularities can then be removed with a dental grinding machine, and the eye can be polished with pumice and an electric buffing wheel. Finally, the ocularist places the artificial eye in the patient's socket and compares it with the natural one.

The National Examining Board of Ocularists is the only certifying organization for the field. Its standards are set by the American Society of Ocularists (ASO). The society does not sponsor apprenticeships, though some of its members do have apprenticeship programs. The length and requirements vary from program to program. An applicant might, for example, need to have a high school diploma, and the program might take four years to complete. In general, apprentices begin with simple tasks and are gradually trained in the specialized jobs of the field. Some apprentices have previous experience in the fine arts, medical illustration, optometry, or another prosthetic field. Those training as ocularists can become apprentice members of the ASO.

It is anticipated that a growing number of Americans will have health insurance, a trend that could boost the demand for ocularists.

For more information on training programs and apprenticeships for ocularists, write to the American Society of Ocularists, listed below. This organization can direct interested persons to accredited ocularists in their geographic area. Additional information might be available from your state's bureau of apprenticeship training. The bureau's address is found in the last section of this encyclopedia.

American Society of Ocularists
690 Market Street, Suite 920
San Francisco, CA 94104
415-399-0747
ATTN: Toni Zappone

Apprentices train under the supervision of a Board Approved Diplomate (an individual certified by the NEBO and the Board of Directors of the ASO).

To sit for the initial NEBO certification examination, an ocularist must have completed an apprenticeship program or been principally engaged as an ocularist for 10,000 hours.

Orthotics Technicians

Orthotic devices, sometimes called orthopedic appliances, are braces used to support weak joints or muscles or to correct physical defects, such as a spinal deformity. A knee brace, for example, is a common orthotic device. Patients fitted with orthotic devices may have been injured in an automobile accident or sporting activity, in warfare, or in numerous other ways. *Orthotic technicians* are skilled craft workers who make, fit, and repair these devices under the guidance of an *orthotist*. In a similar field, *prosthetic technicians* construct artificial limbs and other prosthetic devices.

In general, orthotic technicians do not work with patients. Patients are examined by an orthotist, who then decides the appropriate treatment for the injury or defect. It is the orthotic technician, however, who actually constructs the device. The technician might begin by reading diagrams or other specifications made by the orthotist and by deciding which materials and tools are needed to build the orthotic device. Among the commonly used tools are hammers, anvils, drills, welding equipment, and saws. The orthotic device is built around a structural framework, which is usually made of metal or plastic. To form structural components, technicians might cut, bend, and weld pieces of metal and then drill holes in the pieces and rivet them together.

To assure a proper fit, the technician might shape this framework around a cast model of the patient's injured or defective body part. The model is usually made in two basic steps. First, the orthotist creates an impression of the body part, and then the technician pours wet plaster or molten plastic into the impression, forming a cast model. When the framework is properly shaped, it might be padded and covered with such materials as rubber, felt, plastic, or leather. The device must then be tested for freedom of movement, alignment of parts, and functional stability. Orthotic technicians also maintain and repair such devices; this might involve making adjustments, for example, or replacing parts.

There are no state licensing requirements for orthotic technicians. Even so, the American Board for Certification in Orthotics and Prosthetics (ABC) has established a set of minimum requirements and an examination. Those who are certified by the ABC usually have the best job opportunities.

The board recognizes two major paths for gaining certification. For either, applicants are usually expected to have at least a high school degree or GED. The first path requires the applicant to graduate from a formal training program approved by the National Commission of Orthotic and Prosthetic Education. These programs, found at vocational schools, colleges, universities, and hospitals, last one or two years and award an associate's degree or a certificate. Students study anatomy, the use of materials, and numerous other subjects and receive supervised clinical experience.

The other path, similar to an apprenticeship, is to work two years under the supervision of an ABC-certified orthotic technician. Trainees are initially assigned simple tasks and are gradually trained to handle specialized work. Those seeking such an apprentice-like arrangement should contact the ABC for a list of certified practitioners.

The exam, required for all people who want certification, is divided into two sections. The first is a one-hour written test covering such subjects as terminology, anatomy, componentry, safety practices, and materials. The second is a seven-hour practical test assessing the applicant's ability to handle the basic tasks of the field, including metalwork, plastic fabrication, leatherwork, and layout. In most cases applicants cannot take the test without having first completed one of the two paths described above. The board, however, occasionally waives this requirement for foreign-educated applicants and for people who have had other types of learning experiences that relate to orthotics. Applicants who pass the exam are given the title *registered orthotic technician.* Those who are trained in prosthetics as well and pass the prosthetics exam are called *registered prosthetic-orthotic technicians.*

The employment outlook for orthotic technicians is good. Factors affecting this outlook include the increasing elderly population and an anticipated growth in the number of people with health insurance. Moreover, the development of new types of orthotics could increase the number of potential recipients.

Orthotic technicians generally work in clean, well-lighted, and well-ventilated offices and workshops. They use hand and power tools, which present some risk of injury, but this risk is reduced by following established safety practices. Many technicians derive satisfaction from knowing their work provides an important medical service.

For more information on training programs and apprenticeships for orthotics technicians, write to the organization listed below. Additional information might be available from your state's bureau of apprenticeship training. The bureau's address is found in the last section of this encyclopedia.

 American Board for Certification in
Orthotics and Prosthetics
1650 King Street, Suite 500
Alexandria, VA 22314
703-836-7114
ATTN: Ingrid T. Thomas

This organization can provide a 200-page booklet of accredited training facilities and certified practitioners.

• • •

Preschool Workers

Preschool workers nurture and teach children five years old or younger. They might help children with their basic needs, such as eating or dressing, or organize activities that foster their physical, emotional, intellectual, or social growth. In planning activities they must be aware of the developmental stages that children go through. An average three-year-old child, for example, has different motor skills and reasoning abilities than a four-year-old. Preschool workers who handle educational activities are sometimes called *preschool teachers.* Those who are responsible for basic care are often called *child care workers.* The majority of preschool workers, however, both teach children and help with basic care.

Many preschool workers are employed by preschools or day care centers. About half, though, are self-employed and work out of their homes as *family day care providers.* Preschool workers who are certified by the Council for Early Childhood Professional Recognition are given the title *child development associate,* or *CDA.*

Preschool workers typically begin the day by greeting children and helping them get ready for the upcoming activities. In the winter, for example, children often arrive wearing boots, hats, coats, and mittens, and workers might help them remove these outer garments. They might also try to cheer up kids who arrive cranky or nervous about being away from home. In general, preschool workers must be sensitive to the emotional needs and problems of children.

The daily schedule is often formed around storytelling, music, and simple arts and crafts projects. Also taught might be practical skills, such as how to eat properly and how to clean up after oneself, as well as skills important for their intellectual development, such as seeing and recognizing patterns. Activities might be interspersed with playtime and rest periods. Preschool workers have meetings with parents in which they discuss the child's progress and any special problems.

Educational requirements for becoming a preschool worker vary from state to state. Some positions require only a high school degree (or GED), while others require college training in child development or early childhood education. In some schools and child care centers, preschool teachers must have a bachelor's degree in education or a related field.

Many states, however, require a CDA credential for preschool positions. There are two paths for getting this credential. The first is to enroll in a one-year "CDA Professional Preparation Program" managed by the Council for Early Childhood Professional Recognition. Similar in some respects to an apprenticeship, CDA programs require about 480 hours of work experience, 120 hours of seminars (taken at a local school or college), and weekly conferences with instructors. Students specialize in either a "center-based setting" (working in a state-approved child development center) or a "family child care setting" (working out of one's home). Those in the former must also choose between working with infants/toddlers (from birth to age three) or preschool children (ages three to five). Additional training is available for those who want to work in a bilingual setting. All applicants must be at least 18 years old and have a high school degree (or GED). After completing the program, the candidate is given a final evaluation at the work setting, usually lasting about three months, in which the candidate must demonstrate a mastery of various skills essential to child care. Parent questionnaires and an oral interview are also part of the evaluation process.

Already experienced preschool workers can sometimes become a CDA without going through a CDA Professional Preparation Program. To follow this more direct path, an applicant must be at least 18 years old and have a high school degree (or GED), 480 hours of experience working with children (within the last five years), and 120 hours of formal child care education and training (also within the last five years). The formal education and training requirement can be met in numerous ways; on-the-job experiences, for example, sometimes apply. Once the above requirements are met, the candidate must undergo a formal observation, an oral interview, and a written assessment (a two-hour multiple-choice exam). This process might take only a few months to complete.

Some states might also have formal apprenticeship programs for preschool workers. Washington State, for example, has apprenticeship programs for *child care specialists* (3,000 hours of on-the-job training plus 144 hours of related instruction) and *child care technicians* (2,000 hours of on-the-job training plus 144 hours of instruction). These positions, however, are available only to those already employed by the Washington State public school system. Apprenticeships might also be available on a more informal basis from such organizations as Head Start, which encourages the low-income parents of the children in their classes to learn child care skills.

The number of employed preschool workers is expected to grow much faster than average, in part because of an anticipated increase in the number of children under five years old. Child care services, moreover, will continue to necessary for families with only one parent and for those in which both parents work. Because there is a relatively high turnover among preschool workers, job openings should be plentiful for qualified applicants.

Preschool workers spend much of their day on their feet. They must be enthusiastic and attentive to the needs of children. Although the job can be physically and emotionally draining, many find working with and helping children a rewarding experience.

For more information on training programs and apprenticeships for preschool workers, write to the organizations listed below. Additional information might be available from your state's bureau of apprenticeship training. The bureau's address is found in the last section of this encyclopedia.

 Council for Early Childhood Professional Recognition
1341 G Street, NW, Suite 400
Washington, DC 20005
800-424-4310

 National Head Start Association
201 North Union Street
Suite 320
Alexandria, VA 22314
703-739-0875

Railroad Workers

Trains remain an important means of transportation for passengers and cargo. Some trains make long voyages across the country, for example, while others maintain routes entirely within a city, metropolitan area, or other defined boundary. Among the most common railroad jobs are *brake operator, conductor,* and *engineer.* Most railroad workers are employed by railroad companies. The remainder work for manufacturing firms, mining companies, and state and local governments.

Working under the direction of a conductor, brake operators perform a variety of tasks, including the physical labor involved in adding ("coupling") and removing ("uncoupling") railroad cars at a train station or railroad yard. Before a train departs, they inspect the train to ensure that the handbrakes are released, that all couplers and air hoses are fastened, and that the airbrakes work correctly. They look for signs of trouble, such as sticking brakes or overheated bearings. When a problem is found, they might make minor adjustments or report the need for major repairs.

Brake operators often work as flaggers in stations and yards; for example, they use flags and lights to indicate when an engineer can start or stop a train. They might also throw the switches that turn trains from one track to another. In passenger trains some operators help passengers on and off trains and help conductors with collecting tickets. Brake operators are sometimes called *brakers, brake couplers, yard couplers,* or *switch tenders.*

Conductors also have a wide range of responsibilities, including the supervision of train and yard crews. On freight trains they record the contents and intended destination of all the cars and must ensure that each is removed at the correct stop. They generally receive this information from a dispatcher, and before departing, the conductor might discuss the route, timetable, and cargo with the engineer. After leaving the station the conductor and engineer periodically talk by means of a two-way radio, discussing such matters as the condition of the track and the presence of other trains. On passenger trains, conductors collect tickets and fares. Other conductors work in railroad yards, where they supervise workers assembling and disassembling trains.

Finally, engineers are responsible for operating the trains themselves. Locomotive engineers, for example, operate freight and passenger trains between stations. They must be familiar with the terminals and yards on their route and be able to recognize and respond to the signal systems. They also must know how the train, as well as its cargo or passengers, will react to acceleration, braking, and curves. The number of cars and the ratio of empty to loaded cars are just two factors that affect how the train will react. Decelerating too fast, for example, could damage cargo or disturb passengers.

While on a trip engineers monitor the train's various meters and gauges that measure speed, fuel, temperature, battery charge, and pressure in the brake lines. In the past *assistant engineers,* sometimes called *firers,* would also monitor the train's instruments and observe the track for signals or obstructions. The position of assistant engineer, however, is in the process of being phased out, and the responsibilities are being taken over by brake operators.

Other types of engineers exist. *Rail yard engineers,* for instance, work in the rail yards, where they help assemble and disassemble trains by moving the component cars. *Dinkey operators* work in mines or industrial sites, where they operate trains that haul coal, rock, lumber, or other supplies.

Most railroad workers begin as trainees. Applicants generally need to be at least 21 years old and have a high school degree, good hearing, color vision (to recognize signs), and manual dexterity. They might also need to pass a physical exam and a drug test.

Those with no experience usually train to be a brake operator. Brake operators can then move up to become conductors. Engineer positions used to be given to experienced assistant engineers; they are now more often filled by experienced brake operators or conductors.

Like apprentices in other fields, railroad trainees receive both on-the-job and classroom instruction. Beginning brake operators, for example, are trained in coupling and uncoupling railcars, boarding moving trains, signaling, and other tasks essential to the trade. Conductors might in addition learn about timetables, operating rules, and related subjects. Applicants for engineer positions study such subjects as airbrake systems, fuel economy, train handling techniques, and operating rules and regulations. The length of these training programs varies from railroad to railroad. Those for engineers typically last six months.

Workers who complete the training program and pass the required exams are placed on a list called the "extra board." Extra board workers substitute for regular workers who are absent because of illness, vacation, or other reasons. It may take years for an extra board worker to gain a regular assignment. Workers typically gain a regular assignment and all other promotions on the basis of seniority.

Little change is expected in the number of employed railroad workers. Railroads have fared poorly in competition with other modes of transportation, such as planes, trucks, and ships. Larger and faster trains, as well as the introduction of computerized equipment, however, has also restrained job growth, as fewer and fewer workers are needed to perform the same level of service.

Many railroad employees work nights, weekends, and holidays. Some regularly spend many nights away from home. The most undesirable shifts are given to those with the least experience. Railroad work can be strenuous, especially for brake operators. Getting on and off a moving railcar can be both physically demanding and dangerous.

Railroad apprenticeships are normally sponsored by railroad companies, many of whom prefer to reserve information on their programs for current employees. Most of those contacted asked not to be listed in this directory. The organizations listed below, however, may be helpful in directing interested applicants to specific companies in their area or in providing general apprenticeship information. Additional information might be available from your state's bureau of apprenticeship training. The bureau's address is found in the last section of this encyclopedia.

International Brotherhood of Locomotive Engineers
1370 Ontario Street, Mezzanine
Cleveland, OH 44113
216-241-2630

This organization has 669 locals.

• • •

Brotherhood of Maintenance of Way Employees
12050 Woodward Avenue
Detroit, MI 48203
313-948-1010

This organization is affiliated with the AFL-CIO and has 965 locals.

• • •

American Train Dispatchers Association
The Train Dispatcher Building
1401 South Harlem Avenue
Berwyn, IL 60402
708-795-5656

This organization is affiliated with the AFL-CIO.

• • •

Brotherhood of Railroad Signalmen
601 West Golf Road, Box U
Mt. Prospect, IL 60056
708-439-3732

This organization is affiliated with the AFL-CIO and has 161 locals.

• • •

Brotherhood of Railway Carmen Division/Transportation Communications Union
4929 Main Street
Kansas City, MO 64112
816-561-1112

This organization is affiliated with the AFL-CIO and has 560 locals.

• • •

Transportation Communications
International Union
3 Research Place
Rockville, MD 20850
301-948-4910

This organization is affiliated with the AFL-CIO and has 900 locals.

• • •

 United Transportation Union
14600 Detroit Avenue
Lakewood, OH 44107
216-228-9400

This organization has 900 locals.

• • •

Vending Machine Mechanics

Vending machine mechanics install, service, and repair coin-operated vending machines. These machines might sell candy and snacks, for example, or hot and cold beverages, such as coffee or soft drinks. Some vending machine mechanics are responsible for stocking machines as well. Most are employed by vending companies, soft drink bottling firms, or companies that own amusement equipment, such as video games, pinball machines, and juke boxes.

Vending machine mechanics work in the field—traveling from one machine to another—as well as in company repair shops. They typically spend much of their time on preventive maintenance. They lubricate mechanical parts, make minor adjustments, and clean refrigerator condensers. Handles, springs, merchandise chutes, and other basic parts are checked for proper functioning. If it is a beverage machine, mechanics check that the drinks are being properly mixed. They also check the coin and change-making mechanisms. To install a machine, the mechanic follows similar steps to ensure the machine is working correctly. The required water and electrical connections also need to be made.

When a machine breaks down, the mechanic first looks for obvious problems in the machinery, such as a loose wire or a leak. Problems are sometimes difficult to identify, however, and in such cases the mechanic might refer to a troubleshooting manual or wiring diagram and use specialized testing devices. When the faulty parts are found, they are usually replaced and brought back to the shop for repair. Small problems are sometimes repaired at the job site. Among the other possible job duties are stocking the machines, filing reports, and ordering parts.

Vending machine mechanics use a variety of hand tools, including screwdrivers, wrenches, pipe cutters, and soldering guns, as well as power tools, such as drills, saws, and grinding wheels. Testing equipment might include voltmeters, oscilloscopes, and ohmmeters.

Many vending machine mechanics learn the trade informally on the job. They might begin by cleaning machines or handling other simple tasks. The company might then train them to replace defective parts, handle basic repairs, and perform routine adjustments and testing. The next step might be for the trainee to accompany experienced mechanics to the job sites. This training process might take as little as six months or as long as three years. The length of the training period is affected by many factors, including the complexity of the machines, the ability of the trainee, and the trainee's previous education. Most vending machine mechanics have a high school degree or GED. Some junior colleges offer one- or two-year electronics programs for vending machine mechanics.

A number of vending machine mechanics are trained in a formal apprenticeship program established by the National Automatic Merchandising Association (NAMA). The program, however, is run by individual companies, which are given the NAMA guidelines, manuals, and exams. The core of the program is a home-study course that covers such subjects as blueprint reading, basic electricity and electronics, customer relations, and safety practices. At the same time, apprentices are trained on the job in a manner similar to the one described above. Finally, apprentices must pass written and performance tests, graded by the NAMA, to acquire certification in the field. The length of the apprenticeship program varies from company to company.

Little or no growth is expected in the number of employed vending machine mechanics. Public demand for vending machines will likely increase—in part because of a growing number of services and products dispensed by machines—but technological advances will probably make these machines more reliable, restraining job growth for mechanics. Those with a background in electronics will have the best job opportunities, as electronic components are increasingly used in vending machines.

The workshops used by vending machine mechanics are generally quiet, well lighted, and well ventilated. There is some risk of injury from electrical shock or from accidents with tools, but this risk is reduced by following established safety practices. Work areas in the field can be crowded. While working on a machine in front of a supermarket, for example, a mechanic might be surrounded by passing customers.

For more information on training programs and apprenticeships for vending machine mechanics, write to the organization listed below. Additional information might be available from your state's bureau of apprenticeship training. The bureau's address is found in the last section of this encyclopedia.

 National Automatic Merchandising Association
20 North Wacker Drive
Chicago, IL 60606
312-346-0370

This organization can provide information on its apprenticeship training program.

Part 4
Appendices

Appendix I: Glossary

AFL-CIO (American Federation of Labor and Congress of Industrial Organizations) The largest federation of labor unions in the United States, comprising national and international unions in various occupations and industries.

Apprentice A person who is learning a trade or craft by working under the supervision of a skilled craftworker (usually a journeyman).

BAT (Bureau of Apprenticeship Training) National or state organizations primarily serving apprenticeship sponsors in planning, starting, and operating apprenticeship programs.

Certificate of Completion Certificate awarded upon completion of an apprenticeship program.

GATB (General Aptitude Test Battery) A written test covering mathematics, sciences, word usage or other subjects that may be important for the apprentice to know. This is only one of several tests an applicant may encounter. Other tests are more specific to a particular trade and may test such things as mechanical comprehension and visualization as well as math skills.

GED (General Equivalency Diploma) Diploma equivalent to the high school diploma earned by passing a standardized test.

JAC (Joint Apprenticeship Committee) The administrative body of the apprenticeship program, which sets the rules and requirements, determines the need for new apprentices, and interviews applicants. In programs cosponsored by a labor union (or unions) and a company (or association of companies), the JAC usually consists of representatives from labor and management.

JAP (Joint Apprenticeship Program) *See* JAC.

JATC (Joint Apprenticeship Training Committee) *See* JAC.

JATTF (Joint Apprenticeship Training Trust Fund) *See* JAC.

Journeyman Skilled craftworker who has completed a specified number of years of training in a particular craft or trade.

Jurisdiction The geographical area covered by a particular local union or JAC.

Letter of intent An employer's guarantee (normally in the form of a letter) to the apprenticeship sponsor that he or she (1) intends to hire the apprentice and (2) has sufficient work lined up for the apprentice to carry him or her through the term of the apprenticeship.

Oral interview As part of the application process, one person or a small group of people will ask the apprenticeship applicant questions regarding his or her physical health, interest in the trade, and attitude toward the type of work that would be performed. Personal traits such as aggressiveness and sincerity are also noted. The oral interview helps the sponsor determine whether applicants would commit themselves to the work and whether they would be persistent enough to finish the program.

Preapprenticeship training Training offered at some vocational and technical schools and high schools to help potential apprentices acquire the basic skills necessary to qualify for an apprenticeship program.

Probationary period Period of time at the beginning of an apprenticeship during which either the apprentice or the program sponsor can choose to terminate the apprenticeship.

Residency requirement Some apprenticeship programs require that participants live within a certain area (the program's jurisdiction) for a period of time (usually a year or less) before applying to the program, and, once accepted, while participating in it.

SAC (State Apprenticeship Council) State organization similar to the BAT.

Veteran's DD-214 The basic military discharge form issued to those who have successfully completed their military service.

Appendix II: National, Regional, State, and Local BAT and SAC Offices

The Bureaus of Apprenticeship and Training (BATs), as well as the State Apprenticeship Councils (SACs), provide service to existing apprenticeship programs and technical assistance to organizations who would like to establish an apprenticeship program. Although it is not their primary purpose, most can assist aspiring apprentices by directing them to the appropriate organization.

NATIONAL BAT

U.S. Department of Labor
Employment and Training Administration
Apprenticeship and Training
200 Constitution Avenue, NW
Washington, DC 20210
(202) 219-5921
Director: Anthony Swoope

• • •

REGIONAL BATs

REGION I

**Bureau of Apprenticeship and Training
Region I**
11th Floor
One Congress Street
Boston, MA 02114
(617) 565-2288

States Covered by Region I:
Connecticut   Maine
Massachusetts   New Hampshire
Rhode Island   Vermont

• • •

REGION II

**Bureau of Apprenticeship and Training
Region II**
Room 602, Federal Building
201 Varick Street
New York, NY 10014
(212) 337-2313

States Covered by Region II:
New Jersey   New York
Puerto Rico   Virgin Islands

• • •

REGION III

**Bureau of Apprenticeship and Training
Region III**
Room 13240, Gateway Building
3535 Market Street
Philadelphia, PA 19104
(215) 596-6417

States Covered by Region III:
Delaware   Maryland
Pennsylvania   Virginia
West Virginia

• • •

REGION IV

**Bureau of Apprenticeship and Training
Region IV**
Room 200, 1371 Peachtree Street NE
Atlanta, GA 30367
(404) 347-4405

States Covered by Region IV:
- Alabama
- Florida
- Georgia
- Kentucky
- Mississippi
- North Carolina
- South Carolina
- Tennessee

• • •

REGION V

Bureau of Apprenticeship and Training
Region V
Room 758
230 South Dearborn Street
Chicago, IL 60604
(312) 353-7205

States Covered by Region V:
- Illinois
- Indiana
- Michigan
- Minnesota
- Ohio
- Wisconsin

• • •

REGION VI

Bureau of Apprenticeship and Training
Region VI
Room 628, Federal Building
525 Griffin Street
Dallas, TX 75202
(214) 767-4993

States Covered by Region VI:
- Arkansas
- Louisiana
- New Mexico
- Oklahoma
- Texas

• • •

REGION VII

Bureau of Apprenticeship and Training
Region VII
Room 1100, Federal Office Building
911 Walnut Street
Kansas City, MO 64106
(816) 426-3856

States Covered by Region VII:
- Iowa
- Kansas
- Missouri
- Nebraska

• • •

REGION VIII

Bureau of Apprenticeship and Training
Region VIII
Room 465, U.S. Custom House
721 19th Street
Denver, CO 80202
(303) 844-4791

States Covered by Region VIII:
- Colorado
- Montana
- North Dakota
- South Dakota
- Utah
- Wyoming

• • •

REGION IX

Bureau of Apprenticeship and Training
Region IX
Federal Building, Room 715
71 Stevenson Street
San Francisco, CA 94105
(415) 744-6580

States Covered by Region IX:
- Arizona
- California
- Hawaii
- Nevada

• • •

REGION X

Bureau of Apprenticeship and Training
Region X
Room 925
1111 Third Avenue
Seattle, WA 98101
(205) 553-5286

States Covered by Region X:
- Alaska
- Idaho
- Oregon
- Washington

• • •

STATE BATs AND SACs

ALABAMA

Bureau of Apprenticeship and Training (Main Office)
Berry Building, Suite 102
2017 2nd Avenue North
Birmingham, AL 35203
(205) 731-1308
State Director: William D. Fox

Bureau of Apprenticeship and Training (Local Office)
U.S. Courthouse and P.O. Building
Suite B-1A
101 Holmes Avenue
Huntsville, AL 35801-2548
(205) 895-5400
Field Representative: Louis F. Johnson

Bureau of Apprenticeship and Training (Local Office)
3737 Government Boulevard, Suite 103
Mobile, AL 36693-4309
(205) 441-5169
Field Representative: William Allen

• • •

ALASKA

Bureau of Apprenticeship and Training (Main Office)
Calais Building
3301 C Street, Suite 201
Anchorage, AK 99503
(907) 271-5035

• • •

ARIZONA

Bureau of Apprenticeship and Training (Main Office)
3221 North 16th Street, Suite 302
Phoenix, AZ 85016
(602) 640-2964

Bureau of Apprenticeship and Training (Field Office)
Federal Building, Box FB 35, Room 7P
300 West Congress Street
Tucson, AZ 85701
(602) 670-4652

State Apprenticeship Council (Main Office)
Arizona Department of Economic Security
438 West Adams Street
Phoenix, AZ 85003
(602) 252-7771
Supervisor of Apprenticeship Services: Tom Marin

State Apprenticeship Council (Local Office)
7 South Hibbert
Mesa, AZ 85281
(602) 834-7777

State Apprenticeship Council (Local Office)
6666 West Peoria
Peoria, AZ 85035
(602) 486-9891

State Apprenticeship Council (Local Office)
438 West Adams Street
Phoenix, AZ 85003
(602) 252-7771

State Apprenticeship Council (Local Office)
4635 South Central
Phoenix, AZ 85040
(602) 276-5587

State Apprenticeship Council (Local Office)
3406 North 51st Avenue
Phoenix, AZ 85031
(602) 247-3304

State Apprenticeship Council (Local Office)
9801 North 7th Street
Phoenix, AZ 85016
(602) 861-0208

• • •

ARKANSAS

Bureau of Apprenticeship and Training
Federal Building, Room 3507
700 West Capitol Street
Little Rock, AR 72201
(501) 324-5415

• • •

CALIFORNIA

**Bureau of Apprenticeship and Training
(Main Office)**
1301 Clay Street
Suite 1090-N
Oakland, CA 94612
(510) 637-2951

**Bureau of Apprenticeship and Training
(Field Office)**
3350 Shelby Street, Suite 340
Ontario, CA 91764
(909) 466-8685

**Bureau of Apprenticeship and Training
(Field Office)**
5675 Ruffin Road, Suite 310
San Diego, CA 92123
(619) 557-5574

**State Apprenticeship Council
(Main Office)**
455 Golden Gate Avenue
Room 1193
San Francisco, CA 94102
(415) 703-4251
Chief, Division of Apprenticeship Standards:
Gail W. Jesswein

**State Apprenticeship Council
(Local Office)**
2500 Mariposa Street, Room 3080
Fresno, CA 93721
(209) 445-5431

**State Apprenticeship Council
(Local Office)**
107 South Broadway
Room 5034
Los Angeles, CA 90012
(213) 897-1385

**State Apprenticeship Council
(Local Office)**
7700 Edgewater Drive, Suite 255
Oakland, CA 94621
(510) 577-5170

**State Apprenticeship Council
(Local Office)**
2424 Arden Way, Suite 160
Sacramento, CA 95825
(919) 263-2877

**State Apprenticeship Council
(Local Office)**
100 Paseo de San Antonio, Room 125
San Jose, CA 95113
(408) 277-1273

**State Apprenticeship Council
(Local Office)**
28 Civic Center Plaza, Room 525
Santa Ana, CA 92701
(714) 558-4126

• • •

COLORADO

Bureau of Apprenticeship and Training
U.S. Custom House
721 19th Street, Room 469
Denver, CO 80202
(303) 844-4793

• • •

CONNECTICUT

Bureau of Apprenticeship and Training
Federal Building
135 High Street, Room 367
Hartford, CT 06103
(203) 240-4311

State Apprenticeship Council
Connecticut Labor Department
Office of Job Training and Skill Development
200 Folly Brook Boulevard
Wethersfield, CT 06109
(203) 566-4724
Acting Director, Office of Job Training: Jack Guerrera

• • •

DELAWARE

Bureau of Apprenticeship and Training
Lock Box 36, Federal Building
844 King Street
Wilmington, DE 19801
(302) 573-6113

State Apprenticeship Council
Division of Employment and Training
PO Box 9499
Newark, DE 19714
(302) 368-6909
Administrator, Apprenticeship and Training:
Walter Purzycki

• • •

FLORIDA

Bureau of Apprenticeship and Training (Main Office)
City Centre Building
227 North Bronough Street, Room 4140
Tallahassee, FL 32301
(904) 942-8336
State Director: George Belcher

Bureau of Apprenticeship and Training (Jacksonville Office)
Suite 336, Box 35082
400 West Bay Street
Jacksonville, FL 32202-4412
(904) 232-2596
Field Representative: J. Richard Melton

State Apprenticeship Council
Florida Department of Labor and Employment Security
Division of Labor, Employment and Training
Bureau of Job Training
Industry Services Section
Atkins Building, Room 211
1320 Executive Center Drive
Tallahassee, FL 32399
(904) 488-8332

State Apprenticeship Council
Hollywood Regional Office VI/VIII
4205 Hollywood Boulevard
Hollywood, FL 33021-6632
(305) 985-4450
LET Specialist: Thomas A. Flynn

State Apprenticeship Council
Jacksonville Regional Office III
15 Market Street
Suite 300
Jacksonville, FL 32202
(904) 359-6080, Ext.34
LET Specialist: William (Bill) Lauver

State Apprenticeship Council
Orlando Regional Office V
Job Service of Florida
3421 Lawton Road
Orlando, FL 32803-2999
(407) 897-2880
LET Specialist: William E. Livengood

State Apprenticeship Council
Tampa Regional Office IV/IV II
Tampa Employment Center
9215 North Florida Avenue
Suite 106
Tampa, FL 33612
(813) 930-7588
LET Specialist: Jon D. Goins

State Apprenticeship Council
Job Service of Florida
3113 West Colonial Drive
Orlando, FL 32808-8005
(407) 297-2044
LET Specialist: Marvin Woodard

• • •

GEORGIA

Bureau of Apprenticeship and Training (Main Office)
Room 418
1371 Peachtree Street, NE
Atlanta, GA 30367
(404) 347-4403
State Director: Walace R. Johnson

Bureau of Apprenticeship and Training (Local Office)
3604 Macon Road
Suite 24
Columbus, GA 31907-2575
(706) 568-1787

**Bureau of Apprenticeship and Training
(Local Office)**
120 Barnard Street, Suite A-303
PO Box 8121
Savannah, GA 31401-3647
(912) 652-4203
Field Representative: E. Harold Fowler

• • •

HAWAII

Bureau of Apprenticeship and Training
300 Ala Moana Boulevard, Room 5113
Honolulu, HI 96850
(808) 541-2519

State Apprenticeship Council
Department of Labor and Industrial Relations,
Apprenticeship Division
830 Punchbowl Street, Room 334
Honolulu, HI 96813
(808) 586-8877
Administrator: Stanley Honda

• • •

IDAHO

Bureau of Apprenticeship and Training
3050 North Lakeharbor Lane, Room 128
Boise, ID 83703
(208) 334-1013

• • •

ILLINOIS

**Bureau of Apprenticeship and Training
(Main Office)**
230 South Dearborn Street, Room 758
Chicago, IL 60604
(312) 353-4690

**Bureau of Apprenticeship and Training
(Local Office)**
501 Bell Street, Suite 112
Alton, IL 62002
(618) 463-6440

**Bureau of Apprenticeship and Training
(Local Office)**
2350 East Devon
Room 300
Des Plaines, IL 60018
(708) 827-7139

**Bureau of Apprenticeship and Training
(Local Office)**
9730 South Western Avenue
Room 442
Evergreen Park, IL 60642
(708) 425-8220

**Bureau of Apprenticeship and Training
(Local Office)**
100 North East Monroe Street
Peoria, IL 61602
(309) 671-7056

**Bureau of Apprenticeship and Training
(Local Office)**
308 West State Street, Room 403
Rockford, IL 61101
(815) 987-4253

**Bureau of Apprenticeship and Training
(Local Office)**
U.S. Post Office and Courthouse
600 East Monroe Street, Room 14
Springfield, IL 62701
(217) 492-4478

• • •

INDIANA

**Bureau of Apprenticeship and Training
(Main Office)**
Federal Building and U.S. Courthouse
46 East Ohio Street
Room 414
Indianapolis, IN 46204
(317) 226-7592

**Bureau of Apprenticeship and Training
(Local Office)**
211 U.S. Postal Service Building
101 NW Martin Luther King Boulevard
Evansville, IN 47708
(812) 465-6415

Bureau of Apprenticeship and Training (Local Office)
1302 South Harrison Street, Room 132
Ft. Wayne, IN 46802
(219) 423-1470

Bureau of Apprenticeship and Training (Local Office)
610 Connecticut, Room 114
Gary, IN 46402
(219) 881-3530

Bureau of Apprenticeship and Training (Local Office)
611-A Lincoln Way East
South Bend, IN 46601
(219) 236-8295

• • •

IOWA

Bureau of Apprenticeship and Training (Main Office)
210 Walnut Street, Room 715
Des Moines, IA 50309
(515) 284-4690

Bureau of Apprenticeship and Training (Local Office)
131 East 4th Street, Room 340
Davenport, IA 52801
(319) 324-1339

• • •

KANSAS

Bureau of Apprenticeship and Training
444 SE Quincy Street, Room 247
Topeka, KS 66683
(913) 295-2624

State Apprenticeship Council
Department of Human Resources
401 SW Topeka Boulevard
Topeka, KS 66603
(913) 296-4161
Director: Loretta Shelley

• • •

KENTUCKY

Bureau of Apprenticeship and Training (Main Office)
Federal Building, Suite 136E
600 Martin Luther King Place
Louisville, KY 40202
(502) 582-5223

Bureau of Apprenticeship and Training (Local Office)
2033 Regency Road
Lexington, KY 40503
(606) 233-2501

State Apprenticeship Council
Kentucky Labor Cabinet
Division of Employment Standards
1047 U.S. 127 South, Suite 4
Frankfort, KY 40601
(502) 588-4466

• • •

LOUISIANA

Bureau of Apprenticeship and Training (Main Office)
Suite 133 Afton Village Condo
3535 Sherwood Forest Boulevard
Baton Rouge, LA 70816
(504) 389-0263

Bureau of Apprenticeship and Training (Local Office)
U.S. Postal Building
701 Loyola Street
Room 1323
New Orleans, LA 70113
(504) 589-6103
Field Representative: Alfred W. Bostick

State Apprenticeship Council
Louisiana Department of Labor
1001 North 23rd Street
PO Box 94094
Baton Rouge, LA 70804
(504) 342-7820
Acting Director of Apprenticeship: Percy Rodriguez

• • •

MAINE

Bureau of Apprenticeship and Training
Federal Building
68 Sewall Street, Room #408-D
Augusta, ME 04330
(207) 622-8235

State Apprenticeship Council
Bureau of Labor Standards
State House Station #45
Augusta, ME 04333
(207) 624-6430
Director, Apprenticeship Standards: Kenneth Hardt

• • •

MARYLAND

**Bureau of Apprenticeship and Training
(Main Office)**
Federal Building, Charles Center
31 Hopkins Plaza, Room 1028
Baltimore, MD 21201
(410) 962-2676

**Bureau of Apprenticeship and Training
(Local Office)**
Federal Building
129 East Main Street
PO Box 366
Salisbury, MD 21803
(410) 749-8900

State Apprenticeship Council
Department of Employment and Training
Redwood Towers, 11th Floor
217 East Redwood Street
Baltimore, MD 21202
(410) 333-8754
Director, Apprenticeship and Training:
M. Ann Edwards

• • •

MASSACHUSETTS

**Bureau of Apprenticeship and Training
(Main Office)**
11th Floor
One Congress Street
Boston, MA 02114
(617) 565-2291

**Bureau of Apprenticeship and Training
(Local Office)**
Springfield Federal Building, Room 211
1550 Main Street
Springfield, MA 01103
(413) 785-0315
Field Representative: Daniel T. Malone

**Bureau of Apprenticeship and Training
(Local Office)**
120 Front Street, Suite 630
Worcester, MA 01608
(508) 793-0508
Field Representative: Thomas M. Westerman

State Apprenticeship Council
Division of Apprentice Training
Department of Labor and Industries
100 Cambridge Street
Boston, MA 02202
(617) 727-3488
Director: Gay Wilkerson

• • •

MICHIGAN

**Bureau of Apprenticeship and Training
(Main Office)**
801 South Waverly, Room 304
Lansing, MI 48917
(517) 377-1640

**Bureau of Apprenticeship and Training
(Local Office)**
74 North Washington Avenue
Room #2-1-56
Battle Creek, MI 49017
(616) 961-7337

**Bureau of Apprenticeship and Training
(Local Office)**
231 West Lafayette
Room 657
Detroit, MI 43226
(313) 226-6206

**Bureau of Apprenticeship and Training
(Local Office)**
2920 Fuller, NE
Room 106
Grand Rapids, MI 49505
(616) 456-2187

Bureau of Apprenticeship and Training (Local Office)
310 West Washington Street, Suite 208
Marquette, MI 49855
(906) 228-7308

Bureau of Apprenticeship and Training (Local Office)
100 North Warren, Room 1073
North Warren at East Genesee Street
Saginaw, MI 48606
(517) 758-4136

• • •

MINNESOTA

Bureau of Apprenticeship and Training (Main Office)
316 Robert Street
Room 134
St. Paul, MN 55101
(612) 290-3951

Bureau of Apprenticeship and Training (Local Office)
515 West 1st Street
Room 234
Duluth, MN 55802-1302
(218) 720-5404

State Apprenticeship Council
443 Lafayette Road, 4th Floor
St. Paul, MN 55155
(612) 296-2371
Acting Director, Division of Apprentices
Department of Labor and Industry: Jerry Briggs

• • •

MISSISSIPPI

Bureau of Apprenticeship and Training
McCoy Federal Building, Suite 410
100 West Capitol Street
Jackson, MS 39269
(601) 965-4346

• • •

MISSOURI

Bureau of Apprenticeship and Training (Main Office)
1222 Spruce Street, Room 9.102E
Robert A. Young Federal Building
St. Louis, MO 63103
(314) 539-2522

Bureau of Apprenticeship and Training (Local Office)
3333 South National, Suite 303
Springfield, MO 65807
(417) 883-6186

Bureau of Apprenticeship and Training (Local Office)
911 Walnut Street, Room 1100
Kansas City, MO 64106
(816) 426-5389

• • •

MONTANA

Bureau of Apprenticeship and Training
Federal Office Building, Room 396
301 South Park Avenue, Drawer 10055
Helena, MT 59626
(406) 449-5261

State Apprenticeship Council
Apprentice Training, Research and Safety Division
Department of Labor and Industry
PO Box 1728
Helena, MT 59624
(406) 444-4500
Supervisor: Daniel F. Miles

• • •

NEBRASKA

Bureau of Apprenticeship and Training
106 South 15th Street, Room 801
Omaha, NE 68102
(402) 221-3281

• • •

NEVADA

Bureau of Apprenticeship and Training
301 Stewart Avenue
PO Box 1987, Room 311
Las Vegas, NV 89125
(702) 388-6396

State Apprenticeship Council
Capitol Complex
Carson City, NV 89710
(702) 687-4850
Director: Frank T. MacDonald

• • •

NEW HAMPSHIRE

Bureau of Apprenticeship and Training
143 North Main Street
Room 205
Concord, NH 03301
(603) 225-1444

State Apprenticeship Council
Department of Labor and Industries
State Office Park South
95 Pleasant Street
Concord, NH 03301
(603) 271-3176
Director: Jack Jarvis

• • •

NEW JERSEY

Bureau of Apprenticeship and Training
Parkway Towers, Building F
3rd Floor
485, Route 1, South
Iselin, NJ 08830
(908) 750-9191

• • •

NEW MEXICO

Bureau of Apprenticeship and Training
505 Marquette
Room 830
Albuquerque, NM 87102
(505) 766-2398

State Apprenticeship Council
New Mexico Department of Labor
501 Mountain Road, NE
Albuquerque, NM 87102
(505) 841-8989
Director, Apprenticeship and Training: Jim Fulcher

• • •

NEW YORK

Bureau of Apprenticeship and Training
Leo O'Brien Federal Building
North Pearl and Clinton Avenue, Room 809
Albany, NY 12202
(518) 472-4800

State Apprenticeship Council
New York State Department of Labor
State Office Campus
Building #12, Room 223
Albany, NY 12240
(518) 457-6820
Acting Director: Sandy Powell

• • •

NORTH CAROLINA

Bureau of Apprenticeship and Training
Somerset Park
Suite 205
4407 Bland Road
Raleigh, NC 27609
(919) 790-2801

**State Apprenticeship Council
(Main Office)**
Department of Labor
4 West Edenton Street
Raleigh, NC 27601
(919) 733-7533
Director: Kenneth Pittman

**State Apprenticeship Council
(Local Office)**
500 West Trade Street
Suite 433
Charlotte, NC 28202
(704) 342-5477

**State Apprenticeship Council
(Local Office)**
PO Box 5364
Fayetteville, NC 28305
(910) 486-1441

**State Apprenticeship Council
(Local Office)**
PO Box 732
Maiden, NC 28650
(704) 428-9187

• • •

NORTH DAKOTA

Bureau of Apprenticeship and Training
New Federal Building, Room 428
657, 2nd Avenue, North
Fargo, ND 58102
(701) 239-5415

• • •

OHIO

**Bureau of Apprenticeship and Training
(Main Office)**
200 North High Street, Room 605
Columbus, OH 43215
(614) 469-7375

**Bureau of Apprenticeship and Training
(Local Office)**
201 Cleveland Avenue, South West, Room 208
Canton, OH 44702
(216) 489-4483

**Bureau of Apprenticeship and Training
(Local Office)**
550 Main Street, Room 7031
Cincinnati, OH 45202
(513) 684-2112

**Bureau of Apprenticeship and Training
(Local Office)**
1350 Euclid Avenue
Room 440
Cleveland, OH 44115
(216) 522-3823

**Bureau of Apprenticeship and Training
(Local Office)**
301 West First Street
Room 305
Dayton, OH 45402
(513) 225-2725

**Bureau of Apprenticeship and Training
(Local Office)**
234 Summit Street
Room 706
Toledo, OH 43604
(419) 259-6390

**Bureau of Apprenticeship and Training
(Local Office)**
City Centre One
Suite 410
100 Federal Plaza East
Youngstown, OH 44503
(216) 743-0186

State Apprenticeship Council
Ohio State Apprenticeship Council
2323 West 5th Avenue
Room 2140
Columbus, OH 43216
(614) 644-2242
Executive Secretary: Mary Ann Walters

• • •

OKLAHOMA

**Bureau of Apprenticeship and Training
(Main Office)**
Room 305, 51 Yale Building
5110 South Yale
Tulsa, OK 74135
(918) 496-6770

**Bureau of Apprenticeship and Training
(Local Office)**
Alfred P. Murrah Federal Building
Room 526
200 NW Fifth
Oklahoma City, OK 73102
(405) 231-4814
Field Representative: Cynthia S. McLain

• • •

OREGON

Bureau of Apprenticeship and Training
Federal Building, Room 629
1220 SW 3rd Avenue
Portland, OR 97204
(503) 326-3157

**State Apprenticeship Council
(Main Office)**
Oregon Bureau of Labor and Industry
Apprenticeship and Training Division
State Office Building, Room 32
800 NE Oregon Street
Portland, OR 97232
(503) 731-4072
Director: Quint Rahberger

**State Apprenticeship Council
(Area Office)**
Salem/Albany (Area II)
3865 Wolverine NE: E-1
Salem, OR 97310
(503) 378-3287

**State Apprenticeship Council
(Area Office)**
Eugene/Springfield (Area III)
165 East 7th Room 220
Eugene, OR 97401
(503) 686-7582

**State Apprenticeship Council
(Area Office)**
Coos Bay/Roseburg (Area IV)
320 Central Avenue, Room 510
Coos Bay, OR 97420
(503) 269-4576

**State Apprenticeship Council
(Area Office)**
Medford/Grants Pass (Area V)
700 East Main, Room 105
Medford, OR 97504
(503) 776-6201

**State Apprenticeship Council
(Area Office)**
Pendleton (Area VI)
200 SE Haley, Suite 308
PO Box 730
Pendleton, OR 97801-0730
(503) 276-7884

**State Apprenticeship Council
(Area Office)**
Bend (Area VII)
1250 NE 3rd Room B-105
Bend, OR 97701
(503) 388-6331

PENNSYLVANIA

**Bureau of Apprenticeship and Training
(Main Office)**
Federal Building
228 Walnut Street
Room 773
Harrisburg, PA 17108
(717) 782-3496

**Bureau of Apprenticeship and Training
(Local Office)**
307 Mid-City Tower
12 East 9th Street
Erie, PA 16501
(814) 452-4918

**Bureau of Apprenticeship and Training
(Local Office)**
1436 Federal Building
1000 Liberty Avenue
Pittsburgh, PA 15222
(412) 644-2937

**Bureau of Apprenticeship and Training
(Local Office)**
PO Box 8796
Philadelphia, PA 19101
(215) 596-4176

**Bureau of Apprenticeship and Training
(Local Office)**
20 North Pennsylvania Avenue, Room 2028
Penn Place
Wilksburg, PA 18701
(717) 826-6511

**Bureau of Apprenticeship and Training
(Local Office)**
Berkshire Knoll
1125 Berkshire Boulevard
Room 240
Wyoming, PA 19610

State Apprenticeship Council
Apprenticeship and Training
7th and Forster Street, Room 1303
Harrisburg, PA 17120
(717) 787-3687
Director: Raymond Vaughan

• • •

RHODE ISLAND

Bureau of Apprenticeship and Training
Federal Building
100 Hartford Avenue
Providence, RI 02909
(401) 528-5198

State Apprenticeship Council
Apprenticeship and Training
Department of Labor
220 Elmwood Avenue
Providence, RI 02907
(401) 457-1858

• • •

SOUTH CAROLINA

Bureau of Apprenticeship and Training (Main Office)
Strom Thurmond Federal Building
1835 Assembly Street, Room 838
Columbia, SC 29201
(803) 765-5547

Bureau of Apprenticeship and Training (Local Office)
Federal Building
334 Meeting Street, Room 313
Charleston, SC 29403-6427
(803) 727-4326

• • •

SOUTH DAKOTA

Bureau of Apprenticeship and Training
Oxbow I Building, Room 204
2400 West 49th Street
Sioux Falls, SD 57105
(605) 330-4326

• • •

TENNESSEE

Bureau of Apprenticeship and Training (Main Office)
Airport Executive Plaza
1321 Murfreesboro Road, Suite 541
Nashville, TN 37217
(615) 781-5318

Bureau of Apprenticeship and Training (Local Office)
Joel Solomon Federal Building
900 Georgia Avenue, Suite 63
Chattanooga, TN 37402
(615) 752-5112

Bureau of Apprenticeship and Training (Local Office)
530 Gay Street, Suite 221
Knoxville, TN 37901-1531
(615) 545-4189
Field Representative: Sheila A. Kelley

Bureau of Apprenticeship and Training (Local Office)
Federal Building
167 North Main Street, Suite 209
Memphis, TN 38103-1821
(901) 544-3300
Field Representative: George R. Beasley

• • •

TEXAS

Bureau of Apprenticeship and Training (Main Office)
VA Building
Room 2102
2320 LaBranch Street
Houston, TX 77004
(713) 750-1696

Bureau of Apprenticeship and Training (Local Office)
2320 LaBranch Street
Room 2101
Houston, TX 77004
(713) 750-1699
Field Representative: Billie Grotzinger

**Bureau of Apprenticeship and Training
(Local Office)**
Federal Building
PO Box F13276
205 East 5th Street, Room B-18
Amarillo, TX 79101
(806) 376-2276
Field Representative: Steven Opitz

**Bureau of Apprenticeship and Training
(Local Office)**
Frito Lay Building
Exchange Park
6300 Forest Park Road, Suite 224-B
Dallas, TX 75235
(214) 358-3781
Field Representatives: Raymond J. Federle, Wendell Sullivan

**Bureau of Apprenticeship and Training
(Local Office)**
Federal Building
819 Taylor Street, Room 10G04
Fort Worth, TX 76102
(817) 334-3486
Field Representative: John A. Piekarski

**Bureau of Apprenticeship and Training
(Local Office)**
4550 Jimmy Johnson Boulevard, Room 115
Port Arthur, TX 77640
(409) 727-1780
Field Representative: Frank Herring

**Bureau of Apprenticeship and Training
(Local Office)**
10127 Morocco Street, Suite 112
Northchase 1
San Antonio, TX 78216
(210) 229-4592
Field Representative: Bill G. Donaho

• • •

UTAH

Bureau of Apprenticeship and Training
Administration Building, Room 1051
1745 West 1700 South
Salt Lake City, UT 84104
(801) 975-3650

• • •

VERMONT

Bureau of Apprenticeship and Training
Federal Building
11 Elmwood Avenue
Room 629
Burlington, VT 05401
(802) 951-6278

State Apprenticeship Council
Department of Labor and Industry
120 State Street
Montpelier, VT 05602
(802) 828-2157
Director: David G. Lagala

• • •

VIRGINIA

Bureau of Apprenticeship and Training
400 North 8th Street
Room 10-020
Richmond, VA 23240
(804) 771-2488

**State Apprenticeship Council
(Main Office)**
Department of Labor and Industry
13 South 13th Street
Powers-Taylor Building
Richmond, VA 23219
(804) 786-2381
Director: Robert S. Baumgardner

**State Apprenticeship Council
(Local Office)**
Virginia Department of Labor and Industry
Brookfield Square
966 West Main Street
Suite #4
Abingdon, VA 24210
(703) 676-5465

**State Apprenticeship Council
(Local Office)**
Virginia Department of Labor and Industry
104 Annhurst Drive
Danville, VA 24540
(804) 836-8412

**State Apprenticeship Council
(Local Office)**
Virginia Department of Labor and Industry
11211 Waples Mill Road
Suite 302
Fairfax, VA 22030
(703) 359-1167

**State Apprenticeship Council
(Local Office)**
Virginia Department of Labor and Industry
3704 Old Forest Road
Suite "B"
Lynchburg, VA 24501
(804) 386-4705

**State Apprenticeship Council
(Local Office)**
Virginia Department of Labor and Industry
2551 Eltham Avenue
Suite"H"
Norfolk, VA 23513
(804) 858-6700
Tidewater Regional Supervisor: James L. Davis

**State Apprenticeship Council
(Local Office)**
Virginia Department of Labor and Industry
13 South 13th Street
Richmond, VA 23219
(804) 786-3259
Richmond and Northern Virginia Regional Supervisor: Harry P. Seay

**State Apprenticeship Council
(Local Office)**
Virginia Department of Labor and Industry
1314 Peters Creek Road, Suite 130
Roanoke, VA 24017
(703) 562-3580
Southwest Virginia Regional Supervisor: Connie M. Perry

**State Apprenticeship Council
(Local Office)**
Virginia Department of Labor and Industry
Broadmoor Plaza Office Center
Route 340
Suite 101
Stuarts Draft, VA 24477
(703) 337-3225

WASHINGTON

**Bureau of Apprenticeship and Training
(Main Office)**
1400 Talbot Road South
Suite 100
Renton, WA 98055
(206) 277-5214

**Bureau of Apprenticeship and Training
(Local Office)**
711 Vine Street
Kelso, WA 98626
(206) 577-2200

**Bureau of Apprenticeship and Training
(Local Office)**
500 North Morain
Suite 1110
Kennewick, WA 99336
(509) 735-0104

**Bureau of Apprenticeship and Training
(Local Office)**
PO Box 1406
Mt. Vernon, WA 98273
(206) 428-1350

**Bureau of Apprenticeship and Training
(Local Office)**
East 3901 Main
Spokane, WA 99220
(509) 456-2923

**Bureau of Apprenticeship and Training
(Local Office)**
1305 Tacoma Avenue South
Suite 305
Tacoma, WA 98401
(206) 596-3931

**State Apprenticeship Council
(Main Office)**
Department of Labor and Industry ESAC Division
PO Box 44530
Olympia, WA 98504
(206) 956-5320

**State Apprenticeship Council
(Local Office)**
Department of Labor and Industries
Section of Apprenticeship
300 West Harrison Street, #502
Seattle, WA 96119-4081
(206) 281-5511

• • •

WASHINGTON, DC

State Apprenticeship Council
DC Apprenticeship Council
500 C Street, NW, Suite 241
Washington, DC 20001
(202) 724-7246
Director: Frances Barry

• • •

WEST VIRGINIA

**Bureau of Apprenticeship and Training
(Main Office)**
Federal Building
550 Eagan, Room 303
Charleston, WV 25301
(304) 347-5141

**Bureau of Apprenticeship and Training
(Main Office)**
Palace Furniture Building
168 West Main Street
Room 500
Clarksburg, WV 26301
(304) 623-0916

• • •

WISCONSIN

**Bureau of Apprenticeship and Training
(Main Office)**
Federal Center, Room 303
212 East Washington Avenue
Madison, WI 53703
(608) 264-5377

**Bureau of Apprenticeship and Training
(District 13)**
Prairie Professional Park
6921 Mariner Drive, 1st Floor
Racine, WI 53406
(414) 886-2917

**Bureau of Apprenticeship and Training
(District 19)**
Federal Center, Room 303
212 East Washington Avenue
Madison, WI 53703
(608) 264-5377
State Director: Terrence Benewich

State Apprenticeship Council
Bureau of Apprenticeship Standards
Department of Industry, Labor and Human Relations
7201 East Washington Avenue, Room 211-X
Madison, WI 53707
(608) 266-3133

State Apprenticeship Council
Bureau of Apprenticeship Standards
Department of Industry, Labor and Human Relations
District 1
c/o Chippewa Valley Technical College
620 West Clairemont Avenue, Room 7A
Eau Claire, WI 54701
(715) 833-6444

State Apprenticeship Council
Bureau of Apprenticeship Standards
Department of Industry, Labor and Human Relations
District 2
c/o North Central Technical College
1000 Campus Drive
Wausau, WI 54401
(715) 675-3331, Ext. 225

State Apprenticeship Council
Bureau of Apprenticeship Standards
Department of Industry, Labor and Human Relations
District 3
c/o Wisconsin Indianhead Technical College
600 North 21st Street
Superior, WI 54880
(715) 394-6677

State Apprenticeship Council
Bureau of Apprenticeship Standards
Department of Industry, Labor and Human Relations
District 11
c/o Western Wisconsin Technical College
325 North Eighth Street
Technics Building, Room 118
LaCrosse, WI 54602-0908
(608) 785-9176

State Apprenticeship Council
Bureau of Apprenticeship Standards
Department of Industry, Labor and Human Relations
District 14
2125 Commercial Avenue
Madison, WI 53704
(608) 246-7900

State Apprenticeship Council
Bureau of Apprenticeship Standards
Department of Industry, Labor and Human Relations
Milwaukee Office
State Office Building
819 North 6th Street, Room 260
Milwaukee, WI 53203
(414) 227-4398

State Apprenticeship Council
Bureau of Apprenticeship Standards
Department of Industry, Labor and Human Relations
Appleton Office
1825 North Bluemound Road
PO Box 2277
Appleton, WI 54913
(414) 832-5303

• • •

WYOMING

Bureau of Apprenticeship and Training
American National Bank Building
1912 Capitol Avenue, Room 508
Cheyenne, WY 82001
(307) 772-2448

• • •

Appendix III: DOT Index

This list of job titles and occupational classification numbers is provided so that users can explore the occupational description further as defined by the U.S. Department of Labor. The classified numbers refer to those used in the *Dictionary of Occupational Titles* (Government Printing Office, U.S. Department of Labor, 4th edition, 1991). The *Dictionary of Occupational Titles* lists occupations by their DOT number and is a standard reference tool found in the collections of most public libraries.

Air conditioning and refrigeration mechanic   637.261-014

Asbestos worker   869.684-082

Auto glass installer   865.684-010

Automotive mechanic   620.261-010

Automotive painter   845.381-014

Baker   313.381-010

Bank note designer   142.081-010

Barber   330.371-010

Bartender   312.474-010

Bindery worker   653.

Blacksmith   610.381-014

Boilermaker   805.261-014

Bookbinder   977.381-010

Breeder   041.061-014

Bricklayer   861.381-014; 861.381-026

Building maintenance repair   899.381-010

Cabinet maker   660.280-010

Cable splicer   829.361-010

Candymaker   520.685-050

Carpenter   860.381-022

Carpet layer   864.381-010

Cement finisher   844.364-014

Cement mason   844.364-010

Chemical technician   008.261-010

Child care worker   313.361-014

Combination welder   819.384-010

Composer   971.382-018

Compositor   973.381-010

Construction laborer   869.664-014

Cook   313.361-014; 526.685-010

Cooper   764.684-022

Corrections officer   372.137-010

Cosmetologist   332.271-010

Crane operator   921.663-010

Decorator   142.051-014

Die maker   601.280-010

Diesel mechanic   625.281-010

Dispensing optician   299.474-010

Drafter   007.261-010

Drywall finisher   842.664-010

Drywaller   842.381-010

Electrical instrument repairer   729.281-026

Electrician   824.261-010; 825.381-030

Electronics mechanic   828.261-022

Electronics technician   003.161-014

Elevator constructor   825.361-010

Embalmer   338.371-014

Emergency medical technician   079.374-010

Environmental service technician   029.261-014

Erection machinist (millwright)   638.261-014

Facilities custodial service technician (maintenance mechanic)   899.261-014; 899.381-010

Farrier   418.381-010

Firefighter   373.364-010

Fitter   805.361-014

Floor covering installer   864.481-014

Forester   040.061-034

Forger (heat treater)   504.382-018

Foundry   011.061-010

Front end/back end mechanic   620.281-038

Funeral director   187.167-030

Gaming dealer   343.467-018

Gasfitter   953.364-010

Glazier   865.381-010

Graphic designer   141.161-018

Gunsmith   632.281-010

Hardwood floor layer   860.381-022

Heavy equipment mechanic   620.261-022

Heavy equipment operator   859.683-010

Horse trainer   419.224-010

HVAC mechanic   637.261-014

Hydroelectric power plant operator   952.362-018

Instrument mechanic   710.281-026

Instrumentation technician   003.261-010

Insulation worker   863.364-010

Ironworker   801.361-018

Jig and fixture builder   693.281-030

Jig and fixture tool maker   601.281-026

Joiner   860.381-050

Laborer   869.664-014

Last model maker   761.381-018

Lather   842.361-010

Leatherworker   783.684-026

Legislative lobbyist   165.017-010

Lighting and sound technician
   962.362-014

Line installer   821.361-018; 822.381-014

Lineman   821.261-014; 821.361-026

Loftsperson   661.281-010

Machine repairer   638.281-014

Machinist   600.280-022

Mailroom   209.587-026

Maintenance electrician   829.261-018

Maintenance engineer   828.261-022

Maintenance machinist   600.280-042

Maintenance mechanic   638.281-014

Marble mason   861.381-030

Marble setter   861.381-030

Marine electrician   825.381-034

Meatcutter   316.684-018

Mechanic   805.361-010

Mechanical engineering technician
   007.161-026

Medical transcriptionist   203.582-058

Metallurgical technician   011.261-010

Millwright   638.281-018

Mold maker   518.664-010

Molder   518.361-010

Motion picture machine operator
   960.362-010

Museum curating and administering
   102.017-010

Nondestructive tester   011.261-018

Nursing assistant   355.674-014

Ocularist   713.261-014

Operating engineer   859.683-010

Orthotics technician   712.381-034

Outside machinist   623.281-030

Painter   144.061-010; 840.381-010

Painter (marine)   840.381-014

Paperhanger   841.381-010

Pattern maker   600.280-050

Pattern setter   661.281-022

Piano tuner   730.361-010

Piledriver   859.682-018

Pipecoverer   863.381-014

Pipefitter   862.381-018

Plasterer   842.361-018

Plumber   862.381-030

Police officer   375.263-018

Power plant operator   952.382-018

Preschool worker   313.361-014

Press operator/platemaker   972.381-026

Pressman   611.482-010

Printer   979.382-018

Production controller   221.167-018

Protective signal installer   822.361-018

Real estate appraiser   188.167-010

Refrigeration mechanic   862.281-026

Rigger   921.6664-014

Rigger (marine)   806.261-014

Roofer   866.381-010

Sandblaster   503.687-010

Screw machine operator and setter
   604.280-014

Security officer   189.167-034

Sheetmetal worker   804.281-010

Shipfitter   806.381-050

Shipwright   860.381-062

Shoe repairer   365.361-014

Soft floor layer   861.381-034

Sound and communication technician
   829.281-022

Sound technician   829.281-022

Sprinkler fitter   862.281-022

Stage technician   962.261-014

Stationary engineer   950.382-026

Steamfitter   862.381-018

Steamfitter helper   862.684-022

Stone cutter   771.381-010

Stone mason   861.381-038

Stone setter   861.381-042

Surveyor   018.167

Taper   842.664-010

Tax return preparer   219.362-070

Terrazzo worker   861.381-046

Tile finisher   861.664-018

Tile setter   861.381-054

Tin smith   804.281-010

Tool and die maker   601.280-046

Tool designer   007.061-026

Tool maker   601.280-042

Tooling inspector   601.281-022

Truck driver   905.663-014

Tuckpointer   869.664-014

Vending machine mechanic   639.281-014

Waste water treatment plant operator
   955.362-010

Waterproofer   869.664-014

Welder   805.381-010

Job Index

Acoustical ceiling installer:
　　Carpenters, **134**
Air conditioning and refrigeration mechanic:
　　Pipe Trades Workers, **384, 388, 390-391, 403, 414**
　　Sheetmetal Workers, **485-488**
　　Appendix III: DOT Index, **783**
Ambulance attendant:
　　Emergency Medical Technicians, **644, 656-657**
Architectural glazier:
　　Glaziers, **263**
Asbestos worker:
　　Asbestos Workers and Insulators, **38-56**
　　Colleges and Technical Schools, **600-601**
　　Appendix III: DOT Index, **783**
Assistant engineer:
　　Railroad Workers, **750-751**
Auto glass installer:
　　Glaziers, **257, 262**
　　Appendix III: DOT Index, **783**
Automotive machinist:
　　Machinists, **303**
　　Mechanics, **323-324**
Automotive mechanic:
　　Mechanics, **324, 327, 331-332**
　　Appendix III: DOT Index, **783**
Automotive painter:
　　Painters and Paperhangers, **363**
　　Appendix III: DOT Index, **783**
Automotive trades worker:
　　Mechanics, **323**
Baker:
　　Cooks, Chefs, and Bakers, **166-172**
　　Appendix III: DOT Index, **783**
Bank note designer:
　　Additional Occupations, **569**
　　Appendix III: DOT Index, **783**
Barber:
　　Colleges and Technical Schools, **599-602**
　　Cosmetologists, **603, 605-607, 614, 617, 620-621**
　　Appendix III: DOT Index, **783**
Bartender:
　　Additional Occupations, **570**
　　Appendix III: DOT Index, **783**
Basic EMT:
　　Emergency Medical Technicians, **638-672**
　　Beautician (See Cosmetologist)

Bindery worker:
　　Printing Industry Workers, **441, 443, 445, 449, 452, 455, 457-459**
　　Appendix III: DOT Index, **783**
Blacksmith:
　　Boilermakers, **59**
　　Additional Occupations, **570-571**
　　Crafts and Trades Workers, **623, 625-629**
　　Appendix III: DOT Index, **783**
Bladesmith:
　　Gunsmiths, Gunmakers, and Bladesmiths, **731-733**
Boilermaker:
　　Boilermakers, **57-64**
　　Shipbuilding Industry Workers, **514**
　　Additional Occupations, **570**
　　Appendix III: DOT Index, **783**
Bookbinder:
　　Printing Industry Workers, **442, 446-447, 453, 455**
　　Appendix III: DOT Index, **783**
Brake coupler:
　　Railroad Workers, **749**
Brake operator:
　　Railroad Workers, **749-751**
Braker:
　　Railroad Workers, **749**
Breeder:
　　Additional Occupations, **576**
　　Appendix III: DOT Index, **783**
Bricklayer:
　　Bricklayers and Stone Masons, **66-84**
　　Colleges and Technical Schools, **599-601**
　　Appendix III: DOT Index, **783**
Broom maker:
　　Crafts and Trades Workers, **626**
Building maintenance repairer:
　　Mechanics, **325**
　　Appendix III: DOT Index, **783**
Cabinet maker:
　　Carpenters, **94, 106, 110, 122-123, 132, 141**
　　Colleges and Technical Schools, **601**
　　Crafts and Trades Workers, **629**
　　Appendix III: DOT Index, **783**
Cable splicer:
　　Electricians and Line Workers, **186, 211**
　　Appendix III: DOT Index, **783**

Candymaker:
Cooks, Chefs, and Bakers, **171**
Appendix III: DOT Index, **783**

Cardiac technician:
Emergency Medical Technicians, **645, 652**

Carpenter:
Carpenters, **86-145**
Shipbuilding Industry Workers, **511**
Colleges and Technical Schools, **596-597, 599-602**
Crafts and Trades Workers, **626**
Appendix III: DOT Index, **783**

Carpet layer:
Carpenters, **87, 109, 127**
Appendix III: DOT Index, **783**

Carriage smith:
Additional Occupations, **571**

CC lather specialist:
Tool, Die, Mold, and Pattern Makers, **545**

CC mill:
Tool, Die, Mold, and Pattern Makers, **545**

Cement finisher:
Cement Masons, **156, 159, 161-162**
Appendix III: DOT Index, **783**

Cement mason:
Cement Masons, **146-165**
Colleges and Technical Schools, **601**
Appendix III: DOT Index, **783**

Chemical technician:
Additional Occupations, **571**
Appendix III: DOT Index, **783**

Coatings and service technician:
Painters and Paperhangers, **369**

Combination welder:
Welders, **563**
Appendix III: DOT Index, **783**

Commercial builder:
Carpenters, **92**

Commercial electrician:
Electricians and Line Workers, **196**

Composer:
Printing Industry Workers, **441, 454**
Appendix III: DOT Index, **783**

Compositor:
Printing Industry Workers, **450**
Appendix III: DOT Index, **783**

Conductor:
Railroad Workers, **749-751**

Construction electrician:
Electricians and Line Workers, **191, 195-196, 225, 227, 237**

Construction equipment operator:
Operating Engineers, 339-341, 343, 345, 356

Cook:
Cooks, Chefs, and Bakers, **167-172**

Corrections officer:
Additional Occupations, **572**
Appendix III: DOT Index, **784**

Cosmetologist:
Colleges and Technical Schools, **599-602**
Cosmetologists, **603-621**
Appendix III: DOT Index, **784**

Crane operator:
Operating Engineers, **343**
Appendix III: DOT Index, **784**

Culinary arts worker:
Cooks, Chefs, and Bakers, **171**

Cylinder corrector:
Printing Industry Workers, **453**
Decorator:
Painters and Paperhangers, **362-363, 370, 372, 375**
Appendix III: DOT Index, **784**

Die maker:
Tool, Die, Mold, and Pattern Makers, **539-540, 542, 544, 546-552, 554, 556-558**
Colleges and Technical Schools, **597, 599-602**
Appendix III: DOT Index, **784, 786**

Diesel mechanic:
Mechanics, **322, 328**
Appendix III: DOT Index, **784**

Digital mechanical engraver:
Printing Industry Workers, **453**

Dinkey operator:
Railroad Workers, **750**

Dispensing optician:
Dispensing Opticians, **630-633**
Appendix III: DOT Index, **784**

Drafter:
Tool, Die, Mold, and Pattern Makers, **543**
Additional Occupations, **572**
Appendix III: DOT Index, **784**

Drywall finisher:
Drywallers and Lathers, **173-174, 177-178, 180-181**
Appendix III: DOT Index, **784**

Drywaller:
Carpenters, **88**
Drywallers and Lathers, **173-183**
Appendix III: DOT Index, **784**

Electric serviceman:
    Electricians and Line Workers, **227**
Electrical contractor:
    Electricians and Line Workers, **190, 210, 217, 237**
Electrical designer:
    Electricians and Line Workers, **215**
Electrical instrumentation technician:
    Electronics Technicians, **249, 255-256**
Electrician:
    Electricians and Line Workers, **184-247**
    Laborers, **291**
    Colleges and Technical Schools, **596-602**
    Appendix III: DOT Index, **784-785**
Electronic instrument and control technician:
    Electronics Technicians, **249-252, 254**
Electronics mechanic:
    Electronics Technicians, **249, 251, 254**
    Appendix III: DOT Index, **784**
Electronics technician:
    Electronics Technicians, **253-254**
    Appendix III: DOT Index, **784**
Elevator constructor:
    Additional Occupations, **574**
    Appendix III: DOT Index, **784**
Embalmer:
    Funeral Directors and Embalmers, **712-730**
    Appendix III: DOT Index, **784**
Emergency care attendant:
    Emergency Medical Technicians, **667**
Emergency medical technician (See EMT)
EMT Critical care:
    Emergency Medical Technicians, **652**
EMT:
    Emergency Medical Technicians, **635-672**
    Firefighters, **682, 684, 696-697**
Engineering model maker:
    Tool, Die, Mold, and Pattern Makers, **543**
Equipment operator (See also Heavy equipment operator):
    Operating Engineers, **339-341, 343-345, 347, 350-352, 354, 356-358**
    Appendix III: DOT Index, **784**
Erection machinist (See also Millwright):
    Carpenters, **109**
    Appendix III: DOT Index, **784**
Experimental machinist:
    Machinists, **305**
Fabricator:
    Carpenters, 108
    Tool, Die, Mold, and Pattern Makers, 554
    Welders, 564
    Colleges and Technical Schools, 601-602
Farm worker:
    Crafts and Trades Workers, **626**
Farrier:
    Additional Occupations, **574**
    Appendix III: DOT Index, **784**
Feeder operator:
    Printing Industry Workers, **461**
Fiber optics installers:
    Electricians and Line Workers, **186, 191**
Field ironworker:
    Ironworkers, **271-273, 280-281**
Fire medic:
    Firefighters, **684**
Firefighter:
    Emergency Medical Technicians, **636**
    Firefighters, **674-702**
    Appendix III: DOT Index, **784**
Fireman oiler (See also Laborer):
    Laborers, **295**
Firer:
    Firefighters, **689**
    Railroad Workers, **750**
First responder:
    Emergency Medical Technicians, **649, 659-660, 669**
Fitter:
    Pipe Trades Workers, **379, 384-388, 390, 395, 399, 401, 405, 408-409, 412, 414-418, 421, 426**
    Colleges and Technical Schools, **601**
    Appendix III: DOT Index, **784, 786**
Floor covering installer:
    Carpenters, **87, 94-95, 102, 114, 116, 122, 127, 141**
    Colleges and Technical Schools, **601**
    Appendix III: DOT Index, **784**
Forester:
    Crafts and Trades Workers, **625**
    Appendix III: DOT Index, **784**
Foundry:
    Tool, Die, Mold, and Pattern Makers, **556, 558**
    Colleges and Technical Schools, **601**
    Crafts and Trades Workers, **629**
    Appendix III: DOT Index, **784**
Front end/back end mechanic (See also Automotive mechanic):
    Mechanics, **330**
    Appendix III: DOT Index, **784**

Job Index

Funeral director:
Funeral Directors and Embalmers, 712-730
Appendix III: DOT Index, **784**

Funeral service:
Funeral Directors and Embalmers, **715, 717, 720, 722-729**

Gaming dealer:
Additional Occupations, **575**
Appendix III: DOT Index, **784**
Garage mechanic (See Automotive mechanic)

Gardener:
Crafts and Trades Workers, **626**

Gas and linesman:
Electricians and Line Workers, **227**

Gas serviceman:
Electricians and Line Workers, **227**

Gasfitter:
Pipe Trades Workers, **400**
Appendix III: DOT Index, **784**

General warehouse worker:
Additional Occupations, **576**

Glazier:
Carpenters, **94**
Colleges and Technical Schools, **601**
Appendix III: DOT Index, **784**

Graphic designer:
Crafts and Trades Workers, **625**
Appendix III: DOT Index, **784**

Gunsmith:
Crafts and Trades Workers, **629**
Gunsmiths, Gunmakers, and Bladesmiths, **731-733**
Appendix III: DOT Index, **784**

Hairdresser (See also Cosmetologist):
Cosmetologists, **605, 620**

Hairstylist (See Cosmetologist)

Hardwood floor layer:
Carpenters, **93**
Appendix III: DOT Index, **784**

Heating and air conditioning mechanic:
Pipe Trades Workers, **379-380, 384, 388, 390-391, 399, 401, 403, 414**
Sheetmetal Workers, **483-489, 506**

Heavy equipment mechanic:
Mechanics, **321, 323**
Operating Engineers, **339-345, 347, 351-352, 356**
Appendix III: DOT Index, **784**

Heavy equipment operator:
Operating Engineers, **342, 350-351, 357**
Appendix III: DOT Index, **784**

Heavy metal fabricator:
Tool, Die, Mold, and Pattern Makers, **554**

High voltage electrician:
Electricians and Line Workers, **231**

Horse trainer:
Additional Occupations, **576**
Appendix III: DOT Index, **784**

Hull outfit designer:
Shipbuilding Industry Workers, **513**

HVAC designer:
Pipe Trades Workers, **398**

HVAC mechanic:
Pipe Trades Workers, **385-386, 392-394, 398, 400-401, 403, 420**
Sheetmetal Workers, **497, 504**
Colleges and Technical Schools, **597, 600**
Appendix III: DOT Index, **784**

Hydroelectric electrician:
Electricians and Line Workers, **224**

Hydroelectric power plant operator:
Electricians and Line Workers, **224**
Appendix III: DOT Index, **784**

Industrial electrician:
Electricians and Line Workers, **199, 239, 245**
Colleges and Technical Schools, **597, 599-602**

Industrial electronics control mechanic:
Electronics Technicians, **254**

Industrial equipment mechanic & production machine mechanic:
Mechanics, **321-323, 331**

Industrial maintenance mechanic:
Mechanics, **331**
Colleges and Technical Schools, **597**

Industrial millwright:
Carpenters, **131**

Industrial plumber & pipefitter:
Pipe Trades Workers, **385**

Inside construction electrician:
Electricians and Line Workers, **196**

Inside wireman:
Electricians and Line Workers, **190, 192-194, 201, 204-205, 208-209, 212-213, 219, 226, 231-232**

Instrument mechanic:
Electronics Technicians, **256**
Appendix III: DOT Index, **784**

Instrumentation technician:
Electronics Technicians, **249, 251, 255-256**
Colleges and Technical Schools, **600-601**
Appendix III: DOT Index, **784**

Insulation worker:
Asbestos Workers and Insulators, **44**
Appendix III: DOT Index, **784**

Interior systems carpenter:
Carpenters, **87, 127**

Intermediate EMT:
Emergency Medical Technicians, **638-643, 647-654, 656-657, 659-672**

Ironworker:
Ironworkers, **268-289**
Colleges and Technical Schools, **596, 600, 602**
Appendix III: DOT Index, **784**

Jig and fixture builder:
Tool, Die, Mold, and Pattern Makers, **542, 554**

Jig and fixture tool maker:
Tool, Die, Mold, and Pattern Makers, **542**
Appendix III: DOT Index, **784**

Joiner:
Carpenters, **87, 90, 97, 115, 120, 129, 131**
Colleges and Technical Schools, **597**
Crafts and Trades Workers, **626**
Appendix III: DOT Index, **784**

Laborer:
Laborers, **291-292, 295, 297-298**
Appendix III: DOT Index, **783, 785**

Lampworker:
Additional Occupations, **577**

Last model maker:
Tool, Die, Mold, and Pattern Makers, **545**
Appendix III: DOT Index, **785**

Lather:
Carpenters, **88, 95, 100, 122, 125, 141**
Drywallers and Lathers, **173-183**
Appendix III: DOT Index, **785**

Leatherworker:
Additional Occupations, **585**
Appendix III: DOT Index, **785**

Lift truck mechanic:
Mechanics, **335**

Lighting and sound technician:
Theater Workers, **517-518, 520**
Appendix III: DOT Index, **785-786**

Line installer:
Electricians and Line Workers, **186-187, 189-190, 227**
Appendix III: DOT Index, **785**

Lineman:
Electricians and Line Workers, **189, 206, 223, 225, 227, 229, 236**
Colleges and Technical Schools, **600-601**
Appendix III: DOT Index, **785**

Loftsperson:
Tool, Die, Mold, and Pattern Makers, **542**
Appendix III: DOT Index, **785**

Machine repair technician:
Machinists, **305, 308**
Mechanics, **322, 334-335**
Colleges and Technical Schools, **597, 601**
Appendix III: DOT Index, **785**

Machinist fabrication technician:
Machinists, **310**

Machinist:
Machinists, **301, 303-307, 310-311, 313-314, 317-318**
Tool, Die, Mold, and Pattern Makers, **545**
Colleges and Technical Schools, **599-602**
Appendix III: DOT Index, **784-785**

Maintenance craftworker:
Tool, Die, Mold, and Pattern Makers, **549**

Maintenance electrician:
Electricians and Line Workers, **185, 197, 217, 237, 243**
Appendix III: DOT Index, **785**

Maintenance engineer:
Operating Engineers, **342, 351**
Appendix III: DOT Index, **785**

Maintenance machinist:
Machinists, **301, 311, 313-314**
Appendix III: DOT Index, **785**

Maintenance mechanic:
Mechanics, **322, 324, 329-336**
Appendix III: DOT Index, **784-785**

Maintenance millwright:
Carpenters, **143**

Maintenance pipefitter:
Pipe Trades Workers, **389, 420**

Maintenance tool maker:
Tool, Die, Mold, and Pattern Makers, **557**

Maintenance worker:
Additional Occupations, **584**
Appendix III: DOT Index, **783-785**

Marble mason:
Tile Setters, **531, 535**
Appendix III: DOT Index, **785**

Marble setter:
Tile Setters, **527-533**
Appendix III: DOT Index, **785**

Marine electrician:
Electricians and Line Workers, **215**
Appendix III: DOT Index, **785**

Marine joiner:
　Carpenters, **97**
Marine machinery:
　Mechanics, **331**
Marine pattern maker:
　Tool, Die, Mold, and Pattern Makers, **542**
Mason:
　Bricklayers and Stone Masons, **67-71, 75-76, 82-83**
　Cement Masons, **146-165**
　Colleges and Technical Schools, **599-602**
　Appendix III: DOT Index, **783, 785-786**
Meatcutter:
　Additional Occupations, **577**
　Appendix III: DOT Index, **785**
Mechanic (See also specific kinds, such as Automotive):
　Mechanics, **321-337**
　Appendix III: DOT Index, **783-786**
Mechanical engineering technician:
　Additional Occupations, **573, 578**
　Appendix III: DOT Index, **785**
Medical transcriptionist:
　Additional Occupations, **578**
　Appendix III: DOT Index, **785**
Metal forger:
　Additional Occupations, **579**
Metallurgical technician:
　Additional Occupations, **579**
　Appendix III: DOT Index, **785**
Meter and instrument technician:
　Electronics Technicians, **255**
MICT:
　Emergency Medical Technicians, **646**
Mill-cabinet worker:
　Carpenters, **126**
Millwright:
　Carpenters, **90, 92, 94, 96-97, 99-102, 104-109, 112-114, 116-119, 122-125, 127, 129-144**
　Colleges and Technical Schools, **597, 599-602**
　Appendix III: DOT Index, **784-785**
Mold maker:
　Tool, Die, Mold, and Pattern Makers, **538-559**
Mortician:
　Funeral Directors and Embalmers, **718, 721-722**
Motion picture machine operator:
　Theater Workers, **524**
　Appendix III: DOT Index, **785**

Museum curator and administrator:
　Crafts and Trades Workers, **625**
　Appendix III: DOT Index, **785**
Musical instrument maker:
　Musical Instrument Tuners and Repairers, **734-738**
Nondestructive tester:
　Additional Occupations, **579**
　Appendix III: DOT Index, **785**
Nonmember association manager:
　Theater Workers, **522**
Nursing assistant:
　Additional Occupations, **580**
　Appendix III: DOT Index, **785**
Ocularist:
　Ocularists, **739-740**
　Appendix III: DOT Index, **785**
Off-Broadway manager:
　Theater Workers, **522**
Oil well driller:
　Additional Occupations, **580**
Operating engineer:
　Operating Engineers, **338-358**
　Appendix III: DOT Index, **785**
Ornamental ironworker:
　Ironworkers, **269, 271, 282**
Orthotics technician:
　Orthotics Technicians, **741-743**
　Appendix III: DOT Index, **785**
Outside electrician:
　Electricians and Line Workers, **197**
Outside lineman:
　Electricians and Line Workers, **225**
Outside machinist:
　Machinists, **301, 304-305, 313**
　Appendix III: DOT Index, **785**
Painter:
　Painters and Paperhangers, **359-377**
　Colleges and Technical Schools, **597, 599-601**
　Appendix III: DOT Index, **783, 785**
Paperhanger:
　Painters and Paperhangers, **359-377**
　Appendix III: DOT Index, **785**
Paramedic:
　Emergency Medical Technicians, **638-645, 647-672**
　Firefighters, **695, 702**
Pattern maker:
　Tool, Die, Mold, and Pattern Makers, **538-559**
　Colleges and Technical Schools, **597, 601**
　Appendix III: DOT Index, **785**

Pattern setter:
    Tool, Die, Mold, and Pattern Makers, **558**
    Appendix III: DOT Index, **785**

PCC restoration:
    Tile Setters, **532**

Piano tuner:
    Musical Instrument Tuners and Repairers, **735, 737**
    Appendix III: DOT Index, **785**

Pile driver:
    Carpenters, **91, 96, 117, 125, 130, 134, 141**
    Appendix III: DOT Index, **785**

Pipe designer:
    Pipe Trades Workers, **398**

Pipe trades:
    Pipe Trades Workers, **378-428**

Pipecoverer:
    Pipe Trades Workers, **389**
    Appendix III: DOT Index, **785**

Pipefitter:
    Pipe Trades Workers, **379, 382-387, 389-391, 393-398, 400, 403, 405-420, 422-424, 426-428**
    Shipbuilding Industry Workers, **511**
    Colleges and Technical Schools, **596-597, 599-601**
    Appendix III: DOT Index, **785**

Plant services mechanic:
    Mechanics, **330**
    Plasterer:
    Plasterers, **429-439**
    Appendix III: DOT Index, **785**

Plumber:
    Pipe Trades Workers, **379, 382-388, 390-402, 404-406, 408-422, 425, 427-428**
    Welders, **563**
    Colleges and Technical Schools, **596-597, 599-602**
    Appendix III: DOT Index, **785**

Pointer/Cleaner/Caulker:
    Bricklayers and Stone Masons, **75**
    Appendix III: DOT Index, **786**

Police officer:
    Additional Occupations, **581**
    Emergency Medical Technicians, **636**
    Appendix III: DOT Index, **785**

Power and substation electrician:
    Electricians and Line Workers, **211**

Power plant operator:
    Electricians and Line Workers, **224**

Powerline installer:
    Electricians and Line Workers, **192**

Prepress worker:
    Printing Industry Workers, **441-443, 445, 447, 449-451, 454-459, 462**

Preschool worker:
    Preschool Workers, **744-749**
    Appendix III: DOT Index, **785**

Press assistant:
    Printing Industry Workers, **461**

Pressman:
    Printing Industry Workers, **444-463**
    Appendix III: DOT Index, **786**

Printer:
    Colleges and Technical Schools, **600**
    Crafts and Trades Workers, **626, 629**
    Appendix III: DOT Index, **786**

Printing:
    Printing Industry Workers, **440-463**
    Appendix III: DOT Index, **783**

Process technician:
    Additional Occupations, **583**

Production controller:
    Additional Occupations, **583**
    Appendix III: DOT Index, **786**

Production machine mechanic:
    Mechanics, **321-323, 331**

Protective signal installer:
    Electricians and Line Workers, **191**
    Appendix III: DOT Index, **786**

Public school workers:
    Additional Occupations, **583**

Radio and TV repairer:
    Electronics Technicians, **252**

Radio communication technician:
    Electronics Technicians, **252**

Rail yard engineer:
    Railroad Workers, **750**

Railroad worker:
    Railroad Workers, **749-753**

Real estate appraiser:
    Additional Occupations, **584**
    Colleges and Technical Schools, **598**
    Appendix III: DOT Index, **786**

Resident firefighter:
    Firefighters, **679-680**

Residential electrician:
    Electricians and Line Workers, **190**

Restoration worker:
    Bricklayers and Stone Masons, **75**

Rigger:
    Shipbuilding Industry Workers, **511, 513, 515**
    Appendix III: DOT Index, **786**

Rodman:
  Ironworkers, **287**
Roofer:
  Roofers and Waterproofers, **464-481**
  Appendix III: DOT Index, **786**
Sandblaster:
  Bricklayers and Stone Masons, **67, 71**
  Appendix III: DOT Index, **786**
Screw machine operator & setter:
  Tool, Die, Mold, and Pattern Makers, **550, 558**
  Appendix III: DOT Index, **785-786**
Security officer:
  Additional Occupations, **584**
  Appendix III: DOT Index, **786**
Sheetmetal worker:
  Sheetmetal Workers, **482-508**
  Colleges and Technical Schools, **597, 599-602**
  Appendix III: DOT Index, **786**
Ship propeller finisher:
  Shipbuilding Industry Workers, **514**
Shipboard worker:
  Electricians and Line Workers, **231**
Shipbuilding industry worker:
  Shipbuilding Industry Workers, **510-516**
Shipfitter:
  Shipbuilding Industry Workers, **511, 513-515**
  Colleges and Technical Schools, **597**
  Appendix III: DOT Index, **786**
Shipwright:
  Shipbuilding Industry Workers, **511, 515**
  Appendix III: DOT Index, **786**
Shoe repairer:
  Additional Occupations, **585**
  Appendix III: DOT Index, **786**
Soft floor layer:
  Carpenters, **125**
  Appendix III: DOT Index, **786**
Sound and Communication technician:
  Electronics Technicians, **254**
  Appendix III: DOT Index, **786**
Sprinkler fitter:
  Pipe Trades Workers, **386, 390, 399, 401, 405, 408-409, 412, 415-416, 421, 426**
  Colleges and Technical Schools, **601**
  Appendix III: DOT Index, **786**
Stage technician:
  Theater Workers, **517-524**
  Appendix III: DOT Index, **786**

Stained glass glazier:
  Glaziers, **264**
Stationary engineer:
  Mechanics, **332**
  Operating Engineers, **340-343, 348-349, 356-357**
  Appendix III: DOT Index, **786**
Steamfitter helper:
  Appendix III: DOT Index, **786**
Steamfitter:
  Pipe Trades Workers, **379, 382, 384-388, 394-395, 399, 402-403, 405-406, 411, 413, 417, 420-422, 425-426**
  Welders, **563**
  Colleges and Technical Schools, **599-602**
  Appendix III: DOT Index, **786**
Stone cutter:
  Cement Masons, **160**
  Appendix III: DOT Index, **786**
Stone mason:
  Bricklayers and Stone Masons, **67-68, 82**
  Appendix III: DOT Index, **786**
Stone setter:
  Tile Setters, **530-532**
  Appendix III: DOT Index, **786**
Structural ironworker:
  Ironworkers, **269, 273, 280**
Surveyor:
  Additional Occupations, **586-587**
  Appendix III: DOT Index, **786**
Switch tender:
  Railroad Workers, **749**
Taper:
  Drywallers and Lathers, **173, 176-178, 183**
  Appendix III: DOT Index, **786**
Tax return preparer:
  Additional Occupations, **587**
  Appendix III: DOT Index, **786**
Temperature control technician:
  Pipe Trades Workers, **401**
  Terrazzo worker:
  Tile Setters, **527-535**
  Appendix III: DOT Index, **786**
Theater worker:
  Theater Workers, **517-524**
Tile finisher:
  Tile Setters, **527, 529**
  Appendix III: DOT Index, **786**
Tile setter:
  Tile Setters, **526-537**
  Appendix III: DOT Index, **786**

Tin smith:
    Additional Occupations, **588**
    Appendix III: DOT Index, **786**

Tool & die gauge technician:
    Tool, Die, Mold, and Pattern Makers, **538-559**

Tool & die maker:
    Tool, Die, Mold, and Pattern Makers, **538-559**
    Colleges and Technical Schools, **597, 599-602**
    Appendix III: DOT Index, **783-784, 786**

Tool and mold maker:
    Tool, Die, Mold, and Pattern Makers, **542, 545, 548, 551, 553, 557**
    Colleges and Technical Schools, **601**
    Appendix III: DOT Index, **784, 786**

Tool design drafter:
    Tool, Die, Mold, and Pattern Makers, **543, 550**
    Appendix III: DOT Index, **786**

Tooling inspector:
    Tool, Die, Mold, and Pattern Makers, **554**
    Appendix III: DOT Index, **786**

Toolroom machinist:
    Machinists, **317**
    Colleges and Technical Schools, **602**

Truck driver:
    Operating Engineers, **358**
    Additional Occupations, **589-590**
    Appendix III: DOT Index, **786**

Tuckpointer:
    Bricklayers and Stone Masons, **75**
    Appendix III: DOT Index, **786**

TV cable installer:
    Electricians and Line Workers, **214**

Universal operator:
    Operating Engineers, **346**

Utility line installer:
    Electricians and Line Workers, **190**

Vehicle mechanic:
    Mechanics, **336**

Vending machine mechanic:
    Vending Machine Mechanics, **754-757**
    Appendix III: DOT Index, **786**

Video production assistant:
    Theater Workers, **521**

Waste water treatment plant operator:
    Operating Engineers, **343**
    Appendix III: DOT Index, **786**

Waterproofer:
    Roofers and Waterproofers, **464-481**
    Appendix III: DOT Index, **786**

Welder:
    Mechanics, **326**
    Pipe Trades Workers, **397, 422**
    Shipbuilding Industry Workers, **511**
    Welders, **560-568**
    Colleges and Technical Schools, **597, 600-601**
    Appendix III: DOT Index, **783, 786**

Welding equipment repairer:
    Welders, **566**

Wildland firefighter:
    Firefighters, **679**

Wireman (See also Inside wireman):
    Electricians and Line Workers, **188-190, 192-194, 201-202, 204-206, 208-209, 212-213, 219-220, 222, 225-226, 231-234, 238**

Wood crafter:
    Carpenters, **128**

Yard coupler:
    Railroad Workers, **749**

State Index

Alabama:
- Asbestos Workers and Insulators, 41
- Boilermakers, 59-60, 63
- Carpenters, 90
- Drywallers and Lathers, 175
- Electricians and Line Workers, 188
- Painters and Paperhangers, 361
- Pipe Trades Workers, 382, 426
- Printing Industry Workers, 444
- Sheetmetal Workers, 485, 503
- Theater Workers, 519
- Welders, 563
- Colleges and Technical Schools, 601
- Cosmetologists, 605, 611
- Emergency Medical Technicians, 638, 641
- Firefighters, 678
- Folk Arts, 705
- Funeral Directors and Embalmers, 715
- Appendix II: BATs, 766-767

Alaska:
- Carpenters, 90-91
- Cement Masons, 149
- Cooks, Chefs, and Bakers, 169
- Drywallers and Lathers, 176
- Electricians and Line Workers, 189
- Glaziers, 259
- Ironworkers, 271
- Operating Engineers, 342
- Painters and Paperhangers, 362
- Pipe Trades Workers, 383
- Plasterers, 431
- Roofers and Waterproofers, 467
- Sheetmetal Workers, 485
- Theater Workers, 520
- Cosmetologists, 605, 615
- Emergency Medical Technicians, 639, 641, 668
- Firefighters, 678
- Folk Arts, 706
- Funeral Directors and Embalmers, 715
- Appendix II: BATs, 766-767

Arizona:
- Carpenters, 91
- Electricians and Line Workers, 189-190
- Ironworkers, 271-272, 274
- Pipe Trades Workers, 384
- Roofers and Waterproofers, 468
- Sheetmetal Workers, 486
- Additional Occupations, 576
- Colleges and Technical Schools, 596
- Cosmetologists, 605, 611, 615
- Emergency Medical Technicians, 640-641
- Firefighters, 678
- Folk Arts, 706
- Funeral Directors and Embalmers, 715
- Appendix II: BATs, 766-767

Arkansas:
- Bricklayers and Stone Masons, 69
- Carpenters, 92
- Cement Masons, 150
- Roofers and Waterproofers, 468
- Cosmetologists, 606, 611, 615
- Emergency Medical Technicians, 640-641, 669
- Firefighters, 678
- Folk Arts, 706
- Funeral Directors and Embalmers, 716
- Gunsmiths, Gunmakers, and Bladesmiths, 732
- Appendix II: BATs, 766, 768

California:
- Asbestos Workers and Insulators, 41-43
- Boilermakers, 59, 63
- Bricklayers and Stone Masons, 69-70
- Carpenters, 93-96, 118
- Cement Masons, 150-152
- Cooks, Chefs, and Bakers, 169-170
- Drywallers and Lathers, 176-180
- Electricians and Line Workers, 191-195
- Glaziers, 259-260
- Ironworkers, 271-274, 280-281
- Laborers, 293
- Machinists, 303
- Mechanics, 323-324
- Operating Engineers, 342-344
- Painters and Paperhangers, 362-364
- Pipe Trades Workers, 384-388
- Plasterers, 431-432
- Roofers and Waterproofers, 468-470
- Sheetmetal Workers, 486-488
- Theater Workers, 520
- Tile Setters, 528-529
- Tool, Die, Mold, and Pattern Makers, 541
- Welders, 563
- Additional Occupations, 577-578, 584-

587, 589
Colleges and Technical Schools, 596
Cosmetologists, 606
Emergency Medical Technicians, 641
Firefighters, 678-679
Funeral Directors and Embalmers, 716
Ocularists, 740
Appendix II: BATs, 766, 768

Colorado:
Asbestos Workers and Insulators, 43
Carpenters, 96-97
Electricians, 195-197
Glaziers, 260-261
Operating Engineers, 344
Pipe Trades, 388-389
Roofers, 471
Sheetmetal Workers, 489
Cosmetologists, 606
Crafts and Trades Workers, 625
Emergency Medical Technicians, 642-643
Firefighters, 679-680
Folk Arts, 706
Appendix II: BATs, 706, 766, 768

Connecticut:
Carpenters, 97-98
Electricians and Line Workers, 197
Electronics Technicians, 251
Glaziers, 265
Machinists, 303-304
Mechanics, 324
Painters and Paperhangers, 364
Pipe Trades Workers, 389-390, 417
Printing Industry Workers, 444
Roofers and Waterproofers, 471
Sheetmetal Workers, 489
Shipbuilding Industry Workers, 513
Tool, Die, Mold, and Pattern Makers, 541-542
Welders, 563
Additional Occupations, 572
Cosmetologists, 607
Emergency Medical Technicians, 641, 643, 668
Firefighters, 680
Folk Arts, 706
Funeral Directors and Embalmers, 716
Appendix II: BATs, 765, 768, 771

Delaware:
Ironworkers, 274
Cosmetologists, 607
Emergency Medical Technicians, 644
Firefighters, 680

Folk Arts, 706
Funeral Directors and Embalmers, 717
Appendix II: BATs, 768-769

Florida:
Carpenters, 98-100
Drywallers and Lathers, 180
Electricians and Line Workers, 198-201
Glaziers, 261
Ironworkers, 274
Laborers, 293, 298
Painters and Paperhangers, 364-365
Pipe Trades Workers, 390-392
Roofers and Waterproofers, 472
Sheetmetal Workers, 490-491
Theater Workers, 520
Tile Setters, 528
Additional Occupations, 570, 583
Cosmetologists, 603, 605, 607, 611, 615
Emergency Medical Technicians, 641, 644
Firefighters, 680
Folk Arts, 706
Funeral Directors and Embalmers, 717
Appendix II: BATs, 766, 769

Georgia:
Asbestos Workers and Insulators, 43
Bricklayers and Stone Masons, 70
Carpenters, 100
Electricians and Line Workers, 201-203
Laborers, 292
Machinists, 304
Mechanics, 325
Operating Engineers, 344
Painters and Paperhangers, 365
Pipe Trades Workers, 392
Roofers and Waterproofers, 472
Sheetmetal Workers, 491
Theater Workers, 521
Tile Setters, 530
Tool, Die, Mold, and Pattern Makers, 542
Welders, 564
Cosmetologists, 607, 611, 615
Emergency Medical Technicians, 641, 645
Firefighters, 681
Folk Arts, 706
Funeral Directors and Embalmers, 717
Appendix II: BATs, 765-766, 769-770, 777

Hawaii:
Asbestos Workers and Insulators, 44

State Index

Bricklayers and Stone Masons, 70
Carpenters, 101
Cement Masons, 152
Ironworkers, 275
Operating Engineers, 345
Painters and Paperhangers, 366
Plasterers, 432
Roofers and Waterproofers, 472
Sheetmetal Workers, 491
Tile Setters, 530
Cosmetologists, 608
Emergency Medical Technicians, 641, 645
Firefighters, 681
Folk Arts, 707
Appendix II: BATs, 766, 770

Idaho:
Carpenters, 102
Electricians and Line Workers, 203-204
Cosmetologists, 608, 611, 615
Emergency Medical Technicians, 646-647
Firefighters, 681
Folk Arts, 707
Funeral Directors and Embalmers, 718
Appendix II: BATs, 766, 770

Illinois:
Bricklayers and Stone Masons, 71
Carpenters, 102-103
Cement Masons, 153
Drywallers and Lathers, 180-181
Electricians and Line Workers, 204-207, 230
Ironworkers, 275-276
Laborers, 293
Machinists, 305
Mechanics, 325
Operating Engineers, 345-346
Painters and Paperhangers, 366
Pipe Trades Workers, 393-394
Plasterers, 433
Printing Industry Workers, 445
Roofers and Waterproofers, 473
Sheetmetal Workers, 492
Tile Setters, 530
Tool, Die, Mold, and Pattern Makers, 542
Additional Occupations, 584
Colleges and Technical Schools, 596
Cosmetologists, 603, 608, 611
Emergency Medical Technicians, 641, 647, 668
Firefighters, 681-682

Folk Arts, 707
Funeral Directors and Embalmers, 718
Railroad Workers, 752
Vending Machine Mechanics, 757
Appendix II: BATs, 766, 770-771

Indiana:
Asbestos Workers and Insulators, 44
Bricklayers and Stone Masons, 71-72
Carpenters, 104-105
Cement Masons, 153-154
Electricians and Line Workers, 207-211
Electronics Technicians, 251
Glaziers, 261
Ironworkers, 276-277
Machinists, 305
Operating Engineers, 346
Painters and Paperhangers, 367
Pipe Trades Workers, 394-395
Plasterers, 433-434
Printing Industry Workers, 445-446
Roofers and Waterproofers, 473-474
Sheetmetal Workers, 492-493
Theater Workers, 521
Tile Setters, 531-532
Tool, Die, Mold, and Pattern Makers, 543-544
Additional Occupations, 571, 573, 578, 579
Cosmetologists, 609
Crafts and Trades Workers, 625
Emergency Medical Technicians, 648
Firefighters, 682-683
Folk Arts, 707
Funeral Directors and Embalmers, 718-719
Appendix II: BATs, 766, 770-771

Iowa:
Asbestos Workers and Insulators, 44
Bricklayers and Stone Masons, 72-73
Carpenters, 105
Drywallers and Lathers, 181
Electricians and Line Workers, 211-212
Electronics Technicians, 252
Ironworkers, 277
Mechanics, 325
Painters and Paperhangers, 367
Pipe Trades Workers, 395-396
Printing Industry Workers, 446
Sheetmetal Workers, 493
Tool, Die, Mold, and Pattern Makers, 544
Additional Occupations, 582
Cosmetologists, 609
Emergency Medical Technicians, 641,

648-649, 668
Firefighters, 683
Folk Arts, 707
Funeral Directors and Embalmers, 719
Appendix II: BATs, 766, 771

Kansas:
Bricklayers and Stone Masons, 73
Carpenters, 105
Cement Masons, 154-155
Electricians and Line Workers, 212
Pipe Trades Workers, 396
Printing Industry Workers, 446-447
Roofers and Waterproofers, 474
Sheetmetal Workers, 493
Tool, Die, Mold, and Pattern Makers, 545
Additional Occupations, 570, 580
Colleges and Technical Schools, 596
Cosmetologists, 609
Emergency Medical Technicians, 649-650
Firefighters, 684
Folk Arts, 707
Funeral Directors and Embalmers, 719
Appendix II: BATs, 766, 771, 773

Kentucky:
Carpenters, 106
Electricians and Line Workers, 212-213, 228, 230
Pipe Trades Workers, 396-397
Printing Industry Workers, 448
Roofers and Waterproofers, 474
Additional Occupations, 574
Cosmetologists, 610
Crafts and Trades Workers, 625
Emergency Medical Technicians, 641, 650, 668
Firefighters, 684
Folk Arts, 707
Funeral Directors and Embalmers, 719-720
Appendix II: BATs, 766, 771

Louisiana:
Asbestos Workers and Insulators, 45
Bricklayers and Stone Masons, 73-74
Carpenters, 106-108
Cooks, Chefs, and Bakers, 169-170
Electricians and Line Workers, 213-214
Electronics Technicians, 252
Glaziers, 262
Ironworkers, 278
Laborers, 294
Operating Engineers, 346
Painters and Paperhangers, 368
Pipe Trades Workers, 397-398
Roofers and Waterproofers, 469, 474
Sheetmetal Workers, 493
Cosmetologists, 606, 610-611, 615
Emergency Medical Technicians, 651
Firefighters, 684
Folk Arts, 707
Funeral Directors and Embalmers, 720
Appendix II: BATs, 766, 771

Maine:
Carpenters, 108, 119
Cooks, Chefs, and Bakers, 171
Electricians and Line Workers, 215-216
Glaziers, 262
Machinists, 305
Mechanics, 326
Operating Engineers, 347
Pipe Trades Workers, 398-399
Printing Industry Workers, 448
Sheetmetal Workers, 494
Shipbuilding Industry Workers, 513
Theater Workers, 521
Tool, Die, Mold, and Pattern Makers, 545
Welders, 564
Cosmetologists, 610-611, 615
Crafts and Trades Workers, 626
Emergency Medical Technicians, 641, 651-652, 668
Firefighters, 685
Folk Arts, 708
Funeral Directors and Embalmers, 720-721
Appendix II: BATs, 765, 772

Maryland:
Asbestos Workers and Insulators, 45-46
Boilermakers, 60
Bricklayers and Stone Masons, 74
Carpenters, 108-110
Cement Masons, 155
Cooks, Chefs, and Bakers, 169
Electricians and Line Workers, 188, 216-218, 230
Electronics Technicians, 251
Glaziers, 262
Ironworkers, 278
Laborers, 294, 297
Machinists, 303, 306-307
Mechanics, 323, 327
Operating Engineers, 347
Painters and Paperhangers, 361, 369
Pipe Trades Workers, 399-403, 422

Roofers and Waterproofers, 474
Sheetmetal Workers, 494-495
Shipbuilding Industry Workers, 513
Theater Workers, 521
Tile Setters, 532
Tool, Die, Mold, and Pattern Makers, 541, 546
Welders, 565
Additional Occupations, 572-575, 580-582, 586
Cosmetologists, 611
Crafts and Trades Workers, 626
Dispensing Opticians, 633
Emergency Medical Technicians, 641, 652, 655, 664, 668-669
Firefighters, 685
Folk Arts, 708
Funeral Directors and Embalmers, 721
Gunsmiths, Gunmakers, and Bladesmiths, 733
Railroad Workers, 753
Appendix II: BATs, 765, 772

Massachusetts:
Asbestos Workers and Insulators, 46-47
Bricklayers and Stone Masons, 75
Carpenters, 110-111
Cement Masons, 155-156
Glaziers, 265
Ironworkers, 278
Machinists, 312
Operating Engineers, 348
Pipe Trades Workers, 382, 404
Printing Industry Workers, 449
Roofers and Waterproofers, 475
Sheetmetal Workers, 496
Theater Workers, 523-524
Tile Setters, 532-533
Tool, Die, Mold, and Pattern Makers, 553
Additional Occupations, 575, 581, 585
Cosmetologists, 611, 615
Crafts and Trades Workers, 626-627
Emergency Medical Technicians, 641, 652-653, 668-669
Firefighters, 685-686
Folk Arts, 708
Appendix II: BATs, 765, 772

Michigan:
Asbestos Workers and Insulators, 47-48
Boilermakers, 60
Bricklayers and Stone Masons, 76
Carpenters, 112-113
Cement Masons, 157
Electricians and Line Workers, 218-220, 230
Machinists, 307-308
Mechanics, 328
Operating Engineers, 348-349
Painters and Paperhangers, 370
Pipe Trades Workers, 404-407
Plasterers, 434
Printing Industry Workers, 449-450
Roofers and Waterproofers, 475
Theater Workers, 522
Tool, Die, Mold, and Pattern Makers, 547-548
Additional Occupations, 570, 572, 574, 584, 588
Colleges and Technical Schools, 597
Cosmetologists, 612
Emergency Medical Technicians, 641, 653, 668
Firefighters, 686
Folk Arts, 708
Funeral Directors and Embalmers, 721
Railroad Workers, 752
Appendix II: BATs, 766, 772-773

Minnesota:
Bricklayers and Stone Masons, 76-77
Carpenters, 114
Cement Masons, 157
Electricians and Line Workers, 220-221
Ironworkers, 279
Laborers, 294
Painters and Paperhangers, 370
Pipe Trades Workers, 408
Plasterers, 434
Printing Industry Workers, 450
Roofers and Waterproofers, 475
Cosmetologists, 611-612, 615
Emergency Medical Technicians, 641, 654
Firefighters, 686
Folk Arts, 708
Funeral Directors and Embalmers, 721
Appendix II: BATs, 766, 773

Mississippi:
Carpenters, 114-115
Electricians and Line Workers, 221-222
Painters and Paperhangers, 371
Pipe Trades Workers, 408
Sheetmetal Workers, 496
Welders, 565
Colleges and Technical Schools, 597
Cosmetologists, 611-612, 615
Emergency Medical Technicians, 641, 654, 665, 668

Firefighters, 686
Folk Arts, 708
Funeral Directors and Embalmers, 722
Appendix II: BATs, 766, 773

Missouri:
Asbestos Workers and Insulators, 48
Boilermakers, 60
Bricklayers and Stone Masons, 69, 77
Carpenters, 115-116
Cement Masons, 158
Electricians and Line Workers, 223
Glaziers, 263
Ironworkers, 279-280
Machinists, 308
Operating Engineers, 349-350
Painters and Paperhangers, 371
Pipe Trades Workers, 409
Printing Industry Workers, 450-451
Roofers and Waterproofers, 475
Additional Occupations, 583
Cosmetologists, 612
Emergency Medical Technicians, 641, 655, 668
Firefighters, 686
Folk Arts, 708
Funeral Directors and Embalmers, 722
Musical Instrument Tuners and Repairers, 738
Railroad Workers, 752
Appendix II: BATs, 766, 773

Montana:
Bricklayers and Stone Masons, 77-78
Carpenters, 117
Electricians and Line Workers, 223
Operating Engineers, 351
Plasterers, 435
Printing Industry Workers, 451
Tile Setters, 533
Cosmetologists, 611, 613, 615
Emergency Medical Technicians, 640-641, 655, 668
Firefighters, 686-687
Folk Arts, 708
Funeral Directors and Embalmers, 722
Railroad Workers, 752
Appendix II: BATs, 766, 773, 779

Nebraska:
Bricklayers and Stone Masons, 78
Carpenters, 118
Electricians and Line Workers, 223-224
Laborers, 295
Cosmetologists, 613
Emergency Medical Technicians, 656
Firefighters, 687
Folk Arts, 709
Funeral Directors and Embalmers, 722-723
Appendix II: BATs, 765-766, 769, 772-774, 776

Nevada:
Asbestos Workers and Insulators, 49
Bricklayers and Stone Masons, 78-79
Carpenters, 118-119
Cement Masons, 159
Cooks, Chefs, and Bakers, 171
Electricians and Line Workers, 224-225
Electronics Technicians, 252
Glaziers, 263-264
Ironworkers, 274, 280
Machinists, 309
Mechanics, 328
Operating Engineers, 343, 351-352
Painters and Paperhangers, 372
Pipe Trades Workers, 409-410
Plasterers, 435
Roofers and Waterproofers, 475-476
Sheetmetal Workers, 496
Theater Workers, 522
Tile Setters, 533-534
Additional Occupations, 570, 575, 578, 581, 584, 586, 589
Cosmetologists, 611, 613, 615
Emergency Medical Technicians, 641, 656, 668
Firefighters, 687
Folk Arts, 709
Appendix II: BATs, 766, 774

New Hampshire:
Carpenters, 119
Colleges and Technical Schools, 598
Cosmetologists, 611, 614
Emergency Medical Technicians, 641, 657, 668
Firefighters, 687
Folk Arts, 709
Funeral Directors and Embalmers, 723
Appendix II: BATs, 765, 774

New Jersey:
Carpenters, 119-121
Roofers and Waterproofers, 476
Sheetmetal Workers, 497
Theater Workers, 522
Additional Occupations, 577
Cosmetologists, 611, 614
Crafts and Trades Workers, 628
Emergency Medical Technicians, 641,

State Index

657-658, 664, 668
Firefighters, 687, 689
Folk Arts, 709
Funeral Directors and Embalmers, 723
Appendix II: BATs, 765, 774

New Mexico:
Asbestos Workers and Insulators, 49
Bricklayers and Stone Masons, 79
Carpenters, 121
Ironworkers, 281
Roofers and Waterproofers, 476
Sheetmetal Workers, 497
Cosmetologists, 611, 614
Crafts and Trades Workers, 625
Emergency Medical Technicians, 641, 658, 668
Firefighters, 687-688
Folk Arts, 709
Funeral Directors and Embalmers, 723-724
Appendix II: BATs, 766, 774

New York:
Bricklayers and Stone Masons, 79-80
Carpenters, 122-123
Cement Masons, 159-160
Drywallers and Lathers, 181-182
Electricians and Line Workers, 226
Machinists, 309
Painters and Paperhangers, 372
Pipe Trades Workers, 411
Plasterers, 435
Printing Industry Workers, 452-453
Roofers and Waterproofers, 476
Sheetmetal Workers, 498-499
Theater Workers, 519, 522
Tile Setters, 534
Tool, Die, Mold, and Pattern Makers, 548
Additional Occupations, 584
Colleges and Technical Schools, 598
Cosmetologists, 611, 615
Crafts and Trades Workers, 628
Emergency Medical Technicians, 641, 658-659, 664, 668
Firefighters, 688
Folk Arts, 709
Funeral Directors and Embalmers, 724
Appendix II: BATs, 765, 774

North Carolina:
Boilermakers, 61
Carpenters, 123
Cement Masons, 160
Electricians and Line Workers, 227
Electronics Technicians, 253

Glaziers, 264
Machinists, 309-311
Mechanics, 329-330
Pipe Trades Workers, 412
Printing Industry Workers, 453
Theater Workers, 523
Tool, Die, Mold, and Pattern Makers, 549-551
Additional Occupations, 571
Colleges and Technical Schools, 597
Cosmetologists, 611, 615
Emergency Medical Technicians, 641, 659-660, 668-669
Firefighters, 688-689
Folk Arts, 709
Funeral Directors and Embalmers, 724
Appendix II: BATs, 766, 774-775

North Dakota:
Carpenters, 124
Electricians and Line Workers, 227
Ironworkers, 281
Pipe Trades Workers, 413
Printing Industry Workers, 454
Cosmetologists, 611, 615-616
Emergency Medical Technicians, 641, 660, 669
Firefighters, 689
Folk Arts, 709
Appendix II: BATs, 766, 775

Ohio:
Asbestos Workers and Insulators, 50
Carpenters, 124-125
Cement Masons, 160
Electricians and Line Workers, 204-208, 213, 218, 227-230, 238, 241
Electronics Technicians, 253
Glaziers, 259
Ironworkers, 282
Operating Engineers, 352-353
Pipe Trades Workers, 413-414
Plasterers, 436
Printing Industry Workers, 454-457
Roofers and Waterproofers, 477
Shipbuilding Industry Workers, 514
Theater Workers, 523
Tool, Die, Mold, and Pattern Makers, 551-552
Additional Occupations, 579, 588
Colleges and Technical Schools, 598
Cosmetologists, 616
Crafts and Trades Workers, 628
Emergency Medical Technicians, 641,

661-662
Firefighters, 690
Folk Arts, 710
Funeral Directors and Embalmers, 725
Railroad Workers, 752-753
Appendix II: BATs, 766, 770, 775

Oklahoma:
Asbestos Workers and Insulators, 51
Boilermakers, 61-62
Bricklayers and Stone Masons, 80
Carpenters, 125-126
Cement Masons, 161
Drywallers and Lathers, 182
Electricians and Line Workers, 230
Electronics Technicians, 254
Glaziers, 264
Ironworkers, 282-283
Laborers, 295
Operating Engineers, 353
Painters and Paperhangers, 373
Pipe Trades Workers, 414-415
Plasterers, 436
Roofers and Waterproofers, 478
Sheetmetal Workers, 499-500
Tile Setters, 535
Additional Occupations, 574, 589
Cosmetologists, 611, 615-617
Emergency Medical Technicians, 641, 662-663, 668
Firefighters, 690
Folk Arts, 710
Appendix II: BATs, 766, 775

Oregon:
Carpenters, 87-144
Cooks, Chefs, and Bakers, 167-172
Electricians and Line Workers, 185-247
Ironworkers, 269-289
Laborers, 291-298
Pipe Trades Workers, 379-428
Plasterers, 429-439
Printing Industry Workers, 441-454, 456-462
Roofers and Waterproofers, 465-481
Sheetmetal Workers, 483-508
Theater Workers, 517-524
Cosmetologists, 617
Emergency Medical Technicians, 663
Firefighters, 690
Folk Arts, 710
Funeral Directors and Embalmers, 725-726
Appendix II: BATs, 766, 776

Pennsylvania:
Asbestos Workers and Insulators, 51
Boilermakers, 62
Bricklayers and Stone Masons, 80
Carpenters, 127-128
Electricians and Line Workers, 231
Electronics Technicians, 254
Glaziers, 259, 265
Machinists, 312
Mechanics, 330-331
Operating Engineers, 354
Painters and Paperhangers, 373
Pipe Trades Workers, 415-416
Plasterers, 436
Printing Industry Workers, 457-460
Roofers and Waterproofers, 478
Sheetmetal Workers, 501-502
Shipbuilding Industry Workers, 514
Theater Workers, 523
Tool, Die, Mold, and Pattern Makers, 552-553
Welders, 566
Additional Occupations, 576, 579
Cosmetologists, 611, 615, 617
Emergency Medical Technicians, 641, 658, 663-664, 668-669
Firefighters, 690-691
Folk Arts, 705, 710
Funeral Directors and Embalmers, 726
Appendix II: BATs, 765, 776-777

Rhode Island:
Asbestos Workers and Insulators, 52
Bricklayers and Stone Masons, 81
Carpenters, 128
Cement Masons, 161
Electricians and Line Workers, 233
Glaziers, 265
Ironworkers, 283, 287
Laborers, 296
Machinists, 312-313
Mechanics, 331
Operating Engineers, 355
Painters and Paperhangers, 373
Pipe Trades Workers, 390, 417
Plasterers, 437
Printing Industry Workers, 460
Roofers and Waterproofers, 479
Sheetmetal Workers, 502
Shipbuilding Industry Workers, 515
Theater Workers, 523
Tile Setters, 535
Tool, Die, Mold, and Pattern Makers, 553

Additional Occupations, 577, 590
Cosmetologists, 617
Emergency Medical Technicians, 641, 664, 669
Firefighters, 692
Folk Arts, 710
Funeral Directors and Embalmers, 726
Gunsmiths, Gunmakers, and Bladesmiths, 733
Appendix II: BATs, 765, 777

South Carolina:
Ironworkers, 284
Operating Engineers, 355
Cosmetologists, 611, 615, 618
Emergency Medical Technicians, 641, 665, 669
Firefighters, 692
Folk Arts, 710
Funeral Directors and Embalmers, 726
Appendix II: BATs, 766, 777

South Dakota:
Bricklayers and Stone Masons, 81
Cosmetologists, 611, 615, 618
Emergency Medical Technicians, 641, 665-666, 668
Firefighters, 692
Folk Arts, 710
Funeral Directors and Embalmers, 727
Appendix II: BATs, 766, 777

Tennessee:
Carpenters, 129
Electricians and Line Workers, 232-233
Ironworkers, 284
Painters and Paperhangers, 374
Plasterers, 437
Printing Industry Workers, 460-461
Roofers and Waterproofers, 479
Sheetmetal Workers, 503
Additional Occupations, 574, 585
Cosmetologists, 611, 615, 618-619
Crafts and Trades Workers, 625
Emergency Medical Technicians, 641, 666, 668
Firefighters, 692-693
Folk Arts, 710
Funeral Directors and Embalmers, 727
Appendix II: BATs, 766, 777

Texas:
Asbestos Workers and Insulators, 52-53
Bricklayers and Stone Masons, 82
Carpenters, 129-130
Electricians and Line Workers, 232, 234-235

Electronics Technicians, 254
Laborers, 296
Painters and Paperhangers, 374
Pipe Trades Workers, 418
Sheetmetal Workers, 497, 503-504
Theater Workers, 524
Tile Setters, 535-536
Additional Occupations, 587
Colleges and Technical Schools, 599
Cosmetologists, 611, 619
Emergency Medical Technicians, 641, 667, 669
Firefighters, 693
Folk Arts, 711
Funeral Directors and Embalmers, 728
Gunsmiths, Gunmakers, and Bladesmiths, 732
Musical Instrument Tuners and Repairers, 738
Appendix II: BATs, 766, 777-778

Utah:
Asbestos Workers and Insulators, 53
Boilermakers, 62-63
Carpenters, 130
Electricians and Line Workers, 236
Ironworkers, 285
Machinists, 313
Pipe Trades Workers, 419
Theater Workers, 524
Colleges and Technical Schools, 599
Cosmetologists, 611, 619
Emergency Medical Technicians, 641, 667-669
Firefighters, 693
Folk Arts, 711
Funeral Directors and Embalmers, 728
Appendix II: BATs, 766, 778

Vermont:
Electricians and Line Workers, 236-237
Pipe Trades Workers, 419
Sheetmetal Workers, 504
Tool, Die, Mold, and Pattern Makers, 553
Cosmetologists, 611, 615, 619-620
Emergency Medical Technicians, 641, 668
Firefighters, 693
Folk Arts, 711
Funeral Directors and Embalmers, 728
Appendix II: BATs, 765, 778

Virginia:
Asbestos Workers and Insulators, 54-55
Boilermakers, 63-64

Carpenters, 131, 135
Cement Masons, 149
Cooks, Chefs, and Bakers, 172
Drywallers and Lathers, 175
Electricians and Line Workers, 230, 237-238
Ironworkers, 285
Laborers, 294, 296-297
Machinists, 313
Mechanics, 331-332
Painters and Paperhangers, 375-376
Pipe Trades Workers, 419
Printing Industry Workers, 461
Sheetmetal Workers, 485, 504-505
Shipbuilding Industry Workers, 513, 515
Tool, Die, Mold, and Pattern Makers, 554
Welders, 566
Additional Occupations, 577, 579
Cosmetologists, 611, 615, 620
Crafts and Trades Workers, 629
Emergency Medical Technicians, 669
Firefighters, 694
Folk Arts, 711
Funeral Directors and Embalmers, 729
Orthotics Technicians, 743
Preschool Workers, 748
Appendix II: BATs, 765, 777-780

Washington, DC:
Asbestos Workers and Insulators, 41
Bricklayers and Stone Masons, 69
Carpenters, 90
Cement Masons, 149, 162
Cooks, Chefs, and Bakers, 169
Drywallers and Lathers, 175
Electricians and Line Workers, 187, 239-240
Electronics Technicians, 251
Glaziers, 259
Ironworkers, 271, 287
Laborers, 292, 294, 296-298
Operating Engineers, 342, 357
Painters and Paperhangers, 361
Pipe Trades Workers, 382, 402-403, 422
Plasterers, 431
Printing Industry Workers, 444
Roofers and Waterproofers, 467
Tile Setters, 529
Welders, 563
Additional Occupations, 569-570, 576-577, 589
Cosmetologists, 620

Emergency Medical Technicians, 641, 669-670
Firefighters, 698
Folk Arts, 705, 711
Gunsmiths, Gunmakers, and Bladesmiths, 733
Preschool Workers, 748
Appendix II: BATs, 765, 780

Washington:
Asbestos Workers and Insulators, 41, 54-55
Boilermakers, 63-64
Bricklayers and Stone Masons, 82
Carpenters, 131-135
Cement Masons, 162-163
Drywallers and Lathers, 182-183
Electricians and Line Workers, 238-239
Electronics Technicians, 255
Glaziers, 265-266
Ironworkers, 286-287
Laborers, 297
Machinists, 314
Mechanics, 332
Operating Engineers, 355-357
Painters and Paperhangers, 375
Pipe Trades Workers, 420-421
Plasterers, 438
Roofers and Waterproofers, 480
Sheetmetal Workers, 505
Shipbuilding Industry Workers, 515-516
Theater Workers, 524
Tile Setters, 536
Tool, Die, Mold, and Pattern Makers, 554
Additional Occupations, 583, 587, 590
Colleges and Technical Schools, 599
Cosmetologists, 607-608, 615, 620
Emergency Medical Technicians, 669-670
Firefighters, 694-698
Folk Arts, 711
Funeral Directors and Embalmers, 729
Appendix II: BATs, 766, 779-780

West Virginia:
Asbestos Workers and Insulators, 55
Boilermakers, 64
Bricklayers and Stone Masons, 83
Carpenters, 135-136
Cement Masons, 163
Electricians and Line Workers, 230, 240
Glaziers, 266
Ironworkers, 282, 288
Laborers, 298

State Index

Operating Engineers, 357
Painters and Paperhangers, 375-376
Pipe Trades Workers, 422
Plasterers, 438
Roofers and Waterproofers, 480-481
Sheetmetal Workers, 505
Additional Occupations, 590
Cosmetologists, 621
Emergency Medical Technicians, 641, 664, 669, 671
Firefighters, 698-701
Folk Arts, 711
Funeral Directors and Embalmers, 729
Appendix II: BATs, 765, 780

Wisconsin:
Asbestos Workers and Insulators, 56
Bricklayers and Stone Masons, 83-84
Carpenters, 136-144
Cement Masons, 163-164
Electricians and Line Workers, 241-247
Electronics Technicians, 255-256
Glaziers, 266
Ironworkers, 288-289
Laborers, 298
Machinists, 315-318
Mechanics, 332-337
Operating Engineers, 357-358
Painters and Paperhangers, 377

Pipe Trades Workers, 422-428
Plasterers, 438-439
Printing Industry Workers, 462-463
Sheetmetal Workers, 506-507
Tile Setters, 537
Tool, Die, Mold, and Pattern Makers, 541, 554-558
Welders, 566-567
Additional Occupations, 572
Colleges and Technical Schools, 599-602
Cosmetologists, 611, 621
Emergency Medical Technicians, 641, 671-672
Firefighters, 686, 701-702
Folk Arts, 711
Funeral Directors and Embalmers, 730
Appendix II: BATs, 766, 780-781

Wyoming:
Carpenters, 144
Cement Masons, 157
Electricians and Line Workers, 231
Ironworkers, 289
Cosmetologists, 621
Emergency Medical Technicians, 641, 669, 672
Firefighters, 702
Folk Arts, 711
Appendix II: BATs, 766, 776, 781